P9-CLF-123

# Sheryl Crow

## No Fool to This Game

**RICHARD BUSKIN**

BILLBOARD BOOKS
an imprint of Watson-Guptill Publications/New York

*For Melanie*

Senior Acquisitions Editor: Bob Nirkind
Edited by Sarah Fass
Cover designed by Michelle Gengaro-Kokmen
Interior designed by Cheryl Viker
Graphic production by Ellen Greene

First published in 2002 by Billboard Books, an imprint of Watson-Guptill Publications,
a division of VNU Business Media, Inc., 770 Broadway, New York, NY 10003
www.watsonguptill.com

Library of Congress Cataloging-in-Publication Data

Buskin, Richard.
  Sheryl Crow : no fool to this game / Richard Buskin.— 1st ed.
    p. cm.
Includes discography, filmography, videography, and index.
  ISBN 0-8230-8432-9
  1. Crow, Sheryl. 2. Singers—United States—Biography. I. Title.
  ML420.C955 B8 2002
  782.42164'082—dc21

                         2002008615

Manufactured in U.S.A.

1 2 3 4 5 6 7 8 9 / 09 08 07 06 05 04 03 02

# Contents

# Acknowledgments

This is not an authorized biography, as attested to by the fact that during the more than two years it took to research and write the book, Sheryl Crow declined my requests to interview her, the members of her family, and her manager. Nevertheless, I wish to extend my heartfelt thanks to Sheryl, as well as to Stephen "Scooter" Weintraub and Pam Wertheimer at W Management, for enabling me to speak with many of Sheryl's closest friends and associates, none of whom would have agreed to be interviewed without first obtaining the go-ahead from her. The upside to Sheryl's lack of involvement in the project was that it did allow me to write what I hope is an impartial and balanced account of her life, without feeling the need to simply please or appease the main subject. At the same time, if it wasn't for her sense of fairness in advising people that they should feel free to speak with me, I could never have achieved my objective.

This became all too clear early on, when Sheryl's hometown of Kennett, Missouri, virtually shut its doors on me. Without exception, every person who was approached to do an interview—friends, acquaintances, former teachers—basically said the same thing: "It shouldn't be a problem, but let me just run it by the family...." For me, this was a problem, because said family had previously been burned by tabloid journalists who'd come to town digging for dirt, and the Crows had expressed anger at the neighbors who had talked to them. Therefore, when my requests were run by Sheryl's family, they weren't exactly enthused, and not one single Kennettite or former resident, I quickly discovered, wanted to risk harming his or her friendship with them. The result: zero interviews relating to Sheryl's childhood. I did have a problem.

"Forty percent of that speaks to the fact that the people are from Kennett, but sixty percent of it speaks to the fact that there's no one here who Sheryl or her family have done anything wrong to," her friend Brian Mitchell later told me. "People really do try to leave her alone when she comes back for a visit. They go out of their way to let her know that she's got free reign around here."

Indeed, while I was more than a little frustrated by the situation, it was hard to be angry. I mean, who could blame these people? To risk ruining a friendship in return for just seeing their names in print—it wasn't worth it. I'd thought that at least a few egos might succumb to the temptation, but I was wrong. The degree of loyalty and integrity displayed by the Crows' acquaintances was both admirable and amazing. Hats off to Kennett, and time to gargle toilet water for me.

It didn't take a genius to figure out that I'd encounter the same kind of difficulty when requesting interviews with people who knew Sheryl through her work. The only difference this time around was that instead of saying "Let me run it by the family," they'd say "Let me run it by her management." It was like hitting a brick wall. I had to engineer a meeting with said management, and eventually I did. Before acquiring a publishing deal, I knew that the Crow camp wasn't enamored with the idea of an unauthorized biography, but I'd been told that no one would stand in my way. Now it was clear that, without Sheryl actually green-lighting people to speak with me, I'd have hardly anyone to talk to aside from the kind of peripheral characters who populate tabloid exposés—the "observers" and "close sources" who few people, including the main subject, have ever heard of. That wasn't the route I wanted to take, and I'm grateful that Scooter, Pam, Sheryl, and Sheryl's father Wendell took a chance by trusting me when I assured them of this.

Before I got to that point, a trio of key people did accede to my interview requests: producer/engineer Hugh Padgham and manager Dennis Muirhead, both of whom have been longtime and valued acquaintances of mine; and A&M Records' former Senior Vice President of A&R, David Anderle, who agreed to an initial talk with me after first obtaining clearance from Sheryl's management. My sincere thanks to all three for helping to get the ball rolling.

A very special debt of gratitude is owed to Allen J. Wiener, whose tremendous help in terms of background research and setting up many of the interviews was, quite simply, invaluable. During the early stages of this project, it was Allen who, more often than not, had to endure the refusals and, in some cases, brusque attitudes or disappearing acts, of the numerous people who'd run his requests by Sheryl's family or her management. He never gave up, however, and it was partly due to his tenacity that the project remained on track.

I am extremely grateful to everyone who consented to my interviews, including those who sought Sheryl's approval to speak with me, and others who had their own just reasons for trepidation about going on the record. This book would have been a wasted effort without the words of the following people: David Baerwald, Bill Bottrell, Al Cafaro, Ann Cash, Wyn Cooper, John Cossette, James Finch, Bob FitzSimons, Raymond Herbert, Ched Hieronymus, Jimmy Iovine, Wayne Isaak, Mary Jackson, Shelle Jensen, Rory Kaplan, Betsy Lenger, John Marx, Ken McClure, Brian Mitchell, Sharon Monsky, Fred Moreadith, Bobby Muller, Jay Oliver, Greg Phillinganes, Darryl Phinnessee, Ira "Rocky" Powell, Patrick Rains, Mike Rechtien, Robert Richards, Seth Riggs, Dan Schwartz, Trina Shoemaker, Jo Beth Skaggs, Randy Sosin, Judy Stakee, Carlotta Tarver, Jeff Trott, Scott Tutor, Deborah Welsh, Billy Wilkerson, and Todd Wolfe.

Originally, I intended to reproduce some of Sheryl's lyrics in order to illustrate her progress as a songwriter, as well as to embellish certain points that she has made in television, newspaper, and magazine interviews. These lyrics had to be excised just before going to press, however, when, contrary to the request made by the rights department at Sheryl's music publisher, Warner/Chappell, her legal representative suddenly insisted on seeing the entire manuscript of the book in order to decide whether or not to grant permission. Given the time constraints, it was impossible to satisfy this demand, which exemplified the kind of control issues that are endemic to the entertainment-related legal profession. (Song lyrics can be viewed at numerous Sheryl Crow Web sites.)

Meanwhile, a special thanks goes to Bob Nirkind. In his role as Senior Acquisitions Editor at Billboard Books, Bob not only believed in this project right from the start, but he also lent his support to help navigate the initial obstacles and served as my best advisor regarding the book's content. His continued involvement made a very positive difference, as did the astute and much appreciated editing of Sarah Fass.

Thank you, once again, to my agent, Linda Konner, whose faith in this project aided its inception, and whose ongoing support helped bring it to fruition; and to Mark Lewisohn, a great friend and trusted sounding board.

Others who I wish to thank, for helping me with photos, research materials, or the arranging of interviews, are: Ward H. Billings, Tchad Blake, Lori Earl, Ritch Esra, Christopher O. Ferguson, Francis Goodrow, "Papa" Jim Harrel, Bob Iuliucci, Allan Kozinn, James Leasing, Wayne Martin, Stephanie Miles, Jeff Mintz, *Pollstar* magazine, Jon Rubin, Karen Scott, J.C. and Betty L. Skaggs, David Stark, Terry Wang, and the research staff at the Evanston Public Library in Evanston, Illinois.

Finally, love and thanks to my wife Dorothy-Jean, who was beside me through the many ups and downs of this project, and our daughter Melanie, whose sweetness, laughter, singing, and dancing made it all worthwhile.

# Introduction

*"Her story is more Rashomon-like than anyone else I ever worked with during my twenty-seven years at A&M. Everyone, including Sheryl, has their own perception of events and things get real fuzzy, but it's worth putting up with a lot of stuff to get this story right."*
— David Anderle

Akira Kurosawa's 1950 cinematic classic, *Rashomon*, centers on the alleged rape of a woman and the murder of her husband in ancient Japan, as described to investigators by the wife, the dead man (through a medium), and a bandit who is arrested for the crime. Each of their self-serving testimonies differs, while an apparent lack of objectivity also casts doubt over the seemingly accurate recollection of an eyewitness. The relativity of truth and the subjective nature of human perception are among the film's major themes, and as A&M Records' former A&R (Artists & Repertoire) chief, David Anderle, pointed out to me back in October 1999, they also have particular relevance to the story of Sheryl Crow.

Many of the anecdotes regarding Sheryl do have countless different versions, and they've been relayed to me with such conviction that it's often difficult to ascertain which, if any, are accurate. None, one, several, all? In such cases, I've allowed the different parties to tell the stories in their own words. Provided with the relevant details, the reader is just as qualified as I am to draw his or her own conclusions.

At the same time, while different people see different sides of Sheryl—some adore her, some don't—there is clear agreement with regard to her incredible drive, determination, and strength of character. From early childhood through to the present day, all who know her allude to these qualities, for even among the overachievers of the high-profile worlds that she inhabits, Sheryl stands out as one of the most driven. And this is remarkable, not only because she grew up in a small town and quickly learned how to survive and thrive in the cutthroat environs of the big city, but also because the extent to which she pursues her goals is unsurpassed, while the skill with which she cultivates the right professional relationships and navigates the music-industry jungle demonstrates a priceless natural ability.

"She's as strong-willed as anyone I've ever worked with," confirms Anderle, who signed Sheryl to A&M Records. "She's tough. She's as tough as Zappa, tough as Jim Morrison, tough as Brian Wilson or any other people I've been close to. She's as tough as Kristofferson when he was drinking. She's as tough as they are because she really believes in what she is doing. She is a true believer and a manipulator, and that's fine because she would be nowhere near where she is now if she wasn't like that."

"She thinks like a man," adds longtime friend Brian Mitchell. "Doesn't look like one by any means, but I've always had that take on her. She understands what, in the given circumstances, is important to immediately take care of, and she'll do so without emotion."

The fact that Sheryl's father, Wendell, is a self-made and highly self-motivated attorney provides a clue to who she inherits both the drive and the guile from, but while he's been content to achieve his aims within a small town, his daughter has carried her ambition to much of the world. In that regard, her life has been an undeniable success, although it's not clear how much true and lasting happiness she's derived from the journey thus far.

"Sheryl's a hundred thousand matches," says recording engineer Trina Shoemaker. "Some are burning, some have yet to be struck, and some have burned out completely. She's always alight, there's always some kind of a flame burning, whether it's a flame because she's in a bad mood and you're gonna get your ass chewed out before she writes a genius lyric, or a flame because she picks up an instrument that she says she sucks on, and when she plays it you're like, 'Jesus, if that's sucking, what's great?'"

Still, while *No Fool to This Game* focuses on one woman's life, it also captures numerous other people, neither sinners nor saints, trying to attain their own (not necessarily materialistic) versions of success—sometimes hurting each other in so doing, but basically just trying to survive. A snapshot of the music business in the 1990s, this book recounts how an individual with innate ambition taps into a natural talent to shape her own destiny, while also impacting the lives of others; how collaborative effort can achieve memorable results, even if the collaborators don't always have a rounded perspective of who or what was involved in the creative process; and how minor and, in the grand scheme of things, relatively unimportant events can get blown out of all proportion to highly detrimental effect, while life's most important issues are overlooked. In essence, it's about not seeing the forest for the trees, and of how the truth in its simplest form is often far more palatable than—and equally impressive as—the truth that is created to satisfy a contrived image.

As in *Rashomon*, everyone has a personal take on things and everyone has his or her own truth, even though there is actually only one immutable, often elusive truth. Accordingly, this biography presents numerous—but probably not all—perceived truths relating to Sheryl Crow, and somewhere in there the real ones might just stand up. During an ultra-image-conscious age, we want to be told that our heroes are better than we are. Or, to put it more succinctly, totally flawless. Most of the sins that are revealed in media-contrived character assassinations or kiss-and-tell bios are fairly routine, but it's evidently gratifying to ignore our own failings while passing judgement on those of others. The hypocrisy of convenience: It adds up to big business.

Celebrity biographies often veer towards either one of two extremes: that in which the subject's life, and all of the events contained therein, are apparently of extreme interest to the entire globe—"The world was waiting for the release of her next record. When it hit the stores, the world applauded…"—or the hatchet job in which as many salacious incidents as possible are compiled between the book's covers, transforming the subject into a crucifiable villain. It is disingenuous for the authors of these works to point out that they've detailed the good as well as the bad, thus presenting a balanced picture. The bad grabs the attention far more easily than the good or the downright ordinary, so perhaps it would be better to balance things from the reader's perspective. No easy task, but within these pages I'm going to give it a try.

It was Sheryl Crow's music that inspired me to write her biography, and ultimately it will be the music, rather than the personal relationships or professional maneuverings, for which she'll be most widely remembered. I hope this book provides appropriate insight and a greater understanding about the creation of that legacy.

Richard Buskin, Chicago, 2002

# *Prelude*

The date: September 15, 1992. The place: Toad Hall, Pasadena, producer Bill Bottrell's home studio a few miles northeast of Los Angeles. Walking into the facility's high, long, faux-stone room, with its neo-Gothic lighting, tapestry-draped walls, and opulent array of classic recording equipment, Sheryl Crow is entering a musical environment unlike any she's encountered during her six years in L.A. Though neither she nor any of the other people present have a clue as to what they're about to let themselves in for, it's a session that will change all of their lives.

For the best part of a year Toad Hall has served as a regular meeting place for an eclectic bunch of musicians—eclectic, that is, in terms of their volatile personalities as well as their varied abilities and musical tastes. Among them are gifted lyricist-composer David Baerwald, an initiator who can be relied on to provide plenty of creative sparks; multi-instrumentalist Kevin Gilbert, whose all-around talents also include songwriting and vocals; drummer Brian MacLeod, described by Bill Bottrell as the collective's "hipster, a conceptualist with ideas that are in the moment"; and bassist Dan Schwartz, who, according to Bottrell, is "the bringer of artistic elitism, the beholder of the art." On the periphery of this core group are the likes of bassist David Ricketts and guitarist Jeff Trott. More than a band, this is a scene, with varying permutations of the afore-mentioned gathering at Toad Hall on Tuesday nights simply to write songs, record the results, and see what develops.

Given this potent cocktail of talents and egos, it's Bill Bottrell's job to bring all of the disparate forces together. As characterized by Dan Schwartz, everyone involved has "an incredible amount of drive, just not necessarily driving in the same direction." In many ways, it's like a scene straight out of *Spinal Tap*, and tonight, with a cast featuring Bottrell, Baerwald, Gilbert, Ricketts, and MacLeod, there's a new character being thrown into the mix.

Sheryl Crow, a thirty-year-old singer-songwriter who has toured as a backup vocalist for both Don Henley and Michael Jackson, has already been recommended to Bottrell by no less than three people: her boyfriend, Kevin Gilbert, who has col-laborated with Bottrell on a number of projects and works out of a room adjoining Toad Hall; Robert Richards, who manages several of the "Tuesday Music Collective" members; and David Anderle, the head of A&R at A&M Records, who signed Crow to the label eighteen months ago and whose neck is now on the line due to the shelving of her first album to the tune of $450,000. Bottrell has heard that album, a collection of characterless, anachronistic "rock chick" tracks, and quickly pigeon-holed it as just the kind of material he's recently been trying to get away from—"all packaging and nothing inside." Nevertheless, the voice enveloped within the pro-duction has definite quality, and Sheryl has some decent songwriting credentials, so when Gilbert called earlier in the evening and asked if he should bring her along, Bottrell was all for it.

From Sheryl's standpoint she has nothing to lose. Having poured plenty of time and emotion into that first album, she's now out on a limb, with no career momentum and certainly no clearly defined artistic direction. For his part, Bill Bottrell is open to working with anyone who might help him achieve his creative goals. A producer, engineer, songwriter, and musician with a long list of credits to his name, Bottrell has turned his back on contemporary recording methods and on what he perceives as overblown superstar projects in favor of employing old techniques with new artists—working live, working more immediately, leaving things raw, never doing demos.

"Everything gets recorded and everything is potentially a master," he says, while also alluding to "leaving things looser and going for the proverbial three minutes of magic in a room."

Having spent the past decade working with African American R&B acts, observing how they tap into their musical roots, Bottrell has determined that his own soul comes from Appalachia and country music. "Good records come from places," he says. "Places like the South, Chicago, Appalachia. They have identities that are local. So, while I grew up with pop music in all its glory as a suburban kid in L.A., I had to learn how to find what it is that I do as a writer and a singer and a musician, and hence as a record producer, and that's how I acquired a connection to country music."

He's not the only one. David Baerwald ascribed a country connection to Sheryl Crow during a recent A&M-contrived songwriting session with the south Missouri native, and there are also clear strains of Appalachia in the directness, easy harmonies, and storytelling attributes of several songs on Baerwald's own album, *Triage,* which Bill Bottrell has produced. Yet, for the longest time, Bottrell has been flirting with an "alternative country" sound that draws on his rock sensibilities. Tonight at Toad Hall it will all come together.

Forewarned by Kevin Gilbert that she's in for a unique musical experience, Sheryl has an open mind and a positive attitude, and she's quickly presented with the opportunity to show what she's made of. First she takes the lead on "I Love This Man," a German-cabaret-type song with a complex chord structure, in which a prostitute in a bombed-out hotel pledges devotion to her pimp. The number is pure Brecht, but the lyrics are pure Baerwald, and so is his unilateral decision to then break with TMC convention by introducing a preconceived song idea into the proceedings. After all, a basic rule of the Tuesday night gatherings is that the participants enter the studio with no ideas, nothing to champion. Yet, on this particular evening, Baerwald just happens to bring along the galley proofs to an as-yet-unpublished novel by a close friend of his. "That's it," he says referring to the book's title, "*Leaving Las Vegas.* There's our shiny phrase for the evening."

Baerwald begins playing the simple G-C-D chord structure he's already worked on and comes up with the song's first few lines and chorus as if improvising them on the spot. Not exactly what's supposed to happen, but hey, there's nothing wrong with a spot of creative deception. Before long everyone is contributing ideas, Kevin Gilbert supplementing Baerwald's first verse with one of his own.

Reaching for the sound that has become his *cause célèbre*, Bill Bottrell provides the rapidly developing song with a backbone, thanks to a loop that he describes as "a weird punk country groove." Still, there's a problem from the producer's perspective—having initiated the new song, Baerwald is now hogging the microphone. Bottrell responds by taking Baerwald's guitar, sending him over to the keyboards, and swinging the vocal mic back in front of Sheryl.

In her headphones she hears the rhythm track that will end up on the finished record; in her mind she hears colors courtesy of the hallucinogens that she's ingested. Earlier in the session Baerwald and Ricketts took up Gilbert's offer of a couple of hits of acid—apparently he also had a tab for Sheryl. As the LSD kicks in, the two guys get a fit of the hysterics. Sheryl gets inspired. Heeding Bottrell's advice to play down the vibrato in her voice, she responds to the sound of the instruments with a vocal style that matches the mood and fits the music like a glove.

To the producer's way of thinking, Sheryl's singing like no one ever has before, melding a laid-back, devil-may-care attitude with a searing, in-your-face vocal delivery. One moment the lyrics are semi-spoken in a low register, the next they're spit out with a high-octane intensity; the result is a breadth of emotion and naturalism of style that will one day give rise to a host of imitators.

"She made that up," Bottrell will later say. "It came from her, it came from country, it came from 'Missoura,' it came from this crunchy sound that was blaring in her headphones, and it came from the fact that she could barely hear herself."

Inside the singer's head is a melange probably approximating musical chaos, and as the LSD kicks into overdrive the singing just gets better. "Leaving Las Vegas" is the simplest of songs, yet it will serve as the model for not only Sheryl Crow's *Tuesday Night Music Club* album, but also the folk-rock/alternative country/neo-hippie sound with which she'll hereafter be associated. She'll make it her own and she'll run with it.

"That's the only time I dropped acid," Sheryl will later tell *Q* magazine. "The first half of the record was a drunken mess and the second half was the clean-up period. We only did one take of that song and I tried to go back and re-sing it, but I couldn't do it again. I couldn't recreate the energy."

She won't need to. In an inspired moment of semi-contrived brilliance, blending her own vocal and improvisational talents with one man's artistic vision and the creativity of her fellow musicians, Sheryl Crow has found the voice and the direction that will launch her career and help her realize some lifelong ambitions.

It's a hot, muggy night back in southern Missouri. Here in Pasadena things are just starting to warm up.

# CHAPTER ONE

# In the Bootheel
# of Missouri

Heading south towards the Missouri-Arkansas border, the I-55 cuts a crooked line through low-lying flatlands that are within 150 miles of Nashville to the east and the Ozarks to the west. Small towns are bypassed: Jaywye, Portageville, Wardell.... At the Hayti exit a right turn onto Route 84 leads past a gas station listing the prices of unleaded, mid-grade, premium, diesel, and a fifth of Jack Daniels. Welcome to farm country.

As the two-lane highway darts through fields of soybean and cotton, its curbs run parallel to a motley collection of tractors, homes, food shacks, convenience stores, dilapidated auto repair shops, and small houses of worship pronouncing "Exposure to the Son may prevent burning" and "Wrinkled with burden? Come to church for a faith lift." Several churches and businesses are boarded up; others are attached to trailers that function as extra office space. Up ahead, Hayti Heights, then Bakerville, then "Welcome to Kennett. Service, agriculture, industry."

Just over 90 miles north of Memphis, Tennessee, in the southern heel of the Missouri boot, about 20 miles west of the Mississippi River, lies Kennett, population 10,941. Officially part of the Midwest—a misnomer if ever there was one—the city has a definite Southern feel, as do Dunklin County, in which it is located, and the entire Bootheel region.

Kennett's inhabitants speak with a distinct Southern drawl; they feast on fried catfish, barbecue, grits, butterbeans, and black-eyed peas; and they'll invariably shop for goods, services, and entertainment in Memphis rather than trek 200 miles north to St. Louis. Both emotionally and geographically, these people are far removed from the state capital of Jefferson City. In historical terms it's easy to see why.

Located in the southwestern tip of the Bootheel region, Dunklin County was named after Daniel Dunklin, Governor of Missouri from 1832 to 1836. Nearly 50 miles in length and 540 square miles in total area, the county was established in 1845, and Kennett was laid out as its seat the following year. Situated on a Delaware and Shawnee Indian village site, the town was initially known as Chilletecaux, before changing its name to Butler and then, in 1851, to Kennett, in honor of St. Louis mayor Luther M. Kennett. It was incorporated as a city in 1873.

In the meantime, the Civil War divided Missouri, and Dunklin County even went so far as to declare itself the "Independent State of Dunklin" after adopting an 1862 resolution to secede from the union. The following year, Union troops paid a brief visit to Kennett. Guerrilla raiders hung around a while longer. Still, there wasn't a whole lot to fight over. Thanks to liquefaction resulting from the 1811 earthquake in neighboring New Madrid—the most violent trembler ever recorded in North America—the region was a largely uninhabitable mess of swampland and forests; a haven for hunters and trappers, but little else. Then, in 1878, recovery commenced with the arrival in nearby Malden of the Little River Valley & Arkansas Cotton Belt railroad, a branch of which reached Kennett in 1890. Three years later, the state provided for the organization of county drainage districts and levees on the St. Francis River, along the Bootheel's western border with Arkansas. This kick-started a program of land reclamation, leading to the implementation in 1905 of the Little River Drainage System, which utilized canals, levees, and ditches to secure more than two million agricultural acres.

Southern cotton farmers, anxious to escape the devastating effects of the voracious boll weevil, began relocating to the Bootheel, as did black field hands from Arkansas, Mississippi, and Tennessee, and by 1920 they had transformed the region into the northernmost land of cotton. What's more, they had also enhanced its Southern feel, while imbuing it with a solid strain of African-American culture that is evident not only in gastronomic terms, but also in the Bootheel's strong tradition of gospel music.

As Dunklin County developed into a noted cotton, soybean, and livestock farming area, Kennett profited from several local railroads serving both Missouri and Arkansas. This, in turn, helped it evolve into the largest community and trade center for the two-state area. Today, home to producers of electric motors, railcar components, steel, cotton seed, soybeans, and sunflower oil, Kennett is similar in appearance to numerous other modest communities dotted throughout the American heartland—rural yet industrialized, while also melding modern economics with the postbellum South.

A city by designation, this is basically a small town in all other respects, and contained within its borders is the usual array of old-time, mom 'n' pop establishments—the Mitchell Drug Store, Bill Horton's Bar-B-Que, North Delta Cotton, the Kennett Bowling Lanes ("Friday Night All You Can Bowl")—juxtaposed with the inevitable presence of Wal-Mart, McDonald's, Pizza Hut, and Taco Bell. These symbols of corporate America are relatively new intruders, providing their homogenized goods to a tight-knit community that derives much of its news from the eighteen pages of the *Daily Dunklin Democrat*, as well as from the socializing that takes place in the neighborhood's thirty-plus churches.

In this Bible Belt stronghold, people not only share in each other's lives, but also in a past that saw most of their ancestors migrate to Kennett from nearby Bootheel locales or from Missouri's neighboring states. The Crows are no exception. In 1846, the same year that Kennett became the seat of Dunklin County, Sheryl's great-great-grandfather, James L. Crow, was born in Tennessee, the birthplace of both his parents. Growing up to be a farmer, James married a local girl named Rachel, and together they moved to Sikeston in Scott County, towards the northeast of the Missouri Bootheel. There, in 1873, Rachel gave birth to their son Charles, Sheryl's great-grandfather.

Charles A. Crow subsequently became a politician and married Emma Gardner, a native of Campbell in northern Dunklin County, whose father was an Alabama farmer and mother an Arkansas housekeeper. Charles made the move to Campbell, and on November 13, 1911, Emma gave birth to Sheryl's paternal grandfather, Charles Augustus Crow. In 1930, Charles, Jr., married another Campbell native, Naomi Drue Wyatt, whose father, Esco, was a hardware store clerk from Gibson County, Tennessee. Her mother, Winnie Fyffer, was a homemaker from Lawrence County, Illinois.

Taking advantage of local opportunities, Charles worked as a levee contractor, and on New Year's Day, 1932, he and Naomi became the parents of a son who was given both of their last names: Wendell Wyatt Crow. Growing up in Caruthersville, a few miles east of Kennett in neighboring Pemiscott County, Wendell broke with family tradition by going to law school at the University of Missouri in Columbia, having graduated from Caruthersville High School in 1949. During his junior year he had penned the CHS song:

> *Our school to us is e'er our joy and pride.*
> *We love its red and white,*
> *We'll cherish and defend it far and wide.*
> *Uphold its fame and might.*
>
> *Dear school of ours, there'll never ever be,*
> *Another school as good as you.*
> *We'll pledge to you the best that we can give,*
> *And always to our Caruthersville be true.*

After graduating from "Mizzou," Wendell returned home to commence work as an attorney, while dating a Caruthersville girl five years his junior. Born at St. Louis's Bethesda Hospital on May 3, 1937, Bernice Cain started life in the northern part of Missouri. At that time, her father, Charles, was a thirty-three-year-old physician hailing from Tennessee; her mother, Janet Chilton, was born in 1911, in Van Buren, Missouri.

While Janet's father, Oliver Chilton (Sheryl's maternal great-grandfather, born 1884), was a newspaper editor in Van Buren, it was Sheryl's maternal great-grandmother, Sarah Austin (born 1887), who was first among the ancestors to utilize music in a professional capacity, working as a music teacher as well as a housewife. Sarah's granddaughter, Bernice Cain, also grew up with a love for music, and this was something that she shared with Wendell Crow, whom she married on June 30, 1955.

A petite, brunette woman from whom Sheryl would inherit her good looks, Bernice played the piano. Following in her grandmother's footsteps, she also gave lessons to earn some money. Wendell, on the other hand, indulged his passion for the trumpet while working as an attorney. From him Sheryl would inherit a number of self-acknowledged character traits, including tremendous self-motivation and an up-and-down disposition. Generally outgoing, alpha-type personalities, both father and daughter have a propensity for moodiness. Not for nothing is Sheryl adept at pouting with what a writer for the *Times* of London once described as "the sexiest top lip in the business."

"Sheryl is her father, in the best way, with her mother's talent," says family friend Brian Mitchell. "The ambition and career side, as well as her suspicion of the business, come strictly from her father, as do the hotheadedness, the determination, and the sense of self that can tend to be perceived as off-putting by certain people trying to court her. She also has her mother's ability and beauty in all senses of the word. Both parents are very creative. Wendell is well known around Kennett for one thing, and that's being extremely passionate in whatever he does—if the case goes to court, don't get in his way. He takes his work extremely seriously and he's incredibly single-minded, which of course is necessary in his profession."[1]

Although Wendell and Bernice each had serious musical aspirations, economic reality quickly led them in other career directions—those in which steady jobs would produce sufficient income to raise a family and, subsequently, provide their kids with the opportunities that they themselves had lacked.

Born in 1957, the couple's first child, Katherine, was initially raised in Caruthersville, but shortly before Bernice gave birth to Karen Elise in 1959, the Crows relocated to Kennett. After living in a tiny ranch-style property at 505 Maple Street, they moved one block west to a slightly larger brick house at 500 Emerson Street. This was the first place to be called home by Sheryl Suzanne Crow,[2] who entered the world at 9:58 on the morning of Sunday, February 11, 1962, at Dunklin County Memorial Hospital.

In strictly local terms, it's a world whose way of life has changed little during the past forty years. Sure, things are more commercial now. Kennett had no Taco Bell, McDonald's, Burger King, or Pizza Hut when Sheryl was born. Nor was there a 24-hour Wal-Mart Super Center, whose overwhelming presence would irrevocably alter the once-vibrant town square—some say destroy it—by forcing several small, long-established businesses to close down.

"Downtown Kennett was thriving when we were kids," says Sheryl's longtime friend Carlotta Tarver. "There was a Rexall drug store where we'd go for lunch, clothing stores, a dime store. All of them are gone, and the place now seems deserted. It's really sad."

Indeed, among the sole survivors in that central area are the county courthouse and the Mitchell pharmacy, whereas the old Cotton Exchange Bank building now houses a store named the Bank of Antiques. There, in a back room on the second floor, surrounded by toasters, glasses, kettles, pots, sofas, and 8-track cartridges, some second-hand apparel can be found next to a small sign stating, "These clothes belong to singer-songwriter Sheryl Crow. She gives us the hand-me-downs and the profit from sales goes

---

[1] *In a number of articles about—and interviews with—Sheryl, it has been alleged that when she was about ten years old, Wendell prosecuted the Ku Klux Klan for rigging a local election, and that the ensuing death threats necessitated him sitting up all night with a shotgun and the police escorting his kids to school. This story is apocryphal. Neither Wendell nor his law office recall any such case or resulting circumstances during Sheryl's childhood, her school friends don't remember a police escort, and there were no associated reports in the local paper. If Wendell was involved in a case against the Klan, it was while he was still in Caruthersville, before Sheryl was born.*

[2] *An amalgam of* chère, *the French word for "dear," and* sher, *the Sanskrit for "beloved," Sheryl is an English variation of the French name,* Cheryl. *It was at its most popular from the 1940s through the early 1960s.*

to the Delta Children's Home in Kennett." The profit is modest: in this low-key setting, Sheryl's micro-miniskirts, leather pants, designer shoes, T-shirts, and tweed jackets go for anywhere from $10 to $50.

Elsewhere, the run-down stores and ramshackle houses that populated the city during the early '60s still survive. So, too, do the more upscale middle-class homes and the ever-present Kennett Country Club which, throughout the decades, has served as a weekly social haunt for many of the city's older residents. These are just some of the community members who turn up for the Delta Fair in the third week of September, where ladies submit their jams, pies, quilts, and baby pictures for competition, while others watch the rodeo. Everybody goes to the Delta Fair, a microcosm of Kennett life that caters to generational continuity. In recent years the organizers have tried to get Sheryl to sing there. She has declined. Not quite her scene. She's done other good things for the city.

"Very little changes in Kennett," remarks Debbie Welsh, another lifelong friend of Sheryl's, who now lives in Kansas City. "It's still largely the same people living in the same places."

This is probably why, for several years after Sheryl found fame and fortune, Wendell and Bernice continued to reside in the comfortable, unpretentious two-story, five-bedroom brick house to which they had moved shortly after their youngest child, Steven, was born in September 1966. Located on West Washington Street, across from Kennett High School, just a few blocks south of Emerson, this home was filled with music from day one, not least because it had four pianos on which the kids would often practice simultaneously while Bernice monitored their efforts from the kitchen.

Bernice and Wendell played in a local big band, and as many of the Wednesday night rehearsals took place at their house, the kids were exposed to plenty of jazz and swing sounds while they were growing up, along with the contemporary rock that emanated from the radio and hi-fi. As a result, the Crow household stood out even within the music-loving environs of Kennett, where church choirs form an integral part of the social fabric, and amateur and semi-pro musicians come a dime a dozen.

"They were very artsy and musical," Sheryl told author Marc Woodworth for his 1998 book *Solo: Women Singer-Songwriters in Their Own Words.* "When I was a kid, they listened to a lot of big bands, swing bands, and crooners. Don't ask me why, but I really related to that music. I can remember lying down by the Magnavox and listening over and over to Judy Garland singing 'But Not For Me.' I was six years old, and for some weird reason everything about that song represented me. That's my earliest recollection of how music could really strike you at the core."

There would soon be other examples.

"At the Country Club in the early years, everybody would just bring their musical instruments and they might get a session going," Debbie Welsh recalls. "There was a children's room—the old 'be seen and not heard' thing—and we'd be in there while everybody had fun.

"Wendell and Bernice would have jam sessions at home, and I remember them putting us to bed and Sheryl and I sneaking out of the bedroom and sitting on the staircase. Her mom played the piano and sang, her dad was on the trumpet, Ernie Simer was on drums, Leo Benson was on the trombone, and we just sat there for hours, listening to the major jam session that was going down in her parents' living room. At that time we thought they were so old, but they were probably in their mid- to upper thirties, playing improvisational jazz as well as the standards.

"Ernie Simer was the pharmacist in town, while Leo Benson was one of the doctors. He was an extremely close friend of their family, and when he died at a young age it was a very traumatic event in Kennett. Dr. Benson was known for driving around in a blue convertible with his trombone always sticking out of the back seat. He didn't go anywhere without it."

A quarter of a century later, Sheryl would allude to these memories in the song "We Do What We Can" on the *Tuesday Night Music Club* album. Wendell would play trumpet on the track, and Sheryl would subsequently describe Leo Benson, the doctor who delivered both Karen and Steven, as "walking art, very cosmopolitan. He had toured with the Tommy Dorsey Orchestra and knew the Hemingways when they had lived twelve miles from our small, rural town," she told author Marc Woodworth. "My parents, along with Leo and his wife, represented something very interesting and very highbrow to me. After a night out they would come home late to play music and drink. There was this one song, a ballad, that they played. I never knew the name of it, but I would sit on the stairs and listen to that song all night long. It was an instrumental, a really heavy, melancholy tune. It would just break my heart. Later on, as I started picking up songs on the piano, I always gravitated towards the sad ones. One of the first songs I learned was Joni Mitchell's 'Both Sides Now,' but that instrumental ballad my parents would play late at night was one of the earliest things that struck a grand familiarity in me. The experience of hearing that song from the stairs when I was a girl is one that never leaves me.

"Years after Leo died, I dragged out the record—it was a Buddy Rich song—and listened to it. Some music represents people or times, and that song really brought those days and those friends back to me. There was real, identifiable sadness there, not just in my parents but in Leo and his wife as well. They had run with a cosmopolitan crowd of artists and intellectuals before they were forced to move to a small town to make a living. The same was true for my dad, who wanted to be a musician but wound up having kids and practicing law in Kennett, Missouri. They all saw themselves as artistic people in a situation that didn't provide the time or the freedom to be very expressive, but because of their love of music I knew about the power of songs early on."

That she did. A naturally alert child whose earliest memories include going to sleep on her grandfather's cot—"I can remember things from before I could talk," she once told Britain's *New Musical Express* (NME)—Sheryl was just three years old when she treated her folks to a near-perfect imitation of a current chart hit.

"We were in our family station wagon and she starts singing Petula Clark's 'Downtown,' all the words, all the inflections, British accent," Kathy Crow recalled in the 2002 Sheryl-dedicated episode of VH1's documentary series *Behind the Music*. "We just howled, it was so funny, and that was it, it never stopped."

This, after all, was the mid-'60s, when the previously divisive effects of rock 'n' roll had been superseded by cooler heads on the part of parents who not only knew the names of teen-oriented acts, but even admitted to liking some of the music. With pop scaling new heights in terms of record sales as well as its cultural and sociological impact on a broad age range, it wasn't unusual for preschoolers to entertain their folks with renditions of the current hits—in essence, impersonating the new icons while conveying juvenile ambitions of one day emulating their success.

In 1965, the cross-pollination that was taking place between the U.S. and U.K. music scenes resulted in half of the singles that topped the American charts being British. Leading the way in January of that year was former child star Pet Clark with "Downtown," that Tony Hatch–penned paean to Swinging London, whose sights and sounds were even bleeding into the consciousness of Kennett and beyond. Sheryl was a precocious kid with a flair for selling a tune. She and the song were a good match. By the age of four she was also learning to play the piano.

"I really hated it, but I discovered I could play by ear," she told actress Elisabeth Shue in a 1997 conversation for *Interview* magazine. "My parents were the kind that showed you off and made you play in front of their friends. I hated performing from a very early age and I never loved it."

Push a kid in a specific direction—be it related to food, academia, or a perceived talent—and the adult version will possibly harbor some sort of aversion. This may partly explain why, to this day, Sheryl is often quicker to pick up a guitar or bass than sit down at the keyboard, even though it is the latter which she is most naturally adept at playing.

"From the age of six there were piano recitals that we all had to perform for the Wednesday Music Club," recalls Debbie Welsh, whose maiden name was Tate. "You would win your little trophy and move up to a higher level. Well, Sheryl and her sister Karen had so many Wednesday Music Club trophies it wasn't funny, because they always won their recitals. The DNA of the Crow family just exudes musical talent."

It also exudes effort and achievement, and growing up as a middle kid Sheryl felt the pressure, much of it probably self-imposed, which says as much about her personality as it does about the atmosphere in which she was raised.

"I was constantly trying to make everybody happy by getting straight A's and practicing the piano," she told Marc Woodworth. "My role was to take care of everybody, to make everybody feel all right, and to have everybody feel okay with me at all times…. I idolized my parents and needed their approval, but I never got enough because I was working so hard to make them happy that I didn't appear to need it. The desire for approval is an essential preexisting condition for people who want to be in front of a crowd. What else could drive someone to stand on a stage and look to an audience for recognition? Whoever that performer is, that need for confirmation all comes down to the same thing; not getting enough at home. I was the kid who turned into a performer for just those reasons."

Still, despite the inner needs and personal isolation, none of this amounted to the kind of misery and deprivation that puts meat on the bones of tabloid exposés. On the contrary, we're looking at a straightforward childhood in middle America, with a mother who taught Sunday school at the First Presbyterian Church, and parents who took a proactive interest in their children's education and recreation, instilling in them a love of literature as well as of music.

"They raised us to be excited about writing and reading," Sheryl recounted to Woodworth. "Instead of letting us watch a lot of TV, they would read to us. I remember my dad playing all of the characters as he read Mark Twain's *Pudd'nhead Wilson*. That was the kind of thing I grew up with, unaware that other children didn't have the same experience."

Since her days at nursery school, Sheryl has been bonded to a loyal band of girl-friends: her best pal Jo Beth Skaggs, Debbie Welsh, Ann Cash (whose physician father delivered Sheryl), and Carlotta Tarver. From grades one through five, Sheryl attended West Elementary School with Jo Beth and Carlotta; in sixth grade, she and Jo Beth joined Debbie at South Elementary School. Thereafter, all five girls were classmates at the city's solitary junior high and high schools, and with the exception of Carlotta they would also attend the University of Missouri in Columbia.

"Sheryl and I were always focused on being friends and having fun," Jo Beth Skaggs recalls. "After grade four, we were supposed to go to separate elementary schools because she lived on one side of St. Francis—which is the main street running through town—and I lived on the other, yet somehow we talked her parents into having Sheryl go to South School with me."

Jo Beth now likens her childhood relationship with Sheryl to that of Lucy Ricardo and Ethel Mertz, the hapless buddies of *I Love Lucy*. Born just ten days apart, they were close from a very early age, and shared birthday parties were not the only things they had in common.

"Those two were inseparable," says Debbie Welsh. "If one of them bought something, the other one bought it, and I can still picture them going to Cosby's bakery on a Saturday morning, riding on the back of Mr. Skaggs's convertible in their matching pyjamas. They must have been nine or ten, and they were waving to everybody in the town square like they were homecoming queens."

Would-be performers at an early age, Sheryl and Jo Beth hung out together on an almost-daily basis, and they evolved into a threesome whenever Debbie Tate was around. Ann Cash and Carlotta Tarver joined them at various other times.

"It was a good place to grow up," says Carlotta, who lived just a block away from the Crows on West Washington Street. "Things may have been fairly conservative, but people generally got along. You know, I can remember hearing about some racial tensions that had been taking place in St. Louis and wondering what that was about. We had black kids at school but we never really experienced that kind of thing."

And so it went in Kennett, where down-home values ensured a virtual disregard for the transition from Kennedy-era innocence to counterculture cynicism. During an age of hippies, yippies, and acid freaks, this place may have had more in common with Andy Griffith's Mayberry, yet wholesome didn't necessarily equate with bland, as this bunch of kids still benefited from outside influences and a well-rounded upbringing.

"Both Ann and Carlotta's fathers were doctors, and Carlotta's father insisted that we all [go] to the opera with him when we were little," Jo Beth Skaggs remembers. "That comes from having exposure to different places. I mean, we definitely decided that Memphis was the place to go shopping and the place to hang out and go do things—we got our music from Memphis and our style from Memphis and our food from Memphis. So, that was one avenue. Then Sheryl's mother has family in Denver, so when Sheryl was little they'd go skiing there. Debbie has family in Boston and Florida, and I have family in Chicago, so we would scatter during the holidays and then compare notes when we got back."

A regular destination for the Crows was a vacation house at Lake Wappapello, about 50 miles northwest of Kennett. It was there that Sheryl learned to water ski, and where she and her friends would often explore the surrounding dirt roads and paths. From the age of nine, she and Ann Cash also attended Girl Scout camp at nearby Camp Latonka, yet another Native American–sounding locale that provided a change of scenery and variance to the routine of life back in the neighborhood.

Throughout Sheryl's childhood, an alternate source of company was a long line of family dogs. These included a favorite named Buddy, who was around during her junior-high years and whom she would reference in the song lyrics to "A Change" on her eponymous 1996 album. Earlier on, when Sheryl was six, a bite from another four-legged friend had left a small scar near her mouth.

"They took me to the hospital, and I don't know if they'd have sewn it up in the city, but they said that they didn't really sew mouths because there are too many germs," she told *Q* magazine in 1998. "About two weeks later the dog went missing. My grandmother had given him to some farm family. She didn't want to upset me, so she told me he ran away."

Things happen. Some of them go unnoticed, potential disasters that no one is aware of.

"There was a truck called the fogger, which sprayed for mosquitoes around the park and in the neighborhood," says Debbie Welsh, "and we can all distinctly remember getting on our bikes when we were seven, eight, nine, and riding behind that truck so that we could be in the fog. We cannot believe that we now don't have some kind of defects, because it was a pesticide. We thought it was so cool to 'ride the fogger,' and nobody thought otherwise. You see, the benefit of growing up in Kennett at that time was that as young girls we were able to ride our bikes at night, go for walks in the neighborhood, have just a great time, and feel safe."

In a place like Kennett the people invariably share in all of the gossip. They share in their kids' successes, while at the same time there's also the type of bitchery and small talk familiar to any small town; some jealousies, some competition. "Kind of like *Peyton Place*," says Debbie Welsh, "although back then you couldn't have too many affairs in Kennett because everybody knew everybody. There were some people who would stray to Memphis, thinking they could get away with it, but no, everybody knew."

See all, hear all, and in certain cases, tell all—the women in the bridge club were sure to be on the case. This setup could be a royal pain in the ass not only for those whose private foibles became public knowledge, but also for a bunch of free-spirited kids who, like their elders, didn't always comply with the age-old maxim to "do whatever you want, just don't get caught doing it." Still, as Debbie Welsh points out, it did have its benefits.

"If I messed up, I knew that Bernice Crow had the right to spank me, and my mother felt very comfortable that if Sheryl messed up she had the right to discipline her. Now, I don't actually remember a day when I ever got spanked by anybody else's mother, but just knowing they could ensured that we did the right thing. We knew we came from people who cared about us, and so everything was very functional.

"In Sheryl's case, her dad came home for lunch and her mom was always there because of the piano lessons. Kathy Crow and my sister were in the same class, but they were quite a bit older than us and didn't really want us around. We were much closer in age to Karen, but even hanging out with Karen and her friends would have been considered 'uncool,' and then Steven was the boy, so again we didn't interact much with him. However, the Crows are phenomenally close."

And so, for that matter, were Sheryl and Jo Beth, who enjoyed more success practicing their twirling routines than they did attracting boyfriends when they began attending Kennett Junior High.

"We were always lagging in that department," Jo Beth admits. "Of course, at that time you're not interested in any boys of your own age, you're interested in the juniors and seniors. Well, with Sheryl's house located right across from the high school, we would purposely sit around in her front yard, doing our homework, waiting for everybody to come out.

"Our interest in pop music really took off at around that time, and we always had the latest records. I think more than anybody else we listened to what was current. There were no radio stations in Kennett playing the music that we were interested in, so thank God we could pick up the ones in Memphis. Back then we were interested in bands like The Who and the Stones; a lot of classic rock. Sheryl had older siblings and a lot of my other friends had older siblings, and that was what they were interested in."

"As I got older I think I was inspired by writers as much as musicians," Sheryl recalled in a 1996 VH1 TV interview. "I guess that's why I've really gravitated to writers like Dylan.... There are so many other people that came out of that part of the world that I grew up in, around Memphis. You know, Derek & the Dominos, and Delaney and Bonnie, and even George Jones."

"The music played in the Crow household really ran the gamut," continues Jo Beth Skaggs. "Of course, they listened to a lot of jazz, and when we were attending junior high school there would be sheet music everywhere. Every single Carpenters song was out there, and Sheryl would listen over and over and over to every song on [Carole King's] *Tapestry* album. There was a healthy appreciation for all different kinds of music, and it was a very playful environment. Wendell and Bernice would encourage anything—their children were more or less required to learn piano, and then whatever else they were interested in would be fine."

Meanwhile, the girls' broadening range of activities during these formative years was often matched by a creativity that reflected their star aspirations. How about the time when a concrete floor in the Skaggs home was converted into a makeshift skating rink? With a family-room addition yet to be completed, Sheryl and Jo Beth capitalized by pouring a bag of white powdered sugar all over the bare floor. Not the best of surfaces for loops and triple Axels, but it was still easier than trying to freeze a pool of water. Then again, this wasn't necessarily just a spot of mischievous fun…at least not from Sheryl's perspective.

"When I was a kid I wanted to be an Olympic ice skater, the best ice skater," she'd tell Marc Woodworth. "It was that kind of drive to be good. I didn't get into music to be famous and have people look at me. I got into it because I wanted to be great at something."

Which, given the aforementioned need for recognition and approval, basically amounted to the same thing. Regardless, the phrase "great at something" is the key here, for Sheryl would go after the golden ring in a variety of ways during her teen years and, in true Crow fashion, excel in a number of different fields. Music, however, was the driving force, a source of inspiration, her first love.

"There have been very few times in my life when I gravitated to anything other than music," she would state. "I've only felt the pull of music…. I've never really seen myself as anything other than a musician."

CHAPTER TWO

# Superstar

If, for some Americans, the 1960s were a monument to optimism and excess, the early '70s were the come-down after the high: the directionless, anticlimactic follow-up to hallucinogen-based psychedelia, in which the inspired gave way to the contrived, flower power was supplanted by flared pants and platform heels, and peace and love ran headlong into a series of slap-in-the-face reality checks—defeat in Vietnam, a falling dollar, rising unemployment, severe price inflation, and a late-1973 energy crisis coinciding with a Census Bureau report that about one-tenth of all citizens lived below the poverty line. The age of innocence was officially at an end.

Post-Watergate, post-revelations about the CIA and FBI compiling secret dossiers on those considered to be a "threat to national security," America emerged from its worst domestic crisis since the Civil War to celebrate its bicentennial with a mixture of enthusiasm and skepticism. In 1976, those who were in the party mood closed a door on the depression of recent years by way of parades, fireworks, and flags. Others, including the underprivileged and the disaffected, didn't buy into all of the nationalism. Their memories were too fresh. In Kennett, life proceeded pretty much as normal.

September 2, 1976, was not only the first day of Sheryl's freshman year of high school, but also the date of the first rock concert that she ever attended. By that time, disco was having a heavy impact on the singles charts courtesy of tracks such as The Bee Gees' "You Should Be Dancing," Johnnie Taylor's "Disco Lady," The Sylvers' "Boogie Fever," Wild Cherry's "Play That Funky Music," The Miracles' "Love Machine (Part 1)," and KC & the Sunshine Band's "Shake Your Booty." An ominous sign of where this trend might be heading was the success of "Disco Duck (Part One)" by Rick Dees and His Cast of Idiots, yet just before punk infused the scene with a desperately needed shot in the rear end, mainstream rock continued its hold on the album charts.

Leading the pack was the double live set *Frampton Comes Alive!* which, thanks to a seventeen-week chart-topping run, sold over 13 million units to make it the most successful double album to date. And it was Peter Frampton, the boyish-faced guitarist/singer/songwriter and former pin-up with The Herd and Humble Pie, whom Sheryl and her friends traveled to Memphis to see on that summer night.

"God, we were in love with Peter Frampton!" recalls Debbie Welsh. "None of us could drive, so a couple of moms agreed to take six of us girls.... Whenever we'd go to Memphis most of them always left Kennett in rollers, so by the time they got there their hair would look beautiful. Depending on what Sheryl wanted, she went through a lot of hair phases—long straight hair, long curly hair, short straight hair. Anyway, there we were, with Sheryl and Jo Beth in the back of the station wagon, and a car full of junior and senior guys from Kennett came up behind us. Sheryl happened to have a crush on one of them, and I never saw her and Jo Beth hit the floorboards so fast, ripping the curlers out of their hair.

"When we got to the concert, we didn't know what to expect. Joints were flying past us and we were like 'Whoa, what's this?' We weren't used to any of it. We just thought we were in love with Peter Frampton."

"Sheryl and I were totally into it," Jo Beth Skaggs confirms. "We saw some other people who we knew from Kennett, and after we managed to get right in front of the stage my neighbor lifted Sheryl up on his shoulders so that she could wave at Peter Frampton."

"I told my friends I liked him when he was in Humble Pie," Sheryl later informed author Marc Woodworth, "and they just looked at me and asked, 'Who's Humble Pie?'"

By the age of fourteen, Wendell and Bernice Crow's youngest daughter was not only acquiring a better-than-average knowledge of the contemporary and classic rock scenes, but she was also becoming acutely aware of how music might satisfy her inherent need for popular recognition. After two decades of steady evolution, youth-oriented music was in a more esteemed position than ever before—it now dominated the charts to the exclusion of the pre-rock brigade—and pop journalism was at its height; at least, at the zenith of taking both the art form and itself completely seriously. Many teens devoured rock journals like *Creem* and *Rolling Stone,* while flashing a musical knowledge that often drew on the opinions of scribes such as Dave Marsh, Robert Palmer, Greil Marcus, and Lester Bangs. After all, cutting-edge tastes could have a status-enhancing effect within the classroom.

"Being into the right clothes or the right musicians is very important," Sheryl told Woodworth. "I was always a good girl but a bit of an outsider. When you're trying to please your parents, you don't get into too much trouble. The first time I went out with my friends to smoke pot I didn't even get to enjoy it because I felt so guilty. I was also on the periphery because I thought what was going on in music was so dismal—Kansas and Foreigner, all that corporate rock. Everybody knew who the lead singer of Boston was. I just couldn't relate to any of that. I was trying to get my friends into Van Morrison and Derek & the Dominos."

Indeed, The Beatles' landmark 1967 release, *Sgt. Pepper's Lonely Hearts Club Band,* had not only paved the way for numerous other artists' so-called "concept" albums and meisterwerks, but it had also heralded the era of progressive rock; music for the mind as well as the body. Naturally, the quality of these efforts varied wildly. For every Led Zeppelin and Pink Floyd there were countless pale imitators, and by the mid-'70s Sheryl was hardly the only person to be complaining about the void that had been created by the deaths of artists such as Joplin and Hendrix, and the emergence of homogeneous, generic-sounding bands that the record companies were marketing as "supergroups." It wasn't enough to be a star in the '70s; "superstar" was the epithet of choice.

Nevertheless, while Sheryl was fine-tuning her ears to the sounds of what would become known as "classic rock," at the opposite end of the musical spectrum she was also singing soprano at Kennett High in a light, sweet voice that would contrast dramatically with her style of singing today. Her musical education was nothing if not varied.

"In her freshman year we had a freshman chorus," explains Sheryl's former music teacher, James Finch. "Then, in the other three years, we had a mixed high school choir, and there was a girls' sextet that she also participated in. Normally around fifty to sixty kids participated in the chorus and they would meet five days a week. We always did a Christmas concert featuring traditional Christmas music, and then in the spring we would do a variety of pop selections and heavier choral pieces. We used the sextet quite a bit to perform a lighter variety of music for local city groups and clubs, and Sheryl was also a member of what we called a mixed ensemble group, which would rehearse in the afternoon once a week."

"She could sing wonderful harmony as well as the lead vocal," adds Jo Beth Skaggs, who sang soprano alongside Sheryl. "It was kind of funny because I hadn't heard that side of her, but of course her mother has a beautiful operatic voice. She sings 'Ave Maria' almost every year in the Christmas cantata. For such a small town Kennett has this huge talent pool. There are a lot of people with very good voices, and I always thought that Sheryl's was right up there."

Having taught both Kathy and Karen Crow before Sheryl entered his class, James Finch fully expected the youngest sister to conform to the family's established standards. He wasn't disappointed.

"I knew of Sheryl's talents from the choral director at the middle school, so I utilized those talents even [when she was] a freshman," he says. "She could sing quite well—I used her for a solo when we did some pieces from Handel's *Messiah*—and she was also an extremely good accompanist.

"Kathy was very talented, and Karen was arguably even better on the piano than Sheryl. I had this really unique experience of teaching the three sisters. From 1972, when I came to Kennett, through 1980, I always had one of the Crow girls playing or singing for me, and I was really fortunate in that regard, but it would be hard to distinguish between their talents."

"My elder sister was really talented at playing classical piano," Sheryl would say about Karen in a 1998 *Q* magazine interview. "Bach and all sorts. But I had really bad kidney problems and I was in the hospital, and the day of her senior recital they let me out and wheeled me into her recital in a wheelchair. It was such a big deal. And I remember being the focal point instead of her. I remember that so vividly...."

Meanwhile, music wasn't the only source of interest. Prior to her sixteenth birthday, Sheryl shared the frustration of most non-driving American teens confined to that social underclass of fleet-footed adolescent wannabes—relying on parental transport to hang around fast-food joints and shopping malls as a means of networking and killing time...not that Kennett had any shopping malls in which to hang out. There, the local Dairy Queen was where the girls would gather and pose, desperately hoping to catch the eyes of some older guys.

"All of the high school kids hung out at the Dairy Queen, and before we could drive, Sheryl and I felt that we needed to be there too," Jo Beth Skaggs recalls. "So, we would have one of our parents drive us there, but of course we had to get dropped off at the back so that no one could see, and then we'd come strolling up like we'd just walked in the door. Nobody would pay any attention to us."

"It was so sad," says Debbie Welsh. "The freshman girls would all be in tow, walking from Dairy Queen to Pizza Hut, and we'd be so embarrassed that we had to walk. Of course, it would be the same guys who you would see every time, but that was okay. You had your crushes, and your crushes lasted for two years of your life."

Then you turned sixteen, and it was time to cruise for real…Kennett-style. Starting at Parr's grocery store, near where the Crows lived, the weekend ritual consisted of driving on St. Francis to the town square, continuing on Main Street to the Sonic drive-in, circling Sonic, turning back towards town, heading for Parr's, and then circling and starting all over again. In short, it amounted to a strong dose of déjà vu that could well have been contrived by parents trying to keep tabs on their kids. This was not the Sunset Strip.

"We'd do that the whole night," Debbie Welsh recalls. "People would be cruising, and they'd stop at Parr's and talk to you for a while, and you'd all switch cars and do it again. Especially when you were a sophomore or a freshman, you wanted to circle Sonic, because that's where the junior and senior boys were. I can't even believe we used to do that, but we'd cruise for hours and think it was great. We'd pull up the car, sit there, drink beers…well, we didn't drink beer back then, or we did but nobody knew about it—we'd only admit so much."

"There weren't a whole load of new faces," adds Jo Beth Skaggs. "We'd grown up with the same people, and so I guess that's why by the time we reached high school age, we were interested in people with whom we hadn't grown up—it was very hard to be romantic with somebody whom you'd taken baths with."

Sheryl would later tell Britain's *NME* magazine that the worst trouble she got into at around this time was "staying out all night when I was 17. I was on a date and we got caught in a snowstorm." This gives some idea as to how "wild" things could really get— less like a scene out of a juvenile deliquency flick than one from *White Christmas*. Still, the guy's name was Pete, and according to Sheryl he was her "first love," even though she'd already caught the eye of another high-schooler, Brian Mitchell.

"We had attended the same schools together, but I never really got to know her until 1978," Mitchell recalls. "A mutual friend and I went up to the Crows' lake house and met the whole family, and my first recollection of Sheryl is of seeing her in the lake and of noticing her unbelievable beauty. Our friendship just progressed from there, and I ended up taking her to the prom in her senior year, 1980.

"There's just such a dichotomy between what she actually was and what was expected of someone with her talent and looks at that age. She was a standout at high school in every area and for all the right reasons. There wasn't a thing petty about her, there wasn't a thing artificial. She had the talent, had the looks, had the brains, and tons of friends."

"Sheryl is very charismatic, and people of all ages have always been drawn to her," adds Ann Cash. "She's an affectionate person who's really comfortable reaching out to touch people or hug them. If someone was to do something that she liked or thought was good, she'd think nothing of gushing over it and hugging or kissing them on the cheek. From the time we were small, people wanted to be around her, and when we got to our teen years all the guys thought she was the coolest thing ever."

Among them, Brian Mitchell.

"We were hardly ever romantic," he says. "I hung around the family because of Sheryl, but I also hung around Sheryl because of the family. To me, even if there was no aesthetic attraction, they would still be a family that anybody would be drawn to just because of the bond, the love they had, and the way they explicitly showed that love. If there were rivalries or instances of pettiness between the siblings, they were shown, they weren't hidden or skirted around. They had family discussions, and I had never sat through a family discussion where you aired your differences with the intent to solve them."

Still, while the Crow kids evidently thrived within this tight-knit, open-minded atmosphere, Sheryl was increasingly feeling the pressure to be straight-A in everything she did.

"My siblings and I were always expected to do the best we could," she would tell Marc Woodworth. "My dad used to joke that if you showed him a good loser, he'd show you a loser. Although that's a funny saying, it really tells you something about doing the right thing. I'd get so wrapped up in that voice in my head that I didn't really develop my own vision or know how to make my own choices. Even learning how to drive was a major anxiety for me, because I worried I'd do it wrong in front of my father. I'm really close to my dad now and realize that most people have complicated relationships with their parents, but some of his expectations were hard to live up to. For a long time I was someone who went through life not letting myself experience happiness or pain. By closing myself off to emotion, I didn't really have to experience anything."

As a teenager growing up in a small town where the God-fearing inhabitants played mostly by the rules, Sheryl yearned for something more—something offbeat, darker, more theoretically exciting. Unable to make contact with the kinds of individuals and experiences that she was encountering in films and novels, let alone get in touch with her own feelings, she lived vicariously through the characters that she'd create inside her own head—an assortment of mavericks and dropouts who tapped into her self-perceived isolation. Years later, some of these characters would re-emerge in her song lyrics.

"I was raised around farm people who possessed a straightforward ethical code," Sheryl told Marc Woodworth. "I never had a life that touched the underbelly, so early on I imagined myself as a character very different from who and where I was. I pictured myself as a loner, off living like a Jack Kerouac character, or worse, someone out of a Charles Bukowski book; one of those down-and-outers who works at a gas station and has no one, no family. Imagining myself through these characters was a way to approximate something without actually feeling it. There have been occasions when I lost someone or felt real pain, and all of a sudden a character I know or invented became me. That's all part of the process, I guess. But most of the time I couldn't feel anything for myself."

And so, in a world where one of the oldest common denominators is that collective need to stand out from the crowd, Sheryl pressed on with her quest to establish an identity based upon achievement, academic or otherwise. This included spells as a track competitor; a drum majorette; a Freshman Maid, Senior Maid, and Paperdoll Queen; a member of the Pep Club, National Honor Society, and Future Farmers of America; and even as an alto sax player in the school band.

"That was not a typical instrument for a girl to play," says Jo Beth Skaggs. "We all had to pick an instrument to play in the school band during the concert series, and she was really good on sax. I know she took lessons for that—the rest of us didn't take lessons; it just sort of came out.

"Sheryl's got the coolest head in the world. Nothing to her is a big deal. I remember when she was made a drum majorette over everybody at high school, it was like, 'Yeah, okay, great.' Her attitude was 'Well, that's supposed to happen, because I worked really hard for it.' The same with her track activities. I don't want to say that she expected to do well, but she knew she had worked really hard to do it and she had a sense of her own ability. I know sometimes when she didn't achieve personal goals, she would generally be disappointed and unable to understand what had happened."

One such time was during her senior year, when Sheryl's concerted efforts to be crowned Homecoming Queen didn't pay off. Everything had been planned well in advance—she'd seemingly worked herself into all of the right situations—yet even though she made it to the finals the decisive votes went to another girl. That wasn't easy to take, not least because it was an aberration in an otherwise over-achieving existence.

"Becoming the Paperdoll Queen at Kennett High is based solely on photographs," explains Ann Cash. "The selected candidates get to pose for photos, and those are then sent to a celebrity who picks the winner. Rick Dees, who hit the big time with 'Disco Duck,' was once a deejay in Memphis, and it was he who selected Sheryl as the Paperdoll Queen during our senior year."

"When Sheryl put her mind to it, she got it," adds Debbie Welsh. "There were no ifs, ands, or buts about it. If she wanted it, she went out and earned it."

Which is precisely what Sheryl did in terms of her athletic endeavors, ranging from hurdling to running up to seven miles a day as part of a cross-country workout through town or along the St. Francis River.

"When we had the levees we would go out and run those levees," says Billy Wilkerson, Sheryl's former athletic coach and science teacher, who would officiate track and field at the 1984 Los Angeles Olympics. "If they were fairly high levees we would run figure-eights on those, and then when we finished that we would come back and I would line them up and send them off in different categories, running back into town."

"Those workouts weren't easy," asserts Carlotta Tarver, who ran track with Sheryl. "Billy Wilkerson drove us hard and there were times when it could be drudgery. Still, it took place after school, and it was our choice to do it."

"Sheryl was a good cross-country runner," continues Wilkerson, "and as a hurdler in her senior year she was second in the district, which qualified her to go to State. You have a district track meet and then you can go to another one, which is a sectional, and they take three runners from the district and four from the sectional and they'll end up with the sixteen best in Jefferson City. Then you run a prelim there to get into the final eight. Well, Sheryl got into the finals at State and was placed sixth; she clipped a couple of hurdles and that made the difference, but I think she was satisfied.

"The last time they'd had girls' track was back in the '40s, and after I got here and they renewed girls' track in the early '70s she was the first Kennett girl to score a point in the girls' state meet. Sheryl was very dedicated. With mostly anything she went into she was dedicated. In that era I don't know of many girls who really wanted to take on track and field and take it to college."

As it happens, the state finals marked the end of Sheryl's track career, because it was music that she intended to study at the University of Missouri. However, Wilkerson's point is well taken—Sheryl Crow gave everything her best shot, and in the Kennett High School Class of 1980 she and her friends distinguished themselves among most of their contemporaries by being among the few to enter Mizzou.

"Our high school did not teach kids to send them on to college," says Debbie Welsh. "Our high school taught kids because this was where a lot of them would stop, so it taught vocational skills—woodwork class, car-painting class. There were three people in the chemistry class. They offered the high-end classes, but very few people were taking them.

"Six or eight of us left Kennett High School and went on to Mizzou, and we were the ones who were considered scholars. Everybody else went off to junior colleges or two-year schools, but I have to say it also never dawned on me that I could go outside of Missouri. I never thought I could look at the University of Arizona or Northwestern in Chicago. It was not even in my thought process, because we didn't have counselors who thought like that. It was about what factory you wanted to work in, and that to me was the only limitation of the small town; so many people either stay or come back, they don't realize that they can get out if they want to."

Ann Cash doesn't necessarily agree. "For a town our size I think the education level was pretty good, and I don't think most people were being trained to do blue-collar jobs," she says. "We weren't the only people to be considered scholars. Lot of kids in our class made excellent grades and went to Mizzou or other colleges. None of us went to an Ivy League school, but there are several people in Kennett who have."

Cash's mother was a teacher within the Kennett school system, as were those of Debbie Welsh and Jo Beth Skaggs. Creative, independent, career-oriented people, they and their husbands instilled their children with a powerful sense of self-sufficiency. So did Wendell and Bernice Crow.

"All of us, Sheryl included, have very strong female identity role models in our mothers," says Jo Beth Skaggs. "I can remember my own mother saying, 'Get your own bank account, make your own way in the world, and don't rely on a man to do it.' So, although we were all very family-oriented, it was never expected of us to automatically go off and get married and have a family. If that's what we wanted to do, then fine, but it was never thrust upon us, and that was one aspect of life in Kennett. There's a kind of split. I mean, [Kennett native] Sally Stapleton won a Pulitzer Prize in journalism, so that's one avenue you could take, and then there's the other avenue which a lot of my girlfriends took, and that was probably because they didn't have the same exposure to different environments as we had."

They also didn't have Sheryl's resolve and self-motivation. Nobody did. Here was a classic case of the effort to back up the talent, and the talent to back up the effort.

"She had a heck of a drive in whatever she attempted to do," remembers James Finch. "In addition to her choral work we'd always do a spring Broadway musical, and she played piano for two of those; she accompanied *Shenandoah* and *Fiddler on the Roof,* and in 1980 she was also the choreographer for *Damn Yankees.*"

In fact, Sheryl shared the choreography chores with Jo Beth Skaggs, drawing on her experience as a drum majorette to attain the desired results for *Damn Yankees.*

"Just getting the guys to move all at the same time is a heck of an effort," says Finch, "and it's also something for a student to be teaching other students. She had a good way of working with the other kids and working with the director. She clearly could deal with that kind of situation.

"She was really busy musically, active in girls' track, and then she was in bands. If you look at her list of activities in her senior year it's unbelievable. That supposed overnight success that she had, Sheryl worked on it for years. That's what is so impressive. We've probably had people as talented as her at other times, but what really set her apart was the determination to achieve."

In the fall of 1980, that determination accompanied Sheryl to the University of Missouri in Columbia, where over the next four years she would major in voice and piano. From now on there would be a central focus to her life, and while the goals would remain modest, the short-term ambitions would be easily realized.

# CHAPTER THREE

# Mizzou Days

"Some people can sit down and play more notes per ten seconds than almost anyone else, but what you need as a performer goes beyond that," says Ray Herbert. "It goes into communication, and that was a strong aspect of Sheryl's musicality. It wasn't necessarily about virtuosic speed and power—that's not what she was all about—but as far as being able to communicate a piece of music effectively she was really as good as it gets."

Herbert was Sheryl Crow's piano teacher at the University of Missouri from September of 1980 until she graduated just under four years later. During that time he saw "a young lady with a vision. Highly motivated, very quiet, reserved, conscientious, diligent. There was a quiet level of enthusiasm, but I could tell that it was intense. Still waters run deep."

Be that as it may, Sheryl's level of enthusiasm was probably quiet for a good reason. She wasn't exactly bowled over by what she perceived as the attitude of some of the teachers, and neither was she completely at ease with all aspects of life on campus. At the age of eighteen, she was both cognizant of her own abilities and accustomed to the kind of response they would normally produce. However, this wasn't Kennett. The student body of MU was more than twice as large as the entire population of Sheryl's hometown, and it also comprised people whose attitudes were markedly different from those to which she was accustomed.

Located in Columbia, at the midpoint along I-70 between Kansas City to the west and St. Louis to the east, "Mizzou" has managed to attract quality students to its music program over the years despite that program's limited resources and sometimes substandard facilities. In this regard, it has suffered the same plight as numerous other college music departments around the country that need to constantly justify their existence to non-arts-oriented administrators.

"Conditions have improved, but at the time Sheryl was there the pianos were miserable, the practice rooms were small and insufficient, and the space for ensembles was less than adequate," recalls Ray Herbert, who joined the music faculty back in 1967. "As a result, it wasn't easy to inspire and motivate the students, but we managed it.

"One of our responsibilities as professors—like with athletics—was to recruit fine talent, and I was fortunate to have a sort of inside track on Sheryl because of her sister Karen, whom I'd already recruited and who was a huge natural talent. In fact, Sheryl was not of the same level as Karen, but no two people are the same anyway. Karen could have easily been a piano performance major, but she elected to do music education because she had a vocational calling to teach in the public schools."

Sheryl had to audition for her course of study by way of preparing and playing a number of different classical piano pieces. In this way, the faculty would assess whether she and the other students had a reasonable chance to develop and graduate with a view to landing a job in their chosen field.

"Over the course of four years they'd be expected to play Bach, Mozart, Chopin, Bartók, Rachmaninoff—nineteenth-century, baroque, and romantic—as well as twentieth-century music ranging from George Gershwin to Aaron Copland," explains Herbert. "Sheryl passed her audition, and I'd say that she was at the average level for those students who qualified. However, she obviously also had vocal talents, so she studied voice in addition to all of the other components, like music history, and music harmony and theory, which covered chord structure and the grammar of music."

Voice and piano lessons were conducted one-on-one; other performance courses were taught as part of an ensemble, including the insipidly named Singsation, a harmony group consisting of between ten and sixteen voices.

"Sheryl was our accompanist on a trip to Romania and Bulgaria," recalls Ira "Rocky" Powell, the music professor who directed Singsation. "However, she also had a beautiful voice, and so I used her as a soloist for every concert we did over the course of about three years."

As if all of this wasn't enough, general College of Education requirements entailed the study of American history, mathematics, and English, as well as how to discourse on the various subjects from a pedagogical standpoint.

"It was a very full load," admits Ray Herbert. "Just in terms of piano lessons the minimum would be twelve hours a week, and we wouldn't like to see people do much more than eighteen, but Sheryl was pretty much sixteen, seventeen, eighteen hours all the way through. What I taught her would have consisted of several pieces of Bach or Scarlatti; at least one Beethoven sonata, one Haydn sonata, and one Mozart sonata; probably several nineteenth-century pieces, like Brahms or a Chopin nocturne; and then pieces by Bartók, Gershwin, Copland, and Samuel Barber."

It was a well-balanced diet. What's more, even though recitals weren't required in the music education degree program, each semester Sheryl had to play an applied exam for the faculty—otherwise known as the jury—which entailed the memorizing of two or three pieces. At the end of her sophomore year she also had to pass a special test in order to advance to the next level. This wasn't a problem.

"Sheryl had a good sense of phrasing, a really good feel for melodic lines, and a very, very steady rhythmic beat," says Herbert. "She was able to grasp essential concepts and assimilate a piece of music very quickly. She never compared herself to her sister, but I sensed a very competitive streak within her. She was, I think, a real over-achiever, at least in terms of her piano playing. She had a can-do attitude and was extremely focused."

Above and beyond her regular piano lessons, Sheryl also attended all of Ray Herbert's performance classes as a means of acquiring the chops to play in front of an audience. "We actively encouraged her to gain the experience of playing in public," he remembers. "We considered that a very important component of the entire picture."

Sheryl's invaluable grounding in the fundamentals of keyboard playing didn't reflect—but certainly prepared her for—the technological trends that were taking place on the contemporary music scene. The early '80s saw the mass emergence of the synthesizer, which had developed from a complicated, oversized piece of electrical equipment into a more portable and facile instrument. Although still analog and polyphonic, this was capable of producing innovative sounds while inspiring the "futurist" image of various new artists.

Indeed, "new" was often a necessary designation at the dawn of a video-conscious, techno-pop age. Punk had given way to "new wave" (a generic catch-all for just about anyone with exotic makeup and gelled hair) and mainstream middle-of-the-roadies were vying with opulently named "New Romantics" such as Ultravox and Spandau Ballet. Raw energy had been eclipsed by slick images and even slicker devices—in Britain, where bluebeat had been reincarnated as ska, and the mods were enjoying a short-lived revival, a satirical TV show titled *Not the Nine O'Clock News* pretty much nailed the issue; a skit in the form of a colorful music video featured a group of poseurs singing "Nice Video, Shame About The Song."

A decade later, Sheryl Crow would capitalize on a scene that had somewhat redressed the balance between machinery, material, and marketing. In the meantime, she bore down on her studies.

"Whenever I asked her to prepare something, she did it," says Ray Herbert. "When I asked her to go a little farther and push the level of the bar a bit higher, she did it. And when I asked her to come in so that I could give her extra time, she was there. She was eager to learn. I would put it this way: 'Sheryl, if you want to be very good, let's do this. If you want to be superb, let's do this. If you want to be all-world, let's do this,' and it was always the latter that she subscribed to."

Nevertheless, even given her propensity for over-achievement, it appears that at least part of the reason why Sheryl was constantly prepared to go that extra step at college stemmed from a feeling—described to fellow students and, subsequently, mentioned in several press interviews—that she was never accorded the respect she deserved within the music department.

"Some professors maybe didn't take her seriously because she was in a sorority, she was pretty, and she didn't superficially appear as studious as some of the other music majors," says Betsy Lenger (formerly Betsy Remley) who, like Sheryl, pledged herself to the sisterhood of Kappa Alpha Theta on enrolling at MU. "Still, she was smart enough to be able to study and also have a good social life, and I think she had a good time, although she never fully embraced the whole sorority party thing. I don't think that ever fit with her image, even though the particular sorority that we were in catered more to people who were studious."

"This was during that period when people were still wearing preppy clothes on campus, and there was a fun, carefree atmosphere," adds Shelle Jensen (formerly Shelle Stewart), another Kappa Alpha Theta sister who went on to become a long-term friend. "I think Sheryl generally took part in that, although I've also heard her say that she really wasn't all that happy there, and in looking back I would think part of that was because it was too confining for her. She had an artiness and a restlessness about her, and I think when she encountered people who didn't express themselves more creatively it could be frustrating for her.

"Sheryl's musical talent was clearly evident right from the start. She'd sit down at the piano in the sorority house living room and play whatever you asked her to play without music or anything. She really has a gift and she's also extremely driven. I think there's something inside her that has always wanted to prove something, and that may just be a trait that she'll always have, no matter what she achieves.

"Still, a lot of the sorority girls were jealous of Sheryl, and she had quite a few mean things done to her; catty, stupid, girlie things, like pouring alcohol in her bed, group gossiping, and leaving weird notes. It was all about jealousy and not accepting her for who she was; about being unhappy and trying to take it out on somebody else because she appears to have it all and you don't. That kind of thing can hurt when you're eighteen or nineteen years old and still trying to figure out who the heck you are."

"There were definitely people who had problems with her because she was smart and beautiful," Betsy Lenger concurs. "Those are difficult things for some people to deal with, and I think that was a challenge for her."

There were fourteen sororities at MU when Sheryl was there, all vying with one another for scholarships and the best-looking girls. Since Karen Crow was already a member of Kappa Alpha Theta, it was only natural for her younger sister to follow suit—tradition plays a large part in such things, as do the right connections. After attending numerous parties where existing members could determine suitability based upon her résumé—being "rushed," to use the vernacular—Sheryl pledged to Theta, along with Shelle Stewart, Betsy Remley, and childhood friend Ann Cash.

"We went to rush at all fourteen houses, and people are usually cut by at least one of them," says Cash, who was rejected by one of the houses herself. "That's because you might not have ties at a particular house or they just might not be interested in you, but no house cut Sheryl. That's quite a feat."

For their part, Kennett natives such as Jo Beth Skaggs and Debbie Tate each joined other sororities.

"Once you got into your sororities those kinda became your life, so even though I kept in touch with Sheryl and Jo Beth and we would share clothes every now and then, our days of being totally bonded came to an end," says Debbie. "We were moving on now, and Sheryl was meeting new friends and dating, so that started separating us out a little bit. Also, being that we were in different schools [within the university], our classes never crossed paths.... A lot of us stayed up at Mizzou for summer school, and Sheryl and I were roommates there during our junior year, but thanks to our different schedules we still didn't see a lot of each other."

Sheryl initially roomed with Ann Cash in a dormitory at MU—they wouldn't live in a sorority house until their sophomore year—and it was there that Ann first saw Sheryl with a guitar.

"We didn't have very much room in the dorm, and we weren't allowed to put nails in the walls, so we'd hang things from sticky tape strips," Ann recalls. "Sheryl had a really large sticky tape hook over her bed and she hung the guitar there, but the problem was that the tape didn't always stick and the guitar would fall off. We were always concerned that it would fall and smack Sheryl in the face while she was sleeping, but it never did.... I don't remember her ever actually playing the guitar in front of me. I just remember it being there."

At the same time, while Ann Cash was a welcome presence within a new environment, Sheryl also eased her way into college life in the company of the aforementioned Shelle Stewart, who was majoring in home economics and journalism, and Betsy Remley, who was majoring in engineering.

"She was just one of those kinds of people who you're drawn to," explains Shelle. "Very talented, very funny—she's got a great sense of humor, kind of off-the-wall, and I think some of that comes out in her music. Sheryl was just a lot of fun to be with. Whenever we'd go out to the bars or to a frat party we'd be all dolled up, Sheryl would walk in, people's heads would immediately turn to look at her, and all we'd hear from her was, 'Will you hold my purse?' She's just beautiful and she's got that way about her. That's something we still laugh about. She's got her entourage, and it was the same way in college.

"In our freshman year we did the spring break trip, piling into a van and driving to Fort Walton Beach, Florida, where we stayed at some cheapo place, went around the bars, ate the free appetizers during happy hour, and once again ended up holding Sheryl's purse. Still, she was never a party girl. I mean, we all drank beer, but we certainly weren't wasted every night, and she also wasn't smoking pot or doing drugs. On the other hand, she had a funkiness to her, and she always picked these real different clothes to wear."

When the girls went on trips together, one thing they tried to ensure was that Sheryl didn't drive. Or if she did, someone would sit up front beside her, keeping an eye on what was going on. The reason: her tendency to fall asleep at the wheel, or anywhere else for that matter.

"One thing Sheryl's never had a problem with is sleeping," says Jo Beth Skaggs. "She would nod off for fifteen minutes and then wake up and be fine. She can sleep anywhere. I can distinctly remember when we were driving home we'd all be kind of excited about Christmas or whatever, and before we even got out of the city limits she was asleep."

"Sheryl can fall asleep in two seconds in the strangest positions," confirms Ann Cash. "We would study side-by-side in the dorm room, she'd fall asleep, and I wouldn't even realize it for awhile."

The sad irony about these episodes of near-narcolepsy is that, when everyone else was ready to grab some shut-eye, Sheryl had a justifiable fear about dozing off, stemming from an affliction that she shared with her mother—sleep paralysis. This is the condition of being awake yet completely frozen, unable to move or speak, which usually strikes shortly after waking up but can also occur just before falling asleep. Some sufferers have hallucinations where they see ghoulish figures looming over them as they lie helpless in bed, others swear they have been abducted by aliens, and some women might experience the feeling of being raped.

"There would be nights where I would be so afraid to go to sleep," Sheryl told Fred Schruers in a 1996 interview for *Rolling Stone*. "In sleep paralysis, sometimes you get to the point where you are sure you're going to die in the dream, and your breathing stops and all that. It's a bizarre and twisted feeling where you feel completely paralyzed. And then the fear that comes along—it makes your heart race, it makes you sweat."

Sleep paralysis also results in sleep deprivation that may have accounted for at least some of the instances when Sheryl had trouble keeping her eyes open during the waking hours.

"When she started dating Mike Rechtien we would do a lot of things together with all our boyfriends, and if we went to a dance and then on to dinner, it was amazing how Sheryl would just nod off at the table in mid-sentence," recalls Betsy Lenger. "During our senior year we wanted to take an easy class together, so we were in organizational theory, and when we'd try to share notes after a lecture she would have the first three words and then there would be a straight line where she'd just fallen asleep."

The aforementioned Mike Rechtien majored in voice, was in some of the same classes as Sheryl, and as her first serious boyfriend would eventually learn that "she was haunted as she slept. She often told me that she thought she was awake and was screaming for help and no one heard her."

Not that he was aware of this right away, for whereas Shelle Jensen perceived her friend as "beautiful, vivacious, and smiling all the time," Rechtien initially considered Sheryl to be "kind of a cute girl who never smiled. She seemed like an unhappy person and I was a pretty happy-go-lucky guy, already dating a girl, so we didn't really cross paths much until a few years later."

Nevertheless, when they did, Mike paved the way for Sheryl's initial outings as a pop performer. After playing guitar and singing at the local Catholic church during his second year at MU, he formed a band named Cashmere in the summer of 1981 with percussion major Fred Moreadith. By the fall, they were performing their first gigs.

"I think the name Cashmere came from somebody's girlfriend's cat," says Rechtien, who took care of guitar and vocals in the six-piece lineup, alongside Moreadith on drums, lead singer Leslie White, lead guitarist Byron Baker, bass player Jim Redick, and keyboard player Rob Brown.

"All of us were in school together, aside from Byron and Jim, who both worked," Fred Moreadith recalls. "We covered contemporary material, together with a few originals that Mike had written and which we played now and again just for fun. Occasionally we went out of town, but the majority of our jobs were at fraternity parties and in the local bars on campus.

"Leslie White stayed with us almost a year, and when she left the band we replaced her with Sheryl, who was with us during her junior and senior years. We really only had so many choices in the music school, and she just fit the bill. She was very enthusiastic, really wanted to sing with the band, and she had a lot of energy. She was a completely different singer to Leslie, who had more of a trained voice, but Sheryl just kind of fell into it and it was a good fit. A couple of the guys initially questioned her inclusion because she had never been in a band like that before, but it didn't take very long for everybody to see that it was going to work."

"We kind of liked her because she was in the Greek [fraternity/sorority] system, which none of us were, and she seemed to be popular, which meant that we'd probably get a lot more gigs at the frat houses," adds Mike Rechtien. "In fact, although I'd previously thought she never smiled, once I got to know her she was outgoing and a lot of fun, and when she smiled she definitely was pretty cute."

Thanks to this revised attitude and newfound appreciation, Mike had actually taken Sheryl out on a date before she ever joined the band. However, the prospective love match initially got off to a false start.

"She was interested in this other guy who had just broken up with his girl, and I was kind of chasing that girl, so nothing much happened," Mike recalls. "Then, at some point after she joined Cashmere, we started dating seriously. You see, I had already dated Leslie White, so there was a moratorium on us dating within the band, but I started dating Sheryl on the sly anyway.

"One of the numbers that we sang together was 'Endless Love,' and we just nailed that song. At that time I was doing church music and I'd sing at a lot of weddings, and I thought, 'Man, she sings that stuff so well, but she can't sing rock.' It just wasn't there, so we did a lot of male vocal material—Doobie Brothers, Lynyrd Skynyrd—as well as pop stuff by bands like The Go-Go's, Nena's '99 Red Balloons,' and the college kids just loved it."

Among the popular student hangouts in Columbia during the early 1980s were music venue The Blue Note and Bullwinkle's, a bar that offered live music as an added attraction on weekends. It was the latter that booked Cashmere, hoping to bring in many of the students that the band had already been attracting on the college party circuit.

"Back then there were very few clubs in Columbia that had live entertainment," says former Bullwinkle's owner Ken McClure. "Still, Cashmere was a pretty average college band, and without their drawing power within the college community I'm not sure they would have ever played at our place. Bullwinkle's could hold between 700 and 900 people, and the nights they were playing it would usually fill up. During the year that they performed there, they would probably play two nights a month, on either a Friday or Saturday.... I remember Sheryl as always friendly and outgoing, with a very strong personality. Even back then you could tell that she was pretty much in control of her own thing."

The six-piece configuration with Sheryl and Mike on lead vocals lasted a year, before the decision was taken to veer the band's direction away from rock and pop towards more funky and danceable R&B-type material. At that point, Byron Baker, Jim Redick, and Rob Brown all departed. A local musician named Frank Ramos was recruited to play guitar, and while Mike Rechtien took over on bass, Sheryl played keyboards. The two of them continued to share the vocal chores.

"When we first started dating I was also seeing another girl, and at that point I had a lot of fun, but when I started dating Sheryl on her own the relationship turned really difficult," says Rechtien. "We actually ended up getting engaged, and I was ready to pursue the relationship more than stay in the band. However, although Sheryl wanted the relationship, she didn't want to give up the band. In fact, I would have probably stopped playing a long time before we did, but that seemed to be very difficult for her, and I was trying to keep her happy so that our relationship would go well. We'd go out and play places where I didn't want to be, and she was just having the time of her life."

"We may have all had it in the back of our minds that we'd love to go further with it, but really it was just a status thing and a source of income," adds Fred Moreadith. "Mike had aspirations, but he was more into Christian music and so his ideas weren't necessarily the same as everyone else's. Then again, I think Sheryl also wanted to do a little more with the band, and that she was more disappointed than the rest of us when we disbanded and went our own way at the end of the 1983–84 year. We all graduated and so to me it was a natural transition, but I think she was very disappointed because we had a nice camaraderie, we all got along well, we had fun, and we made some money.

"Some people have unrealistic dreams, but if you don't have those you're never going to get anywhere. Well, Sheryl always seemed to have that element, like 'Come on, guys, let's work on some original material,' or 'Let's go play some of the clubs in St. Louis and Kansas City.' It's a case of having a reality base as well as some faith to realize your dreams, and I think she had that kind of edge."

Meanwhile, whereas numerous other music majors went on to earn master's and doctoral degrees, Sheryl sufficed with the Bachelor of Music that was a prerequisite for her to teach within the public school system. At that time, a master's degree and an established concert career would have been the minimum to join a university faculty (today a doctoral degree is the base level), yet according to Ray Herbert this wasn't what Sheryl aspired to.

"As I perceived it back then, her goal was to be a teacher instead of a performer," he says. However, his student may have been conveying mixed signals, for according to the recollections of several of Sheryl's friends, Herbert is wide of the mark.

"It was sort of obvious that Sheryl wasn't ever comfortable or content with most of her career options," says Betsy Lenger. "There were a lot of things that she could have done, because she had good grades and she was a tremendous interview, but I never thought that teaching was something she would want to do. It was clear that she was focused on something else."

Sheryl herself has since asserted that she only attained formal career qualifications in order to appease her parents, and that by her early twenties she was disoriented and mad at the world for having compromised herself. Mike Rechtien agrees.

"There is absolutely no doubt in my mind that she wanted to be famous," he says. "Sheryl is very driven, and recognition was very important to her at the time when I knew her. Of course, at that age it's important to almost everybody, but most people wouldn't go to the extent that she eventually would to try and get it.

"She always talked about going to Los Angeles when we graduated, and I was like, 'There is no way I am going to Los Angeles. I just came to get an education, I want to get a job, that's what I'm here for,' and I'd repeat the things that my father had said: 'You know how many people are out there trying to make it?' I was not at all interested in a musical career. I just wanted to lead a normal life, and I think that's why later on she would have a lot of anger towards me."

Indeed, instead of heading for the West Coast, in the summer of 1984 Sheryl followed her fiancé to St. Louis, where he'd already secured his first job and she would acquire gainful employment teaching music at an elementary school—a conventional duo, heading for earthbound stability in that riverfront city along the banks of the Mississippi. Some of the people who knew Sheryl wondered what the hell she was doing. She may have wondered the same, but she went along with her guy, and within a matter of weeks she would find herself pretty much alone in a place where she'd never intended to be.

Still, this is Sheryl Crow we're talking about—Sheryl Crow, whose well-known determination and resilience are matched by an invaluable knack for turning adversity to her own advantage. Temporarily diverted from her predestined course, she would soon get her bearings and, like a divining rod finding water, begin to zero in on her desired objectives. It would be in St. Louis that Sheryl would make her first important music-business connection, and in so doing she would begin laying the basic foundations for her future career.

# CHAPTER FOUR

# Gateway to the West

In early June of 1984, with a Bachelor of Music degree under her belt, Sheryl and her fiancé moved to St. Louis…and straight into separate living quarters—she just north of the city, he to the west.

"After college, I wanted to try to return to a closer relationship with God," says Mike Rechtien. "I had previously tried to draw Sheryl into that—we'd both once gone to a Christian conference in Dallas with my folks—but instead I'd allowed our relationship to dictate that part of my life. Still, religion was important to us when we were dating. For me it was definitely the reason why we never had sex. I wanted to wait until we got married, and although we were engaged we never really got close to marriage."

Indeed, within a month of Sheryl and Mike relocating to St. Louis, their relationship was basically over. There had been a growing dissatisfaction on both sides, and given the fact that he was making the move to work as a salesperson for a company that manufactured bank checks, and she was making it to be with him yet without a job of her own, it's pretty clear who made the biggest compromise. Twenty-twenty hindsight is a wonderful thing.

"The guy dumped me about four months before we were supposed to get married," Sheryl recalled in a 2002 interview for VH1's *Behind the Music*. "It was actually a really big deal. It really took the wind out of my sails."

"What we had was a codependent relationship, and I guess what made me think twice about continuing it was the way that Sheryl would withdraw," Mike explains. "She was really good at just shutting me out emotionally, so that it felt like she wasn't there anymore. In a sense it was very devastating, and instead of just going, 'Well, this is not good. I'm out of here,' it took me a long time to get to that point. Still, I don't know what went on in her life to cause her to be that way, and believe me, I've certainly got lots of faults.

"I was so excited about starting a career, but Sheryl would want me to come over at nighttime, and that was one of the things that drove me crazy. We lived quite a distance apart, and I'd be thinking, 'I want to go to bed, get up, and be fresh for work.' I just couldn't stand that pressure anymore, so we finally broke up, and I can remember going home to see my folks for the July 4th weekend and feeling like I had just been born again. It was like 'Oh my God, I don't even know who I've been the last two years,' and that wasn't Sheryl's fault, that was just the dynamic of our relationship. I had this incredible feeling of freedom, and I even returned to a greater involvement in church."

So did Sheryl. To the same Grace World Outreach Center, in fact, where she would occasionally run into her former fiancé, and where she also started playing Christian music.

"She got real involved with the music folks there," says Mike. "A lot more than I had, and I'd been going there longer. What's more, she actually started visiting my parents, which was really strange, because I'd always felt like every time we visited them when we were dating she never wanted to be there. Anyway, she was into the Christian music for some time, and I thought, 'Wow, this is fantastic. She's really pursuing her relationship with God.' I was real happy for her, I hoped it was sincere, and I left it at that."

In the meantime, it appears that Sheryl might have also harbored hopes of still pursuing her relationship with Mike. Utilizing the qualifications that she had attained at Mizzou, she eventually landed a job as a music teacher at Kellison Elementary School in the small town of Fenton, southwest of the city, and relocated to the Georgetown Apartments in the nearby Webster Groves neighborhood.

"When Sheryl moved there she wanted me to see the apartment," Mike remembers, "and I just thought, 'Okay, she wants a guy to come and check it out.' The same thing when she bought a car; she wanted me to go and look at it, and I thought, 'Okay, she just doesn't want to get ripped off by the salesman.' So, I did all that stuff and I didn't think twice about it until much later when somebody told me, 'Oh, she did all that because she thought it was going to be your apartment and it was going to be your car.' Looking back, I feel for her, because she went there without a job and she went there because of me, but we just had this unhealthy relationship."

The bottom line: Sheryl was now alone, about 200 miles from home and 2,000 miles from the hallowed City of Angels. She could have bailed out and headed west. Instead, hoping to rekindle her relationship with Rechtien, she decided to stay, and her new job actually proved to be rewarding. Kellison Elementary School served about seven hundred kids from kindergarten through sixth grade, and Sheryl taught voice there, as well as leading a special chorus for the fifth and sixth grades.

"I had a couple of classrooms that were predominantly autistic and handicapped emotionally," she recalled in a 2002 *Rolling Stone* interview. "I guess the biggest impact that my teaching had on me was just watching how music can really get in and seep through the cracks of kids who are really noncommunicative. And the different manifestations of the vibrations of the music are always really interesting to see with a kid— whether it brings out violent tendencies like banging and anger, or whether it's soothing or calming to a child who's extremely hyper."

Former colleagues Mary Jackson and Ched Hieronymus don't recall Kellison having any classes of autistic children during the time that Sheryl was there.

"I grew up in a small town, and she seemed like a small-town girl to me," says Jackson. "Very respectful and easy to get along with. I remember her having a lot of energy, and she was young, and that always adds an extra vibrance to someone's classroom. Music programs can be very mundane, but she seemed to be excited about what she was doing."

"She was a very friendly, genuine person," adds Ched Hieronymus. "There wasn't anything fake about her. She was a young Christian woman, and prayer and faith in God were important to her. She had a very positive attitude, and she also had talents that we didn't know about. I mean, you can have music teachers at school who just bang away on the piano for years, but it didn't take long for me to realize that wasn't her limit and she wanted to try something else. We had similar schedules and so we had a fair amount of time off together in the teachers' lounge, and she would tell me about her ambitions."

These ambitions clearly extended beyond performing church music. "By then I was getting more serious about writing my own material and discovering my own voice, out of self-preservation," Sheryl told Elisabeth Shue in their 1997 conversation for *Interview* magazine. As a result, while teaching at Kellison and going to the Grace World Outreach Center, Sheryl began searching out local musicians, and this ultimately brought her into the orbit of jazz artist, songwriter, and producer Jay Oliver.

By his mid-twenties, Oliver had carved out a solid reputation via his commercial work on jingles, scores, and corporate themes. In addition, he had also built his own studio on the lower level of his parents' home in Creve Coeur, just west of the city. Accordingly, his group of friends and colleagues were basically the hip musicians in town. Jay had formed a songwriting partnership with Roger Guth and Peter Mayer, the drummer and singer/guitarist in a cutting-edge local band named PM, who would subsequently sign a deal with Warner Bros. Records. And at the same time, he was also very close to a trio of musicians who were playing in a popular band run by local singer Ralph Butler—keyboardist Kirk Capella, drummer Tony Saputo, and bass player Terry Jackson. (After becoming the rhythm section for Barbara Mandrell, all three were destined to die in a private plane crash.)

"Kirk Capella called me one day, telling me that I should expect a phone call from this girl who had just come in to see them the previous night," Jay recalls. "She had sat in with them, and later asked Kirk if he knew of a producer she could get in contact with. I remember him telling me, 'She doesn't sing very well, but she sure is cute.' Anyway, she called me, and although I wasn't really looking for an artist at that time, I invited her to stop by a session I was working on.

"When Sheryl walked in, she was wearing a T-shirt and blue jeans, and had long dirty blonde hair and a smile that could melt an iceberg…as well as a 'Jesus Loves You' keychain. I'm sure even today, if you were to get the chance to peer deep inside her soul, past the image and past the weathered, hardened jade, you would most likely see the same spirited innocence she possessed that day she walked into my studio."

Jay and Sheryl became instant friends. Both coming from jazz-impassioned families, they quickly discovered that they had almost identical musical tastes. And so, amid all of Jay's projects, the two of them would squeeze in hours of sitting at the piano, playing and singing, while spending late nights listening to Pat Metheny and Suzanne Vega records.

"Sheryl clearly demonstrated an extraordinary musical sensibility, even though at that time she was not crafted in it," says Jay. "She was like a sponge, and her potential was so obvious right from the beginning. The first song I ever remember her learning on piano was a beautiful piece by [Pat Metheny's keyboard player] Lyle Mays; an awesome song with a very sophisticated harmonic language, and she picked it up real quick. I would look at this girl and think, 'What an amazing paradox!' Her natural talent dropped her into the category of big-league achievers, yet she had the overall image of a small-town, humble country girl, carrying a beautiful sense of naïveté.

"We'd listen to records or bands, and the comments she'd make were really perceptive. It was like the truest definition of 'diamond in the rough,' and she was also just a fun chick, someone fun to hang with, just so cool. 'T-shirt and blue jeans'; that was our motto. Perhaps Sheryl's most poignant attribute was her charm and charisma, and just like she slid right into my world and the scene in St. Louis, it would be just as easy for her to slide into Hollywood and be almost immediately accepted with open arms."

Before long, Sheryl was intent on relinquishing her school job and directing all of her energies towards becoming a professional singer and recording artist. Initially, her mentor wasn't so sure this was a good idea, yet she assigned herself the task of doing nothing but practice, eight hours a day, and to that end the pair of them spent the next few months making tapes of every significant vocal record that Jay could dig up— Aretha Franklin, Stevie Wonder, Rickie Lee Jones, Joni Mitchell, Bonnie Raitt, Sting, U2. Consistent with her past efforts as a student, hurdler, twirler, you name it, Sheryl was applying herself to the nth degree, and just as typically her efforts paid off. Jay decided to take a chance by offering her the lead vocal on a jingle for the back-to-school promotion of a local department store called Famous-Barr.

"Sheryl's voice was really young, but it actually fit pretty well with this particular ad campaign," he says. "It was supposed to have a young and unrefined feel. Well, at that time she had a great ear but the muscles in her voice weren't very developed, causing some pitch inaccuracies. I therefore thought this job would be good for her, because it fit into that Belinda Carlisle/early Madonna sound, and she did really well. I had to bounce a lot of things together, and tweak some timing and pitch issues, but the end product was great. She was perfect."

Thereafter, Jay would use Sheryl for corporate themes and jingles, including a spot for McDonald's which aired regionally, then went national, and earned her several thousand dollars. Featuring Sheryl, Jay, and a number of other vocalists, this ad simply consisted of them singing "Stompers," the name of a then-current Happy Meal toy.

All the while, Sheryl and Jay went to see plenty of local concerts, and as a result Sheryl gradually became a familiar face among the musicians in town. Chief in this regard were Roger Guth and brothers Peter and Jim Mayer from PM, whose repertoire blended pop originals with covers of songs by the likes of The Police, Sting, U2, James Taylor, and The Beatles. One night, when PM was playing a private party, the band members asked Sheryl to sit in with them and handle the lead vocal on the Madonna song "Borderline." She jumped at the opportunity.

"She had previously been shy about singing in front of anyone, including me," says Jay. "On this occasion she had good reason to be nervous, but she walked right up onstage, sang the tune flawlessly, and walked off like she'd been doing this for years."

The members of PM were impressed, and based on Jay's strong endorsement of Sheryl's rapidly improving pitch accuracy and phrasing flexibility, they hired her to sing backup. In turn, she would soon master the art of blending in, while accurately tracking the vowel shapes and phrasing of a lead vocalist; this was a skill that would later prove to be invaluable. At the same time, Jay Oliver continued to hire Sheryl for sessions, mostly as a backing singer, and she quickly learned how to double her own vocals and nail complex harmony parts.

"She was, quite simply, my first choice," he says. "It took a little while longer before I started using her regularly as a lead vocalist—her voice needed to get a bit stronger—but through her intense practice schedule, her rehearsals and performances with PM, and her sessions with me, she was on an accelerated path of improvement, not just as a vocalist, but in an overall sense of musicality."

What's more, Sheryl was now on an accelerated path as a performance artist, and to that end she had made good on her wish to quit her $18,000-per-year day job at Kellison Elementary School.

"I remember her getting into the jingle work and doing some gigs in cafés down on the waterfront, and then one day she came in and said, 'I'm closing out my teaching,'" Ched Hieronymus recalls. "She at least wanted to try having a music career. She knew she could keep the teaching in her back pocket and come back to it if necessary, and she was pretty determined, which kind of surprised me. Sheryl was so sweet and so family-oriented, I would have thought that she'd opt for getting married and settling down."

Wrong. Instead, she immersed herself in the life of a semi-pro musician, playing an assortment of bars, clubs, and dives around St. Louis, and occasionally getting more than she bargained for. One night, she tried to steady a waitress who stumbled while carrying some drinks, took a beer mug flush in the mouth, and chipped her front teeth. A decent capping job would restore them to their former glory, but this wasn't the first time that Sheryl's incisors had suffered the effects of a bar-related collision—about ten years earlier she'd run face-first into a metal bar while playing in the semi-constructed house of a Kennett neighbor. As rock 'n' roll stories go, the drinking bar injury has a touch more romanticism to it.

Meanwhile, at around this time, Sheryl also started seeing Mike Rechtien again, yet for both parties this only served to confirm that they were heading in opposite directions.

"There was nothing there anymore," Mike explains. "I could never satisfy whatever it was that she was hungry for. I've heard Sheryl say that I once told her, 'You'll never be happy if you don't play music for God,' but I didn't mean it was wrong. She was kind of struggling with 'Should I play music that's not God music?' and my response was, 'In the long run I don't think you'll be happy doing that, because you're so into God right now.' I mean, we'd played in the band together, so I could hardly be critical about other types of music!"

In her interview with Elisabeth Shue, Sheryl recalled that Mike had told her, "If you stand up in front of the Lord and say you are going to be my wife and then you sing in bands every weekend, we're not going to make it."

"I have a hard time believing I said that," Mike points out, "because we had broken off the engagement *long* before."

Regardless, Sheryl asserted that their differences turned out to be "a blessing, because if we'd got married one of us would've wound up dead, I'm certain. We split up."

The following year, 1986, there would be more partings of the way. When Sheryl had commenced her relationship with Mike, the other members of Cashmere had overlooked their rule of no intraband romances. However, when she became similarly involved with one of the guys in PM, it resulted in her dismissal as well as a decline in her friendship with Jay Oliver. Disillusioned and running out of reasons to hang around, Sheryl realized that this was the time to either look or leap, to once and for all dispense with the musical ambitions that could satisfy her long-harbored desire for popular acclaim or move to Los Angeles and, at the very least, never have to wonder about what might been. The decision was easy. Emboldened by her jingle work and experience as a backing vocalist, she took the plunge.

"I went home on a Tuesday and told my folks I was leaving," she recounted to Elisabeth Shue, "and I headed straight out to California the Sunday after that."

Lalaland—it would be a fresh start with no ties. And besides, the prospect of a fun-in-the-sun lifestyle seemed far less intimidating than the thought of moving to that other music industry hub, New York City. With $10,000 in savings, Sheryl packed her belongings into a red Renault convertible, drove the 1,850 miles from St. Louis to Los Angeles alone, and, as she told Shue, "landed on the 405 [freeway] about five-thirty in the afternoon, right in the middle of rush hour, and just cried my eyes out. Like, 'What am I doing here? What have I done?'"

The insecurity wouldn't last long. "She had always wanted to go to L.A.," says Jay Oliver. "I'd put together a tape of the jingle work that she had done in St. Louis, and that tape got her pretty far."

"When she went to Los Angeles the one person who she knew was one of my best buddies, Todd Taylor," adds Mike Rechtien. "He was also my sister-in-law's brother, so we were kind of related. He'd met Sheryl during the short time when she and I had gotten back together in St. Louis. He was on his way to study drumming at music school in Los Angeles, and he eventually talked me into moving out there. His roommate was David Huff, the brother of session guitarist Dan Huff, and I therefore stayed with Todd and David. In the meantime, Sheryl had moved out to L.A. and started hanging out with them, and there was also some romantic interest between her and Todd. Well, to me that's kind of taboo. If you've been engaged to somebody I don't think you should pursue romance with his friend-cum-brother-in-law, especially as I was moving into his place a month or two later."

As it happens, during her first few months in L.A. Sheryl moved no less than four times. Redondo Beach was her first stop. Then, responding to a newspaper ad, she rented a room within a house that was inhabited by a couple of city girls whose *modus operandi* was in stark comparison to life in the Missouri slow lane. Drugs, drink, and mucho company; not what the Kennett ex-pat was used to. She moved again, and thanks in part to jingle work—attained by inundating session producers with copies of her demo tape, which was presented in person when they wouldn't take her calls—Sheryl secured an apartment in Sherman Oaks, close to a jazz club named Le Café, where she worked part-time as a waitress.

Located on Ventura Boulevard, Le Café was a popular hangout for musicians, both established and unknown, and as such it enabled the new employee to quite literally bump into the right people. It was at Le Café that Sheryl befriended jazz musician Lee Ritenour, and it was also there that she made her next important connection; a session singer by the name of Darryl Phinnessee, who'd already done plenty of album, film, and commercial work. Sheryl was nothing if not a quick study.

"We started talking and we just kind of hit it off," Phinnessee recalls. "She told me what she was doing, how she was composing her own material, and soon after that we began hanging out. One evening, after we'd been to see a band, we returned to her place, Sheryl sat down at her Fender Rhodes, and when I heard her play and sing I could tell she was talented."

What's more, she had impeccable timing, musical and otherwise. About three weeks after meeting Sheryl in early 1987, Darryl Phinnessee was among the twenty-five singers who received a call from Michael Jackson's people in preparation for the Gloved One's upcoming world tour. This was designed to tie in with the release of *Bad*, his first new album since the record-breaking megasmash, *Thriller*, five years before.

Compared to an outfit like The Beatles, who'd issued thirteen albums and a slew of unrelated singles between 1962 and 1970, Jackson, the biggest star of the 1980s, released just a couple of long-players during his halcyon decade. Pop industry marketing had changed drastically, along with the demands that record companies placed on their major artists, and the result was almost-unprecedented hype surrounding *Bad*. The long-awaited album, promoted as a kind of second coming, inevitably failed to match the critical and commercial achievements of its predecessor, yet it would still spawn four chart-topping American singles during the course of a record-breaking world tour. Undeniably, landing this gig would be a major coup.

Contacted sight unseen based on a recommendation, Darryl Phinnessee auditioned with three other singers to be part of MJ's backup band. However, they were unrehearsed, and their performance failed to impress.

"Michael's production coordinator, Nelson Hayes, videotaped the four of us singing together," Phinnessee remembers. "We were just kind of chanting because we didn't know any of the songs, and so I wasn't surprised when Nelson eventually told me that Michael wasn't satisfied with the audition. It was undisciplined, and that was because the musical director, Greg Phillinganes, was a keyboard player, not a singer. Michael's a singer, I'm a singer, and I know how to determine what singers can do. So, when Nelson Hayes told me that Michael wanted a group that had already been singing together, but one that wasn't particularly well known, I replied that I could assemble the right people for an audition and Michael would think we'd been singing together for twenty years. Nelson said, 'Well, if you can do that, do it. Can you come in tomorrow afternoon?' I said, 'Okay.'

"I already had Sheryl in the back of my mind, plus she had told me she was interested in doing studio work. I knew that Michael and those guys were obviously searching for singing ability, as well as for the right look, and so that night I called Kevin Dorsey, Dorian Holley, and Sheryl, and they came over to my house the next morning. I picked a song that I had performed with another group for a Dolly Parton TV show audition; a Manhattan Transfer–type song called 'Jukebox Saturday Night' that would demonstrate really close harmonies to an experienced vocalist, because not everyone could sing that stuff. And then we picked four of Michael's songs, including 'Off The Wall' and 'Beat It,' which would show diversity in terms of our performing abilities.

"I wanted him to see us singing a cappella and nothing else, so we rehearsed just the verse and chorus background parts with no music. Then we went over to where the band was rehearsing and we were filmed singing that way, and later on Nelson Hayes called me and said that as soon as Michael heard the first song, 'Jukebox Saturday Night,' he went, 'That's them!'"

This recollection doesn't quite tally with Sheryl's own version of events. In several interviews she has stated that she was invited to audition alone after submitting an unsolicited video tape, in which she introduced herself to Michael Jackson and expressed her desire to work with him.

"On our audition tape we did each introduce ourselves," says Darryl Phinnessee. "You know, 'Hi, my name is Darryl, blah, blah, blah....' However, most singers who do a lot of work are also contractors, because we call each other, and so I was telling Sheryl, Kevin, and Dorian, 'Don't tell anybody that I called you. Just leave it kind of nebulous as to how we got this gig. I don't want any of my other friends who are singers to get mad because I didn't call them.' Maybe that's why the story later got distorted."

The night when Sheryl learned that she and her fellow singers had landed the Michael Jackson gig, she immediately called her family and close friends.

"She was extremely level-headed, extremely business-minded," recalls Brian Mitchell. "Not jumping up and down hysterical."

Debbie Welsh was at law school in Kansas City when she received a call from Jo Beth Skaggs: "Jo Beth said, 'You are not gonna believe this one!' I was going, 'What has she done now?' and Jo Beth said, 'She's going to be Michael Jackson's backing singer.' I was thinking, 'What? No way!' but sure enough it was true. Just a short time in L.A. and she makes it."

Sheryl had made it all right, even if it was just onto the first rung of the ladder. As one of the most high-profile concert events of the decade, the sixteen-month *Bad* world tour would provide her with invaluable performance experience, widespread media coverage, several influential new contacts, and firsthand knowledge regarding the backstage machinations of the music biz.

Furthermore, it would reacquaint her with keyboard player Rory Kaplan, whom she'd previously met through Dave Weckl, a jazz drummer and associate of Jay Oliver. Both Kaplan and Weckl had played in Chick Corea's Elektric Band. Now, following his stint on The Jacksons' 1984 *Victory* tour, Kaplan was recruited as a keyboardist for the *Bad* gig alongside Greg Phillinganes and Synclavier player Chris Currell.

"Michael's manager, Frank Dileo, called me around March of '87 and asked me to put the band together," Kaplan recalls. "Greg was not aboard yet, so I auditioned drummers, guitarists, and keyboard players; some really incredible musicians and some really horrible musicians. The group came together within a couple of weeks, Greg joined as the musical director, and it was like the ultimate band for me. Well, one day the backing singers all showed up, and there was Sheryl. I said, 'Sheryl? Do you remember me from Chick Corea?' She said, 'Oh, yeah,' but her attention was on Greg. He was the star musician."

Instant metamorphosis—from churchgoing Missouri schoolteacher to blonde-wigged, leatherette vamp. The Jackson gig would encompass numerous highs and lows, and in the process open Sheryl's eyes to the reality of how she might choose to operate in order to attain a measure of success in her own right. "As distasteful as some of it might have been," she would tell Elisabeth Shue, "it formulated who I eventually became."

# CHAPTER FIVE

# Loud Guitars, Big Suspicions

By the late 1980s the rock industry was geared up for concert productions on the grand scale. The multi-star package shows of two and three decades earlier—featuring at least half a dozen acts on the same bill, performing in ascending order of importance—had gradually evolved into more expansive and expensive productions, yet during the '70s these had often been overly ambitious. This was especially true in terms of the poor acoustics and inadequate staging facilities offered by many outdated venues, not to mention amplification and monitoring equipment that hadn't yet caught up with the state of the art. When The Rolling Stones played London's Earls Court in 1976, for instance, concertgoers got four shows for the price of one, thanks to how the sound often reverberated off each of the walls of the cavernous exhibition center.

A decade later, much of that had changed. Not only was there more sophisticated gear to cope with the variety of acoustic environments, but there was also an all-around slicker support structure. This included the promoters; agents; tour and production coordinators; sound, lighting, and video technicians; set designers; construction personnel; tour, production, and stage managers; transport; accomodation; catering; merchandise; security; legal representation; accounting services; publicity; and sponsorship—all vital components of the modern rock extravaganza. In this regard, Michael Jackson's first-ever solo jaunt was at the top of the pile.

The *Bad* world tour, which commenced on September 12, 1987, comprised 123 shows played over the course of sixteen months in front of about 4.4 million fans in fifteen countries—Japan, Australia, America, Italy, Austria, the Netherlands, Sweden, Switzerland, Germany, France, England, Wales, Ireland, Spain, and Belgium. What's more, the tour set new records in a number of categories; seven sellout shows at London's Wembley Stadium were attended by 504,000 people, while the tour itself grossed in excess of $125 million.

Given this tendency for multiple bookings at a particular venue, the *Bad* tour was unlike most other productions where everyone and everything would ship out immediately following a show. Instead, the MJ gig often afforded its participants the luxury of staying in each location for several days at a time, as well as rest periods at regular intervals.

"For a lot of us it was like a long, paid vacation," says singer Darryl Phinnessee. "Everywhere we went it was like 'Michael Jackson Week,' and there'd be people coming out of the woodwork—store owners presenting their goods, someone with a yacht wanting to take you out, the biggest clubs inviting you over. Just anything and everything you could imagine in terms of people offering you stuff."

During the late 1980s, before his skin turned pale and his cosmetically revamped nose virtually disappeared, before the pedophilia-related allegations and short-lived marriage to Lisa Marie Presley, Michael Jackson was the biggest personality on the showbiz scene. Sporting a visage that bore more than a passing resemblance to Diana Ross, he had established a public persona as the "Peter Pan of Pop"; an asexual, semi-reclusive, perpetually adolescent icon, ensconced alongside Bubbles the chimp within the confines of his home in Encino, California. The tabloid word was that he slept inside a pure-oxygen cylinder. Yet, as weird as his reported lifestyle may have been, he appeared harmless, affable, and untouchable.

Still, Jackson's image was already a mass of contradictions. Espousing peace, love, and tolerance on the one hand, he also used his songs and videos to depict himself as the biggest badass on the block, while a soft-spoken, almost childlike demeanor contrasted with a trademark crotch-grabbing, groin-thrusting style of performance. It was this hard sexual persona that MJ most often chose to convey on stage, and to this end his dancers and backing singers had to conform to type; leather bottoms, skimpy tops, belts, straps, buckles, and chains were all part of the concert getup.

For her part, Sheryl had to don the look of a wild-haired, stiletto-heeled rock chick—an S&M diva, in thigh-high micro-minidress and studded leather jacket. Not exactly her choice of appearance, but then, it wasn't her choice to make. She'd signed the contract and this was the deal. The only thing she requested, once the tour was underway, was to be provided with hairpieces so that her own locks weren't blow-dried into oblivion.

"I constantly felt, 'Wait, this isn't who I am. I want to be doing my own thing, and it's degrading to be standing here, dancing around in a really tight black dress,'" Sheryl told actress Elisabeth Shue a decade later. Nevertheless, well aware of the benefits, she continued to dance around in that really tight black dress. "I was a small-town girl from Missouri," she reasoned, "and singing backup introduced me to a whole different world, as well as the world itself."

Ironically, what it rarely introduced her to was the star of the show, whose self-cultivated "man of mystery" disposition extended to rarely associating with his employees offstage, and making little effort to recognize some of them on it. And all this despite the fact that, each and every night, he and Sheryl would duet on "I Just Can't Stop Loving You," the song that MJ and singer/composer Siedah Garrett had propelled to the top of the U.S. pop charts in September 1987.

"He was never around," Sheryl told *People* magazine in September of 1994. "For all the time I saw him, I could've been on tour with Tom Jones."

"We had a lot of interaction during the first rehearsals, and some interaction at the start of the tour, but that became less as the tour went on," says singer/composer Darryl Phinnessee, whose subsequent credits would include writing the theme music for popular TV sitcom *Frasier*. "We'd always pray before going onstage, so we'd see him then, and then the only other times that we'd see Michael with any consistency would be when we'd go to an amusement park. If a city had a major amusement park, they would close it for him and we would go there, just the entourage. Also, if a place threw a really big dinner, we might see him, but there was not a lot of personal stuff.

"Michael would walk by at the end of the show, point to the band members, and shout out each of their names. However, with us he would just point and go 'Whooo!' He's very methodical, and even in rehearsals he would do the same thing. We rehearsed at Universal for the [opening] Japanese leg of the tour, and when we came back the record had been released, so we added new songs and rehearsed those in Florida. We rehearsed for just under a month, and one day we took it upon ourselves to put cardboard signs around our necks with our names written on them. Well, he came over, and just as he got ready to go 'Whooo!' for whoever was first in line, he looked, kind of stumbled back, laughed, and said, 'Oh, I'm so sorry.' It was a good joke, and after that he knew our names."

Nevertheless, in several 1998 press interviews that Sheryl gave to promote her album *The Globe Sessions*, she still alluded to Jackson's less than personable attitude ten years earlier. "The guy is definitely screwed up, there's no two ways about it," she told U.K. men's magazine, *Deluxe*, while to the British rock publication *Q* she asserted "it's very important to learn the names of those who work for you.... In eighteen months, he never once called me by my name, and in a situation like that the name is every-thing—it's your identity, and if someone can't be bothered to ask you your name then there is no identity. You can't have people give their time and their energy and their lives to you and you don't even know their name. Forget it.

"He didn't speak to me. Someone else would speak to you on his behalf. It was a Woody Allen–type situation. It would be 'Michael wants this, Michael wants that.' But in his defense, watching him every night was amazing. Every evening there would be moments in the show that defied any kind of negativity. He'd go out and do those moves that he'd created and sing that music that no one has done before, and you'd be standing there thinking, 'This is unique.' For that reason I have a lot of respect for him, but his manners need a little work. Being around him was like going by a car crash. You just can't keep your eyes off him and you can't figure out why. Good or bad, there's this weird curiosity, and when he walks into a room the energy shifts."

A year before, Sheryl had taken lessons with voice instructor Robert Edwards. Now, during the course of the *Bad* tour, she also had a quick consultation with Edwards's former teacher, Seth Riggs, who was there to work with Michael Jackson three times a day so that his voice remained in prime condition.

"Touring artists have to be taught how to use their head voice in order to keep from pulling up," says Riggs, whose star-studded roster of clients has included Natalie Cole, Anita Baker, Barbra Streisand, Stevie Wonder, Luther Vandross, and Michael Bolton. In general terms, head voice often equates with falsetto, whereas chest voice refers to the thicker-sounding lower register that is normally associated with someone's speaking range. "Pulling up" refers to carrying the chest voice too high and causing it to sound strained. "When you pull up from the bottom it's very hard on your voice," Riggs continues. "It raises your larynx and you actually go into a swallowing condition, and you don't want to sing half-swallowing."

As a backing singer, Sheryl wasn't experiencing this kind of problem. However, when Seth Riggs spoke with her during the *Bad* tour, he suggested that she should try to utilize more upper range—the "money notes" that can attract attention, generate the most impact, and excite audiences.

"Sheryl's got a lot more voice than she uses," says Riggs. "She has an R&B range that nobody knows about. Being that I was working for Michael, I was glad to help her activate that part of her range, so we went to a room, I vocalized her, and she was up into R&B territory no problem. I said, 'God, Sheryl, listen to what you've got!' She was kind of surprised that she could do it in that manner, but all she had to do was be tricked into it, and she did it very, very well.

"When you're in school what they usually do is teach you all this operatic-style singing, and it's a European form that we as Americans are not necessarily interested in. They don't teach you a thing about pop music. The classical people consider pop to be a little less than respectable. They think of it as being trash; they think of it as being all belted, yelled, or screamed chest voice, and that's absolutely wrong. As a result, Sheryl had to unlearn a lot of stuff that she'd learned at university, but better still, when she did these exercises with me she would run up into R&B range, no problem at all. She went up into Aretha Franklin's range. Oh yeah, she's got it, even though no one knows she does, including herself maybe."

Pepsi-Cola was the sponsor for the *Bad* tour, and the liaison between Michael Jackson and his financial backer was Stephen "Scooter" Weintraub, who was basically serving as the Pepsi rep. Employed by RockBill, a marketing firm specializing in concert tours, promotions, and TV commercial endorsements, matching sponsors with the acts, Scooter had acquired his nickname when working on his first big project, Sting's 1985–86 *The Dream of the Blue Turtles* world tour, which had been sponsored by Honda…you can guess where this is heading. The shows were connected to scooter giveaway contests, and since these occupied a fair amount of his time, Weintraub was assigned his moniker by members of Sting's band. Not that the name Scooter conveys an accurate image of the man. Short and frenetic? Forget it. Scooter Weintraub's tall, slim, and laid-back, with an indolent-sounding voice and a contemplative disposition.

Since 1993, Scooter has been Sheryl Crow's manager, but it was in Japan, during the September/October 1987 first leg of the *Bad* tour, that they first met. "Scooter was also the sponsor rep for Eric Clapton's tour," recalls Rory Kaplan. "Sheryl liked Scooter and was interested in the fact that he was with Clapton."

"He's a very low-key kind of guy who winds up becoming friends with musicians," says guitarist Todd Wolfe, who is managed by Scooter and has known him since they played ball together as kids in Forest Hills, New York. "He's got a keen ear and he knows enough about music to sit and discuss it."

"I realized Sheryl was a Southern American–style musician," Scooter told *Performance* magazine in 1994. "Mostly we talked artistically about things."

As a result of their mutual friendship with Scooter, Todd Wolfe and Sheryl met when the *Bad* tour played the Meadowlands Arena in Rutherford, New Jersey, at the start of October 1988. "She seemed really nice, and I said, 'Anytime you're in town, stop by,'" Todd recalls. Sheryl would subsequently take him up on the offer, and after sitting in with his band, T. Wolfe & the Tornadoes, at a New York club, they would eventually become friends and musical collaborators. In the meantime, it was also while playing the Meadowlands that Sheryl made another useful contact—Wayne Isaak, the Executive Vice President of East Coast operations in the New York office of A&M Records.

"I remember seeing the show and I guess the first time I really saw her was on sort of a news special," says Isaak. "Michael didn't talk much, so they talked to band members, and they talked to Sheryl a little bit."

A few years later, when Sheryl signed to A&M, Wayne Isaak would help to devise her image and promote her in his other role as head of publicity. Then, in 1994, he would leave A&M to become Executive Vice President of Talent and Music Programming at VH1, and utilize Sheryl's videos to simultaneously build both the cable network's core audience and her own following.

Clearly, the *Bad* tour was paying Sheryl dividends in more ways than one—she was gaining experience as a touring artist within a major-league band; acquainting herself with the nonstop grind of life on the road (even if it was the kind of up-market grind that most musicians could only aspire to); meeting people who would play significant and complementary roles in her future career; and actually getting some media exposure in the process....

"Michael Jackson's Secret Girlfriend" screamed a headline in the *National Enquirer,* alongside a photo of Sheryl. Since she was duetting with Jackson onstage every night, it was natural tabloid logic to conclude that they were also making sweet music together behind the scenes. Just as naturally, sister paper the *Globe* took things a step further, alleging that Sheryl was carrying Michael's baby. (Even back in the late '80s this was defying the laws of probability.) Standing in a grocery store in Kansas City, childhood friend Debbie Welsh noticed the *Globe*'s front page and immediately bought every copy in the hope of preventing other shoppers from seeing it. Back on the road, Sheryl wasn't nearly as perturbed.

"She went along with the ride and she thought it was funny," says Rory Kaplan. "She didn't get pissed off. She was really cool about it."

And why not? Even idiotic publicity is better than no publicity. Kaplan agrees. "*I* should have been having Michael's baby!" he asserts.

At the same time, Darryl Phinnessee was hardly surprised by Sheryl's composed reaction to the media gossip. "I think she was very single-minded about making it," he says. "Our own relationship changed somewhat when she got on the tour, and although I hadn't necessarily seen her single-mindedness before that, I certainly saw it afterwards. You know, she started to focus on having a friendly relationship with the band leader, while at the same time almost treating me like I expected something from her for getting her on the tour. It was like she was responding to that without me even doing anything for her to respond to. She stayed friendly, but she was clearly putting distance between us while now focusing on the band leader."

That band leader was Greg Phillinganes, one of three keyboard players on the tour, whose job was to shape the selected band members into the best and most cohesive unit possible. "They not only blended well together, but they also fit in with Michael's request at the time for trying to have a multicultural and multiracial look," Phillinganes observes. What wasn't in the plan was a romance between the musical director and the lone female backing singer.

"It was kind of bad timing on my part because I was married," Greg concedes. Nevertheless, he and Sheryl developed a strong relationship early in the tour, and this incorporated a teacher-pupil dynamic on the musical level.

"In terms of her work and her career, Sheryl was pretty intense," he recalls. "We talked a lot about music, and she was really driven to know and to learn as much as she could. I helped her to the point of even showing her my style of playing and why I do what I do musically. I'd show her different little licks that I had learned through the years, and some of these things she picked up right away.

"Sheryl's very talented, and she's probably a better keyboard player than she might think. Back then she could already play more than one instrument, but while she didn't necessarily focus on keyboards, the things she picked up did help to develop her overall ability insofar as being able to translate her thoughts into songs. At that time she was also developing her writing skills. She'd listen to a lot of Bob Dylan and Joni Mitchell, and we actually did a bit of writing together. I still think 'Nightfall,' the first thing we composed, is a great song even though it was never released."

"Sheryl was doing a lot of writing and Greg was helping her to get her songs together for a deal, for her own project," confirms Rory Kaplan, who often hung out with the couple during the course of the tour. "I had a recording setup in my hotel room—a rack-mounted Akai 12-track, a mixer, keyboards, outboard gear, and a patch bay—and so I would record Sheryl's demos. Well, she wrote this track called 'Little Boy Blue' that Greg produced with her. I played bottle-neck guitar on it, and I remember thinking, 'This song is as good as—if not better than—anything I've heard by Elton John and Bernie Taupin.' I was floored. To this day the melody is in my head. I've never heard her do it on a record, and I wish to God she'd release it."

In 1988, as the *Bad* tour sandwiched European dates in between concerts around the U.S., Sheryl contributed backing vocals to a trio of albums: *Mirror,* by A&M act One 2 Many; *Once In A While* by Johnny Mathis; and an eponymously titled Warner Bros. release by PM. She was beginning to forge a reputation based on her singing abilities, but she also knew that these types of assignments had a limited value insofar as her larger career objectives were concerned.

To maximize her chances of success as a solo artist, Sheryl would not only have to keep honing her songwriting skills, but she'd also have to capitalize on her tour-related opportunities by networking as much as possible with the major shakers—artists who might help her land a record deal, music publishers who might be interested in her compositions, managers and agents who might champion her cause. In essence, anyone with the clout or connections to help her climb the ladder.

Greg Phillinganes, for one, introduced Sheryl to Eric Clapton. During rest periods in the Jackson tour, Phillinganes was playing keyboards for Clapton, with whom he has a close working relationship to this day. "I was all in love with her, so I introduced her to Eric and she definitely aligned herself with him," says Greg. Sheryl's close friendship with Clapton would develop and evolve during the coming years.

Meanwhile, around the start of 1988, she also ran into Robert Kraft, later president of the music division at Twentieth Century Fox, but then a record producer who, on the strength of Sheryl's onstage performances, was interested in recording some demos to showcase her voice. To this end, Kraft called Judy Stakee, his contact at music publishers Screen Gems, and asked if she could supply any songs. Stakee set up a lunch meeting, and before long she would become a key ally in the burgeoning career of Sheryl Crow.

"After lunch at this little Thai restaurant we went back to my office, I played some songs, and Sheryl and I connected on some level," Judy recalls. "For one thing, she'd been the backup singer in PM, and we'd signed them on the strength of some demos which often featured her voice. So, I played her some songs which weren't just run-of-the-mill, she really liked my taste, and we just hit it off.

"After that she went back on the road with Michael Jackson, and the next time she came out she called me and we went and had lunch again. We just kept up this friendship, and during this time, while she was still on the road, I lost my job at Screen Gems and I was out of work for eight months. Well, during those eight months, Sheryl and I probably spent every day together working on how we could get her a record deal."

Unfortunately, not all of Sheryl's efforts to befriend the right people and garner support were quite so successful. In certain cases the wires evidently became crossed and potentially fruitful associations were short-circuited—a case of false promises, mistaken assumptions, or slimy intentions, according to whose version of events should be believed. Five years later, on her *Tuesday Night Music Club* album, Sheryl would pen a song with David Baerwald titled "What I Can Do For You" in which the protagonist offers a novice help in return for sexual compensation.

In interviews immediately following the *TNMC* album's release, Sheryl would assert that the song's lyrics didn't refer to just one person but to a variety of experiences. However, on "The Na-Na Song," co-written with Baerwald, Bill Bottrell, Kevin Gilbert, David Ricketts, and Brian MacLeod, she'd come straight to the point by asserting that she might have furthered her career if she'd serviced the "dong" of Frank Dileo, Michael Jackson's manager at the time of the *Bad* world tour. "The Na-Na Song" would very nearly prompt Dileo to sue, yet even at the tail end of 1988 he had to deal with Sheryl's comments about him to several of her fellow musicians.

"Towards the end of the tour I remember her being upset, although she didn't mention any details," says Darryl Phinnessee, while Greg Phillinganes opines that "it was based on a misunderstanding. I think there were certain things that were not clear between what Frank expected and what Sheryl expected or what she wanted. You know,

Frank might have been expecting more out of Sheryl in return for what he could do for her, while Sheryl was just looking for whatever he could do for her and that was it.

"Things can easily be misinterpreted between women and men, but it was weird because I ended up being in the middle. She would talk to me about him and he would talk to me about her, and it was like, 'Oh, this is interesting. This is all I need. I have my own problems and now I'm hearing this.' When Frank would talk about Sheryl he seemed to be unsure about where he stood with her in general. He obviously knew that she wanted any help that he could give her career, and she obviously saw him as a good choice based upon his relationship with Mike, but I think he might have wanted more at the time than she was willing to give."

Originally scheduled to end in December 1988 with nine sold-out shows at the 45,000-capacity Tokyo Dome in Japan, the *Bad* world tour eventually wrapped with five additional dates in Los Angeles from January 16 to 27 of 1989. Then it was straight back to reality for Sheryl and the other band members—no more room service, limos, wardrobe assistants, makeup artists, troubleshooters, or itineraries. From now on they'd have to become reacquainted with doing everything for themselves. Initially, Sheryl hit the ground running.

"By that time I'd found out that she wrote," comments Judy Stakee. "She had started playing me stuff and asking, 'What do you think of this?' and I'd said, 'You're not going to do anybody else's songs. You've got to do your own stuff!' So, I would go over to her place or she would come over to mine, and I basically served as her cheerleader, encouraging her and telling her she could do it. You know, Sheryl would have done this if she made a dollar or a million dollars. There was a true love of music, and when she sang it was from deep down. It wasn't just a case of 'Oh, you have a nice voice. Oh, you have some great songs.' She was the real deal.

"She was working 24 hours a day, and I hadn't seen a lot of women like that in a long time. Beforehand there had been Pat Benatar and Laura Branigan and Olivia Newton-John, and before them, of course, there had been Joni Mitchell, but for a long time we hadn't seen anybody write their own songs unless they were hard rock. So, when Sheryl came along it was like, 'Wait a minute! Who are you?' The more I got to know her, the more I got to know her as a person, and that's who I absolutely adored. She was a true human being, down to how she treated my family and my friends. In fact, when Sheryl first went on the road, my brother stayed at her apartment and took care of her dog. Her sister also became a very good friend of mine, so we integrated everything and it was more than just the music; it was a whole way of life."

Not that it was the only way of life that Sheryl could imagine for herself. On the flip side was the family-style setup that her parents and siblings had opted for, comprising spouses, kids, and steady jobs. Given her close-knit roots and small-town upbringing, these aspects had definite appeal, and while they jarred with the kind of existence that was requisite for her to pursue her career objectives, Sheryl's inner conflict would sometimes be evident to those around her.

"Because she is so focused there are very few things that illustrate her soul," says Crow family friend Brian Mitchell, "but I remember her visiting Kennett around the time of the Michael Jackson tour, before any of us had any idea as to how big she would be, and when she came home her sister Karen was there with her family, and I could see the feelings welling up inside of Sheryl. There was that instinct to also have a family, and while it didn't kill her or perhaps even upset her daily, you could see that it was something which she really yearned for. That's a side of her that I had never imagined existed, because it's hard for me to think that all of those aspects can exist in one human soul, but there was no faking that. She said, 'I don't want to leave. I want that. I want what Karen has,' and it was real. There would have been no reason to make that up."

Still, despite such moments of personal contemplation, Sheryl didn't veer from her chosen course. After all, the professional goals were the product of inner needs that, in the short term at least, evidently held more sway than her desire to have kids running around a yard surrounded by a white picket fence. That could wait until later.

Instead, when backing vocalists were required in February 1989 for overdub sessions on the album *Off to See the Lizard*, by highly popular, tropical-tinged singer-songwriter Jimmy Buffett, Sheryl hopped on a plane at LAX and flew down to Key West, Florida. Jay Oliver had co-written ten of the songs on the record, and it was he who had recommended her to producer Elliot Scheiner.

"Sheryl came down for four or five days, taking the opportunity to get away from the stress of Los Angeles," Jay recalls. "Elliott also recruited his wife—the actress Diana Canova—Frank Floyd, and Timothy Schmit from the Eagles, taking a gamble that the combined blend would supply the best spirit for the record. I remember telling Elliot that Sheryl had the gift of being a vocal chameleon; that her pitch was accurate and she'd fall right in line with the blend. Well, she did. She blew everyone away, and we all later talked about how good she was, and that this was probably the beginning of a long and winding road to the top. She had just come off the Michael Jackson tour, and I remember her state of anxiety, running around saying something like, 'Now's the time! Now's the time! I've gotta hit before they forget about me!'"

In the short term this makeshift mantra appeared to pay off. Returning to Los Angeles after finishing the Jimmy Buffett assignment, Sheryl got together with Judy Stakee for a Chinese meal at Chin Chin in Brentwood.

"It was a Sunday evening, and she said, 'I had this wonderful idea on the plane. I need to work with a guitar player. I need to work with somebody like Don Henley,'" Judy remembers. "Of course, I was like, 'Okay, sure,' but I told her that a friend of mine worked over at HK Management and I would call her in the morning and find out what was going on. Well, Monday morning came, and before I even got around to calling my buddy, Sheryl phoned me and said, 'HK Management just called me. They want me to try out as a backup singer for Don Henley.' I said, 'Wait, wait. You just talked about this and it happened? We were talking about this for the first time ever last night, and they called you this morning?'"

In fact, with the impending release of his third solo album, *The End of the Innocence*, and the accompanying concert tour just a few months away, the former Eagles drummer was on the lookout for backing vocalists. After being sent a reel of Sheryl's Michael

Jackson work, Henley told his management to contact her, and the result was that she sang backup on the track "If Dirt Were Dollars" and made it onto his tour.

"Being on the road with him, I think, was for me really insightful, because he would travel with the band, and I just saw the difference that it made," Sheryl told David Wild in a 2002 television interview for the Bravo cable network's *Musicians* series. "He always took us out for dinner, it was like a big family...."

According to author Marc Eliot in his book *To the Limit: The Untold Story of the Eagles,* an unnamed source who went on the *End of the Innocence* tour observed that when Don Henley encountered Sheryl, "he couldn't get over what a fox she was and began to wine and dine her. The only problem for him was, at the time she was more interested in her solo career than a relationship and just wasn't interested, which of course made him want her all the more. Everybody knew he was going nuts because he couldn't get her. There weren't that many girls at any given party in L.A. that would have ever said no to an offer from Don Henley.... She sang on his album and agreed to go out on the road with him, but they had no romantic affair."

Regardless, the most important point is that Henley would become Sheryl's friend, her supporter, and her advisor. He'd try to get her a record deal and even a lawyer to broker that deal, and when he learned that some of her compositions were being pitched to major artists such as Phil Collins and Eric Clapton, Don counseled Sheryl to retain those songs for herself.

"He just kind of put his energy where his mouth was," Sheryl told David Wild. "He stood by me, made a lot of phone calls, got a lot of people interested in me, got my songs around."

Even when Sheryl would sign with A&M and embark on her first album, Don Henley would serve as her constant ally and sounding board. In the meantime, also fulfilling that role was Judy Stakee, who was prepared to go out on a limb to help her friend capitalize on her recent touring credits and strike while the iron was hot.

"While I was out of work we tried to get Sheryl a record deal, and she did a couple of showcases at [a small club in Santa Monica called] At My Place which were very well attended," Judy recalls. "She had Greg Phillinganes in her band, Don Henley came to one of the events, and he brought different people along. As a result she was offered a deal by Irving Azoff at Giant Records, but in her mind Irving was making the deal as a favor to Don. It was very generous and Sheryl appreciated it, but none of the A&R people knew who she was or what to do with her, and so she just didn't think it would be the right marriage.

"She also said she would wait to see where I ended up before signing a publishing deal, and that's what happened. When I came to work for Warner/Chappell, I signed her. Sheryl was the first person I ever signed who wasn't just a songwriter; she was also an act. I believed in her as an artist so much, she could have sung the Yellow Pages and I would have bought them."[1]

---

[1] *A standard composer's requirement is to form a separate publishing company and affiliate it with a Performing Rights Society: either ASCAP, BMI, or SESAC. Accordingly, in 1989, Sheryl affiliated herself with BMI and made a play on her own name to form Old Crow Music.*

Still, not all was smoothness and light. Sheryl's relationship with Greg Phillinganes, always awkward given his marital situation, had basically fizzled when the *Bad* tour ended. Thereafter, his attempts to sustain or resuscitate Sheryl's interest were invariably rebuffed.

"I was still trying to keep things going when she went on the road with Don Henley's band, but it was kind of unhealthy," Greg admits. "I remember sending her flowers at every stop, every gig that she did, but she wasn't interested.... I would like to think that what we had was genuine, but I'm sure there was also a self-serving element to it. Sheryl was very intent on aligning herself with people who could help her, but at the time I was a bit messed up emotionally and I felt—or I wanted to feel—that there was something genuine to what we had. For a period of time there might have been, but it didn't last. It always seemed to me that Sheryl was searching for something more; searching for her own identity, which she would find a few years later."

"That whole situation between Greg and Sheryl was pretty sad," adds Rory Kaplan. "It was a very sad thing for everybody. Sheryl went into a depression, and she blamed Michael and Frank Dileo, but I don't believe that for a second. The fact that a marriage broke up, and she and Greg had a falling-out, is what really went down. And it was sad, because [Greg's wife] Carla was loved by everybody, Greg was loved by everybody, and so was Sheryl, but their passion took them a little bit over the top and at the end of the day it destroyed some great friendships."

Nevertheless, shattered relationships weren't the sole reason for Sheryl falling into an extended funk. For one thing there was the deflating realization that seemingly generous offers might be disingenuous when considering what was expected in return. And for another, her attempts to sustain career momentum appeared to be running out of steam. In 1989, Sheryl sang backup on the *Late Nite* album by solo artist (and founding member of Journey) Neal Schon, as well Steve Thomson's eponymous release for CMC, yet the next twelve months would seem like a fallow period compared to the relative excitement of the preceding two years.

With hindsight it is clear that the ensuing time spent writing and forging new relationships would ultimately help Sheryl Crow ascend to the next level, yet there was no way for her to know this back then. At the age of twenty-seven she could justifiably fear that, in a youth-oriented business where people routinely break through in their late teens and early twenties, any chance of stardom was already gone. The frustration of trying to launch a solo career, and launch it quickly, started getting to her.

"I went through a period of six or eight months of not getting out of bed," Sheryl recalled in a 1996 VH1 interview. "I mean, not showering, not doing anything, of having food brought in and just being so depressed and so despondent."

In reality she probably didn't spend quite so long holed up inside her bedroom—the dates of her gigs and meetings throughout 1989 and 1990 preclude that. Yet, the extent of Sheryl's depression was such that even her mother initially couldn't shake her out of it.

"My mom and I are very close, but she would call and say, 'You're a cute girl, you're smart, you've got everything in the world going for you,' and that would just make it worse," Sheryl told *Rolling Stone*. "Because then it makes you even loathe yourself more for being sick."

Besides, how often does a dejected kid want to listen to the biased support and unwavering belief of a loving parent? "I just wanna be depressed. Stop finding me reasons to be optimistic." Sheryl, already given to mood swings, was going through the biggest downer of her life so far, and it would take more than homegrown talk therapy to turn things around.

"I just got lost, you know, and it was scary for me," she recalled in a 2002 interview for VH1's *Behind the Music*. "I would go to bed thinking, 'I just don't want to wake up,' and I would wake up and I would be mad."

With the aid of antidepressants and professional therapy sessions, Sheryl began to turn things around, yet getting back on her feet was a gradual process.

"I know when I first moved from Memphis to Los Angeles at the start of '90 it was a particularly hard time for Sheryl," says Jo Beth Skaggs, who nevertheless didn't realize that her friend was in the midst of a full-blown depression. "She was still kind and gracious and let me crash over at her apartment many times, and if friends came into town she would go out with us, but that was probably the only time when I felt that maybe she wasn't herself. She was just very sullen, she looked like she'd gotten thinner, and she didn't have that usual sparkle in her eyes. She was very quiet and not very forthcoming or gregarious."

Soon that would change. Sheryl would start reassembling the pieces of her life—the contacts, credentials, talents, and self-belief—and with some invaluable assistance she would pry open the door to her solo career.

# CHAPTER SIX

## The Real Deal

While Sheryl was coping with her depression she did virtually no session work, but she did at least make her professional acting debut…as a Catholic schoolgirl. If this sounds like somewhat unlikely casting, then it fit perfectly with the bizarre premise of *Cop Rock*, a brutal crime TV show in which murderers, pimps, drug addicts, and their captors would break into song at the slightest opportunity. Described by one critic as a "shotgun marriage of musical fantasy and inner-city mayhem," this brainchild of Steven Bochco—the otherwise-successful producer of *Hill Street Blues*, *L.A. Law*, and *NYPD Blue*—aired on ABC from September 26–December 26, 1990.

Networking in Hollywood—in future years, post-fame, Sheryl would make some altogether more notable appearances on the small screen, portraying herself on shows such as *Ellen*, *TFI Friday*, *The Naked Truth*, and *The Late Jonathan Ross*. However, these were just lighthearted addenda to her musical interests, and back in 1989 and 1990 she took some positive steps in that regard by hooking up with a couple of musicians who, after relocating to L.A., briefly collaborated with her as songwriters. One was her friend Jay Oliver; the other was guitarist Todd Wolfe, whom she'd met through Pepsi rep Scooter Weintraub during the course of the Michael Jackson tour.

Todd's band, T. Wolfe & the Tornadoes, performed a mixture of blues standards and originals at clubs in New York City, and when Sheryl had sat in with them on a few occasions she'd displayed a natural flair for that vein of music.

"She would just sing, and do anything from a straight blues to something like 'Chain Of Fools,'" Todd recalls. "You know, she doesn't like to do the blues thing, but it's in her voice, and she'd get up and she'd nail it. She'd always wow them. She'd do two or three numbers, get it down, and not think anything of it. I mean, that even happened when we were playing at Manny's Car Wash, a famous blues club in New York City which is now closed. She dropped by one night and the place went nuts. We got her up there and she sang 'Have You Ever Loved A Woman' and 'Going Down,' and she didn't think it was happening but the crowd was going crazy. I'd go, 'Come on, it's good!' I guess she always felt she was cheating, but she could get up there and belt it."

Judy Stakee, who had signed Sheryl to a publishing deal at Warner/Chappell, was acutely aware of Sheryl's flexible vocal talents—of her ability to sing blues, R&B, country—but she was also cognizant of the need for her to channel those abilities in a specific direction and establish her own identity.

"The thing that most backup singers have a hard time with is 'who am I?' because they're such chameleons," Judy asserts. "My whole thing is, 'You've got to figure out who you are and what you're about and what you want to say,' and I think that's what I hit her over the head with the most."

During this period in 1989 and 1990, Sheryl moved several times, from Brentwood to West L.A., then to a building near the intersection of La Brea and Franklin where she was spooked by a prowler in the middle of the night. Her next stop was a vintage building on the southwest corner of Fountain Avenue and Crescent Heights, in the heart of West Hollywood, close to L.A.'s version of the action.

"In those days we'd have breakfast at [West Hollywood restaurant] Hugo's at least three to five times a week, and we would just go over stuff," Judy Stakee recalls. "She'd come by the office with Scout [a labrador-greyhound mix that Sheryl had rescued from an animal shelter], saying, 'I've got a new song to play you,' and I'd visit her after work. She also lived in my condo for a couple of months, so we were always going over songs. 'What do you think of this? What do you think of that?' I was a sounding board for a while there, and of course I tried to put her with different writers, a couple of whom are probably now kicking themselves for not doing it. She's a great writer on her own, and the only reason I wanted her to co-write was because she was new to the songwriting world, and it would be good for her to hang out with other writers and experiment."

Sheryl heeded the advice. While sitting in with T. Wolfe & the Tornadoes at a Manny's Car Wash gig in November 1989, she encouraged the band's leader to move to Los Angeles, where they could write some material, demo it, and see what happened. Todd, until then a nine-to-fiver, had already been looking for ways to make music his full-time career, and this sounded like a worthwhile opportunity. Later that month he drove to L.A. and found a place to stay, and shortly thereafter he and Sheryl were writing songs together.

"I would come up with some of the music and she would kind of formulate it, write some lyrics and things like that, and we came up with four or five numbers," he says. "Then we went in and demo'd everything, and we thought it was great. I still have the tape—she wrote 'the kick-ass band' on the tape's label—but I guess after hearing a few people in the business tell her, 'Ah, it's not happening,' she was off to the next project."

This Crow/Wolfe material has never been released.

"Sheryl and I actually did one little showcase," Todd continues. "I don't recall the band members, although Greg Phillinganes had come and jammed with us—but nothing ever came out of it, alongside people passing on the demo. That was in late '90. There was a group of Sheryl's friends from St. Louis out there, including Jay Oliver, and they even had a house in Manhattan Beach where they all stayed and which they called the 'St. Louis Embassy.'"

In fact, although Jay hadn't informed Sheryl about his move to Southern California, she called him the moment that he arrived at his new living quarters in April 1990. "I was quite literally opening the tailgate of the truck that I had rented to move all of my gear," Jay recalls. "The phone rang and it was Sheryl. This could only be some kind of synchronicity. I mean, how did she know? And how did she get that number so quickly? She was saying, 'Hey, I can't believe you're here! Let's get together and let's write!'"

True to form, Sheryl wasn't wasting any time, least of all her own. Jay Oliver assembled a 4-track setup in Manhattan Beach, including all of his MIDI, synth, sampling, and computer gear, and when it became clear that more tracks were required, Sheryl invested in an 8-track Tascam machine that utilized regular cassette tapes. It was here that the two of them began writing the material that would be included among her first solo recordings: "Father Sun," "Indian Summer," "Near Me," "Love You Blind"—all synth-based, mid-tempo numbers.

"When Sheryl came in with 'Near Me,' which I think was the first of the batch, it was so different," says Judy Stakee. "Not R&B, but not pop. I'd say, 'Who is that? It doesn't sound like anybody else.' At that point it was like, 'Okay, whatever you've got here, keep going.'"

"She used to work really hard at trying to become a great writer, and I've got to hand it to her," adds Jay Oliver. "She wasn't one of those people who expected everything to be hand-delivered to her just because she was cute and charismatic. She worked at it, and I really give her great credit.

"In all, we wrote maybe fifteen or twenty songs together, and it was a very equal collaboration. Then there were times when she would bring in her own material as well as co-writes with other musicians. She still brought them to me to produce the demos, and that's where the line got fuzzy. At that time, I didn't have enough experience to realize that doing countless free demos of other people's music is a labor of love which builds little to no equity. Sheryl had a free supply of professional demos, and although my productions were very good, they were based on the previous decade's computer and MIDI technology, which was on its way out of the trend…and didn't come back until 2000. As a producer with a studio, you have to be conscious of just who and what becomes the fruit of your labors. But frankly, I was simply driven by the music and my belief in Sheryl as an artist and a friend. All in all, it was a great learning experience, and the wisdom I acquired from it is now invaluable."

At the same time, Sheryl and Jay enjoyed collaborating on their own material, and so for a while they continued to write together. This helped both of them learn the craft. However, as Sheryl neared her ultimate destiny, Jay also perceived her becoming a little more stressed, a little more volatile, a little more sensitive to outside comments, while in another sense her drive became stronger.

"It's kind of like being stripped of all your clothes and thrown into the ocean," he says. "You've got to sink or swim. Sheryl started waking up to the fact that she was out there and she just had to go all the way. As her own artistic direction and artistic spirit began to develop, she became less and less flexible and malleable, and that's completely understandable. We started to butt heads a little bit more—not so much musically, but in other ways—and there was a little bit more politicking and some stuff that was a little more manipulative and underhanded. She had to do what she had to do, and I absolutely respect that, but because of those elements it was no fun anymore for me. We weren't just a couple of kids kicking around and writing some songs.

"I hadn't written with too many other people, so at that point it had been an easy ride for me, and I still wasn't aware of what it's like to hunker down and say, 'Okay, this is my job, this is what I do. I'm diving full-on naked into the abyss of Hollywood.' There is politics, there is manipulation, with this vacuum of people all vying for their own validations and their own glories. I just don't like that stuff, and I've never aquiesced to it. So, when that started to enter the picture, I started to back out, and it came to a time when I finally told her that I didn't want to write with her anymore for her own project. However, I really wanted to write with her for other people, because there wasn't any of that other stuff going on. It was easier, looser, and we had fun with it.… One of the last tunes we wrote was a real nice ballad called 'Destiny,' which a band called Bell, Book & Candle recorded for an album that went to number one in Germany."

Meanwhile, "What Does It Matter?" a ballad that Sheryl had penned on her own, was added to "Father Sun," "Near Me," and "Love You Blind" for a four-song demo tape that Jay and she produced, and which Sheryl and Judy Stakee then used to try to land a record deal. The package appeared to be a good one—an attractive singer-songwriter with decent stage and studio credentials and a professionally recorded batch of original songs. Still, this was 1990, before the advent of Triple A (adult album alternative) radio, and, as the two women quickly learned, most A&R people at the major record companies were now looking towards bands that were merging '70s-style stadium rock with angry lyrics and heavy riffs—a style of music that would come to be known as grunge, evolving out of and appealing to an age group that would be dubbed Generation X.

Paul Atkinson at MCA, Jay Landers at CBS, Jason Flom and Kevin Williamson at Atlantic; all were impressed when Sheryl Crow walked into their offices, but none of them quite knew what to do with the material that they heard on her demo tape.

"She'd be told, 'Oh, we've got the perfect thing for you,'" Judy Stakee recalls. "'We'll put you with this writer and this writer and this writer…' and we'd walk out and say, 'I don't think so.' They all recognized Sheryl as a great singer, but no one got the fact that she was an amazing songwriter and musician."

Enter Hugh Padgham. Acclaimed for his work with acts such as Genesis, The Police, Phil Collins, Sting, David Bowie, and Paul McCartney, the British, Grammy Award–winning producer/engineer had forged a solid relationship with A&M Records, a company that counted Sting among its roster of artists. A&M's co-founders, Herb Alpert and Jerry Moss, had been talking to Padgham about the possibility of his becoming a part-time house producer, to take charge of A&M projects or to simply record other artists in the label's Hollywood facility, which had once served as Charlie Chaplin's film studio. What's more, a year or so earlier the company's temporary head of A&R, David Anderle, had also implored the producer to help the industry by working with more new artists. In early 1991, while he was mixing Sting's *Soul Cages* album at A&M, Hugh Padgham stumbled upon the opportunity to fulfill Anderle's request.

"Sting and I hadn't been out for about ten days since we'd got to L.A.," Hugh recalls. "Then we were invited to Billy Idol's gig, and although we didn't make the gig we did make the party afterwards. It was in this mud-wrestling club, and as I was waiting to get in I bumped into a friend of Phil Collins's wife, Jill. Her name was Megan [Taylor] and she had Sheryl in tow with her, so I got them into the party and we just hung around and talked. Sheryl told me that she was a singer, and when she found out that I was a record producer it was like 'Oh, I'll play you my demos.' So I said, 'Well, look, I'm working at A&M. Just drop them in there and I'll have a listen.' A day or two later she dropped the tape in, and I listened to it and I thought, 'Wow, this is really, really good!'

"She was a good keyboard player, she sounded great, she was writing these really good songs, and I just thought, 'She will be a star.' She looked terrific and her vocals were brilliant. The only thing that I was concerned about was her name. I thought, 'Oh, I'm not sure if Sheryl Crow sounds very good, what with all of the connotations relating to a crow. Maybe she should have a stage name....' but I soon got over that."

Hugh quickly ran into Sheryl several more times, either by chance or by design. After they met to talk about her work, they also encountered one another at the recording sessions for *Rooms in My Fatha's House,* an album by percussionist/singer/ songwriter Vinx, which Sting was producing on his own Pangea label, and to which Sheryl was contributing backing vocals. (For contractual reasons, she would be credited as Cheryl Crowe on the finished record.)

Impressed with Sheryl's evident talent, her appearance, and her general demeanor, Padgham immediately thought of presenting David Anderle with her demo tape. First, however, the producer played it to his manager, Dennis Muirhead, along with the demo tape of another artist. Muirhead preferred the latter.

"To me, Sheryl just sounded like a 'rock chick'," he recalls. "It was pretty heavy rock music for the time and I certainly didn't like it much, but Hugh did. Shortly afterwards I met her with Hugh in a bar on the Sunset Strip, and it was clear right from the start that she was a go-getter. I mean, you can just tell when somebody has got that sort of determination and drive to succeed. It's something that I'm always looking for when I'm trying to decide whether to sign a producer or work with an artist, and so at that stage I saw it as a very positive sign."

At 10:45 on the morning of Monday, March 4, 1991, Hugh Padgham walked into David Anderle's office at A&M and said, "Do you remember that conversation we had?" Anderle did. "Well," Padgham continued, "I think I've found somebody."

David Anderle was no slouch himself when it came to mining fresh talent. Having served as both a talent director at MGM/Verve Records and co-founder of the Beach Boys' Brother Records label, he'd headed the A&R department at Elektra before moving to A&M. In the process, he'd introduced music fans to the likes of Frank Zappa, The Doors, Tim Buckley, Bread, and Van Dyke Parks, while producing artists ranging from Judy Collins, Rita Coolidge, Bonnie Bramlett, Kris Kristofferson, Booker T. Jones, and Chris de Burgh to the Ozark Mountain Daredevils and the Circle Jerks. Now here he was, listening to a possible new discovery by one of the most successful and influential producer/engineers of the 1980s.

"Hugh played me Sheryl's tape and I really loved it," states Anderle, who met with A&M CEO Al Cafaro at four o'clock that afternoon and handed him a copy of the recording. He also gave a copy to Jerry Moss. The following day Cafaro called Anderle while he was listening to it in his car. He too loved what he heard. Moss concurred.

"My impression was along the lines of 'Here's somebody who is very talented, who has the potential to be a star based upon who she is, and she can sing really well,'" Al Cafaro remembers. "It was worth a shot."

Launched with just a couple of hundred dollars in 1962 by trumpeter/producer Herb Alpert and producer/promo man Jerry Moss, A&M had initially been a standard record company specializing in middle-of-the-road pop music. During the 1970s the roster had expanded to incorporate British rock acts such as Joe Cocker, Procol Harum, and The Move, while a licensing agreement with Island Records secured the U.S. rights to Spooky Tooth, Fairport Convention, Free, Jimmy Cliff, and Cat Stevens. A deal with Humble Pie evolved into the solo career of Peter Frampton, and along with the signings of groundbreaking American acts such as Phil Ochs and The Flying Burrito Brothers, A&M developed the multi-platinum careers of Frampton, Stevens, Supertramp, The Carpenters, Carole King, Quincy Jones, Captain and Tennille, Bryan Adams, The Police, Sting, and Amy Grant.

Boasting an eclectic roster that also included Captain Beefheart, The Tubes, Joe Jackson, Suzanne Vega, John Hiatt, and the Neville Brothers, A&M became the most successful independent record company in history, described by *Rolling Stone* as "one of the classiest in the business, where music really did come first. It was a company known for its commitment to its artists." Nevertheless, in 1989 Alpert and Moss sold A&M to the PolyGram Corporation for around a half-billion dollars. (They would continue in management positions until their joint departure in June 1993.) Now this organization was interested in acquiring Sheryl Crow. There could be no doubt that she'd be in good company.

"Things moved quickly when it came to signing Sheryl," says Al Cafaro, himself a one-time promo man, who'd become A&M's CEO in December 1990. "I had seen her and knew of her, and I knew that she was looking for a deal. I remember being at [Hollywood restaurant] Spago with a few people and being introduced to Sheryl, and I remember being immediately impressed with the fact that she was not only a beautiful woman, but that she was definitely sharp, smart, and wanted it. You know, it was very clear that this was a woman who was going to make something happen. Now, I don't mean to sound like a sage, because it wasn't until I heard her sing and heard her music that I started putting it into the context of this is somebody who we should sign, but she definitely had that spark.

"She schmoozed in a very clear and compelling way, not in any tacky or insincere way. It was just spot-on. It was exactly what you would hope an artist is going to be; it's the look in the eye, it's listening to what people are saying, it's saying the right thing, it's being engaged with you in conversation and being completely aware of the surroundings and what's going on. Just really smart, sharp stuff, and she was gorgeous too, which is, of course, always part of the impression that someone makes and, in the context of having a career, an important attribute. It cannot possibly overcome any lack of talent in my judgement, but who you are and how you present yourself is a critical part of this."

Clearly, by the time Al Cafaro had been handed Sheryl's demo tape he was already interested in hearing her music. "I didn't know that Hugh Padgham was tied to it," he says. "I just knew that Hugh thought this was a woman of talent. It was certainly an important endorsement."

For his part, David Anderle was hooked. "I don't even know what it was about Sheryl that got me, but she got me so quick, and it had to do with a combination of the sound of her voice and what she was writing," he explains. "I really liked the songs a lot and I loved her voice. I called Hugh and I said, 'Look, we're really interested in this and I'd like to sign her. Do you want to tell her or do you want me to tell her?' He said, 'I think you should call her, because I think it would be a wonderful thing for her to get that call from a record company.' I said, 'Fine,' and so I called and asked her to come in."

When the A&M execs liked something, they moved quickly—David Anderle had first heard the demo tape on the Monday, Al Cafaro had listened to it on the Tuesday, and on that Wednesday, March 6, at 4:00 P.M., Sheryl Crow had her first meeting with Anderle. She was accompanied by Judy Stakee, who had given a copy of the tape to A&M's Vice President of A&R, Larry Hamby, at the same time that Hugh Padgham had handed Anderle his copy. All bases were being covered, and on all sides it was love at first sight.

"When Sheryl walked in the office it was all over," Anderle recalls. "As soon as I saw her I knew that, from my point of view, it was all there. And I can't even pinpoint what it was about her. It's just there, and it's always there with Sheryl.

"She was sitting on a couch across from me, we had a bit of a conversation, and physically her appearance just kept changing. It was late afternoon, the sun was coming through the windows in my office, and there were trees outside, so there were a lot of shadows. Well, she would be looking at me and she'd be one person. Then she would turn her head to say something to Judy and, what with the way the sun was hitting it, her hair would be straggly and she'd kinda look as if she just came in off the ranch or something. Then she'd look the other way and she would look beautiful. All of that was going on the whole time I was talking to her. I was just sitting there and I was watching that, and as I'm a visual person that meant a lot to me, along with everything else. I believe in that kind of stuff. She reminded me very much of Bob Dylan in that they never look the same all the time. She would go from being really kind of sexy to not very sexy to having a sort of country feel to having a kind of hippie look, and I found that incredibly fascinating.

"I basically asked her three questions: I asked her if she wanted to make a record and she said, 'Yes'; I asked her if she was ready to make a record now and she said, 'Yes'; and I asked her if she would like to make one with us and she just turned to Judy, and Judy said something like, 'Oh my God, I've always wanted to be in a meeting like this!' That was it. She didn't have a lawyer, she didn't have a manager, she only had Judy, so we suggested that she get a lawyer and a manager and we went from there."

"David knew every song, every lyric, every chord change, and we both knew immediately that this company was different," adds Judy Stakee. "We then met with Al Cafaro, and he impressed us immensely when he started reciting lines from Sheryl's songs. As we walked around the A&M lot that day everyone we came across knew about her. They had circulated her demo tape to some of the key employees, and so when they met her they already knew the songs. As a result she eventually signed with A&M, and we went to Chaya Brasserie for our celebration dinner with Timothy Drury, who was a keyboard player for Don Henley."

"I remember Sheryl calling me in hysterics," says Jay Oliver. "She was saying, 'I can't believe I got a record deal! I can't believe I got a record deal!' She came down to where I was living in Manhattan Beach and we celebrated."

Not too surprisingly, Sheryl celebrated her achievement with a quite a few people in the spring of '91. After all, up to that point she may have been in L.A. less than five years, but she'd packed a lot of effort into that time; a lot of singing, songwriting, strategizing, networking, knocking on doors, and general hard graft. What's more, there had been plenty of effort expended in that direction preceding her move to the West Coast, from her musical activities in high school and college through to her stage and studio experience in St. Louis. Sheryl was twenty-nine years old when she finally secured a recording contract. Compared to numerous other artists destined for stardom, her route to success was long and fairly circuitous, and there was still a way to go.

In due course, she would be managed by Morty Wiggins, an exec at Bill Graham Management, and recording sessions for her first album would begin in the early fall. However, before Sheryl had much chance to focus on her own career, she went back on the road, playing keyboards and singing backup for a progressive rock band named Toy Matinee.

Initially the brainchild of composer/keyboardist Patrick Leonard, whose songwriting and production credits included Madonna, Bryan Ferry, and Julian Lennon, Toy Matinee had been formed in 1988 with a nucleus of Tim Pierce on guitar and Guy Pratt (who'd played in a post–Roger Waters lineup of Pink Floyd) on bass. Leonard subsequently began writing songs that melded British pop sensibilities with prog rock and '70s-style jazz fusion, and when he was invited to judge a national "battle of the bands" contest sponsored by Yamaha, he encountered singer/songwriter/guitarist/keyboard player Kevin Gilbert performing with a post-modernist outfit named Giraffe. Gilbert's band won the competition, and shortly thereafter he and Leonard discovered a shared passion for '60s pop and conceptual rock. Kevin Gilbert joined Toy Matinee, he and Patrick Leonard teamed up as songwriters, and drummer Brian MacLeod completed the lineup.

In 1990, Toy Matinee released a self-titled album on Reprise Records. Produced by Bill Bottrell and featuring nine well-crafted songs in the Steely Dan vein, it nevertheless failed to make any impact whatsoever. Internal disagreements quickly led to the band members going their separate ways, but Kevin Gilbert wasn't immediately resigned to giving up the ghost. In early 1991, he decided to promote the album by taking it on the road with an entirely new lineup: Marc Bonilla joined him on guitar, Spencer Campbell played bass, and Toss Panos was behind the drums, but while requests started coming in for them to appear at various clubs, they initially didn't have anyone to fill in on keyboards.

"I hunted all over the place for a keyboardist for a long time and this girl at my publishers [Judy Stakee] had sent me tapes of Sheryl Crow," Kevin Gilbert recalled in a 1994 interview with *Music News Network*. "I had known her from songwriting. She was the only person who could play 'King of Misery,' the keyboard part, so I gave her the gig and we went out."

The songwriting that Gilbert alluded to was a track titled "All Kinds Of People," which he and Sheryl had co-penned with bass player Eric Pressly as part of her ongoing efforts to find compatible composing partners. The number would be included on her unreleased first album, although by the time Sheryl landed the Toy Matinee job, she knew Kevin far better than just as an erstwhile co-writer—they were already romantically involved. Still, as Judy Stakee points out, Sheryl was initially hesitant about joining the Toy Matinee tour.

"The reason she did take it was that she had never programmed her own keyboards before," Judy states. "She decided to do it so that she would be forced to learn. She was constantly pushing herself and putting herself in those situations that would enable her to become a better musician."

An in-house video of Toy Matinee performing at the Roxy on the Sunset Strip in May '91 shows Sheryl standing towards the back of the stage, behind the keyboards, dressed all in black, a large crucifix hanging around her neck. At this point, neither she nor Kevin Gilbert could have realized how much their relationship would soon impact both of their lives.

A native of San Mateo, California, Gilbert had studied classical piano at an early age before turning his attention to pop and progressive rock. After spending a year at UCLA, he moved to Sunnyvale and formed Giraffe, which released a couple of albums on the independent Still Life label. Then, in 1989, he relocated to Los Angeles. The following year he got together with producer Bill Bottrell for the *Toy Matinee* album (which, courtesy of the aforementioned tour and a promo video featuring actress Rosanna Arquette, would eventually sell nearly 200,000 copies). Gilbert sublet the space adjacent to Bottrell's Toad Hall studio in Pasadena, created his own recording setup named Lawnmower & Garden Supplies, and, thanks to Bottrell, landed a gig playing high-speed sequencer on the Michael Jackson single "Black Or White."

Kevin Gilbert was a man of considerable talent, great intensity, dark thoughts, and volatile mood swings. Partnering all this with the headstrong personality and variable disposition of Sheryl Crow could produce explosive results, and it did. During the next few years Kevin would contribute in no small part to Sheryl's eventual success and subsequent vilification, yet in the short term he'd also provide her with emotional support and creative input.

In July 1991, the Patrick Swayze/Keanu Reeves action movie *Point Break* was released, featuring an MCA soundtrack that included Sheryl's recording of "Hundreds of Tears," a rock ballad that she'd co-written with musician/producer Bob Marlette. Sheryl had met Marlette when they both worked on Neal Schon's *Late Nite* album a couple of years earlier—she was drawing on the talents of a wide array of collaborators while trying to develop her own skills as a songwriter. "Hundreds Of Tears" had subsequently been among the tracks that Sheryl had demo'd with Jay Oliver, and it was then thanks to the efforts of Judy Stakee at Warner/Chappell that it was included on the *Point Break* soundtrack. "That's why it's always good for composers to have a publishing deal," Judy asserts.

That same month, Sheryl flew to New York to meet with Hugh Padgham, who had to oversee the mastering of Sting's *Soul Cages* album before commencing pre-production on Sheryl's record. The purpose was to discuss strategy. Both agreed that the demos she'd produced with Jay Oliver were decent enough to use as a starting point for the recordings proper. So, as a means of saving time and money, they'd retain these and simply replace the parts that weren't quite up to the mark.

"In terms of the instrumentation the demos weren't brilliant quality," Padgham explains, "and so where, for instance, there had been a fake piano, we would put on a real piano. We also planned to overdub real drums, put on some more guitar, and do the vocals properly."

Expediting matters would be the assortment of crack session musicians who Padgham could call on at a moment's notice—people with whom he'd already worked and who he knew he could trust: Vinnie Colaiuta on drums, Pino Palladino on bass, Dominic Miller playing some of the guitar parts. Sheryl would sing, play piano and Hammond organ, and she'd also be able to count on the contributions of former Toy Matinee guitarist Tim Pierce and long-time mentor Don Henley. It was Henley, of course, who'd previously recommended that she not have her compositions recorded by other artists. Sheryl could have done with the publishing royalties, yet she'd heeded his advice. During the coming months, Henley's influence would become even more evident.

The project was initially allotted a budget of around a quarter of a million dollars, and the tape was scheduled to start rolling at A&M's state-of-the-art facility in mid-September. Everyone, it appeared, was on the same wavelength, Sheryl and Hugh sharing a common vision as to the direction that the music should take…. Things rarely turn out the way they're planned.

# CHAPTER SEVEN

# *A False Start*

A&M's Studio A—a popular venue over the years for numerous top recording artists who were either signed to the label or intent on using this prime Hollywood facility. It was here, in the fall of 1991, that work commenced on Sheryl Crow's debut album.

Laid out as a self-contained suite, with its own entrance and client lounge, Studio A afforded relative privacy while housing a control room with a choice combination of state-of-the-art and classic equipment. The vintage Neve 4972 console, purchased from the AIR Studios Montserrat facility of famed record producer George Martin, overlooked a 1500-square-foot live area with 20-foot ceilings that was connected to a pair of isolation booths along the right-hand wall and a smaller vocal booth on the left. During more than two decades, many major sessions had taken place in this room, including that for the 1985 all-star charity single, "We Are The World."

Still, even prior to A&M's acquisition of the property, the facility had enjoyed a colorful history. This began in 1917, when screen legend Charlie Chaplin purchased a five-acre parcel of land on the corner of La Brea and De Longpre Avenues. Chaplin's intention was to build his own film studio just south of his brother Sydney's mansion on the corner of La Brea and Sunset Boulevard. When completed in 1918, the Chaplin Studios resembled an English village, with a series of gray Colonial-style cottages, a brick Tudor mansion facade, and a ten-room house, backed by several acres of orange and lemon groves. Behind the Tudor facade were soundstages, a developing plant, an editing suite, and offices.

Between 1918 and 1952, the "Little Tramp" shot seventeen of his films on the La Brea lot, including classics like *The Kid*, *The Gold Rush*, *City Lights*, *Modern Times*, *The Great Dictator*, and *Limelight*. Then, in 1953, following Chaplin's relocation to Switzerland, the facility was sold to Kling Studios (which produced the *Superman* TV series), before falling into the hands of several different owners: Red Skelton, CBS, and, in November 1966, the A&M Record Company/Tijuana Brass Enterprises, Inc.

While the original five-acre lot was reduced to just under half that size when the Chaplin family home was sold to make way for what is now a shopping center, Jerry Moss and Herb Alpert duly converted two of the soundstages, as well as Chaplin's swimming pool, into a multi-facility tracking/mixing/mastering complex. In 1969, the Los Angeles Cultural Heritage Board designated the site a historical cultural monument, thus protecting certain other buildings from being altered.

Fast-forward to mid-September of 1991, when Sheryl, Hugh Padgham, and assistant engineer Rob Jaczko were joined by Jay Oliver inside the Studio A control room. Jay had been responsible for engineering the demos that now served as the template for Sheryl's first album, so it was only natural that he should be hired to come in for a week with all his own gear and lay down the basic tracks.

"Hugh was there for the first day, but then he went off to do some work with Sting, so I transferred all of the parts onto tape and I was out of there," Jay recalls. "As I perceived it, Sheryl was handling a lot of the production herself, and I thought the dynamic in the studio between her and Hugh was fine."

Indeed, there were plenty of positive signs during the early stages of recording. Co-producers Padgham and Crow were like-minded in their approach, there was a good atmosphere among the musicians, and things were progressing at a brisk pace.

"We'd had quite a lot of preparation beforehand, and to start with we had bloody good fun on the sessions," asserts Hugh. "You know, Vinnie Colaiuta was an absolute hoot. When he was in the studio playing drums, I remember having a really good time and laughing constantly. There certainly were no bad feelings at all, and even though Sheryl let me do my thing, there was never a question during the sessions of me doing anything that she didn't want to do. It was more like a co-production anyway, and then I happened to do the knob-twiddling as well."

For his part, David Anderle justifiably assumed that the record's sound, feel, and overall direction would be similar to that which he'd heard on the demo tape.

"Sheryl was a songwriter, and so it wasn't going to be a case of an artist being manipulated to sing songs by other people," he says. "I knew her identity would be together and that Hugh certainly knew what he was doing, so they went away and made the record."

At the beginning of October, Sting celebrated his fortieth birthday with a party on an A&M soundstage following a concert performance at the Hollywood Bowl. Sheryl was invited to the star-studded event, and it was Padgham's manager, Dennis Muirhead, who swung by her apartment and drove her to the studio. Once there, he got an up-close view of Sheryl's no-nonsense networking skills.

"A lot of well-known people were there," Muirhead recalls, "including Bob Dylan dressed in his shepherd gear and using a walking stick as he wended his way through the crowd with a trail of people behind him. Anyway, from the minute we arrived, Sheryl was quite clearly going to work the room. We did that together for not terribly long, and then she basically split from me and I didn't see her again."

Rarely, it appears, did Sheryl not seize the opportunity to interact with anyone who might help further her career, be it now or at some later date. Nevertheless, back in the studio, sharing an unfamiliar environment with an established record producer, she wasn't quite so assertive. Mindful of Padgham's status and experience, as well as the opportunity he'd presented her with, Sheryl largely acceded to his choices in terms of the sound while overdubs were taking place. However, as the sessions progressed, she began to realize that what she'd let herself in for was a sonic treatment that bore many of the hallmarks of Padgham's work with Sting, Genesis, and Phil Collins—clean, highly polished and, as in the case of the latter two, heavily layered, with little front-and-center space in which to highlight her vocals. In no way did this conform to the more rough-hewn edges of Sheryl's self-image or ignite the music that she and Jay Oliver had conceived.

"What you have to realize is that the songs had been incepted in a manner where they were integral with the production," Jay points out. "The material had been written using my studio gear, and I had a certain way of playing and working with these interesting sounds that were purely synthetic. They kind of sounded like drums and kind of sounded like guitars, but they couldn't be replaced by humans. They had their own identity and were never intended as substitutes for human tracks. Because of the nature of the sound, because of the way it was played, and because it was quantized by a computer, it just had a characteristic that couldn't be reproduced in any other way. If you tried to play it, the result wasn't as good; it sounded watered down.

"What's more, all of that stuff that I did had a dated production sensibility, and therefore—although I wasn't cognizant of this—Sheryl, Hugh, and David Anderle were all saying, 'That's good, but we need to be cutting-edge. We need to do something new,' and in retrospect I would have said the same thing. I don't think anyone said it was bad, but where they went wrong was trying to keep the same songs and replace everything with real instruments to make them work. That was a mistake, the wrong move. They tried to take something and turn it into something else, and by the time it became something else it was so watered down that it had not only lost the integrity of the original demos, but it was also just plain confusing. There was no focus in any way."

For a rerecording of the Crow-composed ballad "I Will Walk With You," Todd Wolfe attempted to recreate a dobro guitar part that he'd played on the original demo. Even that wasn't easy.

"When we'd done the original version in a studio in North Hollywood, I'd played the dobro in a bathroom, sitting next to a urinal," Todd explains. "Bathroom acoustics are amazing, and they reeled in this big boom mic which was coming through the door. Well, when they redid the tune with Hugh Padgham, they wanted some kind of really bare acoustic—stone or stuff like that—so they chose the basement, and there I was down in the basement at A&M trying to recreate that dobro part.... Our demo version of that song is better than the one which ended up on the album. It blew it away. It was just more inspired and it didn't have that session-y feel. I felt like all of the guys were hot-dogging it too much on the album version."

Still, in addition to the problems encountered when trying to recapture the spirit of the demos while replacing synth sounds with piano and supplemental guitars, the major source of discontent for Sheryl was the album's intended focal point—her own voice. Somehow, it just didn't have the right feel—it lacked punch and emotion—

yet she couldn't convince Hugh Padgham of this. The solution? Bring in Jay Oliver once again. After all, hadn't he achieved all of the right results on a Tascam 8-track back in Manhattan Beach?

"Sheryl wasn't happy with what she'd done," Jay confirms. "They had probably tried a million things and then thought, 'Well, let's get Jay back. Maybe he has some magic formula.' So, I went back in there for one or two songs that she wanted to re-sing, and I tried to recreate what I had done. Hugh wasn't there for that, and so from his perspective it may have been kind of an unauthorized experiment. Later on I was told that, when he heard the results, he immediately dismissed them as unusable, saying the miking wasn't good enough. Well, I completely bow to whatever Hugh says—he's such an expert—but I will say that it sounded fine to me. Then again, I also can't vouch for what he said. That's just what I was told."

At the same time, A&M's then-CEO, Al Cafaro, believes that during the recording sessions with Hugh Padgham—some of them at the Townhouse studios in London, which Padgham helped build as a staff engineer during the late '70s—Sheryl probably did communicate her dissatisfaction in her own way, but that the producer may not have been tuned in to this.

"With all due respect to Hugh, I don't know if his antenna for a dissatisfied artist, particularly a new female artist, might have been all that acute at the time," Cafaro says. "Sheryl could very easily have been giving signs—acting a bit passive-aggressive and a bit moody—which someone else might have picked up, and I'm not saying this to fault Hugh but simply to explain what the dynamic might have been. You know, Hugh's going along, doing his job, working hard, thinking everything's fine, maybe not reading exactly what's going on; Sheryl's probably a bit reticent because it is Hugh Padgham and this is her first record, even though she's been in the studio and around artists before. So, I think it was probably a combination of both."

Either way, as the recording sessions ended and Hugh Padgham embarked on the mix, tensions arose between artist and producer, and Sheryl's insecurities came to the surface. There can now be little doubt that somewhere along the way, possibly right at the start, their wires had become crossed. Consequently, with little apparent control over a product that would bear her name and might make or break her career, Sheryl was feeling as if she'd been blindsided and backed into a corner.

"Towards the end, things started to get a bit weird with Sheryl," Padgham admits. "She would get very frustrated because she was always totally paranoid that her voice was out of tune, and I particularly remember going home and feeling pissed off during the mixing stage. I got the feeling that it was a case of 'Oh Christ, if it's a little bit out of tune, what's Don Henley going to think?' Unfortunately, in those days there weren't things like Auto-Tune [a computer software plug-in that can correct pitch]—if she was really upset about something it would be so easy to fix now. It was a pain in the arse having to hook up harmonizers, and having the harmonizers on faders to change the voltage that changed the pitch of the machine."

Padgham wasn't wrong in his estimation of Sheryl's deference to the views of Don Henley. In fact, as her concerns increased and she felt as if these were falling on deaf ears, Henley took it upon himself to intercede between Sheryl and the record company.

"Don and I have known each other for years," says David Anderle, "and during the making of the Hugh Padgham record I got a call from him, asking me if I thought it was good enough…which is how Don always does anything anyway, gentleman that he can be. Sheryl had probably been complaining to him at that point. Then there was a series of occasions when Don would call, or Sheryl would say, 'Well, Don doesn't like it! Don doesn't think it's good enough!' The fact that I had so much respect for Don did help; I can say that much. If it had been somebody else it may not have worked so well. Don and I talked very creatively about it, but he was definitely A&R'ing her record."

And Hugh Padgham was still co-producing it alongside Sheryl, even though their conflicting viewpoints were now making that an increasingly difficult and unpalatable task.

"Sheryl was more whiny-moany than animated and heated," Hugh recalls, "but she was definitely a pain in the arse about her vocals. This was probably because, after years of trying to get a record deal, she really didn't have the self-confidence. Still, as far as I was concerned, she was being sort of over-the-top anal about everything, because to me her performances were great in the first place.

"There again, we also didn't have ten or eleven killer songs. We maybe had seven, eight, or nine songs that I thought were really good, and I remember going back into the studio and doing another number. I was getting frustrated because I was trying to get back home to London and now I'd have to spend another week in Los Angeles. I'd had enough of her and she'd probably had enough of me, so I suppose what we had was a falling out, but without a full-on slanging match."

"That's because I was in the middle," adds David Anderle who, after Hugh Padgham had finished the album on February 13, 1992, and delivered it to him the next day, felt it was "not raw enough."

"I thought it was a little too Sting- and Phil Collins–like," he says, "and when I played it around to a few people on the lot whose taste I appreciated, I didn't get the response I wanted. Then I talked to Sheryl, and Sheryl said she thought the record was too slick; she wanted to remix some of it and asked me to call Hugh, which I didn't really enjoy, but Hugh was a friend and so I said, 'Okay, I'll do that.' I called Hugh, who I think was on vacation at the time, and I told him what we were planning to do as best I could. I mean, that was a very hard position to be in. I knew that he was hurt and disappointed, but that was the role I played and I felt the same way [as Sheryl did] about the record."

On March 9, after Anderle had sanctioned Sheryl's request to give her musician boyfriend Kevin Gilbert the chance to remix the record at Andora Studios in Los Angeles, Anderle sent a note to Hugh Padgham back in London stating: "What bothers me most about the L.A. mixes is a feeling that they are generally over-mixed. The vocals, except for 'You Want It All,' 'I Will Walk With You,' and 'What Does It Matter?' are mixed too close to the track. This gives the record a sense of it being a band record as opposed to a singer-songwriter's record. The mixes also lack the rough-edged simplicity usually associated with a first record. The few mixes Sheryl has attempted with Kevin have this simplicity and focus. This is why I would like to continue remixing with her and Kevin. I feel secure their mixes and your mixes will work well together."

So secure, in fact, that only one of Padgham's mixes, "Love You Blind," actually made it onto the version of the album that, by early March of 1992, was slated for a September 22 release. Either that or A&M didn't have the stomach to shelve a project which was already $135,000 over budget and estimated to exceed $441,000, a sizeable figure for a debut record. In any case, *Sheryl Crow* (A&M 75021 5393 4) made its initial appearance on a test-pressing cassette with the following track running order:[1]

PROGRAM ONE

All Kinds Of People (Crow/Gilbert/Pressly)

Father Sun (Crow/Oliver)

What Does It Matter? (Crow)

Indian Summer (Crow/Oliver)

I Will Walk With You (Crow)

Love You Blind (Crow/Oliver)


PROGRAM TWO

Near Me (Crow/Oliver)

When Love Is Over (Crow)

You Want It All (Crow/Lunn)

Hundreds Of Tears (Crow/Marlette)

The Last Time (Crow)

On Borrowed Time (Crow)

A press folder was subsequently prepared to accompany a possible distribution of the tape to radio stations and other media outlets. This contained an artist photo and a creatively factual publicity release that read as follows:

---

[1] *Over the years there has been confusion among Sheryl Crow fans as to the precise names of some of the songs—the test pressing cassette listed "Father Sun" as "Father, Son," while a five-track Warner/Chappell publisher's demo cassette listed "Near Me" as "I Only Want You Near Me," and "On Borrowed Time" as "Borrowed Time." However, the titles listed here have been reproduced from the album credits approved by Hugh Padgham on May 15, 1992, and the revised credits approved by Sheryl Crow on May 29, 1992. The aforementioned publisher's demo, titled* Sheryl Crow Songs, *supplemented "Near Me," "On Borrowed Time," "What Does It Matter?" and "Hundreds Of Tears" with "The Real Life," an outtake from the album sessions.*

<u>SHERYL CROW</u>
"She's one of the best singers there is
right now. Period, bar none."
—Don Henley

Although her much-admired vocal talents garnered her the coveted back-up slots on the road with Don Henley and Michael Jackson, Sheryl Crow is a composer first and foremost. Her self-titled A&M debut is filled with stirring and luminously romantic songs all written or co-written by Crow.

<u>SHERYL CROW</u>, produced by Crow and Hugh Padgham, features tracks that range from turbulent rockers to affecting balladry. The band, fronted by Crow's piano and Hammond organ work, includes Dominic Miller, Vinnie Colaiuta, Pino Palladino and many of the musicians who played with Crow during her days as a performer in St. Louis. Don Henley guests on the song "What Does It Matter."

Although Crow has had a hugely successful career recording and touring with artists as varied as Joe Cocker, Stevie Wonder, Bruce Hornsby and Bonnie Raitt, the songs on <u>SHERYL CROW</u> were written when her career had reached a temporary impasse and her personal life was at a low. "I wasn't doing sessions. I was barely making the rent," she explains. "A lot of them were written after a three-year, really rocky relationship…They're dark pop songs."

Sometimes dark, always powerful and stirring, <u>SHERYL CROW</u> is the work of a movingly original pop music artist.

Out on A&M September 22.

In truth, the tracks on this album are rarely powerful or stirring—the "rockers" are anything but turbulent, and the ballads certainly aren't all that affecting. Instead, Alannah Myles meets Roxette in an uninspired union of generic, wailing guitars and competent but characterless lead vocals. The production is slick and sterile, the songs tame and undistinguished, lurching from pseudo-gospel to '80s synth-pop, with the featured artist lost somewhere in between. This is not a particularly bad album; it's just forgettable, and Sheryl Crow bears little resemblance to the artist who's since merited multiplatinum sales, numerous Grammy Awards, and widespread critical acclaim. There are instances when the quality of her voice does manage to rise above the formulaic arrangements—most notably on "Father Sun" and "On Borrowed Time"—yet these are few within the context of a dozen tracks. File under "dispensable."

Meanwhile, Hugh Padgham balked when he saw early drafts of the album credits, attributing the "additional production" of "All Kinds Of People" and "Father Sun" to Kevin Gilbert, the additional production of "Love You Blind" to Jay Oliver, and the mix in its entirety to Gilbert.

"A&M had actually decided that they needed to completely redo 'Love You Blind,' so Sheryl and I went over to Andora Studios, I brought in my gear again, and we redid the song from scratch," Oliver explains. "As I remember it, I knew going into the session that I was going to be given a co-production credit, and I recall Hugh knowing that too. He was there, and it was an interesting moment where we were both saying things at the same time. I thought we did pretty well together. The Kevin Gilbert mixes, on the other hand, were done without Hugh's knowledge."

Accordingly, on May 11, after several revisions had already been made to the album credits, Sheryl felt obliged to write Padgham a note expressing her hope that he wasn't too upset:

"It's been very agonizing with the production credits being revised at the eleventh hour, and I regret that the finishing of this record has been so complicated. I have to partially take blame for that, not knowing the complications my experimenting would cause. I think the album is really good and I hope it's one you feel good about and are proud of."

This message is interesting in terms of how Sheryl's positive comment about the album flies in the face of the events that were soon to follow. Nevertheless, it is in line with the positive noises that she was making—at least to certain people—while the project was still on track during the late spring and early summer of 1992.

"The mastering you did is wonderful," Sheryl wrote in a note to Bob Ludwig at Masterdisk in New York on May 13. (A month earlier Ludwig had sent a note to Hugh Padgham stating, "Really nice record, what a fantastic singer…I think this could be a big hit.") Around this time, Sheryl also penned the thank-yous that she wished to be included in the album's liner notes, beginning with these two paragraphs:

> I would first like to say I thank God for listening, but especially for sending me to planet Earth by way of the most wonderful people I've ever known—my mother and father, sisters and brother. I'm sending this music upward!

> I would also like to express my deepest, most heart-felt gratitude to the following: to Hugh Padgham for hearing something in my music that others didn't hear and for having the determination to get it onto tape; to Judy Stakee for wearing so many hats and not minding; to Scooter, my most honest critic and friend; to Kevin Gilbert for being my ears when mine fail me and for believing in making music no matter what; to Don Henley for your support and encouragement (la!); to Kevin Wall at whose door I camp; and to Jay Oliver for your patience and vision.

"With that first album Sheryl was grabbing at an amazing, amazing opportunity," says Judy Stakee. "Getting the record deal was the easy part, and I don't think she understood that; I certainly didn't. It was like, 'Yes! We've got a record deal!' You think, 'This is the most wonderful thing. How can I not trust that all of these people who've made all of these records are going to ensure that the album's going to turn out the way it's supposed to?' Up until the very end we all had those hopes that something would be fixed. Sheryl kept telling herself, 'Well, it is kinda different and I'm not too sure, but I'm gonna go with it.' She wanted this to work. At the same time, she had never made a record before. She had been in the studio before, but this was all new to her."

The production credits, which underwent four revisions between the first draft of March 10 and the version approved by Sheryl on May 29, finally settled on her and Hugh Padgham as co-producers, Padgham as the engineer, and Kevin Gilbert as the mix engineer on all but "Love You Blind," with Gilbert and Jay Oliver accorded their aforementioned "additional production" credits.

Then, suddenly, all bets were off. According to David Anderle, both he and Al Cafaro were in total agreement with Sheryl that the album was misrepresentative of her artistic talent and appeal, and that as such it wouldn't serve her well in trying to reach an audience. Still, what appears puzzling is the fact that after being remixed by Gilbert and Crow in March, the album was then mastered by Bob Ludwig the following month and placed on the release schedule.

"I don't ever remember it being scheduled," states David Anderle. "You get into a period where you play it, you listen to it, you check it out, and so on, and you do all of the liner notes and credits months ahead of time. The fact that someone came up with a release date doesn't mean it was coming out in my eyes. The only time I thought it had a chance to come out was when they were working on it. I would be the first person to say that if I had pushed to put that Hugh Padgham record out it would have failed, and I would have been just as responsible as anyone else."

In an April 1999 interview with the *Chicago Tribune's* Greg Kot, Sheryl asserted that she "had to go in and plead with the label not to release it. The producer brought me to the label, but we never had a common mind-set on what kind of album it should be. I wanted to make a rock album and he wanted to make a lush album based on my demos, which were very slick. I thought if the label put that out, it would make the wrong first impression and it would be impossible for me to tour behind it."

Al Cafaro, on the other hand, doesn't recall having to be convinced by Sheryl that the album should be scrapped.

"Frankly, I was the one who uttered the words first," he says. "It would not have been her, because she would not have been confident about what the outcome of that would be.

"I don't know if I'd regarded it as '80s music when I first heard the demo going along in my car. I subsequently came to that conclusion upon hearing the record submitted by Hugh; not so much that the music was dated aesthetically, but that it was very AOR [album/adult-oriented rock], which at the time was not a real active format. Given the nature of the marketplace and the radio stations where we'd need to play it, I was immediately concerned: 'What are we going to do with this record?'

"It wasn't to do with the quality—there was some quality songwriting—but it gave me reason to pause, and as I was contemplating how we would navigate this situation it came to my attention for the first time that Sheryl was very unhappy with the record. Not only that, but she had been unhappy with the whole process, and I believe it was David [Anderle] who made me aware of this. I was still reasonably new to the process at this time, but I've got my legs, I know how to talk to artists, and I've pretty much got a sense of purpose and of what my job is. So, I was very keen on us talking things through and having us all understand the reasons behind our thought process and decision making. As I recall, we sat and started talking about it with Sheryl, and I was probably honest but pulling my punches a little bit as to where we might go with this record. You know, 'This is really good, but....' Still, we immediately got right to the issue; that Sheryl wasn't happy either, and that, by the way, she didn't really feel it represented who she was."

This must have been a tough conclusion to reach, not least for the A&M brass who had signed Sheryl on the strength of some demos that weren't all that far removed from the finished album. In essence, this record featured the exact same songs with rerecorded vocals and replaced instrumental parts. So, if the compositions themselves had a dated feel, as Jay Oliver acknowledges, why wasn't this apparent before a huge pile of cash was flushed down the toilet?

"I think one of the reasons for that is the natural sort of process that you go through when you sign an artist," says Al Cafaro. "It's always about the possibilities and the excitement and the enthusiasm, and I think there's sort of a suspension of disbelief in the process. That, coupled with Hugh Padgham's involvement and what we believed Hugh could do—and maybe unfairly so, maybe we expected too much—put us in a situation where it's easy to hear things differently the second time around. I mean, I've had that happen to me when I'm listening to the exact same thing. So, I think it was probably a function of that process, and then it became 'What are we going to do?'

"I'm sure that, had the record been received wonderfully, everybody's perception would have been very different. However, I didn't get the impression that there was anything at all disingenuous or self-serving about Sheryl's concerns. When I heard those concerns I heard real concerns, and I responded in a very sort of forthright fashion. I was not at all skeptical, and part of that was due to the fact that Sheryl was compelling in terms of her feelings about it, and part of it was also down to my instincts and David's as well. We would always err on the side of what the artist felt, because at the end of the day it was the artist who had to sell it, sing it, and be judged by it.

"Keep in mind that even through this process the woman is compelling; she's bright, she's involved, she's smart. This is not someone who is shrugging her shoulders and saying, 'I don't know, I don't think.' So, when we had that moment in time—'Okay, that's how you're feeling. Well, geez, I feel that way too. What do we need to do?'—it was pretty clear to me that if we were to release that album we really didn't have an opportunity to be successful. Having said that, I also don't remember hearing it and thinking, 'Oh, this is terrible, this is dreck.' It was very much a case of 'Yeah, this is a pretty good record, and yeah we've got some good songs here, but you know what, there's just no home for this right now.'"

Quite a few people within A&M shared this view, as evidenced when copies of the album were circulated and feedback invited. Among the disapprovers was Wayne Isaak, A&M's Executive Vice President of East Coast Operations and head of publicity in the New York office. Isaak liaised with the various departments, obtained bookings for the company's artists on the major radio and TV shows, and generally tried to maximize marketing and promotion opportunities in the Tri-State area, while also keeping track of the national situation on an executive level.

"Part of what I did was to meet new artists, figure out who they were, and start developing their story," he explains. "I lived in New York, but I went to Los Angeles on business, and when Sheryl first signed with the company, she came over to the A&M offices and we just sort of sat down and talked for a while. In the early '90s rock was big, with Guns N' Roses and the like, and when I met Sheryl she struck me as a rock artist with a little bit of mid-South roots. She had enough of 'Missoura' in her to give her something I like, which is a kind of charm, and something other than just your average, slick sort of L.A. musician, trying to get a deal and trying to make it. I'd heard one song that she and Hugh had demo'd, and I really liked her. I mean, I liked her as a person."

Nevertheless, when Wayne Isaak listened to the finished album, he didn't hear much of either 'Missoura' or Sheryl the rock artist. Instead, like practically everyone else, he felt that it lacked the essence of who she was. "That record didn't bring out Sheryl's indigenous quality or her roots," he says. "My opinion was that she had more and it really wasn't brought forward.

"Back in the early '80s, there was an opinion that when you develop an artist, you can have the first album and get them out there. By the early '90s, however, we were already taking the approach that is very prevalent now—you'd better have some singles, you'd better make the best record you can, because it's gonna take years of marketing that record to even have a shot at breaking it. And that's really what we collectively decided from the hardcore business standpoint, that the singles weren't on the album, and that the sound didn't reflect this really energetic, great voice and this charismatic person."[2]

David Anderle concurs: "When Sheryl delivered the record I personally felt that it was a little too shiny. Initially, from the few people who I shared things with, I wasn't getting any reaction—it just didn't feel right—and she came in and I talked to her about it. She said that she thought it was a little too slick, and she wanted

---

[2] *Wayne Isaak recalls receiving advance copies of the album in his New York office, and mailing these to "probably twenty or thirty writers, just saying, 'This is a great artist, see what you think of the music.' At that point the decision [to shelve the record] hadn't been made, but we got information back within a couple of weeks saying, 'Well, wait a minute, this isn't coming out.' So I called all of the people and said, 'Look, just throw it away, it's not done. There will be tracks coming out of it.'"* The unreleased Sheryl Crow *album would subsequently surface on bootleg CDs.*

permission to go in with Kevin and tart it up a bit, and I gave her permission to do that. She wasn't saying, 'Pull it.' From the beginning she was talking about wanting to make the changes and wanting to remix it.

"I went down to a couple of the sessions with her and Kevin and watched them working on it, but there was no way they could really do anything, because Hugh imprints a lot of what his thing is on the tape. The material that was on the record had been demo'd, recorded, and reworked, so those songs were pretty much cooked. I thought to try to strip them down again would be impossible, and I'm sure Sheryl did too. So, that's when we scrapped it."

Well, almost. In fact, before the final nail was hammered into the coffin of the aborted *Sheryl Crow* album, David Anderle understandably wanted to have some idea as to a viable and, most importantly, cost-effective alternative—A&M certainly wouldn't be dipping into the kitty for another half-million dollars to record an entirely new collection of songs.

Time drifted on. With no visible solution, Anderle's concern grew, as did his anger at Sheryl, who he thought was avoiding him. In fact, she had good reason for maintaining a low profile—shelving the album was probably more gut-wrenching for her than it was for A&M. It was like shelving the past three years of her life, and amid the feelings of ire, disappointment, and humiliation, Sheryl now had to pick herself up and start all over again…if she could figure out how.

First off, she'd already ditched her manager, Morty Wiggins (interestingly, Wiggins would subsequently join A&M as a Senior Vice President of Marketing), and handed the reins to Robert Richards, who'd handled the careers of numerous major artists. Sheryl had been introduced to him by her friend, Scooter Weintraub, who, like Richards, consulted for Radio Vision International, a company that produced network television specials and syndicated them worldwide.

Richards's current roster of clients included the band Wire Train, A&M artist David Baerwald, and David Ricketts, Baerwald's partner in a duo named David & David. Bill Bottrell, a producer/engineer with credits ranging from Madonna to Michael Jackson, had helmed Wire Train's *No Soul No Strain* album, as well as Baerwald's second solo record, *Triage*. Working out of his own Toad Hall studio facility in Pasadena, a short distance from Los Angeles, it would be Bottrell who'd serve as the key figure in the resurrection of Sheryl Crow's career.

"One result of my producing the Wire Train and Baerwald albums simultaneously was that all parties to both records had started coming around to Toad Hall whenever they felt like it," Bottrell explains. "I went week-to-week, back and forth on those projects, in addition to occasional Michael Jackson sessions where whoever was there might get to play an instrument. Also, just to add to the chaos, Kevin Gilbert was working next door and wanted me to produce his solo record."

Given the proximity of Gilbert's studio to Toad Hall, it might seem inevitable that Sheryl would eventually run into Bottrell, yet this actually occurred in a more roundabout way.

"David Baerwald and I were starting an outfit called the Tuesday Music Collective," Bottrell says. "We didn't have any goals, we just wanted to write songs and record them. Well, being that all these people were dropping by—Jeff Trott, Kevin Hunter, Brian MacLeod, Baerwald—everybody sort of joined up and started working together. We had a core group and a fringe group, basically made up of Wire Train, Baerwald, and Dan Schwartz."

Trott, Hunter, and MacLeod were all members of Wire Train. Baerwald and Schwartz had already collaborated on the former's *Triage* album. Nevertheless, on the first couple of Tuesdays, it was only Bottrell, Baerwald, and Kevin Gilbert who gathered at Toad Hall to make music, before the producer began to hear about this singer named Sheryl Crow.

"One day, during a meeting with David Anderle about Dave Baerwald's record, he mentioned Sheryl to me," Bottrell recalls. "Then I was at a rehearsal studio in the [San Fernando] Valley, listening to Wire Train prepare for their tour, and Robert Richards got all up in my face about Sheryl. Kevin was there, and he started in too."

Each of the men who were championing Sheryl's cause had a vested interest in her; Gilbert as her boyfriend, Richards as her manager, Anderle as the man who needed her to justify his faith in her talent. Indeed, uncertain about A&M's ongoing commitment to his client, Richards made it his immediate priority to ask Anderle and Al Cafaro their intentions while proposing a way of jump-starting her career.

"Before meeting David, Sheryl and I powwowed about this and I briefly talked to Bill Bottrell," Richards explains. "Basically, the concept was to advise A&M to dump the financial responsibility of that first album, give me a certain figure, and I'll deliver the Tuesday Music Club with Bill Bottrell to make a new record. It would be a great start for this new artist."

"There was a period of time when I didn't know how to handle the situation," admits David Anderle. "I didn't want to say to the label that we had a problem, I wanted to see if I could figure it out, but time was going on, I wasn't talking to Hugh, and Sheryl wasn't talking to me. Sheryl and I had been very close during the making of the record, and I knew she wasn't happy with the result. Then, when Robert Richards became involved with her, he called me and said, 'Look, we've got to get this thing going. Her career has stalled, and I have this idea to put her to work with this guy Bill Bottrell. I'd like to get a meeting together.' At that point I was just really unhappy with the whole situation, and probably in hindsight I might have been more unhappy because I didn't know what to do with this stalled album.

"I was trying to keep the problem from Al [Cafaro], and I don't think Al was even thinking about it at the time. I was trying to manage the situation while I could figure out what the heck to do, and I think that's where my problem was with Sheryl; I just wasn't secure about what I wanted to do and I wasn't getting anything from her. I would see her coming to visit other people on the lot, but she never came up to say 'Hello.' Anyway, Sheryl, Robert Richards, and I had lunch—she and I were sitting next to each other in a booth, he was sitting on the other side of the table—

and he said, 'Okay, we have to get this thing together, we have to move on, we have to figure out what to do,' and I said something to the effect of, 'Well, before we do that I've got to get something off my chest,' and I looked at Sheryl and said, 'You know, right now I don't like you. I'm mad at you.' I think she was rather shocked, and I was shocked that she was so shocked, because I had figured she would have known that."

"Sheryl has a way of making people want to go the extra step for her," says Robert Richards. "That's not a calculated thing, but people quickly recognize 'There's a talent here, and a voice, and we can all go out and conquer the world,' and some of them might get their feelings hurt. They might feel that they put in a special effort for Sheryl and didn't get enough back, but that happens to anybody at any time within any group of people. I know that David Anderle cared very much about her and was putting a lot of effort into her career, and Sheryl was probably just afraid to see David because she felt she may have failed him the first time around. However, she was never unhappy with David. He was like a father to her."

Accordingly, once the A&R chief had explained the reason for his anger, he and Sheryl put their misunderstanding behind them and resumed business. Anderle continues the story:

"I turned to Robert and said, 'What do you have in mind?' and he said, 'Well, I know Bill Bottrell, and I think he could make the record that you guys want. He can make it for X amount of dollars because he has his own studio,' and so I said, 'Okay, fine, we should have some meetings.' It was Robert who took me out to Pasadena to meet with Bill Bottrell."

Nevertheless, during this meeting with Anderle, the producer was non-committal, and even disapproving when, at one point, he was asked to simply record a single that could be added to the Padgham album.

"My wife, Betty, was basically my manager," Bottrell explains. "She rejected the idea of me recording a single that would be added to the album, and she was right."

The concept of supplementing a commercially challenged record with a new single might have been mentioned by David Anderle, but this would have amounted to sticking a Band-Aid on a broken leg, and he knew it. What's more, he was also aware that if Bill Bottrell utilized his own well-equipped studio, a brand new album could be produced at a pretty reasonable price. This is what Anderle now proposed. Bottrell said he'd get back to him.

On Tuesday, September 15, 1992, Kevin Gilbert called the producer and suggested bringing Sheryl to that night's TMC session. Sensing that the all-male Collective might benefit from some feminine input, Bottrell agreed.

"We were trying to be liberated people, '90s kinds of people, with the music we were doing, [but] we had no women there," Gilbert jokingly told L.A. radio hosts Mark Thompson and Brian Phelps (known as Mark & Brian on KLOS 95.5) on the April 7, 1995, broadcast of their syndicated morning show. "You know, what is this? Here are five white men—yeah, we're *very* liberal!"

"Sheryl showed up the third week, but it wasn't in the spirit of making an album for her," Bill Bottrell confirms. "I just wanted to see who she was, because everyone had been talking about her, and what she brought was her voice and her attitude. She was melodic; she had good vocal ideas and good vocal expression. As I said, at that point there was no goal for us, we were just guessing, and she was another one of the guessers."

That night, the first two verses of "Leaving Las Vegas" were recorded and completed. Bill and Sheryl would supply the words to the bridge and the third verse at a later date, yet the producer was immediately aware of the singer's potential, which went far beyond what he heard on the album that Sheryl had made with Hugh Padgham.

"I went to her home, and she played me the mixed album and she played me the demos," Bill recalls. "I told her I thought the demos were better. They weren't drastically different, but there was a little more life in them. There again, I knew the material wasn't what I would do.... Sheryl expressed to me the fact that she was hoping to somehow save the Padgham album."

Bottrell was thinking otherwise. Having come face to face with her ability during the "Leaving Las Vegas" session, as well as that for "Solidify" the following week, he was quickly warming to the idea of making Sheryl the focus of a TMC-associated project. He therefore called David Anderle and they set up another meeting in Pasadena. After listening to both recordings, the A&R chief immediately wanted to seal the deal.

"I said, 'Look, I really think you should do this,'" Anderle recalls. "I told Bill, 'Sheryl is a fantastic artist and it would be perfect for you to take her into the studio and let things develop, but I also have to insist that this figure we have is the figure you're going to stick with.' I knew I could probably get that amount of money to do it, but he couldn't spend a penny more. He said he could do that and wanted to do that, and I said, 'Fine.'"

According to David Anderle's recollections, the budget being offered to produce an entirely new album was in the region of $200,000. Bill Bottrell asserts that it was closer to $150,000.

"I was committed to low budgets," Bill explains. "You see, I thought the normal record industry system was not just a waste of money, but it made the music worse and it took opportunities away from hundreds of young musicians who should get a share of that money. They could make a great album with a hundred thousand bucks, and I made the Baerwald, Wire Train, and various other records all for under $150,000. That's how I wanted to work because I believed in it, and I was cocky. I knew I could sell the back end [earn royalties] and make money. I was making millions of dollars off the back end. I didn't even get much advance money working with Michael Jackson. I barely survived, but I took the back end and did great. By the time I was working on the Sheryl record I was a millionaire, so it was working for me."

At last, armed with a definite plan of action, David Anderle returned to the A&M lot and had a meeting with Al Cafaro.

"I said, 'I think we should scrap the first record, because we're going to have to spend a lot more money to do videos, a lot more money to put her on the road, and I don't think we're going to get the results we want,'" Anderle recalls. "I then explained that for this extra amount of money we could do another record from scratch, and the sum total of the whole thing would give us what we wanted."

"At that time none of us knew what the new record was going to do," adds Robert Richards, "but we were looking to establish Sheryl with 250,000 units of sales by being very practical and very smart, attaching the right dollars to getting her launched."

And so it was that the A&M execs decided to abort—and therefore see no financial return on—a debut project for which their company had shelled out close to $450,000. This was motivated by a combination of two things—their own reservations about the album and, as events were to prove, their remarkable faith in the talent and instincts of a new signing.

"I was hearing from people in town that I was about to be dropped," Sheryl recalled in a 2002 episode of VH1's *Behind the Music*, and Bill Bottrell states that he, too, suspected A&M was thinking about dumping her. However, all evidence points to the contrary.

"When I first spoke with both David Anderle and Al Cafaro they made it clear to me that they really believed in Sheryl and wanted to give things another go," says Robert Richards.

"I really tried to assure him of how much we cared about Sheryl," Anderle confirms. "I certainly never wavered for a second from the time I met her."

"It's fairly unusual for a record company to eat almost a half million dollars, but I think the reason it happened was that we all really felt good about Sheryl," adds Wayne Isaak, while according to Al Cafaro, "The decision to shelve the record was made with reassurances to do something else; that this was definitely something we should continue to pursue."

As for Hugh Padgham, he wouldn't have any idea about the recording of a brand new album until its release in August 1993. Thereafter, legal wranglings would ensue between the producer and the company to which he'd introduced Sheryl Crow.

"The deal was for Hugh to produce her first two albums, although she had the right to veto this, in which case he was due compensation," Padgham's then-manager, Dennis Muirhead, explains. "As things turned out, A&M struggled with that clause. Hugh had a written contract for the album that he did, which made reference to the follow-up, and then there was another document on top of that which was never executed, and that was one of the problems. The reason why that document was never put into effect was because after the first album was shelved, we thought it was all over as far as Sheryl Crow and A&M were concerned. Then the next record [*Tuesday Night Music Club*] came out, and so I had to persuade Hugh to make a claim, which we did, and after about a year they ended up settling with us for quite a lot."

For his part, Padgham now has no disagreement with the Crow/A&M decision to pull the album that he produced with Sheryl.

"When I was doing the Sting records at that time they were really sort of perfectly crafted," he states. "Perhaps using the demos as the basic spine of each song wasn't the right way to do it in retrospect. It would have been better to have had the band playing the songs, because we had really good musicians on it. Still, I have to say that by trying to correct every little wart with regard to her vocals, Sheryl was making her own contribution to the album being too perfect. I therefore don't wish to shoulder a hundred percent of the blame for that. It was the two of us, and it was she who then turned around and said, 'No, this isn't really what I want to do,' and I respected that. It was just one of those things.

"It would have been nice to work with Sheryl for another two or three albums, which was what was supposed to happen when she originally signed to the label, but you can't knock the success that she's had, and so, as far as I'm concerned, I wish her the best of luck. The album didn't come out and in retrospect I would imagine it was obviously for the best. You win some and you lose some, but at least I can still say I'm the one who discovered Sheryl Crow."

# CHAPTER EIGHT

# Pasadena Tuesday Nights

Sheryl may have heeded Don Henley's advice to hang onto her own compositions, but as soon as her freshman album had been shelved and its songs worked to death, Judy Stakee began shopping them around to other artists who might wish to record them. The first takers were Wynonna Judd, who included "Father Sun" on her 1993 album *Tell Me Why*, and Celine Dion, who cut "Love You Blind" as the B-side of her 1992 single "If You Asked Me To." In 1996, Tina Turner included a version of "All Kinds Of People" on her *Wildest Dreams* album, while several other numbers from Sheryl's aborted record were covered overseas: "All Kinds Of People" by both Jill Johnson in Denmark and Anita Hegerland in Sweden, and "What Does It Matter?" by Danish artist Sanne.

"Those songs had been written after coming off the road with Michael Jackson and Don Henley, and for Sheryl they were no longer applicable," Stakee explains. "We were getting away from synthesized music, and for her there was no way of making them relevant anymore.

"When Sheryl first came on the scene, Brad Rosenberger, the Vice President of Film and Television at Warner/Chappell, was sending her stuff to music supervisors, really getting them pumped up about this new girl. In fact, Sheryl had just come on the marketplace when Mitchell Leib was supervising *Boys on the Side*. Mitchell sent her a script and said, 'I'd love for you to do something.'"

The movie, eventually released in 1995, featured a soundtrack that included Stevie Nicks's performance with Melissa Etheridge of the Sheryl Crow/Todd Wolfe composition "Somebody Stand By Me," as well as Sheryl's rendition of Derek & the Dominos' "Keep On Growing."

"Sheryl had a lot of people behind her, and that's where I believe we really helped," says Stakee. "We helped in marketing her and getting everybody in this industry behind her."

At the same time, despite the setback regarding her intended debut, Sheryl didn't have to wait long before embarking on an entirely new project. The shelved album had been tentatively scheduled for release in September 1992, and that same month she began working with the guys in the Tuesday Music Collective.[1] Once more, she had a solid support system, not least in the form of the troupe's innovative leader, Bill Bottrell.

---

[1] *The band's original name was the Tuesday Music Collective. This soon evolved into the Tuesday Music Club and, by the time of the album's completion, the Tuesday Night Music Club. Some people still refer to it as either TMC or TNMC.*

Originally a guitarist, Bottrell began engineering after leaving college in 1974. Eventually he became a producer, and by 1992 he'd amassed some impressive credits: the co-production of Thomas Dolby's *Aliens Ate My Buick* album; the engineering of tracks on Tom Petty's *Full Moon Fever*; the engineering of Madonna's *Like a Prayer*, the co-production of her songs on the *Dick Tracy* soundtrack, and production of the movie soundtrack to *Truth or Dare* (titled *In Bed with Madonna* outside the U.S.); and the co-production of three songs on Michael Jackson's *Dangerous* album, including the hit single "Black Or White," which was among the tracks that Jackson and Bottrell co-wrote. Nevertheless, it was largely as a result of these experiences that, by the time he encountered Sheryl, Bill had turned his back on superstar projects.

"The way the records were being made was just too humongous," he says. "You know, I spent two years pretending I was working on certain Michael Jackson songs, because that's the way it's done in those circles, when really I was just using the original vocal that he did and, with the exception of certain sections, most of the original sounds. I knew how I wanted to make that record, and it wasn't the way those people were making it."

Consequently, once Bottrell had made enough money to be more selective about his work assignments, he initiated a project that conformed to his own ideals, hoping it might fulfill some of his musical ambitions. David Baerwald was his initial partner in the Tuesday Music Collective, and it wasn't long before everyone else jumped on board, including Sheryl.

With the songs conceived pretty much on the spot, Bottrell rolled tape while the assembled musicians rehearsed, arranged the music, and played together as a band. Then, whenever possible, and conforming to the approach of a bygone era, he selected the best complete performance rather than compile a song out of numerous different takes. The vibe was his main concern, and he therefore focused on attaining the optimum live results, even if lyrical revisions required the punching-in of certain vocal parts at a later date.

"This way of working is fraught with problems," Bottrell explains. "You'd be writing a song, the tape would be rolling all the time, and you'd get something really magic, but the third verse would just be made-up crap, and you'd never get it right before getting that magic. So, we'd have to go back, rewrite some words, and punch them in, although never because of the performance. I could still remember people doing that when I'd started engineering back in '74, especially as the studio that I'd worked in was kind of ten years behind the times. I remembered it as being much more fun, and as CDs started coming out and people started rereleasing old material, I would buy some old albums and listen to them, and I just decided that way of working produced all of the great American pop music, whereas the other way was not holding up its end of things.

"The TMC sound was my sound; in the early days the songs were coming from this group, and the alternative country thing was something that I'd been waiting to do for the longest time. All the way through the '80s I had worked with black R&B acts, and I'd learned a whole lot about music and soul and digging to find what one naturally does, as opposed to just making a record in the Hollywood sense. At the end of that time, as I was finishing up with Michael Jackson, rap was coming out and there was a trend towards a new black separatism. It was this wholly black form which didn't need white guys in there doing stuff, and I understood that, and I also understood that when I went off on my own I could sit there and try to make music that sounded black in order to do something soulful—because I was kind of good at it—but I realized 'I'm supposed to find where my soul comes from,' and that is Appalachia and country music.

"Ever since then, almost everything I've done has been based in these roots. When you grow up in L.A., which is the media capital of the world and the dream factory, you take for granted this idea of things being conceived, written, and pieced together to become these modern myths. But somehow, as I grew older, I started to realize that good records never come from that."

Accordingly, Bill Bottrell and his TMC colleagues were now attempting to produce songs that were more closely aligned with their own musical and ethical leanings, if not necessarily their geographical roots. The venue for this quest was Bill's Pasadena studio, Toad Hall, which he'd assembled at the tail end of 1990 and the start of 1991. Located on El Molino Avenue, close to the famed Pasadena Playhouse, and comprising a long, high-ceilinged room with gothically inspired decor (a second, adjoining room was added in 1992), Toad Hall was markedly different in both appearance and atmosphere from the usual L.A. facility. A wall of books blended with tapestries, while antique tables contrasted with a mixing console that was in the main recording area rather than in a separate control room. However, it wasn't just the furnishings that made the facility unique.

On successive Tuesday nights in the late summer and early fall of 1992, the afore-mentioned atmosphere was embroidered with an ensemble of notable talents, mercurial temperaments, and barely restrained egos that could vie with star-studded gatherings at the most celebrated studios: David Baerwald, Bill Bottrell, Sheryl Crow, Kevin Gilbert, Brian MacLeod, Dan Schwartz. Sometimes it was as if Bottrell, let loose in the lab, was attempting to see what would happen if he mixed industrial-strength acids with a few drops of nitroglycerin. The unpredictable results could very well be interesting, but one shake and the entire roof might come off the place.

Before examining how each of the songs came together, it's worth taking a look at the personalities behind them, for these were crucial to not only the creative process but also to the controversial events that were to follow. In the latter regard it wouldn't be fair to single out any one participant as the major perpetrator, but suffice it to say that the working relationship between Baerwald and Gilbert could turn into an egotis-tical challenge, the personal relationship between Crow and Gilbert was severely strained, and Baerwald enjoyed picking on both while having his "little nervous break-down" and incurring the wrath of self-appointed mediator Schwartz.

From Schwartz's perspective, Gilbert and Baerwald's sense of self-importance was throwing the whole "collective" concept out of whack—their musical focus was being submerged by the kind of "lead-singer egos" that fuel the need, and are necessary, to stand center stage, grab the spotlight, and dominate the proceedings. Then again, from Baerwald's standpoint, what Schwartz perceived as ego, he considers to have been "exuberance and excitement and joy" over the creative process.

"To call this ego is to call everything ego," Baerwald says. "Every creative act is an act of ego. I think Bill was confident about the way he wanted the record to sound, I think Kevin had a lot of insights into Sheryl that gave him the ability to write in a language that she could sing and believe in, I think Dan and Brian provided a really good rhythm section, and I know I believed in the stories and characters that we were creating. All of us had very different skills. I could take the first verse and chorus of "Leaving Las Vegas" and dump it right in Kevin's lap, and he'd know exactly what to do with it. I could throw him the ball and he would shoot, both musically and lyrically. He was brilliant. He was really fast and he could think on his feet."

At the same time, there was no small irony in the fact that Sheryl—still recuperating from her shelved-album debacle, grateful for the new opportunity, and trying to deal with the sometimes-intimidating atmosphere—initially suppressed her own ego to the point where individuality had to be virtually coaxed out of her. It was this, in conjunction with the aforementioned variety of male temperaments, that comprised one aspect of the highly complex, multifaceted TMC dynamic. Another was the camaraderie, inventiveness, and accomplished musicianship that would lead to inspired collaboration and memorable results.

Everyone brought something to the table: Bill Bottrell was the conceptual instigator, creative nurturer, and technological craftsman who saw the songs through to completion; Sheryl Crow was the featured artist with the engaging voice and dexterous ability to field whatever ideas were thrown her way; Kevin Gilbert was the brilliant, fast-thinking multi-instrumentalist who could take those compositional ideas down any number of different avenues; David Baerwald was the dynamic lyricist and innovator who could provide the collective with its motivational spark; Brian MacLeod was the consummate drummer and wordsmith, whose ironic, off-center take on both the material and the recording process instilled the sessions with much of their energy; and Dan Schwartz was the musical elitist whose high-impact bass helped underpin several TMC tracks, and who invariably tried to ensure that there was integrity to the art.

"I thought we all had a good idea for the making of that album, but as it turned out, we had about five good ideas," Baerwald remarks. "Basically, I had this dream, which I realized was about the Tuesday Music Club: I'm in a zoo, looking at the monkey cage, and this monkey climbs up a tree and starts gibbering. That's me. Then he takes a big shit in the palm of his hand, and throws it on the ground and starts jumping up and down like a lunatic. Then all of the other monkeys start doing it, and it turns into this big shit parade. Well, that was us; a bunch of gibbering chimps, and Bill was in there going, 'Hmm, this is a very nice turd. Let's polish this up and do something with it!' And I really mean that in the best way. I think all true creative moments have aspects of that, especially group sessions. Go check out a television writers' session, or a Sun Ra concert. It's just enthusiasm and pride and excitement."

"When it all came together, everybody was into it," says Dan Schwartz. "Nobody had to be told to shut up or to speak up, and so while ego was often an issue, that wasn't always the case."

"What happened there was a unique situation," adds A&M's then–Executive Vice President of East Coast operations, Wayne Isaak. "You had an exceptional producer, a catalytic sort of combo of collaborators, and a situation for them to try a whole different approach than what had been going on with Hugh Padgham. That period was when all of them innocently—and in the wonderful early stages of working together—just went for it. Sheryl had a lot of specific talent, and even though she'd been in bands and had played with some awesome musicians, this was finally a moment to kind of have it built around her."

Robert Richards agrees: "Those guys really got behind Sheryl and made her feel like part of this big family. They gave her the freedom to express what she was really confused about, because she'd just made an album where she thought she'd been expressing herself to this other producer, and that hadn't worked out. Having been smacked down the first time out, she was a bit apprehensive and extremely insecure, and so I think it was great for her to have this support system."

The flip side was that, from Sheryl's perspective, said system might not have always felt all that supportive. For one thing, she had to deal with regular critiquing by her perfectionist boyfriend, Kevin Gilbert. "I use to bug him about his perfectionism," Brian MacLeod recalled in a 2001 interview with Wayne Perez for the official Kevin Gilbert Web site. "So did Bill Bottrell. 'That's bullshit! You're over-thinking.' He couldn't help himself. Those kind of intellectual minds, they're going five times as fast as yours and mine. They can't stop." At the same time, Sheryl also had to contend with the over-assertiveness of David Baerwald, whose improvisational talents could be matched by his off-the-wall behavior.

"Back then I admit I was pretty aggressive about getting my ideas out there, but that's what it was about," Baerwald now states. "It was like a basketball game—you're supposed to run around, and pass and shoot. That's what it's all about. You know, Bill had a professional agenda, Sheryl obviously had a professional agenda, and we were just having fun. One of the things about me is that, whether I write well or not, I write fast, but I'm usually ready to change it too. I mean, it's not like I'm saying, 'Here's the Bible.' I'm just saying, 'Here, try it,' but I will also throw things out there, and I see absolutely no reason to be ashamed of that.

"The stuff I am embarrassed about is walking into the studio with a bunch of declassified CIA documents, grabbing somebody by the shirt collar, and yelling at them to take a look. I was doing that all over town. Still, you have to remember, this was the time when the super-corpo shit was really hitting the fan and we were watching the walls close around us everywhere—musically, politically, sexually. You had Reagan and Bush and [William J.] Casey and Darryl Gates and Iran-Contra and crack cocaine and the riots of '92, and in music all of the megamergers and the dehumanization which that brings. It was the end, I thought. Everything was turning into dog shit, and so Tuesday was our day to be gregarious and loud and just let it all hang out. At least, it was for me.

"I had a bunch of hang-ups, my house was sort of a meeting place for all of these wannabe libertarian anarchists, and I ended up kind of becoming one of them. I admit that I was going utterly mad, but it was an utterly mad time. I was totally paranoid and my manners became a little bit brusque, which wasn't helped by the fact that I was drinking a lot. I didn't get the fact that this was a business. The rest of the guys were all trying to create something, and in retrospect I can see how having somebody as voluble and volatile and death-driven and wordy and nihilistic as me would drive everybody crazy. Bill asked me to write the Tuesday Music Club manifesto, so I did this sort of 'situationist' thing about Reichstag fires and terrorism and propaganda and psychological warfare, and then Bill took my things and said 'or not' at the end of them. I knew this wasn't a radical cell. It was a bunch of musicians. Most of the time, when I said things to them about politics they'd say, 'You're fucking crazy,' and they were right, if uninformed. I was really extreme, and I owe everybody apologies for some of my behavior."

That having been said, David Baerwald also formed some quick opinions about Sheryl Crow after their first meeting. This didn't take place at Toad Hall, but at his home in Venice Beach, before TMC was even incepted. A&M had arranged for the two of them to get together and write some material, but although this resulted in a song titled "What I Can Do For You" that would find its way onto the *Tuesday Night Music Club* album, there were hardly any feelings of instant kinship.

"At that time, Sheryl was a very different kind of character to the one who emerged later," Baerwald comments. "She was dressed all in white, and my first impression was that she was really uptight, straight, and ambitious."

Still, uptight or not, Sheryl didn't arrive mute-mouthed or empty-handed. Instead she recounted her alleged experience of sexual harassment by Michael Jackson's manager, Frank Dileo, and then she produced a rough composition alluding to this.

"She actually had some lyric focusing on herself as this poor, innocent thing, and I thought, 'Oh God, this is really boring,'" Baerwald recalls. "So I said, 'Why don't we try taking it from his point of view?' and I just pretended I was Frank Dileo and wrote this awful kind of threatening come-on."

Then and there, using an Akai 12-track machine, David and Sheryl recorded a demo. "I actually remember putting this brutal harmonizer on her voice so that she sounded like Darth Vader," he says. "However, I didn't think much of the whole thing. To my mind it wasn't even a song."

Regardless, David was at least aware of Sheryl's vocal talents, and this awareness increased sharply once they began working together as part of TMC. Still, he felt that something was missing.

"Sheryl was a pro jingle and backup singer with this very nice tone and control," he says. "Without question she was really good, but there was no persona, no place to hang your hat in terms of writing stuff. Then again, she was really game. I mean, she would do just anything, which on one level is great. It's really fun to have this great singer doing whatever idea is floating around the room, but at a certain point you need to know where home is, regarding the person you're writing for or with."

To this end, it didn't take long for Dave Baerwald to switch over to wind-up mode and set about testing the limits of Sheryl's amenable attitude. After all, he reasoned, she might be willing to sing his lyrics about pimps and prostitutes—which were his cynical, sub-contextual allusion to the relationship between the A&M hierarchy and their ambitious artist—but surely this straightlaced go-getter from southern Missouri would reach her breaking point if he threw some really down-and-dirty words her way. There's nothing like a challenge....

"I thought Bill was in on this, but he denies ever knowing about it," Dave remarks. "Basically, Sheryl was agreeable to everything, but there was no back to it. We needed a back wall and needed for her to have an opinion. I thought, 'Let's just throw really heinous things at her until she finally can't take it anymore and says, "No!" We needed her to provide us with a backstop if we were going to make it real. So, I would come up with all of these really scabrous things about being in vomit up to her knees, just horrible stuff, to get her to say, 'No, I'm not going to sing that!' You know, 'So you're in the stall of the toilet in the men's room at the truck stop, there's puke everywhere, and you're giving head for a quarter! Whaddya think of that?' I wanted to see her fight back a little, and finally she did...big time! One night, she got really hurt by some of the rudeness and ran into the bathroom and started crying. Bill and I were sitting on the couch and we just sort of looked at each other and said, 'Uh, maybe we've gone a little far here.' She was a bit steelier after that and I tried to back off a little, but it was hard for me not to tease her."

And Dave also found it difficult, according to Dan Schwartz, to refrain from locking horns with Sheryl and Kevin Gilbert over their respective contributions to the record. As it happens, both of these people were quite capable of standing up for themselves, yet Schwartz, already harboring his own bias following a falling-out with Baerwald during sessions for the latter's *Triage* album, took it upon himself to defend them.

"That album credit which Sheryl gave me for 'gadgets, gossip, and God-like bass,' comes from me partly being self-delusional," Dan concedes. "David was so aggressive, and so wrapped up in his own ego, that he was constantly having a go at Kevin and Sheryl about how incompetent they were."

"I've heard all about these ego battles that Kevin and I had, but I didn't know about them at the time!" Baerwald insists. "We never had words during that project, and I didn't get on Sheryl and Kevin's case. Kevin and I had a very, very simpatico relationship. I mean, I was in awe of him, and I know he respected me. It was Dan who couldn't help stirring things up. If I had any battles, they were with *him*!"

Dan Schwartz's recollection is different: "I remember one night in particular when everybody had left the studio except David, Bill, and me. We were listening to a song and David said, 'Kevin never gets to the emotional center of anything.' I could have just killed the guy. I thought, 'You don't either!' The next morning I was on the phone with Bill, and Sheryl was also calling me. You see, Sheryl had this habit of leaving TMC sessions early and calling me up on Wednesday morning, really pissed off, and mostly she was pissed off at David. I'd be on the phone to people, trying to play Henry Kissinger, and of course all it did was get me in trouble. In the end, everybody just pointed at me, and I can now look back and go 'Yeah, it was totally stupid of me,' because it wasn't my problem. You know, if Sheryl and David wanted to duke it out, fuck it; let 'em duke it out! However, partly because Sheryl's a girl and she was the only girl there, I was trying to be the white knight.

"In terms of my own bias, I was tremendously biased against David for his behavior because of how he dealt with me personally towards the end of my participation in *Triage,* and Bill was extremely angry with me for getting involved in all this, for believing myself to be the peacemaker. He'd be yelling at me on the phone, and I remember one night when we were about to leave the studio, Bill and David just kind of confronted me: 'So, are you gonna knock this shit off or what?' I said, 'Fuck, no! Absolutely not! Not until David gets off their backs.' David's an extreme character— when he's pissed off, he's *really* pissed off. When he's having fun, he's *really* having fun. Not that I can necessarily tell the difference.

"There was already tremendous tension between Kevin and Sheryl, which I was not aware of at first, because they were in the midst of breaking up. You know, the genesis of the song 'No One Said It Would Be Easy' is partially about that. So, I don't blame David for the tension. My tension was with David, and it was my own decision to appoint myself as Kevin and Sheryl's defender. I mean, Sheryl would be on the phone to me, bitching about this and that, and I'd try to take action in response, and then she'd be yelling at me for trying to take action. It took me a good month to figure out where it was at: 'All right, I'm holding David at fault here, but everybody's at fault. I can deal with my own fault by stopping this.' So, I removed myself from that whole thing by no longer wanting to be anybody's defender.

"What I finally realized was, as much as I saw David as this snarling creature, and Kevin and Sheryl as these unhappy underdogs, my view of all this had nothing to do with the truth. Kevin and Sheryl could hold their own against anybody."

Amid this clash of personalities, Bill Bottrell was trying to put a record together, and he quickly learned how best to use the musicians' contributions. For one thing, they had enough respect for his professional credentials to pretty much do as he said, and for another he was the person with his fingers on the faders as well as on the tape machine once each session was over.

"It was my studio, I knew how to run it, and I was doing most of the engineering," he states. "It was my show as they came in the doors. Certainly, David and Kevin would go at it with egos, but I could break that up anytime I wanted by moving the mic to somebody else. Nobody would question it.

"With all their posturing, chest-beating, and shouting, David, Kevin, and Dan were never truly aware of how they were intimidating and shutting down Sheryl. As a producer, I would ordinarily kick someone like that out of a session immediately. The producer has to look out for the fragile egos, encourage the insecure singer, and so on. But I was happy with the powerful chaos that would develop from the sessions with those guys, and Sheryl and I soon got used to the fact that on Wednesday through Friday we could erase their bluster in a single three-minute wipe.

"David, Kevin, and Dan were only used by me for the things I wanted. David's lyric style infused the whole record, but not his lyrics, and he only played a couple of instruments. Dan's bass can be heard on five songs, but his uncompromising approach to art and commerce was a constant. Kevin's music survived erasure only when we needed technical prowess, and these occasions were rare, but check out the piano on 'We Do What We Can,' among others. Still, even then I spent days editing the MIDI notes he played into my sequencer. Many songs feature just Sheryl and me, writing and performing. This is how we grew to trust that, whatever happened while the guys were there, our fragile and insecure music would have the last word.

"If there was any mayhem in the studio, it was orchestrated by me, but I don't think it was mayhem. I think it was the best work those people ever did up to that point, and they don't even know how it came together. David has made a career out of claiming he made that record, and he doesn't know how it was made. Kevin knew how it was made, but as he had a big ego he wasn't about to tell anybody. Sheryl knows how it was made, but she wasn't about to tell anybody, and that was not ego, that was strict business sense. That was her in collusion with the record company which owned a product in the form of this person, Sheryl Crow. They didn't own me, they didn't want to know about me. They didn't want to know about other people."

None of this was yet an issue on September 15, 1992, when Sheryl turned up for her first TMC session. That night, she was immediately given the chance to display her vocal chops when the lineup of David Baerwald on guitar, Kevin Gilbert playing keyboards, David Ricketts on bass, and Brian MacLeod on drums, launched into "I Love This Man," a number inspired by the Kurt Weill/Bertolt Brecht opera, *The Rise and Fall of the City of Mahagonny*.

"It had a really complicated, really demanding chord change, and Kevin gave it this gorgeous kind of pseudo-orchestral-arrangement," Baerwald recalls. "It was a German cabaret song about this prostitute living in a bombed-out hotel, talking about how much she loves her pimp. I just thought it was funny. A German guy there translated all this stuff for us, but it was a really demanding piece of music. The chords would end up being used for 'We Do What We Can,' which was a lot slower and had a beautiful Bill Bottrell lyric."

Again the initiator, Baerwald next suggested playing a simpler song based around a G-C-D chord structure—"Leaving Las Vegas" broke the TMC rule of not bringing any preconceived ideas into the studio, while taking its title from a book written by Baerwald's longtime friend, John O'Brien.

"John had given me the galley proofs," Dave explains. "I'd read them and thought it was a very evocative book with a beautifully written female character and really good title, so I came to the session with the idea of using this as the starting point. I didn't know Bill had a rule about showing up with no ideas. My whole thing was, 'Let's do something really dumb, where we don't have to remember a bunch of chords, and let's call it "Leaving Las Vegas." How about this for a verse and a chorus idea?' That was about it, and then Bill came up with this wild loop which was really hard to play to."

David Baerwald and John O'Brien were born in the same small Ohio town, within days of one another in July 1960. Twenty-two years later, they met as neighbors in Venice, California, and quickly discovered that they had plenty in common.

"We both had long, kind of horsey faces," Baerwald would recall in a 1996 *L.A. Weekly* article, "we both drank too much, we both wrote about the discarded, the hopeless, and the lost. Like a lot of people those days, we were kind of human garbologists, hoping to find some inherent truth about ourselves in what our culture threw away. The FBI looks through dope dealers' trash to find out what's up; we did the same, only in our case it was the people who got thrown out who told the story. Poets, hustlers, thieves, magicians, barflies, hookers, dealers, blah, blah, blah. Hardly the most original of concepts, but John, especially, deserved an A for effort. Trouble is, with that line of research, the researcher can get pretty swallowed up, it's only a matter of time, really, if you're doing it right."

In other words, the kinds of loners and drifters that populated Sheryl's imagination during her teen years were the exact individuals who Dave and John were actually hanging out with during their twenties and thirties—the netherworld of L.A. culture, its fringe characters and nearly-people. Eventually, O'Brien turned into one of them, drowning his personal demons in an ocean of booze as he sailed down the fast track to oblivion. His first published novel, *Leaving Las Vegas*, documented the self-destruction, and Baerwald's autographed copy bore the inscription: "Dear David, Here's the text for your song. Never abandon me as your friend."

These words would come back to haunt Baerwald, but in the meantime he was off on his own trip, both literally and figuratively. At the start of the aforementioned "I Love This Man"/"Leaving Las Vegas" session, he and David Ricketts each took a hit of LSD, and by the time they got around to working on the second number they were feeling and seeing the effects.

"I just couldn't stop laughing," Baerwald recalls. "You know, the first name of the band was the Tuesday Music Collective, an experiment in not having a front man, anarcho-syndicalism, and just letting it all hang out. Well, one of the things that cracked me up when we were doing 'Leaving Las Vegas' was that two Tuesdays before that we'd been Captain Beefheart and the Magic Band, and then all of a sudden we were Fleetwood Mac, and I thought this was hilarious, though also kind of sad and scary. Every time I closed my eyes I would see this kind of sad Vegas Fourth of July parade, with all of these tattered flags and Bermuda shorts. Both Dave and I were laughing hysterically. He couldn't look at me, 'cause every time I caught his eye he just fell about laughing. I don't even know how he got through the bass line—it was really good playing—because it was all I could do to play that weird Matrix 1000 line. I was just incapacitated."

Given this state of affairs, it wasn't surprising that Bill Bottrell had already pointed the vocal mic away from the song's initiator and towards the woman whose talents he wanted to explore. In turn, Sheryl responded with a performance that would serve as a stylistic blueprint for both the *Tuesday Night Music Club* album and her future career—

laid-back, in-your-face; singing one moment, drawling the next. During the course of a single evening, courtesy of Bottrell's artistic vision, the inventiveness of her fellow band members, the ingestion of some mind-warping chemicals, and her own intuitive flair, Sheryl Crow took a complete left turn from anything she'd ever done before, and in the process she found a musical identity. Not a contrived image conforming to a clichéd persona, but a more natural self that tapped into her Southern roots and rock-influenced aspirations.

"Sheryl's vocal style was simply her responding to the sound of the instruments," Bottrell explains. "She made up that sound based on the context she was in, no doubt about it. It was the complete opposite of everything she'd been doing on the previous album; just chaos going on in her head, musical chaos, but I believe this sound was probably very, very inspirational. What we had going in the headphones was virtually what you hear on the radio today. We did lots and lots of takes, and she got what I thought was drunker and better. It was later on, when she felt more comfortable and started slipping back into some old habits, that I had more opinions on how she sang. You know, vocal histrionics; vibrato that sounded like Bonnie Raitt, textured notes, Mariah Carey shit. I had some rules, and that had no place within the context of what we were doing."

According to Sheryl's own recollections, she too had taken some acid. Nevertheless, tequila and beer were the usual infusions of choice at the TMC sessions.

"I've never been like a person that was into drugs, but I can drink," Sheryl admitted in some outtake interview footage from VH1's *Behind the Music*. "I can seriously drink, and that is not a big part of my life anymore.... It took me out of myself, and I felt like my creative juices were just flowing if I just had some wine and turned on the mic.... I don't really rely on that so much anymore and I don't really enjoy being smashed. It's not fun, and I don't think my best work comes from that anyway, but at that time it kind of freed me up to say what I wanted to say."

After "Leaving Las Vegas," the next track to evolve out of a Tuesday night session was "Solidify," a funky mid-tempo number that would end up being credited to no fewer than seven composers: Crow, Hunter, Bottrell, Baerwald, Gilbert, Ricketts, and MacLeod.

"That started with a guitar loop and a drum loop and a song called 'California Motor Madness Zoom Zoom Zoom,'" Bottrell recalls. "A killer song, it was great, but David [Baerwald] was singing it and I'd just had a year of him singing on *Triage*. After 'Leaving Las Vegas' I'd started thinking, 'Man, we can make Sheryl's album this way. This'll be cool.' We had the groove—David and Kevin [Gilbert] played guitars, and I looped it in a machine with some other loops I had—but we only had one verse and David sang it four times. The loop just kept going and going, and that was what we ended up with at the end of that evening.

"The words were about dirty streets, prostitutes in hotel rooms, and things like that, and we were all sort of down on that idea, so I took the song, sped it way up, put some guitars on it, and made the music sound similar to how it sounds now. Kevin Hunter came in to write the words with me and Sheryl, so what we were specifically doing was developing this germ of an idea that TMC had worked on. Hence all of the writers on the damned song. You know, everybody has to get credit. You can't take the work that came out of the TMC session, totally change it, and not give them credit, and that's what I had to bear in mind for a lot of the numbers.

"So, 'Solidify' eventually was Sheryl, Kevin [Hunter], and me, and we laid it down in one session. Kevin came up with the first verse, built around how Sheryl felt about working with David Baerwald: you know, why should she 'solidify'? We sat down and she started describing this experience of writing separately with Baerwald at his house and how she felt. In fact, I have a version with me singing it, and that was after we wrote the new words. Maybe I was trying to show her how it should go…It's me sounding like Curtis Mayfield, which is cool. To this day I'm very proud of it."

Next up was "Strong Enough," a wonderful, introspective ballad that begins with David Ricketts's rolling guitar riff, segues into Sheryl Crow's lilting melody, and focuses on the strains placed on a relationship by PMS.

"David had this beautiful guitar piece, again working around D9, and for some reason Bill wanted to record it in the lounge," Dave Baerwald recalls. "So, we all set up in the lounge, which had this beautiful copper table, and we got this group thing going."

"Brian, Kevin [Gilbert], David Baerwald, David Ricketts, Sheryl, and I were all there on that particular Tuesday night," states Bill Bottrell. "Kevin and Sheryl had mics—maybe David [Baerwald] too—to sing ideas, and Kevin came up with the B section. The tune was pretty much Sheryl's. She sang the 'strong enough' refrain in a stream of consciousness, and I said, 'That should be the hook.' Gilbert and Baerwald contributed lyrics, I contributed the first couple of lines, setting the tone of the thing, and it was almost done that night. We didn't record it. It was like a demo—it wasn't played well—so a few days later we came back in, sat down, and worked on the master take."

"I think Kevin came up with the 'strong enough' line, and we just riffed on that for a while," adds Baerwald. "There were words floating around, but nothing really codified. Then, at some point Bill said, 'Dave, go away and write a lyric.' I think he just wanted me to stop playing the guitar because I couldn't figure out that pesky nine chord; towards the end of that record I'd start feeling a little bit like a mule. You know, 'Here Dave, shut up and write me this lyric.' I might have started getting a bit grouchy about that.

"Anyway, there was this gay bar called The 49er across the street, and I went in there and it just so happened that there were these two gay guys arguing. I basically made notes of what they were saying to each other, put these together in stanza form, and then went back to the studio and said, 'Hey, guys!' It was great. It kind of reminded me of the newsroom; you know, 'Copy!'"

Along with "Leaving Las Vegas," "Strong Enough" represented the true collaborative nature of the early TMC sessions, as described (and exaggerated) in Sheryl's sleeve notes on the album—"For the last year or so I've spent most Tuesday nights with a group of musicians, or shall I say artists, at Toad Hall…." Not strictly accurate, but it conjured up the desired image.

"The myth that was put out about these people sitting in a room and coming up with things wasn't entirely true," states Bottrell. "It was our ideal, and it happened with 'Leaving Las Vegas' and 'Strong Enough,' but that was all. Those were the only ones that came out that way, with the people in the room all working together. The Tuesday nights were one thing, and then there was this circle of people who also kept coming by on every other night of the week, and that's when the rest of the songs were done without the Tuesday night rules.

"For instance, 'Run, Baby, Run' wasn't the Tuesday Night Music Club. That came out of a tough session with David [Baerwald], Sheryl, and me sitting down and writing songs. I'd had the music for a couple of years, David had this lyrical poem which he'd written called called 'Run, Lily, Run,' and we started sticking them together, but it wasn't easy. They didn't quite fit; we made them fit. Sheryl helped make them fit, and it was an amazing day.

"Those words fit perfectly from the start!" maintains Baerwald. "I was actually pissed off about that one too, because they did change it in a way that I thought just bowdlerized it and made it a lot less punchy. But it wasn't a phrasing issue, because the phrasing remained the same. You know, nobody was saying, 'Wow, there are too many syllables here.' It was more like 'We've got to make this a little mellower because it's too real.' I thought, 'You're wimping out on me here!'"

"Run, Baby, Run," featuring Sheryl's haunting lead vocal, Bill Bottrell's atmospheric guitar lines, Dan Schwartz's expressive bass playing, and Kevin Gilbert's adept drumming, is another of the *Tuesday Night Music Club* highlights. Yet, even after the lyrics were finished and the parts had been played, Bill still had plenty to do in terms of post-production.

"I put a lot of work into that song, especially during the mix," he says. "It was always very crude. Being that I never do a demo, I worked and worked and worked on the thing, trying to turn this crude version into a finished version, and unfortunately I can still hear all of that effort on the record. I've heard it way too many times."

"For me, 'Run, Baby, Run' was the best musical memory of the album," says Dan Schwartz, who laid down his bass line after all of the other parts had already been recorded. "I did it in one pass, sitting alone with the engineer Blair Lamb, who overcompressed the bass beyond description. That's why you practically can't hear it. Still, I remember how incredible I felt playing that part—the vocal was great, the song was great, and Kevin's drumming was really inspiring, even though it turned out that it had been very edited. That moment of playing bass meant so much to me.

"Later on in the process, Bill really agonized over what to do with the guitar on that song, because David Baerwald's playing had great energy, a great vibe, a great feel, but it didn't sit right. Bill has this thing where he wants to retain whatever was played when the vocal was performed. To him, when the vocal goes down, that's the moment, and you leave everything that's there, which is why, for instance, you get the meandering organ on 'Leaving Las Vegas.' He really agonized over replaying the guitar on 'Run, Baby, Run,' but I sat there and supported him while he experimented with whether or not he could make it sound a whole lot better, and ultimately he did."

"I think that by the end we had a fabulous song," adds Bottrell. "That first line of David's, about being born the day Aldous Huxley died, is unbelievable. We eventually decided to start the album with that verse."

At this point during the recording of the album, Sheryl landed a gig singing backup at Bob Dylan's thirtieth-anniversary concert. Staged on Friday, October 16, 1992, at Madison Square Garden in New York, the tribute featured Dylan standards performed by artists such as George Harrison, Johnny Cash, Stevie Wonder, Willie Nelson, Neil Young, Eric Clapton, John Mellencamp, Kris Kristofferson, Tom Petty, Lou Reed, Roger McGuinn, and, of course, the man himself. Sinead O'Connor, appearing just a couple of weeks after not-too-diplomatically ripping up a photo of Pope John Paul II on NBC's *Saturday Night Live*, was booed off the stage. Sheryl was one of the backing singers on Chrissie Hynde's version of "I Shall Be Released," and she sang as part of the chorus for the O'Jays' rendition of "Emotionally Yours." On future all-star occasions she'd be among the headliners; to those who knew Sheryl at around this time it was clear how much she wanted this.

"She was a girl who was just going to make it," asserts David Baerwald. "She wanted to be famous big time. She'd been in that world and watched all those guys like Henley and Sting and Michael Jackson—all of those really super-pro guys who are serious personalities in the music business. Well, she's not stupid. She learns everything, it's amazing. She's serious business, and I think you have to be that way. She's super-canny, she's a really good singer, she's a total pro, she's a great politician, she's pretty, and she's ruthless as all hell.

"I remember a party at Sheryl's apartment on the corner of Crescent Heights and Fountain. Bill was there, Kevin was there, and Don Henley was there, along with a bunch of other guys. I was on the couch talking to [drummer/producer] Stan Lynch, and I watched her talk to Bill, and she had a kind of Bill vibe. Then, she turned around, left Bill, and started walking across the room towards Kevin, and she developed a Kevin vibe. She talked to Kevin for a while, turned away from him, walked over to Henley, and developed a Henley vibe. I was thinking, 'Wow! That is a fucking actress, man! That is pro!'"

On election night of that year—Tuesday, November 3—a few of the TMC members gathered at Toad Hall, watched TV, and jammed on some new material, including the basic feel to "All I Wanna Do" and "The Na-Na Song." Bill Bottrell then filed both of these numbers away, intending to work on them at a future date.

"I have a lot of that session on video," he says. "Later on, we all came back and worked on 'All I Wanna Do,' and once again David had these lyrics and this whole force behind it. It was called 'I Still Love You' and I thought it sucked. I was never buying that, but I waited until he went home and then Sheryl and I began working on it."

"I was obsessed with the pedal steel, even though I couldn't play it to save my life, and if you play an E9 pedal steel you automatically get this kind of cool jazz chord," Baerwald explains. "You can just slide it around, and it's jazzy, but it still sounds sort of country, so Brian [MacLeod] and I were saying, 'Come on, let's do a country disco thing.' That was the initial idea, based around the chord changes that naturally come out of playing pedal steel without the pedals, and that four-on-the-floor disco beat. Bill actually ended up replacing the pedal steel because I can't play the thing."

Bottrell also rewrote the chords. "I worked alone a lot on the music, making it into a song form," he recalls, "but we still didn't have lyrics, and that went on for months and months. Then, way at the end, I pulled out a Wyn Cooper poem which provided all of the verses, and Sheryl sang or spoke that right into the mic, and I made a chorus out of the line about just wanting to have some fun. I also wrote the lyric about the sun coming up over Santa Monica Boulevard, except that I had 'Sunset Boulevard' and Sheryl changed it to 'Santa Monica.'"

Vermont-based writer Wyn Cooper was largely unknown before his poem "Fun," published by Ahsahta Press in 1987 as part of his collection, *The Country of Here Below*, was utilized for "All I Wanna Do"—the book was still in its first printing of a mere five hundred copies when Bill and Kevin stumbled upon it in Cliff's Books, around the corner from Toad Hall. Some of Cooper's phrases were altered, a few lines deleted, and an ironically upbeat refrain added, yet the subject matter—masterfully conveyed via lyrical imagery and Sheryl's conversational vocal style—still focused on a couple of no-hopers watching the world go by their local bar.

"I wrote the poem in Salt Lake City in 1984," Cooper says. "It was based loosely on a bar there called The Twilight Lounge, although that didn't look out onto a car wash. It was mostly made up, utilizing a line that a friend of mine had said to me the night before; 'All I want to do is have a little fun before I die.' The next day I wrote that line down and kept going, and I wrote the whole poem in just a couple of hours. Bill and Kevin thought it fit in with the sort of underbelly-of-society characters that were populating some of the album's other songs.

"After Sheryl recorded the vocal, Judy Stakee called me, quickly followed by Bill. Judy told me how my poem had been set to music for this new artist called Sheryl Crow, and she asked, 'Is that okay with you?' Well, I was just so thrilled that somebody had even found my book, I said, 'Yeah, go ahead!' She subsequently offered me a thousand dollars for the publishing, and we did a deal for two thousand dollars.

"I didn't know who Sheryl Crow, Bill Bottrell, or any of the other guys were, and I didn't do any research to find out. Sheryl seemed a little upset that I hadn't been treated entirely fairly. I talked to her lawyer, but he didn't think that he or Sheryl could do anything about it, so I just let it go."

The deal that Cooper did with Warner/Chappell was termed a "single song agreement," whereby he assigned the publishers 50 percent of his "All I Wanna Do" royalties in return for just $2,000. However, he did hang on to the other 50 percent.

"I could have made more money," he says, "but it's turned out just fine. I don't have to work anymore."

"All I Wanna Do" would not only serve as Sheryl's breakout single, but also prompt instant media interest in Wyn Cooper, who'd even recite his poem onstage during a couple of her concerts. Still, in late 1992, that kind of thing was unimaginable. Bill

Bottrell was not even halfway through his work on the TMC album, and his next order of duty was to complete "The Na-Na Song," which was the other number that had been worked on during the election-night jam.

"Kevin and Sheryl wrote all of these stream-of-consciousness lyrics, and she sang them over that original demo," he recalls. "When it came to the line about Frank Dileo's 'dong,' she said, 'I'm a little worried about saying this,' and I said, 'Well, is it true?' She said, 'Yeah,' and so I said, 'Well, then, you can sing it.'"

Which Sheryl did, much to the record company's consternation a little further down the line.

A Dan Schwartz guitar riff during a writing session between him, Sheryl, Kevin, and Bill gave rise to the troubled-relationship ballad, "No One Said It Would Be Easy." It was Sheryl who came up with the title line, while she, Kevin, Dan, and Bill composed the verses all during the course of one long day.

"Sheryl asked me to write something like 'Norwegian Wood,'" remembers Dan, whose appreciation of—and influence by—Beatles music was self-evident. "My response was that I'd rather write something like 'We Can Work It Out,' because at that time I was really in love with John Lennon's right-hand rhythm-guitar strumming on that song. Bill said, 'Yeah, go that way with it,' and so although we were generally told not to come in with something, I had the okay here to go away and develop an idea. That night, I used one of the dulcimer tunings of my big hero, the English folk singer Martin Carthy, to work this thing out at home, and what I came up with was very much a cross between both approaches: a big right-arm strum like the one on 'We Can Work It Out,' together with the kind of climbing-and-descending, very folky, Indian melody that you might imagine hearing on a dulcimer."

When Dan encountered Sheryl in the lounge at Toad Hall the following day, the first words out of her mouth were "Kevin hates me." Ditto when Schwartz ran into Gilbert: "Sheryl hates me." This acrimonious state of affairs immediately prompted Dan to contemplate his own impending marriage. Then he, Sheryl, and Bill discussed the impossibility of relationships, and this quickly became the song's theme.

"We went downstairs to start working on it," Dan recalls, "but when I played Bill what I'd done the night before he said, 'Nah, we can't use that. It's too folk. Come up with something else.' So, we did the usual thing; we rolled tape and I just started improvising on an electric guitar that was miked. Basically, I worked out the song on my own—the little introductory riff and verse and bridge—and I was fishing for a chorus, so Kevin, who was playing bass, said, 'Let's try turning the verse around.' As far as I was concerned, I was copying the feel of the whole thing from Martin Carthy's version of a Leon Rosselson song called 'Palaces Of Gold.' So, that's where the music came from, and then we sat there for the day and wrote the lyrics, most of which came from the other three while I contributed some lines. We cut the whole basic track that night, and when I came in the next day Bill was already busy overdubbing all of the electric guitars."

"What I Can Do For You," the Dileo-related product of Sheryl and Dave Baerwald's pre-TMC writing session in Venice Beach, was also completed in a single session, with

Bill playing synthesizers while David played guitar, before a far more lengthy work process began on that jazzy, evocative snapshot of Sheryl's youth, "We Do What We Can," featuring the trumpet contributions of her father, Wendell Crow.

"Sheryl came in with a song called 'Flying Over Egypt,' which she'd written with Jay Oliver, and that was the first glimmer that I ever had of her songwriting," says Dan Schwartz. "Only Bill, Sheryl, and I were there, and as she was playing this for us I was looking at Bill with wide eyes, like 'Holy shit! What's this?' because it really surprised me. We got her experimenting on a little digital keyboard that was plugged into a piano module running to DAT, and we asked her to explore some chordal ideas. Well, over the course of twenty minutes she went through all these different ways of playing piano, and there was one moment that she hit, when Bill and I locked eyes. I remember I was sitting on the couch like I always did, he was over at the console, and we looked at each other like, 'Wow, here's something!' It seemed to have so much more substance to it than anything else. I went over to the machine and made a note of the numbers, so we'd be able to refer back to the DAT.

"Sheryl got up from the piano, and there were all of these microphones set up around the room, and so we gradually got her to talk about her family. Somehow we patched the mic into the DAT and began recording without Sheryl knowing. We recorded about an hour to an hour-and-a-half of her reminiscences about her family and about her father, and at the end of a day in which we'd seemingly accomplished nothing, we gave her the DAT and said, 'Go home and listen to this and start writing.' As far as we knew, when she came in the next day she'd written a bunch of words, but Kevin later said, 'It wasn't that easy. I sat up with her all night working on this.' Anyway, with the four of us gathered there, we played Kevin that little piano improv of Sheryl's, and that became the basis for the mood of 'We Do What We Can.' It didn't actually appear in the song, but it suggested the contemplative jazz direction."

"It took a long time to complete that song, trying to get it right, trying to come up with a bridge," adds Bill Bottrell. "It never had a bridge, and it was months later that I came up with one—the music and the lyrics—and recorded it with Brian."

"Can't Cry Anymore," an appealing mid-tempo rocker with Bill's Keith Richards–type guitar licks, included Jeff Trott among the backing vocalists. Jeff, then a guitarist with Wire Train and later to become one of Sheryl's most prolific and successful songwriting partners, first encountered her when he dropped into Toad Hall to collect some of his equipment. At that time, singing harmonies wasn't part of his shtick.

"I was carrying this [Farrington] Baritone guitar and Sheryl was curious about it," he remembers. "She said, 'Well, play something,' so I just started playing this tune and, being that she liked what she heard, she stopped what she was doing and we ended up writing a song called 'On The Outside.' I came up with the music for that, and like a week later she said, 'Hey, you remember that thing we were doing the other day? Well, I finished it.'"

Although it didn't make its way onto the *Tuesday Night Music Club* album, "On The Outside," a moody number constructed around Jeff's guitar, Bill Bottrell's pedal steel, and Sheryl's Bonnie Raitt–type vocals, would be included on *Songs in the Key of X*, a 1996 CD featuring music from and "inspired by" TV's *The X-Files*.

"Around that time I was sort of an alternate Tuesday Night Music Club guy," Jeff continues. "I wasn't an official member or anything, but if one of them couldn't make it Bill would call me up and say, 'Do you wanna come down and hang out and do some playing?' So, that's kind of how I really got to know Sheryl. When you're in a community of players using the same studio, you run into one another and say, 'Hey, if you've got some time, maybe you can sing background on this track....' That's actually how I gained my first experience singing harmonies, on 'Can't Cry Anymore.' I wasn't really known as a background vocalist, but Sheryl gave me a shot. I mean, she knew I was into The Beatles, so she figured, 'Well, he must know something about harmonies.'"

Along with "I Shall Believe," "Can't Cry Anymore" was one of the last two numbers recorded for the *Tuesday Night Music Club* album. Both were originated by Sheryl, and then completed by her and Bill. However, it was becoming increasingly clear that Sheryl's main compositional strength lay not so much in conceiving songs as in refining them, embellishing them, and making them her own. This is a talent all in itself, just as some people have a gift for coming up with ideas but not necessarily bringing them to fruition.

"I almost never experienced Sheryl initiating an idea, and even if she did it was still sort of sketchy, which was fine with me," Bill remarks. "I don't judge that either way. It works as well as anything else. Finishing things off is sometimes way more valuable than coming in with a hundred bad ideas."

In the case of "I Shall Believe," which was eventually selected as the record's closing track, Sheryl wrote some basic lyrics and the music for the verse before Bill added the B section. She came up with more words during a trip to the local sushi bar, and the number was recorded that same day. "Can't Cry Anymore," on the other hand, comprised Sheryl's lyrics and Bill's musical improvisations.

"I like the song 'Cathy's Clown'," he explains. "So, I overlaid a bastardization of the rhythm to 'Cathy's Clown' onto this song that she had, added a B section, and she came up with more words to go with the B section."

This, in summary, was the chronological order in which the album's tracks were recorded, yet there were also three other completed songs that never made the final cut: "All By Myself," "Volvo Cowgirl 99," and "Reach Around Jerk." Almost inexplicably, the first of these was a cover of the Eric Carmen hit ballad, which itself drew on the music of Sergei Rachmaninoff's Piano Concerto no. 2. If Sheryl's career was now taking a left turn from all that she'd done before, "All By Myself" represented a well-produced (if thankfully short-lived) return to the kind of material she'd performed with Cashmere at the University of Missouri. Quite simply, Bill Bottrell wanted to cover all the bases during the project's early stages, recording a pop standard that could be a single should the album lack any other commercial material.

"We spent a lot of time on that track," he says. "Mostly me and Sheryl. By the time the album was done I was pretty sure that was not a contender, but I did have to consider it."

The song ended up as the B-side of the "Run, Baby, Run" single in the U.K., where "Volvo Cowgirl 99" was also released as the B-side of the "What I Can Do For You" single. This was an upbeat remake of "The Na-Na Song," containing the same lyrics and, in Bottrell's opinion, a much better vibe. At least, that's how he feels about it now. Struggling to make a decision back in the spring of 1993, he finally went with the original version because he thought it worked better within the song sequence that he'd chosen.

"I wasn't totally happy with 'The Na-Na Song,' so we got together about three quarters of the way through the project with the expressed intent of using the same words and writing some new music," Bill recalls. "Kevin, David, Brian, Dan, Sheryl, and I were all there. It was actually a rare moment when we had a purpose and a session. It was daytime, it wasn't the Tuesday Night Music Club; we were going to try to do something, and it was very successful. The title 'Volvo Cowgirl' was a phrase I came up with, describing my wife at the time, and David just added the '99' for incongruity.

"'Reach Around Jerk' was a little further along in the process, on a day when just Dan, Sheryl, and I sat down in the studio. Dan was on bass and I was on guitar, and we started strumming the tune while Sheryl began singing. I ended up playing slide and acoustic and drums on that track, while Dan played bass and electric. Sheryl wrote all the words, and they were pointedly about somebody—she was a little vague as to who, but it was definitely a bitter song, and the bitterness didn't really go with the rest of the album."

"It could be about any one of us or none of us," adds Dan Schwartz. "The political stuff could be about David and the 'button-down shirts' could be about me. We're probably all in there…. It was a two-day affair, and I believe that song died the day we finished it, when Blair Lamb said the intro reminded him of one to a Led Zeppelin track. At that point I recall seeing the look on Bill's face, and I realized, 'Okay, this one's dead."

Again, the U.K. proved to be a receptive outlet—"Reach Around Jerk" made it onto the four-song CD single of "Run, Baby, Run."

And so it was that the *Tuesday Night Music Club* album was truly born—not as the result of a group of artists gathering on the same night every week for a solid year, but out of their collaborative efforts on a few Tuesdays to begin with, and then sporadic sessions at various times, followed by the ongoing endeavors of Sheryl and the record's producer.

"On a lot of the songs, Sheryl and I played all of the instruments, and that goes against the myth," Bill Bottrell remarks. "I mean, the album did grow out of the musicians meeting once a week, but man, there were just months and months of sweat put in mostly by me and, secondarily, Sheryl, and then months and months more put in by me, trying to choose the songs, put them in an order, and mix them."

"Bill with his fucking brilliance would fix stuff," Brian MacLeod confirmed in his interview with Wayne Perez. "Fix tunings. The guy was a genius. Him and Kevin both. Because Kevin couldn't help himself, he was always looking over Bill's shoulder. They would always fine-tune the songs and make them more perfect."

"Bill and Sheryl worked their butts off," adds Dave Baerwald. "Bill in particular. You know, taking some of those jams, with no beginnings or ends, and sampling pieces of them—that was so much work on his part, the most tedious, awful work, pre–Pro Tools. Now it's a lot easier to do that kind of stuff, but in those days he did it all with the 24-track, [an Akai] S1000, and a half-inch tape machine, and it took a lot of time. Boring, hard work."

In the meantime, while much of this toil was taking place at Toad Hall, David Anderle was sweating it out in his office on the A&M lot. According to the then–head of A&R, it was a long time before Bill Bottrell would allow him to hear the fruits of TMC's efforts. According to Bottrell, it was Anderle who didn't appear to be interested in listening to the tapes.

"David Anderle, to me, was always a mystery," he says. "I never knew what he or Al Cafaro were doing. They were very secretive with me. Anderle was never banned from the studio. I do have a policy of no tapes going out of the studio, so I wouldn't send tapes over to A&M for people to listen to in their offices. There again, people don't like to drive out to Pasadena from Hollywood, but I always looked forward to having them come out, turn the lights down low, and crank up the work I was doing. David Anderle having to wait to hear things may have been because of scheduling and the long trip out to Pasadena.

"At first I didn't have a contract, but I knew that they wanted me to do the album, so I just got started. Then, a couple of weeks after Anderle had come and asked me to do the project, he took a tape of 'Leaving Las Vegas' as is and 'Solidify' as is, which were from the first two sessions, and I couldn't get him to return my calls for the next couple of months."

"That is completely wrong," counters Anderle. "Totally, absolutely, completely wrong. After having convinced Al Cafaro to proceed with another $200,000, my neck was on the line. I was hanging on the end of a limb, and I had no idea what was going on out there. I was totally trusting Bill. Whatever he says is his world, but that's certainly not mine. I was desperate to hear what they were doing, and we only had a couple of phone calls. I called up, and on both occasions he specifically said, 'Nothing is ready to be heard yet.' I kept saying, 'You know, Bill, I produce records, so you don't have to present finished stuff to me. I can hear things in progress and judge what's going on.'

"I felt like a fool to my label—'Duh, they won't let me in!'—and finally I got angry. I called him and said, 'Look, man, I know you don't want to share this stuff until it's done, but I've got news for you—I've been a record producer and I'm a painter, so I understand how to see things before they're finished. That's the advantage you have working with me, and what's more, my balls are on the line. You're going to let me hear this shit!' He said, 'Come on out,' so I went out one night to his studio and they played me the stuff, and it was incredible, absolutely incredible.

"Sheryl was there and she looked very different. She was now wearing cowboy boots and things like that. Anyway, they played me some stuff, and I had the distinct feeling that because my reaction was as positive as it was—my mind was being blown—they were playing me even more stuff; they were playing me partial tracks without vocals, and you have no idea how happy I was that night. Oh my God, was I thrilled when I heard that stuff!

"Sheryl was just standing looking nervous, smoking a lot. When she saw my reaction to the music I think she was happy, but I mean Sheryl's not a whoopedy-doo girl. She's not whoopedy-doo at all. I just hugged her and said, 'I am so proud of you! This is so good! This stuff is great! I am so happy!' I also said, 'This is unbelievable. Where did this come from? Why didn't we get this before?' and she said, 'Well, you know, I went over to England with Hugh Padgham, one of the really giant, great guys. What am I going to say to him? Who am I to tell him that something is wrong?' I said, 'You're absolutely right.'

"So, that's my reading of it, and my reading of it is very clear. What's more, Bill had a reputation for being very secretive about his stuff and very protective of his stuff, and I was trying to battle through that too. I was continually trying to explain to him that I was different from the other guys he may have been dealing with at other record companies, because I'd had so many years of producing records myself and dealing with the label wanting to come down and hear my stuff. He should have been comfortable with me being there, so I absolutely have no idea how he remembers it being that way. He was the last person I would not return a phone call to. A lot of what was going on with me at that point was in his hands, in his studio. The last thing I would do was avoid a phone call from him!"

For his part, Bottrell backs up his version of events by citing the fact that he initially had to fund the TMC project out of his own pocket.

"There was no money, and I believed Sheryl Crow was being dropped from the label during that time," he states. "They wouldn't return my calls, and they certainly weren't giving me any money. When we did 'Strong Enough' I would have been very anxious to play it for Anderle, because by now I was completely sold on the thing. However, given my past experience with record companies, I assumed the whole project was about to be cancelled. Anderle would be studiously avoiding my calls, and the check-writing woman at A&M would be hinting about how it was out of her control and she couldn't do a thing. I was months into formally making Sheryl's record before I extracted a commencement check from A&M. After that, if I didn't return their calls it was probably due to overwork and priorities."

The lack of advance funds certainly gave Bottrell just reason for concern. However, several key players categorically refute the notion that the company was considering the termination of its relationship with Sheryl Crow.

"We never really felt like that was a front-burner issue," David Anderle insists. "We had obligations to do other records anyway. As I recall, it was a two-album deal that we had made. So, although I'd love to look like the sage and the guy who, out of the kindness of his heart said, 'Let's make another record,' that really wasn't the case. We knew that we had a business deal here that we were going to have to work out, and as long as we felt that we were making some sort of progress towards that end I was perfectly content to shelve the record and try to get the right record."

Al Cafaro agrees with Anderle's take on things: "It was clear to David and me—and I vaguely recall having these meetings with him where we would talk about it and both start shaking our heads—that we thought, 'This girl's got something. This girl's got it. We've got to get the right record.' As I recall, there was a period of time when David wasn't telling me what was going on, but my relationship with him was always one of trust. I'm sure David was reaffirming to me that there was something going on here and we would know about it soon, but his job certainly wouldn't have been on the line. We collaborated on things, and I would have viewed this as my failure as well."

"Bill was a hundred percent wrong if he thought they were looking to drop Sheryl from the label," adds Robert Richards. "A&M were extremely supportive and very excited about the potential of this new project, because they realized that Sheryl was working with talented people. In my recollection, it wasn't the kind of studio situation where you wanted to go down and hang out with them. You just wanted them to get on with what they were doing, and Bill created a scenario with the studio that was very artist-oriented. You know, 'This is our home,' and if people who weren't part of the recording process dropped in, it might disrupt the flow. Bill liked things to keep moving forward and he didn't like the vibe to change, so you were very cautious about walking into Tuesday Night Music Club sessions, especially under these circumstances, because he was given a tight budget to work with and he was committing all of his time to it. If he went over, it would come out of his own pocket.

"In my view, David Anderle was a huge supporter, and he waited for Bill to say when he could come and have a listen. He really put himself on the line, as did I, and people were waiting to see that it wasn't just a case of getting finagled into spending more money. You know, these guys were different kinds of human beings and extremely talented musicians, and everybody believed that there was something special going on, but they were a little nervous at the same time. There was a lot to gamble on positively, but it was still a gamble, and in my dealings with record companies I've never seen one of them flush away half a million dollars and then give more to go back and make another album. It was an interesting show of support."

Unfortunately for Robert Richards, he didn't feel the same way about Sheryl's attitude towards him when, about halfway through the production of *Tuesday Night Music Club*, he suddenly discovered he was being edged out of the picture.

"Maybe I misjudged her insecurities or securities," he reflects. "I came from Lookout Management and East End Management, where we managed Neil Young, Yes, Tom Petty & the Heartbreakers, The Cars, Devo, Joni Mitchell, Bob Dylan, and Billy Idol, and our whole philosophy was that managers don't hang around the studio. We've got our job to do, the people in the studio have their jobs to do, and you go in when the artist is ready for you to hear something. So, I had a habit of not hanging around the studio. Sheryl would call me six, seven, eight times a day, every day, and we would have very productive conversations—I would talk her out of things or talk her into things, and we'd discuss today's problems, the near future, and the long-term plans. It was typical management stuff, and we had what I thought to be a very close relationship.

"Then, all of a sudden, about halfway through the making of the album, I wasn't getting phone calls. After about a week I didn't know what to make of this, but it was like, 'Great, she's focused on the studio,' until Kevin Wall came down to my office and said, 'Listen, I was at the studio the other day, and Sheryl wants me to get more involved in the day-to-day.'"

Kevin Wall was the founder of Radio Vision International, the TV production/syndication company for which Richards served as a consultant. After doing business with Steve Fargnoli, the manager of, among others, Sinead O'Connor and World Party, Wall had been interested in financing a worldwide management company partnered by Fargnoli and Richards. Now, however, he was positioning himself to take charge of Sheryl's career. Richards was floored.

"Kevin Wall wasn't a manager," he asserts. "He's a great entrepreneur and a great deal-maker, but management wasn't his area of expertise. I was a little confused by this and I didn't take it very well. I basically told him and Sheryl to go fuck themselves—which is maybe what they were telling me—and Sheryl tried very hard to talk to me about it. She really wanted to get together with me and explain herself, but since that experience was absolutely new to me—I'd never been fired by a client before—I was furious and probably over-the-top. I said, 'Sheryl, I am so upset about this, you don't want to be around me right now because I'm just gonna be rude.'

"I even remember about three weeks later, when I thought I was over it and was able to have a conversation, we started talking on the phone and I just went fucking nuts at her. One of the things I said was, 'What the fuck are you doing even thinking about this kind of stuff while you're in the middle of making an album? What are you doing? You're supposed to be in the studio! Why are you thinking about management now?' I felt really bad about getting so mad at her, but I was very unhappy."

So unhappy, in fact, that Richards actually took the rest of his clients and ended his relationship with Radio Vision.

"I didn't feel I could trust them anymore," he says. "Still, Sheryl has obviously made all the right moves for herself since then, and I've got nothing bad to say about her. She's a wonderful person, she's extremely talented, she's unbelievably focused, and she's gonna wind up doing what she believes to be the right thing for her. I liked her a lot, and I don't know exactly what happened when this whole thing fell apart. I think she was confused in the situation. I was quite proud of myself for the unique deal that we made and I wanted to continue working with her, but I believe she was manipulated by Kevin Wall."

As it happened, Wall himself would only handle Sheryl for a few months before also exiting the scene for not being involved enough. At that point, her trusted friend, Scooter Weintraub, would take over the reins, and the game of musical management chairs would finally come to an end. Not that this was the only issue on Sheryl's mind.

As originally formatted, the *Tuesday Night Music Club* album consisted of ten tracks, and "All I Wanna Do" was not among them. Sheryl, considering it to be the weakest effort in the TMC batch, had never laid down a proper vocal, yet David Anderle recalls that he still liked the song, and that it therefore sprang to mind when he heard the finished record and decided that it could do with another upbeat number. He immediately called Bill Bottrell.

"'The Na-Na Song' was about the only thing that really had some kind of a groove going on," Anderle says. "So, I called Bill and said, 'What about that song with the kind of Stealers Wheel feeling to it?' Having grown up in Southern California, we always referred to those kinds of songs as the Pacific Coast Highway songs—driving with the top down on the car, listening to music that really made you feel good. To me, 'All I Wanna Do' definitely had that feel, but Bill told me he thought Sheryl didn't want to finish that because she considered it to be a bit too pop.

"Coming off what she was feeling about the Hugh record, I could totally understand that, except I thought we needed that groove, and I didn't hear it as pop, I heard it as just a cool groove. So, she did finish it, and then later I read in interviews that Sheryl gave her brother credit for the song being on the album…which is fine. That was probably how she saw it, but I know from the record company's point of view that song was something which I insisted on being finished. Even to the extent that if she got pissed at me I didn't care, I just believed so much in that groove.

"Sheryl has her own sense of history, and that was always okay with me. I was just thrilled working with somebody who had that kind of talent. So if, according to her, it's her little brother who pointed out to her that she should include 'All I Wanna Do' on the album, that's fine, because that is her reality and that's her truth and that is a truth. The fact that I called Bill Bottrell and insisted that she finish the song is my truth, and ultimately, who cares? It's her career, not mine. What do I care as long as she's happy?"

In her 2002 television interview with David Wild on Bravo's *Musicians*, Sheryl recalled how she fought for "All I Wanna Do" to be left off the record. However, this time around she didn't credit her brother Steven for changing her mind: "In the end I thought, 'You know what it does? It fills a position.' And I did believe in the song, because it really was a snapshot of what L.A. was like in the '90s, and it was definitely a snapshot of my life at that time."

David Baerwald recalls Anderle championing the cause of "All I Wanna Do." Still, what kind of TMC-related issue would this be without at least one other "truth" thrown into the mix? Bill Bottrell has his own version of events.

"Credit Rich Frankel, the head of A&M's art department at the time, with the existence of 'All I Wanna Do,'" he says. "He championed it and nobody else did. He and only he is responsible for it going on the record. While I was sequencing and mixing the album in April of 1993, trying to choose from fourteen songs, Sheryl was assembling a touring band in St. Louis, and I swear I was getting no help from Anderle. I was behind schedule and Sheryl was getting pissy for the first time. There were these women at the label who had adopted Sheryl as their *cause célèbre*, and I started getting my first glimpse of the spin-battle that would eventually claim almost a decade of my professional life: 'the mean, overbearing, male perfectionists against the strong and talented female victim.' Still, I wasn't turning the album in until I knew it was done.

"I was choosing between 'All I Wanna Do,' 'All By Myself,' 'Volvo Cowgirl,' and 'Reach Around Jerk.' I called Anderle and I forget what he said, but I sure as hell remember he didn't have an opinion. Neither Sheryl nor her increasingly combative defenders of feminine brilliance had an opinion. It was left to me, riding my bike with my Walkman every morning, to work another month sequencing, listening, mixing, listening, until I finally came up with the sequence.

"I knew Rich Frankel from my yearly mixing sessions with Herb Alpert. Rich was part of the family who would always drop by the control room and talk. He was old-school. I knew he'd been around the lot during the making of hundreds of big hit records. He was qualified, in my mind, to say, 'You gotta finish the country disco song.' He was unequivocally stoked on it. He came by Toad Hall at least twice in the later months and insisted we finish 'the country disco song' and put it on the album. The song had been shelved until his enthusiasm brought it back. Then we put Wyn's poem on it and it finally worked."

Dan Schwartz, who was present at many of the mix sessions, concurs with this account. Still, whatever the truth, for Sheryl Crow and, especially, for Bill Bottrell, the *Tuesday Night Music Club* project represented an intense and heavy workload. What's more, for all those involved, it was also a memorable time; a time when a remarkable album resulted from the vital collision of talents and tensions that comprised TMC.

"That record was, for me, a real blessing," Sheryl told David Wild, "and I still have really great…really fond memories of it."

"I liked the band and the sessions were fun," adds Dave Baerwald. "In fact, I still like them, I miss them, and I still miss having Sheryl's voice in my headphones. I loved that. I loved watching Kevin just be fucking brilliant. I loved Brian's humor and drumming, and Bill's unbelievable engineering and spirit. We were really just trying to make a jolly, radio-friendly little record."

# CHAPTER NINE

# Among Strangers' Hands

When David Anderle finally got to hear the *Tuesday Night Music Club* album his relief was palpable. Once Al Cafaro heard it, at Toad Hall in the presence of both Bill Bottrell and Kevin Wall, all A&M bets with regard to Sheryl Crow were definitely on. Cafaro was blown away by the musical results, which bore absolutely no resemblance to Sheryl's previous effort with Hugh Padgham, and it didn't take long for the CEO's enthusiasm to spread like wildfire among the other execs and underlings at the record company.

"I'm not going to tell you I listened to that record and I saw multiplatinum, because that's not true," Cafaro remarks. "When I listened to it I heard a brilliantly written, performed, and produced record that I was absolutely thrilled with—'Leaving Las Vegas' particularly slayed me. I left that studio feeling so wonderful about what had transpired. I felt that Bill had done an incredible job, I felt that Sheryl had achieved a result that was unique and compelling and exciting, and I felt that she should be very proud of it. I know at that point she was cautiously very proud of it."

Once Cafaro gave the record his blessing, the A&M staffers familiarized themselves with its contents and set about devising a marketing strategy. First, the songs had to be listened to on their own terms, but then there had to be some objective evaluation as to what should be done with them.

"If you accelerate into that mode too quickly you rob the artist and the record of the opportunity to inspire," Cafaro explains. "I've always been suspicious of people who listen to records and, on the first time through, are trying to evaluate singles. That's really missing the boat. So, after that exhilarating moment of hearing the record for the first time, I bought very, very big into the fact that we had a great record, I immediately started telling people this, and I recall as people heard it around the company it was all coming back the same way. I think there's a tendency to believe that at record companies it's kind of like the emperor's clothes, where everyone just blindly says, 'That's great.' However, that's really not the way it is, particularly at a place like A&M. The individual was always respected. People could offer opinions, and it all came back gangbusters on this."

A&M released about forty albums in 1993, and while the company may have tried more than most to adhere to the principle that "all artists are created equal, all records are created equal," this obviously wasn't the way things played out. After all, how could it be? The need to make money, in conjunction with the indulgence of personal preferences, precluded it. Fortunately for Sheryl Crow, *Tuesday Night Music Club* immediately found its way onto A&M's unofficial A-list.

"We would try not to differentiate, but when we heard this record it clearly catapulted itself into the front line as something very special," Cafaro admits. "Nevertheless, once again I have to underscore that the enthusiasm is primarily an evaluation of the creative aesthetic, not necessarily the commercial appeal. People may well surmise otherwise, but when I heard this record I didn't say, 'We're going to win Grammys and we're going to sell millions of units!' I just heard an incredible record that was so unique and special that we had a responsibility to do a great job with it and reach an audience. It was by no means a case of me walking away saying, 'We're gonna ring that cash register!'

"It's a case of the extent to which you feel an obligation to the art, because there are some records where you care about the people, you love the people, but the records don't come out the way you hoped and you can't make them better. They are what they are, and you still have an obligation to do your job, but when you hear something that's compelling it's just a higher calling, because it's what you live for."

Certain albums help a record company to create a plan. *Tuesday Night Music Club* did just that, providing the A&M marketing team with rich material while suggesting the route they should take with regard to the featured artist.

"How we proceed is partly driven by the artist and the life experiences," says Cafaro. "You know, what is the biography here? We all have biographies in the eyes of God, who presumably knows everything, and then we all have biographies that we like to talk about. So, you start with the biography that you like to talk about: Who are you and what do we want to accentuate about you? With Sheryl, we had this artist who had been around and worked her way up to this, which was a virtue, but then on the other hand she had also been a backup singer for Michael Jackson, which is not necessarily a marketing point that you want to accentuate. Still, you can't avoid those things. I was always very big on presenting the right side of the artist—the most provocative, compelling side—but I was never one who would try to bury or hide things. I think that's a dangerous place to be in, because I've never felt that you should ask artists to deny a part of themselves."

Sheryl didn't really have any closeted skeletons to hide, but she also didn't have the kind of heart-wrenching, rags-to-hopeful-riches background that makes for great press-release copy. As a result, during the coming months—and, indeed, coming years—there would be plenty of hyperbole and tall tales attached to her struggle for success: how she served her apprenticeship playing in bands "on the beer-soaked bandstands of St. Louis" (to quote the November 14, 1996, issue of *Rolling Stone*); how she quit her job teaching music to autistic children after earning "$42,000" for supposedly singing "It's a good time for the great taste of McDonald's" on a radio jingle; how she left St. Louis for L.A. in "a beat-up old convertible"; how she gatecrashed the auditions to sing backup on Michael Jackson's world tour by sending him an unsolicited video of herself; and how her career was in limbo for a couple of years following the shelving of her first album.

Still, if there were exaggerations or fabrications, none of them were a big deal, and they certainly paled in comparison to some of the more ridiculous, overblown biographies that have been concocted by showbiz publicists (and self-publicists) over the years. What they did was add a rock 'n' roll edge to the story of a small-town girl from southern Missouri. Next came the photos.

"With Sheryl, the images and the subsequent videos were always harder to get than the music," says Al Cafaro. "I think a lot of that had to do with her sense of unease with—and inability to know exactly—what she wanted to communicate."

Rich Frankel, A&M's Senior VP of Creative Services, played a large role in determining what Sheryl's image should be. A company veteran who'd shared a congenial relationship with many of the in-house artists, Frankel could be legitimately characterized as the resident "art dog"; the man who was always looking for something special.

"He wasn't perceived by us as a literal, marketing-driven creative guy," states Cafaro. "The company wasn't really populated in that way. At A&M we would always come to things from a different direction, and when people talked about A&M as being an artist-oriented company that always seemed to make sense and have meaning to me."

For Sheryl, and for those around her, the task of participating in photo shoots and trying to find the right image wasn't an easy one. Still, having suffered through his own photo session after becoming CEO of A&M, Al Cafaro had a fairly clear understanding of what the artists had to endure.

"It's not enough that we ask them to be creative, to be brilliant musically, to perform live," he says. "Now they've got to pose for photo sessions and then they've got to do videos! Who's equipped for this shit? Out of my own experience I had some empathy. Still, having said that, most record companies—including A&M to some degree—work under the assumption that artists should be grateful for the opportunity, and that we are the experts and they should just shut up and do whatever we tell them to do. You know, 'If we think you look best in this, wear it! If we think your hair looks best like this, wear it! If we think this is the best photo, it is!' Certainly there's an element of arrogance involved in that, but I don't know that it's as much driven by arrogance as it's driven by people's desire to contribute and to do their thing. At the same time, people will also put in their ten cents' worth just so they can show they're doing their job, and it's hard to get around that.

"You want people to be involved, you want people to care, but then you always have a fear that it's arbitrary, and that used to drive me nuts. To this day I still have the impression that there are probably too many people involved in the mix at these record companies, and that the process would be better served by fewer people [who are] basically doing what they're told. To someone who is skeptical or cynical about the process this might sound like bullshit, but I can tell you one of the secrets about record companies that escapes most people is that, for the most part, people at record companies really do care and really do live vicariously, to some degree, through those artists and those projects."

Like many fledgling acts, Sheryl was at first uncertain about how she wanted to present herself. Initially, therefore, she agreed to some of the ideas coming her way, and then spoke up later if things didn't feel right. This had been the case with the Hugh Padgham project. She had to learn as she went along, but she was learning fast.

"I went out to the West Coast and interviewed Sheryl, and tried to get a feel for what her story was and what she had to say," recalls A&M's then–Executive Vice President of East Coast operations, Wayne Isaak. "I worked with people, product-managing her, and we started to do interviews. It's really interesting to reflect back on this, because Sheryl had a great voice, and quite a bit of experience from Michael Jackson and Don Henley and playing in bands, so she wasn't just a Johnny-come-lately to the scene. However, early on she was still getting rolling. She always looked great to anybody who met her, but she was still trying to figure out—as we all were—how to present herself photographically, how to style herself. You know, how do we make a video look right for her?

"I think that the main concern, the main goal, was to enhance what was there; to take this woman who was beautiful and sexy and who had great blonde hair and a really unique look, and just make sure that it came across in whatever medium we were presenting her. Still, it wasn't easy, because Sheryl was an artist, so her music was a more important thing, and I think at times this was a load on her. Some female artists, some female musical entertainers, love the fashion part, but for Sheryl it was an extra task."

Briefly during this period of time, Sheryl was managed by both Scooter Weintraub and Kevin Wall, who, according to Isaak, "was an overview sort of manager. His television experience meant that he certainly had a clue as to what was going on, and we hit it off right away.

"One day, I had lunch with Scooter and Kevin, and one of the things we talked about was how I really wanted to get Sheryl on TV early, on no-stakes sort of TV, where she wouldn't necessarily hit a home run but she'd get the experience under her belt. This was about the time when Letterman left NBC and they'd created the Conan O'Brien show for late night, so I booked her to perform on one of Conan's pilot shows. They needed musical guests, so I did that with the guarantee that they would book her back later. She played with their big house band.

"The thing I loved about Sheryl at the time was that she didn't take anything for granted. You know, we talked through a lot of things before she went out. We had all kinds of fall-back plans, like 'If you break a guitar string, or if you hit a note and you really crack on it, here's what you do; you stop! Because if you stop they have to retake it.' So, she did that show, and I fondly remember doing all of that stuff, because Sheryl was so gung-ho. The first six months were really formative."

Meanwhile, there were numerous people with whom Sheryl had to work at the record company. Primarily, these consisted of Al Cafaro, who was involved in all aspects of her career as they pertained to A&M, and David Anderle, who served as an overseer. Then there were the department heads: on the West Coast, J.B. Brenner, VP of AOR Promotion; Bill Gilbert, Senior VP of Sales & Distribution; Jay Durgan, VP of International; Laura Swanson, National Director of Publicity West; Diana Baron, VP/Director of Publicity West; Rich Frankel, VP of Creative Services; Bob Garcia, National Director of Artist Relations; Emily Wittman, National Director of Video Promotion; and Rick Gershon, Director of Information West. On the East Coast there was Wayne Isaak, the VP/Executive Director of Publicity; Jim Guerinot, Senior

VP of Artist Development & Marketing; Rick Stone, Senior VP of Promotion; Lauren Zelisko, Director of Publicity; and Richie Gallo, VP of Sales & Distribution. To varying degrees, these individuals each played a role in shaping and sustaining an artist's career.

"Sheryl would deal with the head of Promotion regarding what's going to happen with radio," Cafaro explains. "The promotion people are important. At the beginning of the project, when you're planning, they're involved but they're not intimately involved. However, subsequent to the release of the record they're very involved. You're going to be spending a lot of time with those people, because they're going to take you out on the road, they're going to take you to radio stations, and they're going to coordinate backstage and meet 'n' greets.

"Then again, the sales people are also important. You'll meet sales people on the road and certainly meet retailers on the road, although this is a little bit less primary than the Promotion Department's involvement. Sheryl would have some interaction with the head of Sales, but this would be a general interaction because he is going to sell the records to where they need to be sold based on other things that happen at the company.

"If the record was scheduled to be a simultaneous international release, that would be a whole separate marketing process, where she would meet with the head of International and then a product manager who deals with the international market-places. Because A&M was an independent record company and historically we made a lot of money outside the U.S., we always maintained a very aggressive International Department.

"Sheryl would deal with the head of Press in a very primary sense, because that person—in this case, she—would have to understand that she's going to be the one who's out there hawking everybody to review the record, to write features, et cetera. Then there's the head of Creative Services, who helps to create the images, set up the photo shoots, get the treatments for videos, do the liner notes, and really put the total package together.

"Sheryl would deal with the marketing department through a product manager, who's kind of like the one-stop shopper within the record company. An artist can go to a product manager and his or her A&R person to generally find out everything that's going on. A lot of things get coordinated via the product manager to the artist. Still, at a company the size of A&M, where there was this intimacy, I would say that Sheryl's primary relationships were with me and David, the head of Press, the head of Creative Services, the head of Marketing and the product manager, and then probably Promotion, Sales, and International, in that order."

At any given time, each of these people would be dealing with five to eight artists who were at a similar stage in their careers, and who were therefore vying with one another for pole position on the exec's list of priorities. In 1993, Sting, Bryan Adams, Soundgarden, and Amy Grant were at the top of A&M's list, and Sheryl now found herself up there courtesy of the hopes that the execs were pinning on her first official album. Not that her networking responsibilities were limited to the record company and its related activities. To really help promote *Tuesday Night Music Club* and build a personal fan base, Sheryl would have to go out on the road, and this in itself would bring her into contact with many other people of influence.

Before the album had even been completed, she'd had a meeting with John Marx at the all-powerful William Morris Agency in Beverly Hills, and within a few months they signed a deal for him to take care of her worldwide concert bookings, excluding the U.K. and Europe.

"I first heard about Sheryl through Robert Richards," Marx recalls. "He was no longer her manager, but he told me that she was laying down tracks in Los Angeles and that I should follow up on this. So, in early '93, she came in with Kevin Wall and played me some of the unfinished songs. I told her that I wanted to become involved with her, and shortly afterwards we finalized the agreement to work together.

"Sheryl knew the business. She'd been on the road with Michael Jackson, and she was very aware of the way things worked. Many artists who come to see us don't know what an agent does, but Sheryl was very much aware of what we do here. I think she was looking for somebody who really believed in her, and somebody who had the necessary connections and insight and track record to be able to work on this aspect of her career. She needed to get on the best opening slots at the right time, and so it was just a matter of us having some headliners.

"For instance, The Eagles were out on the road; she and Don Henley were friendly, and we also represented The Eagles. So, whether they were clients of ours or clients of other agencies, because I'd been doing this for many years I had the relationships out there to be able to at least get her up to bat. At the end of the day, it's the call of the headlining artists as to whether or not they want to take the support act on the road, and often if you don't have the right connections you can't get your artist up to bat."

Still, even though one of John Marx's career traits has been to pick and represent artists on the basis of their musical talents, his colleagues at William Morris initially didn't afford him a strong vote of confidence regarding Sheryl Crow. In essence, they didn't hear what he was hearing, yet instead of being swayed by this, Marx was undeterred.

"At that time, alternative music was king," he says. "So, I think many of the agents were listening to Sheryl's record with alternative ears and saying, 'Where does this fit in? What radio stations are going to play Sheryl Crow?' I knew that it wasn't going to be an easy project, but nothing ventured, nothing gained. For me, Sheryl had great songs, she had charisma, and I chose to place my bet on her. I come from a musical background, so I see myself as someone who has the ears to detect good songs and whether the artist has credibility."

While the album was still being mixed, Sheryl returned to St. Louis to assemble a touring band. Initially, there had been talk that she might be joined by the other members of TMC, but the wires were crossed at both ends.

"At first there were conversations about the TMC 'cabaret tour,' where we'd go out featuring Sheryl, but David would do some songs, Kevin would do some songs, and we'd all be supporting each other," Dan Schwartz remembers. "It was in February of '93 that Sheryl asked me to go on tour, and I ordered a bass and I'm glad to have it, but it became unnecessary that year.

"When the album was delivered, Sheryl told me she had no friends in L.A. except for me, Bill, and Judy [Stakee]. She needed to get away from L.A. and I thought, 'Yeah, that makes sense to me.' But then she told me she was putting a band together in St. Louis, and I said, 'What's the deal here? I thought we were doing something,' to which she said, 'Well, will you go on the road for $600 a week?' I said, 'You know what, I can't afford to do that. I'm getting married in six months.' I wasn't angry; I sort of accepted it as inevitable. I assumed it was A&M's decision, similar to them being unwilling to put up as much money for the album as they had been for the shelved album. They were still hedging their bets all the way down the line."

"We were in a dance," adds Bill Bottrell. "We weren't touring musicians but we wanted to be, and we were all like, 'Well, is there a way we could do this? After all, we are a band, and we're all going to make each other's albums, right?' Sheryl was going, 'Yeah,' and so it was a dance between 'We all wanna do it,' and 'We know the level you're going to start at, and can we afford to give up our other work to do these things?' We were waffling really. Something had to break through and someone had to go, 'Okay, here's what can happen.' That someone should have been a record executive. It should have been David Anderle coming and saying, 'Well, if this is going to be a band, you could do this, it's going to take this long, and you're not going to get paid much.' Then each person could have said yes or no, but that never happened."

In fact, Sheryl did ask Brian MacLeod to join her touring lineup. But, as he explained in his 2001 interview with Wayne Perez for the official Kevin Gilbert Web site, he went with a better offer.

"She took me out to dinner," MacLeod recalled, "and said, 'Brian, will you go on tour with me? I want you to tour with me. I don't have any money and it will be $1,000 a week. We will be in a band and we will be in Motel 6's and you'll have to double up with the bass player.' At the same time she asked me this, Tears For Fears rolled out the red carpet; sending me to London first-class, putting me up in this huge suite overlooking Hyde Park, offering me tons of money.... I remember I didn't sleep for two or three days, pacing back and forth. I said, 'Ya know what? I have never done a big, big stadium tour with a big-name act. Some of those songs are challenging with Tears For Fears.' So I told Sheryl, 'I am supportive of you. I want this record to be great. I'll help you find people, but I'm going on the road with Tears For Fears.' She holds that against me to this day. She was pissed off about that. She brings it up."

Regardless, in the spring of 1993 Sheryl had to make some quick decisions. Meeting with David Anderle in his office on the A&M lot, she informed him of her intention to assemble a touring band in St. Louis.

"She said, 'I don't want to get into one of these situations where I burden the record company by having to pay these outrageous prices to put an L.A. band together,'" Anderle recalls. "She realized she was going to need time."

In a 2002 interview for VH1's *Behind the Music*, Scooter Weintraub put things more succinctly. "We couldn't take the Tuesday Night Music Club on the road, that wouldn't have worked," he asserted. "You couldn't get a record [by] a brand new artist and have, like, four other artists playing in the band."

As Kevin Wall receded from the picture, Scooter began managing Sheryl on his own, and he was heavily involved in helping assemble her touring lineup. The selected musicians consisted of Jon Chalden on drums, Eric Hotter on bass, and Roy Scott Bryan as the utility man who could sing backup and play keyboards, guitar, and, later on, even some percussion and pedal steel. Sheryl herself would sing and perform on keyboards, as well as the guitar which she was still learning to play, and the lineup was completed when her erstwhile co-writer and Scooter's friend, blues guitarist Todd Wolfe, flew in from L.A. in late July.

"I thought it would be a six-month run, but I ended up being with her for close to five years," Todd remarks. "They had set up two or three gigs in the St. Louis area, just to get out and start playing a little bit, so I had about two days of rehearsal. There was a heat wave going on, the Mississippi was overflowing, and the rehearsal room was about 106 degrees, but we just kept playing and playing, and by week's end we went out and did a few gigs in the St. Louis area. That was at the end of July, just before the album came out."

David Anderle, Judy Stakee, and A&M's head of International, Sue DeBenedetti, were among the contingent that flew to St. Louis to see Sheryl's first gig. This took place at Off Broadway, an atmospheric little venue located downtown on Lemp Street. It was a hot and steamy summer night, and by the musicians' own admission, their performance wasn't up to par.

"There were about fourteen people in this small club, eleven of us from the label," David Anderle remembers. "Afterwards, Sheryl came up to me at the bar and she was chagrined about her band and so forth…typical Sheryl. I said, 'Don't worry about it, because as you work and get better you'll be able to draw better players.'

"That gig was where I met Triple A [album adult alternative] people for the first time. A bunch of people from different labels were having a dinner in that town, and I was invited over to join them. They loved Sheryl's record, right from the get-go, and they were actually having arguments as to what the best track was. I said to this young A&R guy who was with me on the trip, 'This is what you dream about, having radio and other record companies arguing about what's the best song on your artist's album!' So, Triple A went for it right away. They loved her. Then again, I also knew there were people at the label who liked this album, so I could relax a little bit with the fact that we were going to get a shot. If Sheryl could just get a shot I knew she would make it, because there was no way she would miss."

The live debut in St. Louis coincided with Sheryl's solo debut on the airwaves. In July, A&M issued "Run, Baby, Run" as a promotional single in the U.S. (it was released as an official single in the U.K., Europe, and Australia). This incorporated an edited version of the song for deejays who might not play a four-minute, fifty-three-second track by an unknown artist, but it didn't stir up much interest.

"We didn't expect 'Run, Baby, Run' to be a hit, but we saw it as a good way to introduce Sheryl to adult alternative radio formats," Al Cafaro explains. "It was also a good track for her to get out there and start touring with."

At the beginning of August, A&M distributed a four-song sampler, *Scenes from the Tuesday Night Music Club,* featuring "Run, Baby, Run," "Strong Enough," "All I Wanna Do," and—following its inclusion on the soundtrack to the Brad Pitt movie *Kalifornia*—"No One Said It Would Be Easy." Again, this disc failed to generate much radio play, although it would help to popularize Sheryl in early 1994. The album itself was released in the U.S. on August 3, and initial sales were slow—a grand total of 139 copies crawled off the shelves during the first week. A&M's execs weren't surprised.

"On some level the record business has changed from then to now," Cafaro remarks. "You know, now the record business is like a skier out of a chute at the Olympic downhill—you'd better hit maximum speed in the first thirty seconds, otherwise you're done. Back then, if given the option, you'd always prefer to take the other path, because you wanted to play it out over a period of time. You wanted there to be some natural sense of discovery, some sort of unfolding. You wanted some people to get it and buy in big. You wanted it to be special to them. You wanted to have people out there believe that they had found something and bought into something first, whereas when you're going right to the mass marketplace it's one taste, one color for everybody. In that case everyone might still appreciate and enjoy it, but I don't know if there's a bond and a sense of ownership with an audience when you go that way.

"I think the reason things have changed is partly because of less desire to take a risk, and some of it has to do with consolidation of media and the fact that you're now dealing with major broadcast chains that own hundreds of radio stations and divvy up the marketplace. You're never going to move a record from this format to that format, because they don't want that record. You know, they own three, four, five radio stations, so each genre is going to take its slice. It's a whole different world. Then there is the function of demographics—you've got a huge bulge in the population of kids who are 'teenyboppers' and they're going to devour stuff very quickly, because they're moving on very quickly.

"Rolling out this record back in 1993 and '94, the reasoning was not all that hard. You have an artist who you've signed because you think she really has talent. She proves it to you by making a collaborative record with a lot of talented people who produce startling results. She is driven to make it work and can pull it off live. And you've got a deep record, so you want to be able to say, 'Okay, we're going to roll this thing out over a period of time.'"

That August, a small review in *Billboard* referred to the *Tuesday Night Music Club* album as "an intriguing solo debut. Crisply played compositions, warmly sung by Crow.... Positive potential for Top 40 and AC [album chart] acceptance."

In October, *Musician* magazine stated that the record "presents a range and level of popcraft rarely on display these days," while a four-star review in the November edition of U.K. music publication *Q* went even further: "Sheryl Crow's debut is an instant and lasting joy. Co-written with excellent musicians at recreational sessions (hence the title), these 11 songs blend roots, melody, emotion, and intelligence. Drawing on blues, R&B, country, funk, and jazz, Crow's nearest reference point is a more together Rickie Lee Jones. The music, led by piano, organ, and rhythm guitar, is stylish but not slick, while her charged lyrics mix irony, imagination, and observation.... Memorable stuff, sung with that unmistakable confidence of an artist who's getting it right all the way down the line."

Despite the positive words, it would actually require a few good breaks and a lot of hard work to ignite sales of the record, but if anyone was up to the task it was Sheryl Crow. From early childhood through high school, college, and the past nine years in St. Louis and L.A., she'd pulled out all the stops and gone that extra mile whenever it was demanded of her (and often when it wasn't). Now, with one failed album project already behind her, she was standing on the precipice, staring at the ultimate prize: the chance to achieve success in her own right. She, of all people, wasn't about to drop the ball.

At the end of August, Sheryl and her band performed at the Triple A convention in Boulder, Colorado, where David Baerwald showed up and played guitar on "What I Can Do For You." Then, following the gig, there was a change of bass player. "Eric Hotter was good, but he never seemed to be comfortable with the material," says Todd Wolfe. The result was that Wire Train's Anders Rundblad joined the lineup, and that September the band hit the road for a proper tour, crisscrossing the country in a fifteen-passenger van while the equipment followed in a U-Haul trailer.

The material being played at this time obviously focused on the new album, but it also included "Father Sun" from the shelved record, not least because Wynonna Judd had covered it the previous year. The plan was to methodically work the *Tuesday Night Music Club* album from market to market, routing the tour in coordination with A&M's marketing department. Performing for just a few people in a tiny club was the nature of the game at this stage, but the idea was to attract attention, rely on word-of-mouth, and play return gigs in front of, hopefully, larger audiences. That way, even the smallest growth in following would be discernible.

"Sheryl was not a big touring act on her own," John Marx explains. "She'd certainly played large venues as a background singer, but she understood the merit of going out there and working the small rooms so that she could feel comfortable on a big stage. You can kill artists by putting them out on a big stage too early. We therefore started off doing a lot of club dates. Generally, when people tour clubs they'll play one date in Colorado, but I remember on that first tour Sheryl did five dates there. She was getting played on Triple A radio, and so we would go and play those secondary markets, in venues with anywhere from a hundred to three hundred seats."

Accordingly, during December of 1993 and January of 1994, you could catch Sheryl Crow performing at the King Edward Hotel in Calgary, Alberta; the Town Pump in Vancouver, British Columbia; the Paradise Lounge in San Francisco, California; Garton's Saloon in Vail, Colorado; the Old Town Pub in Steamboat Springs, Colorado; Ramona's in Taos, New Mexico; and the Cushing Street Bar in Tucson, Arizona.

"She found an audience and it started to build," says Marx. "Sheryl worked harder than most acts ever work. She would play any place where she was getting airplay or where there was a buzz, and on a couple of dates there were only fifty people in a room. That's tough, but I can tell you that I have never had a complaint from Sheryl about any date that I've ever booked her on, and that's unusual. They all want to bitch about something, but she always knew that I had her best interests at heart. You can't guess right all the time—if you play a date in a city that you've booked way ahead of anyone else, and then The Eagles drop on top of you that day, there's not much you can do. However, we always tried to use the information that was available to us in order to gauge where we should put her."

Traveling six to eight hours at a stretch, napping upright in the van when it was someone else's turn to lie down in the back row, sleeping two to a room—the life was hardly glamorous and the work was hard, especially for Sheryl, who not only performed additional acoustic gigs with Roy Scott Bryan whenever she was presented with a promotional opportunity, but also partook in the kind of on-the-road schmoozing and networking that was vital at this stage of her career.

"She was going to radio stations with her acoustic guitar in every town, she was charming those guys, and she wasn't doing it because she was being asked to do it as much as she was doing it because this was part of her dream," David Anderle says. "Then, when radio had a chance to play her record, they all went for it. Again, she never went in there like 'I have to do this.' She went in there like 'Thank God I get an opportunity to play some music on the radio for you guys.'"

"You're dealing with local promotion people and the local sales guy and the distribution people, and again they all want a piece of you," adds Al Cafaro. "You've got people taking you around town when you're out there, you've got people at sound-check, you've got people between sound-check and the gig, you might have a dinner that you have to go to, you'll meet people at that dinner, you'll meet people after the dinner, you'll hang out and have a few beers…you're gonna work!

"You're dealing with a lot of people, and you're dealing with people who believe you should be doing everything. Because it's your career, and if I'm prepared to bust my ass for you as a promotion guy, or go the distance as a publicist and find people to review your record, then you should be willing to work, and certainly Sheryl Crow was willing to work. She worked really, really hard."

The problem was, she'd often work too hard.

"She would start making herself sick," says Cafaro. "And when I say sick, I mean really sick. I'm talking about feeling shitty; tired, rundown, 'My voice doesn't feel good.' What we would do—and Scooter comes to mind as my collaborator and co-conspirator in this process—is tell everybody in the company through the proper channels, 'We're working her too hard. I want less of this, less of this, less of this. Continue to do this, and I want everybody in sync. Don't tell her to do something, because she'll do it! And just because she'll do it doesn't mean it's the right thing to do. She's not going to say 'no.'

"Of course, Sheryl wouldn't be very happy about this, but we'd have it all straightened out, and then she'd go out and be with somebody and say, 'Is there anything else you need to me to do?' They'd go, 'No, no, we're all done.' 'Come on, there's got to be something I can do!' 'Well, I mean, sure, if you want to stop by....' 'Yeah, let's go there!' So, she would do it anyway, and she just worked her tail off."

In the meantime, Cafaro knew that he had his own work cut out regarding the contentious reference to Frank Dileo in "The Na-Na Song." This type of controversy A&M could do without. For one thing, it might not be easy for Sheryl to support her allegations of sexual harassment by Dileo during the *Bad* world tour, and even if she could, the shit was bound to hit the fan once Dileo got to hear about it...which is precisely what happened. With the word "litigation" looming large in everyone's minds, Cafaro got on the phone to Dileo.

"The record was a done deal," Al explains. "However, I knew Frank, so I called him and he was a mensch about it. You know, he sort of flailed and moaned, but ultimately he was okay.... 'The Na-Na Song' was never one of my favorite tracks."

And neither (surprise, surprise) was it one of Frank Dileo's.

"Frank was pissed because his son's teacher discovered it," says Rory Kaplan, who'd played keyboards on the *Bad* tour. "That's a low shot."

Following a radio date in Nashville on December 15, Sheryl and her band took an eleven-day break from their tour. Then, when they reconvened after Christmas, it was with a new bass player and drummer. Sheryl hadn't been pleased with Jon Chalden's drumming, and neither had Anders Rundblad. Unable to resolve his musical differences with Chalden, Rundblad wanted out, and this was made easier when Sheryl and Roy Scott Bryan met bassist Tad Wadhams during one of their joint promotional assignments. Following a jam session involving Wadhams, his drummer-roommate Wally Ingram, and Todd Wolfe, Wadhams and Ingram were invited to become the new rhythm section, and it was at this point, according to Wolfe, that the band really started to jell.

"It was definitely the sum of its parts," he says. "Musically, the strongest guy in the band was Scott Bryan, because he was more of a session guy and he could play anything, whereas Wally, Tad, and I weren't. Still, we'd get out there and rock, and although it wouldn't be great every night—it wasn't as consistent as the lineup she has now—it definitely had something going. It looked like a band, it felt like a band, and we even had an RV instead of a van. We were raising the stakes—an RV and a trailer. That lasted for three or four months, until we finally got our big pink bus.

"Sheryl is kind of a taskmaster. When you have an artist, especially a female artist, out on the road with all the guys, her emotions are going to be more up and down. Some nights she's going to feel it or hear it a certain way, and we'd have to keep on our toes. For me it was tough, because I'd never done anything like this, whereas for a guy like Scott it was easier, because he'd done it a lot. I mean, we were enjoying being out on the road, but musically there were those nights when we'd come off stage and it would be 'What were you doing there? What was going on?' It was good, because in an innocent way we'd blow off steam. Maybe we'd drink a little bit that night and smash some bottles.... Sheryl's like a sister. You know, sometimes you want to smack her upside the head, and sometimes you just want to give her a hug. There are a lot of emotions when you're out on the road. You're like family."

In March of 1994, the *Tuesday Night Music Club* album finally cracked The Billboard 200, charting at No. 173 on the strength of 6,000 copies sold. Then, on April 5, "Leaving Las Vegas" was issued as a single, and on the twenty-third it became the first Sheryl Crow recording to debut on The Billboard Hot 100. Remaining there for ten weeks, it would eventually peak at No. 60, while the accompanying video was accorded limited exposure on VH1. Still, the film deserved better, and it would be played in heavier rotation following the success of Sheryl's next single later in the year.

Directed by David Hogan, the "Leaving Las Vegas" video combined seductive close-ups of Sheryl's mouth and face with wry depictions of Vegas staples located on and around a desert highway: a portrait of singer Wayne Newton, a troupe of showgirls, and a band of Elvis-lookalikes flying overhead. This was a case of eye-catching visuals that bore only a slight connection to the lyrics, but which fit perfectly with the music.

"We got a little more attention when that video came out," says Todd Wolfe with regard to a spring tour on which Sheryl and the band opened for Crowded House, the New Zealand band fronted by Neil Finn. "I don't think it was so much the song as the video. We rode on that a little bit."

They needed to, at least until record sales turned the corner. At that point, Sheryl could climb to the next level as a concert artist, playing larger venues and selling any-where from five hundred to a thousand tickets per show. Sure, a following was starting to develop as she kept returning to the same markets, but she probably wouldn't be head-lining theaters unless her efforts were augmented by the record.

"When Sheryl went out on the Crowded House tour that was a big step, and then 'Leaving Las Vegas' helped too," says John Marx. "That's when we started to catch a little magic. The performances were being well received and there was a good buzz out on her."

Sheryl had actually premiered "Leaving Las Vegas" in front of a nationwide televi-sion audience prior to its release, with an appearance on the *Late Show with David Letterman* on March 21, 1994, the same night as the Academy Awards. She followed that up by performing the song on *Late Night with Conan O'Brien* on April 7. During June, she and the band played in Europe, and the following month they commenced the third annual H.O.R.D.E. tour, which John Marx had booked them onto back in the spring. Standing for "Horizons of Rock Developing Everywhere," this tour featured the likes of Blues Traveler, Big Head Todd and the Monsters, the Dave Matthews Band, and the Allman Brothers playing thirty-one dates over the course of an eight-week period, filling amphitheaters from Maine to California.

Prior to the first concert, members of the Allman Brothers, Blues Traveler, and Sheryl's band visited Shooters, a bar/restaurant complex in the Flats of Cleveland, where, towards the end of a set by local outfit Oroboros, they took over the stage and spent two hours jamming on Allmans songs and old blues material. This, in turn, was a precursor to what became known as the H.O.R.D.E. "jam stage," where many of the musicians would partake in impromptu sessions while the main stage setups were being changed between

**1201 West Washington Street, Kennett, Missouri**
This is where Sheryl lived during most of her formative years, across the road from the High School, in a house with four pianos on which the Crow kids would practice simultaneously during the late afternoons while their mother monitored their efforts from the kitchen.
*Richard Buskin*

**A happy childhood in
small-town America**
Sheryl (*right*), aged seven,
in "traditional" getup for a
Purim party, alongside friends
Carlotta Tarver (*center*) and
Debbie Tate, one of the neigh-
borhood's few Jewish kids.
*Courtesy of Deborah Welsh*

**Jo Beth Skaggs's eleventh birthday party, 1973**
Sheryl, in glasses *(top right)*, is on her best friend's shoulders—both are in their matching pyjamas. Among the other revelers are Carlotta Tarver *(bottom left)*, standing next to Debbie Tate, and on Carlotta's shoulders, Ann Cash.
*Courtesy of Jo Beth Skaggs*

**High school soprano, 1978**
Sixteen-year-old Sheryl *(bottom row, center)* performing as part of the girls' sextet.
*Courtesy of Kennett High School*

**The drum majorette, 1979**
In addition to this activity and her stint as Freshman Maid, Sheryl's overachieving years at Kennett High also saw her taking the titles of Senior Maid and Paperdoll Queen, while participating as a member of the Pep Club, National Honor Society, and Future Farmers of America.
*Courtesy of Kennett High School*

**Hurdling during a district meet, 1979**
Second in the district during her senior year, Sheryl qualified for the state finals.
*Courtesy of Kennett High School*

**The Senior Maid, 1980**
Missing out on the title of
Homecoming Queen was
one of Sheryl's few failures.
"She was really busy musically,
active in girls' track, and then
she was in bands," recalls music
teacher James Finch. "If you
look at her list of activities in
her senior year it's unbelievable."
*Courtesy of Kennett High School*

**Chaste lovers, 1982**
With boyfriend and
eventual fiancé Mike
Rechtien, attending
the "winter formal"
dance at the University
of Missouri-Columbia.
*Courtesy of Mike Rechtien*

**Mizzou days, 1983**
At the annual spring dance,
with Mike, fellow Kappa Alpha
Theta sorority sisters Shelle
Stewart and Betsy Rimley, and
their respective boyfriends.
*Courtesy of Mike Rechtien*

**Cashmere's six-piece lineup, 1983**
(*Left to right*) drummer Fred Moreadith,
lead singer Sheryl Crow, lead guitarist
Byron Baker, keyboardist Rob Brown,
guitarist/lead vocalist Mike Rechtien,
and bass player Jim Redick.
*Courtesy of Mike Rechtien*

**The star attraction at Bullwinkle's...**
Well, almost. Onstage at one of Mizzou's favorite college hangouts.
*Courtesy of Mike Rechtien*

**The first big break**
Performing "I Just Can't Stop Loving You" with Michael Jackson during his 1987–1989 *Bad* world tour. Despite the fact that MJ hardly spoke to her offstage and could barely remember her name, Sheryl was labeled as his "secret girlfriend" and the mother of his baby in tabloid reports.
© *Cliff Lipson/Retna*

**With good friend and loyal supporter Judy Stakee, 1992**
Three years earlier, Judy had signed Sheryl to a publishing deal with Warner/Chappell.
*Courtesy of Judy Stakee*

**Bill and Sheryl**
Despite their smiles in early 1993, the pair's successful working relationship would soon degenerate into mutual antipathy.
*Zhenya Nesterov*

**Toad Hall**
Bill Bottrell's studio in Pasadena, which was markedly different in terms of both appearance and atmosphere from the usual L.A. facility.
*Courtesy of Bill Bottrell*

**Before the fallout**
The Tuesday Night
Music Clubbers: (*top
row, left-right*) Brian
MacLeod, Bill Bottrell,
David Baerwald; (*seated*)
Dan Schwartz, Sheryl
Crow, Kevin Gilbert.
*Zhenya Nesterov*

**The pop star and the poet**
Backstage in 1994 with
Wyn Cooper, whose poem
"Fun" comprised the lyrical
basis for Sheryl's breakout
hit, "All I Wanna Do."
*Courtesy of Wyn Cooper*

acts. What's more, there was plenty of cross-pollination during the shows themselves, with Sheryl, for example, providing vocals on the Allmans' "Midnight Rider."

H.O.R.D.E. '94 was an excellent means of raising Sheryl's profile, and as luck would have it, the start of the tour also coincided with the release of her breakout single. Still, it hadn't been easy deciding which song should fill that role.

"There was a lot of controversy over the choice of 'All I Wanna Do,'" confirms Al Cafaro. "Many people didn't like it, and I'm not going to claim that when I heard the album for the first time I said, "'All I Wanna Do" is the hit song.' However, as we spent time with the album, as we had time to see Sheryl perform, as things were progressing, as 'Run, Baby, Run' did what we wanted it to do, and as 'Leaving Las Vegas' moved into another realm, 'All I Wanna Do' appeared to be the logical choice if we wanted a hit…and we wanted a hit.

"Then again, we didn't know we had lightning in a bottle with 'All I Wanna Do,' because there was a huge internal controversy at the company as to whether or not 'Can't Cry Anymore'—which turned out to be the fifth single—should be the third single instead. In fact, for a senior manager who already had a strained relationship with the company, this was actually the straw that broke the camel's back. He thought releasing 'All I Wanna Do' was some kind of joke that wasn't going to happen, whereas I felt that it had to be the single."

In the middle of this controversy, Cafaro and David Anderle went to see Sheryl playing at the Wiltern Theater in Los Angeles. Also there were Anderle's wife, Cheryl, and Cafaro's wife, Linda, a record-industry veteran who was then working for publishers Private Music. When Linda heard Sheryl perform "All I Wanna Do," she nudged her husband and said, "If that's not the next single, you're crazy!" Spousal advice often helps. Cafaro felt vindicated.

"Seeing the song performed live made it very clear," he says. "It was such a fun song. People weren't sitting down looking at their shoes, they were up and hooting and hollering, and I was not unimpressed with this reality. It's a very thought-provoking song. It's not just a simple 'I wanna have a beer and have some fun.' There's a definite attitude that gives it some irony and makes it substantive, and after experiencing the record and experiencing her performing the song live, I had no doubt that 'All I Wanna Do' was the right choice for the third single. Implicitly that meant it was our best shot at a hit. Number three had to go big, had to be the biggest track on the record, and fortunately by the time we got there that was the way I saw it."

Never a fan of the song in the first place, Sheryl still had to be convinced. Certainly it was catchy, but she was concerned that it was too lightweight and lacked the credibility that she was hoping to establish by way of the album's other tracks.

"My view about that has always been a little bit different," Cafaro states. "I've had this conversation with a lot of artists: 'You wrote it. It's on your record. Come on! It's not like we're asking you to do a remake of "The Peppermint Twist!"' Sheryl, I know, was skeptical. I don't remember her saying, 'Oh my God, no!' but we had a conversation about it and she made me prove it to her—put my ass on the line, if you will.

"By the time we got to that point of making the decision, I was very confident. You know, 'We are going to be okay. We're gonna sell a lot of records. We're not saying number one record, smash hit, a Grammy, we're just saying we've got a hit.' However, as soon as that record came out, the world changed. It was one of those things where you sit back and go 'Wow!' You just love it."

In fact, radio deejays had started showing an interest in "All I Wanna Do" earlier in the year, when they turned to the *Scenes from the Tuesday Night Music Club* four-song promo for a follow-up to "Leaving Las Vegas." This resulted in A&M asking Bill Bottrell to remix "All I Wanna Do" in a couple of shorter versions for radio, prior to its eventual release on July 12, 1994. The biggest-selling single of Sheryl Crow's career to date, it spent six weeks at No. 2 on the *Billboard* chart, climbed to No. 4 in the U.K., was certified gold for American sales in excess of 500,000 units, remained on The Billboard Hot 100 for thirty-three weeks, and was the top Adult Contemporary song of 1994. That September, the *TNMC* album climbed to No. 8 on The Billboard 200.

"'Leaving Las Vegas' impacted alternative, and that got everyone's attention," says David Anderle. "Then 'All I Wanna Do' came out, and MTV and radio decided that Sheryl was the way to go. We had that magic thing that you can never plan: the hit single happening at the same time as Sheryl was really grooving with the live act. It was perfect. It was absolutely perfect."

Unfortunately, what was less than perfect from Sheryl's viewpoint was the "All I Wanna Do" video, which had been conceived in the same way as all of her promos around this time: Meeting with head of Creative Services, Rich Frankel, she'd name the videos that she liked and be provided with the sample reels of directors Frankel ascertained he could get. Sheryl would list what she considered to be the best work, and each of the related directors would then be asked to write a treatment for her video. Al Cafaro, Rich Frankel, Sheryl, and perhaps even the product manager, Kelly Mills, would take a look at these treatments. They'd discuss them, make suggestions, and try to agree on who should get the job. However, it was usually a tortuous process.

"It could take weeks," says Cafaro. "Making videos is a tough thing, because although it's a very collaborative process, it's your ass that's on the line as the artist, and it takes a while to get your sea legs in that setting. Even then, for some artists it's always a challenge, and I don't know that it really corresponds to the creative aspect of the artist either. Sting was the same way; videos were a pain in the ass.

"It's amazing to me how often you end up with things that you didn't expect, and we've all been really, really shocked by videos from time to time. You know, having read treatments, having seen storyboards, it's like 'Huh?' It's a very imperfect process, and if an artist wants to be involved it can be risky, because either you get involved all the way and say yes and no with confidence and then act on it, or you can really be driving a director crazy.

"Sheryl would do the work, but we did have some moments, and we even had a moment for 'All I Wanna Do.' She hated that video. I remember being in the trailer with her at the Woodstock II festival, and it was terrible. She just threw a fit, although it wasn't a tantrum in the sense of any silliness, and ultimately I made the call that we were using the video. To some degree she may have taken an attitude towards me because of this, but I believe she always felt that I was in this with her."

Again directed by David Hogan, who had certainly delivered the goods for "Leaving Las Vegas," the "All I Wanna Do" video was an altogether cheesier affair, featuring Sheryl and her band playing for small change in front of a boarded-up "Roxy" theater. Once more there were numerous close-ups of Sheryl's face and mouth, as well as some bodies floating overhead, but this time around the results were less intriguing than just plain ridiculous.

"I do remember looking at the video myself and thinking, 'What the fuck are all those people doing, floating around up there?'" Cafaro admits. "Sheryl hated it, and I think we took those people out, but that was also a problem. I didn't want to take them out, because that's the way the video was made. From experience I felt like once you take an element out of something that's weird, it can make everything else look really crazy, and that's one of the things I was talking to Sheryl about at Woodstock; 'You're looking up! What are you looking up at?' We were in a trailer, and she was walking around that trailer like the caged animal in the [1996] 'If It Makes You Happy' video."

There were four different versions of the "All I Wanna Do" video. In the final one, the floating people were reinstated. However, this was by no means the last time that Sheryl and the record company would lock horns over videos and photo shoots.

"Photo shoots were a pain in the ass, videos were really, really difficult, and around those kinds of situations she would be very conflicted, because I don't know that she ever really got what she wanted out of it," says Cafaro. "Every now and then we'd have a meeting and I'd have to make certain things clear. You know, 'We've exhausted our options, we can't not have a video. I understand how you feel, but I don't think it makes you look bad. It's non-negotiable.'

"She would ultimately always get there with you, and I think a lot of it had to do with the fact that she wanted to know you believed so fiercely, that you were willing to go to the wall. And I think she trusted me enough to know that if I went there, then I was there because I had to be there, and at some point that was good enough for her and she could walk away. I don't know that we ever really had a situation that was like, 'Shut the fuck up, that's the way it's gonna be! Get the fuck out of my office! We're not talking about it again!' We never really had any sense of estrangement or difficulty in dealing with each other."

Al asserts that, aside from conveying his own opinions, he'd always listen to Sheryl's, not only because she might tell him something he didn't know, but also because she was the artist with her face in the video and on the album cover. Then again, what to do when a meeting might end with Sheryl seemingly accepting his dictum, only for her to return the next day and resume her original stance?

"It drives you crazy," he concedes. "It definitely drives you crazy. But it's interesting, because I remember those things much more fondly than one would think. It's those moments that somehow make it all worth it, because you are sort of engaged in a struggle and you really have to care. You can't browbeat her, and that's one of the things I respect so much about Sheryl. There were times, I guess, when it sort of wore me out, but I'm sure she changed my mind on some things."

"It's tough," adds David Anderle. "And she's tough. I mean, you can have a conversation with her and you can say, 'This is blue,' and she's gonna go, 'No, it's not blue.' 'Sheryl, I swear to God that's blue.' 'It is not blue.' You go on and on, however long it takes, and then finally you go, 'Sheryl, this is blue,' and she'll go, 'Okay, it's blue, but it's the wrong blue. It's not the blue I want.' There have been moments where I've thought, 'You know, I'm not going to put up with this shit anymore,' but then when I've calmed down I've said, 'Of course I'm going to do it, because I really believe in her.' It got to where I wasn't sure I wanted to work with her, but I've never stopped believing in her.

"I understand how fucked up you get with yourself if you can't get what you want— 'Why can't I get this right? I don't understand.' People are going, 'Oh man, that's beautiful!' and you're going, 'No, it's not beautiful. It's bullshit!' I understood that about Sheryl, and I always found myself saying, 'Of course I'm going to get on the phone and deal with her, because she's going to deliver, and I understand her frustration.' As mad as I've gotten with Sheryl, every time I see her I always remember how much I like her. I like her a great deal, but I also can understand how people might have negative perceptions of her. She could really put somebody over the edge.

"I believe Al loves Sheryl. I mean, we would have meetings about her that were really heated, and it was all because we believed so much in her. Not just the fact that we were going to have a hit record—that was not the thing—but she was really making interesting music, and it's always fun when you have an artist who's making really interesting music and selling records too. Al and I worked very hard with one another regarding Sheryl. You know, there were times when we would try to figure out how we would approach her on a certain little thing, to get her to understand what we were thinking, without seeming like 'the record company.' We were very sensitive about that. And then sometimes you have to be 'the record company.'"

Meanwhile, once "All I Wanna Do" became a hit, Sheryl's tour band began to see the changes. All of a sudden, the RV and trailer were replaced by a couple of tour buses and an 18-wheeler truck. And if an important TV assignment came up at short notice, they'd take to the skies.

"We were on the H.O.R.D.E. tour, and we were told to fly to New York and take the Concorde to London in order to take another plane to Frankfurt to do this show called *Love Over Gold*," Todd Wolfe recalls. "The German A&M people were saying, 'You've got to do the show. This is really gonna sell the record,' and we did it. We deviated from the tour—at least we got to fly on the Concorde—and after the show we took a direct flight from Frankfurt all the way to Seattle to meet up again with Blues Traveler. Well, you know what, the album went platinum after that gig in Germany.

"Back then, if you told Sheryl, 'You need to do this and you need to do that,' she and Scooter would go over it and really give thought to certain things. She did a lot of what she was asked to do, and I think that's part of the reason for her success. She was willing to do those things, to work her butt off and go here, there, wherever. We deviated from the tour to do [the VH1 celebrity golf tournament] *Fairway to Heaven,* and then we deviated from that to do the *Love Over Gold* show."

What's more, Sheryl and her band, together with Blues Traveler and the Allman Brothers, also took a quick break from H.O.R.D.E. to appear in front of 300,000 people at the aforementioned Woodstock II festival in Saugerties, New York, on August 12 to 14 of 1994. Performing on the first night, Sheryl managed to avoid the mayhem that ensued on the final day when Green Day took to the stage and became embroiled in a mud-slinging war with the audience. Instead, she just benefited from having her name appear on the same bill as Aerosmith, Blind Melon, The Cranberries, Melissa Etheridge, Peter Gabriel, Metallica, and the Red Hot Chili Peppers.

The success of "All I Wanna Do" changed everything. It placed Sheryl on the musical map, it provided her with a sound and image for the public to latch onto, and it projected sales of the album into the stratosphere. Suddenly, Sheryl Crow was the hot new talent of 1994, and as is necessary in all such situations, it was very much a case of the right person in the right place at the right time: a female rock artist with a country tinge, reminding a generation about its favorite music, now updated, in the wake of rap, hip-hop, and grunge.

This was the upside to the story. However, for every positive image there's a negative counterpart, and in Sheryl's case the professional triumph comprised just one aspect of her life at this time.

CHAPTER TEN

# Metaphorically Incorrect

*"No one tells a lie after he's said he's going to tell one."*
—The Commoner in *Rashomon*

If ever the *Rashomon* analogy is pertinent to the story of Sheryl Crow, it's when trying to explain the demise of her relationship with the members of the Tuesday Night Music Club. Everybody involved has a different version of events.

Over the years, it's generally been reported that Bill Bottrell and his colleagues felt shortchanged by Sheryl taking most of the credit for the creation of her album, and that they retaliated by vilifying her in the press. This is both simplistic and largely inaccurate, however, for while there were some shared opinions and common problems, each of the TMC members had his own grievances and only a few of these were aired publicly.

Misunderstandings, miscommunications, misrepresentations, defensive postures, and fragile egos left the doors wide open for spin doctors and media shit-stirrers, and when the crap hit the fan everyone got spattered, some worse than others. Still, despite all the rumors, assertions, and supposed insinuations, there were no outrageous crimes, and none of the participants revealed themselves to be either sinners or saints. This was simply a case of human beings behaving like…human beings. In line with most disputes, the causes can appear trite and petty to those not involved, yet for the people who were caught in the eye of the storm, the pain and aggravation were very real, and numerous lives were never quite the same.

As previously mentioned, the TMC guys weren't exactly enamored with the methods or—as they perceived them—motives of the major record companies, and there had already been a certain amount of tension between Bottrell and a few of the execs over at A&M. Nevertheless, the first real conflict involving Bill and Sheryl took place when, in the company of Kevin Wall and Betty Bottrell on Saturday, May 8, 1993, he handed her a cassette tape of the finished album during a meeting at the Ben Franks diner on the Sunset Strip.

"Sheryl and I had our moment of truth that day," Bill recalls. "Her attitude towards me changed right in front of my eyes. She had waited and waited for the record to be completed, and the company had been calling, and I'd been saying, 'It's not done, it's not done.' Now finally it was done, and I was saying, 'What are we going to do next?' I don't remember her exact response, except that there were three sentences rejecting my further involvement. Then, holding the cassette copy, she said, 'This is all I've got,' implying I had everything whereas that's all she had. In fact, that was all I had too. The previous three sentences had been something to the effect of 'There is no next. There's no more us. We're done.'

"Kevin Wall had called me to set up that meeting, we'd talked, and towards the end of the conversation he said, 'So, what are you doing next?' You see, there was no next for me. Looking back I can understand that, but I hated the way they handled it, because I felt that Sheryl took whatever she could get from me. She never said no to an idea, be it musical or conceptual or dress or hairdo. She never said no to anything. She took whatever I had to offer until she had the product in her hand, and then she rejected everything I had to offer.

"She shouldn't have taken only what she wanted from me and abandoned all of the other stuff I had worked so hard for. She took from me a sound and my knowledge of twenty years, and it was her job to do that. There was nothing wrong with that, it was my job to give it to her, but she consistently, actively rejected the other part of everything I was doing, which was the philosophical part and the economic part—I wanted to make a hit record and change the record industry, maybe even the world a little. She wanted a hit record, period. She wanted to do the big record industry thing, like the Hugh Padgham album, and she kept that a secret for a year while working with me. She pretended to play along with all of these ideals I had, and then as soon as she had the product and the power she did an about-face. She had the power as soon as she had that product. I could have hemmed and hawed for another year and not turned it in, but she got it and she abandoned all those ideas. You know, to see her at the opening of the Hard Rock Café saying, 'and I won't be leaving Las Vegas until you get here…'—it was heartbreaking."

David Baerwald would have his own problems with Sheryl. However, these didn't relate to music-biz philosophy nor to feeling duped by what she appeared to believe in and whom she purported to be.

"Three songs into that album it was clear," he asserts. "I mean, saying that Sheryl Crow is suddenly going to ascribe to those views is like saying Al Gore is going to join the Black Panthers. It's just not going to happen. I pretty much knew that the first time I saw her, the day we wrote 'What I Can Do For You.' I grew up in L.A., I know a lot of actresses, and there's a certain kind of thing you see in people. She was dressed all in white, and I remember saying to my girlfriend, 'Uh-oh, here comes another one of those.' Which is nothing against any of those people. Most successful actors or show-business people have that. It's not my favorite human characteristic, but what are you gonna do? So, I wasn't pissed off at her for selling out. What could you expect? Selling out wasn't even in her vocabulary. What was she selling out?"

For his part, David Anderle points to a middle ground between Sheryl's motives and Bill Bottrell's expectations of her—a gray area in which the producer thought she'd bought into the entire pro-music, anti-corporate TMC package, and in which she might have thought so, too, until the end of the project brought her overriding ambition back into focus.

"Sheryl is driven," asserts Anderle. "She is the most driven artist that I've been around, which to me is one of her great strengths. During the course of making that record, when they were all there night after night after night, we know what happens in that situation. I've been in that situation. You get into a family environment, you get into an us-versus-them, you get into all that kind of stuff, and if she got into that then I'm sure at the time she was totally into it. And then, when the record was done and it was time for her to get her career going, I'm sure she switched straight into 'This is my career, and I'm gonna do what I'm gonna do to get it going.' Meanwhile, Bill was perceiving this as his Tuesday Night Music Club dream realized, and it was an absolutely no-win situation.

"Her dream was always to be Sheryl Crow, and now she had a chance to become Sheryl Crow. If that's a fault then that's a fault, but we as a label really worked hard to make sure that happened. Sheryl to me is a scrambler. She was always searching for musical answers, and she probably still is to this day, and probably will forever. She needs to be with other musicians who can offer her things. A lot of times Sheryl has to hear music before she can make a judgement on something. She's an absorber, and when somebody is that way there's a tendency to see them as users, because they are, but that doesn't mean they're a negative user. Also, once they get what they want they move on to the next thing, so people see them as abandoners, which they are, but that's not a bad thing.

"Sheryl has her idiosyncratic way of dealing with people, which is kind of bizarre at times, and it leaves a lot open to interpretation if somebody wants to think 'She doesn't care about me anymore.' And she may not, but she also may; she just has to keep moving on. She always needs to have something new musically come into her life, and I think sometimes she gets so absorbed with that, that she may not see the big picture. She may not be aware that maybe this is going to hurt somebody. She is very unsure creatively until the pieces are all there and she can work with them, and then she starts to get really secure. The only thing is, when people work with you they need to know that's the way you are."

Judging by her own statements on the subject, Sheryl is aware of the contradictions that were perceived in her behavior, but apparently not as cognizant about how these might have been avoided. As such, she casts herself as an unwitting victim of circumstances.

"That record really represents a lot of darkness and a lot of pain," she stated in an interview that was published in the September 2001 issue of *Esquire* magazine. "And it was really a blessing and a curse. We were looking back on life with a sense of defeat and a feeling of grandiosity—like we're better and we don't even wanna be successful, because if we're successful, we've become one of them. And then I became successful and I became one of them. And there is no way out of that."

It wasn't until several months after the showdown between Bill and Sheryl at the Ben Franks diner that Dan Schwartz learned about it from Betty Bottrell. According to Betty's version of events, Sheryl had shown up late, spent twenty minutes yelling at Bill in front of everybody there, and then walked out. If this was an exaggeration, it was enough to piss Dan off.

"I called Sheryl up," he recalls. "I said, 'You're out of your fucking mind! What are you doing, calling Bill to a meeting and screaming at him?' You see, in the period between when that supposedly happened and when I was told about it, all I'd heard from Sheryl on the phone from St. Louis was 'You and Bill and Judy are my only friends in L.A.' However, when I confronted her on this, her response was, 'Dan, you and I are too good friends to talk about this.' To me that was like a closed loop. What the hell did it mean?"

It could have meant that, while Bill and Sheryl were struggling to remain on cordial terms—the record company, after all, expected them to collaborate on her next album—she didn't want to involve Dan or have a falling-out with him. Dan now agrees that's a possibility, but at the time he didn't take it that way.

"I felt that it was totally disingenuous and I felt that it was deceptive," he says. "It was an end-of-communication statement and I didn't speak to her for nearly a year. In June of '94, I saw her at Bill and Betty's anniversary party. It was a Saturday night, and Sheryl came right up to me and made small talk about my daughter who'd been born the previous Monday. I'm sure she thought there'd be hostility, because there had been no communication between us and she'd also been so hostile to Bill all through that year, but we made five minutes of small talk and I realized this had nothing to do with anything I care about. I went over to Bill and said, 'Count me out.' That was in June, and in October of '94 she phoned and left a message saying, 'We're starting my second album. I hope you'll be coming down to write songs and play bass.' There was no way."

Still, even before he confronted Sheryl about her treatment of Bill at Ben Franks, Dan had observed what he considered to be ominous signs about Sheryl's approach towards the music and her subsequent attitude towards him. He soon discovered that he'd made some crucial mis-assumptions.

"The issue of friendship is something I fault myself for," Dan remarks. "In late April of '93, about ten days before the record was handed in, Sheryl came over to my house and we drove off to a bunch of places, attempting to buy guitars for her work on the road. At this point she and Kevin were breaking up. He was constantly fighting with her, and from what I understand he was telling her things like 'This isn't your album. You're just the singer on it.' I remember driving east on Ventura Boulevard and her saying, 'Why doesn't Kevin get it? We're a family. It's my turn now, next time it will be Kevin's turn. Maybe then it will be Bill's turn or David's turn again. Maybe it'll even be your turn someday, Dan. We're a family.' I was in heaven, you know, because this person's a good singer, she's a good friend, and I just love the idea that we're a family, that I've finally found a band.

"By the end of that project, I, for one, had completely believed that we'd uncovered the true Sheryl Crow; that she'd either become what you hear on the record as a result of Bill teaching her, or that he and the rest of us, like some sort of head surgeon, had liberated these essential things from inside her. However, once we saw her sing the songs live, it was completely obvious that we'd just believed our own bullshit. At least, I had."

In early September, Sheryl and her road band arrived in L.A. to prepare for their first West Coast gig, opening for John Hiatt at the Coach House in San Juan Capistrano. As a nod to the collaborative force behind the album, Schwartz, Gilbert, and Bottrell would sit in for a couple of the numbers, yet there was immediate friction when they showed up for the rehearsal at SIR Studios on Santa Monica Boulevard. To their ears, the material was being reproduced neither accurately or adequately.

"The band was lousy and Sheryl was adding all of this blues riffing to 'Run, Baby, Run,'" Schwartz remembers. "It sounded terrible, it was out of tune, and she was singing as if that whole album just hadn't been done."

The Coach House gig took place on Tuesday, September 7, and Todd Wolfe recalls it as "a terrible night. Oh man, I didn't dig that! There was a lot of tension because the guys who made the album didn't like us or the way we played, and it was a real drag to play such a nice venue in a beautiful part of California and have that vibe going on."

When it was time for their onstage contribution, Schwartz, Gilbert, and Bottrell replaced their touring band counterparts for a performance of "Run, Baby, Run," with Kevin on drums, attempting to reproduce his playing on the record. The results were less than spectacular.

"The piano, for some reason, got unplugged, and the whole thing just sort of fell apart," Schwartz recalls. "This was Sheryl's first gig in California, but there was no inner musical drive. At this point I still wasn't pissed at her, but I was really getting nervous. Like 'We just did this great record. What's going on here? How could you be singing it this badly?'

"The next day, Judy [Stakee] called and said we wouldn't be needed for that night's gig at the Roxy, and for me it was a relief. I told her, 'I'm really concerned.' She said, 'What is it?' and I said, 'This band sucks. They can't play the music. They're getting it all wrong. The way they're playing the notes they might as well be reading them off paper. There's nothing happening here, and Sheryl's singing with no inspiration and no energy at all. I'm just afraid that they're going to go out there and that's how they're going to represent this record.' A few hours later I got a phone call from Sheryl saying, 'Dan, I don't need this! What I need now is support!' I said, 'Sheryl, I'm not gonna lie to you. I'm not gonna tell you that I think this is all really great. This is all really terrible and it needs to be worked on to make it great.'"

Bill Bottrell remembers that at the Coach House gig, some of the A&M reps objected to the use of TMC members in the stage lineup.

"They were most likely giving their true opinion, because it didn't look right," he says. "You know, 'We don't want to advertise a band. We want to advertise Sheryl Crow.' I understood that. However, they left it all up to her to handle, and it was brutal. On the day of the Roxy gig the guys were told, 'You're not going to do it,' and it was demeaning to each of them. They had stopped everything, rehearsed, gone down to San Juan Capistrano, and played on a couple of songs, and this was a real power-play slap in the face. The whole idea had been to try them out for a guest spot at the Roxy, and it was a brutal way to treat them. I think she was just setting them up for a fall."

Then again, given the pressure that Sheryl must have been feeling at this time—to repay the record company's faith in her, to make the most of her big opportunity, to lead a band for the first time and deliver the goods from center-stage—it's not hard to understand why she'd exclaim "I don't need this" in the face of criticism from the likes of Bottrell, Baerwald, Gilbert, and Schwartz. She'd made her choices regarding the live band, and for better or (in the view of the TMC members) for worse, she now had to get on with doing her own thing. For Sheryl, this amounted to giving the songs a rockier feel as a means of trying to attract audiences. For her *Tuesday Night Music Club* collaborators it amounted to musical sacrilege. The members of the touring band, who never had anything to do with the record and who'd been recruited to provide their own interpretation of the material, were caught in the crossfire.

"For the first eight months to a year, Bill and some of the other cats always had a problem with the way we were playing the music," says Todd Wolfe. "Our attitude was 'We're not those guys.' In the beginning we would try to tread lightly and go, 'All right, how can we get it like that?' but if we'd try to do that it would lose everything. It didn't translate that way. Now, if those guys had gone out and done their thing, they might also have found that they'd take things to somewhere different than they'd done on the album. But, as they were sitting back and watching us, and as Sheryl became more popular, they would really get critical. They'd go, 'Well, they're not doing this and they're not doing that,' but they were talking about different guys who weren't on the record.

"David Baerwald showed up a few times and I know he had his complaints, although never directly to me. We'd hear that they'd been saying we couldn't play and that we were ruining the material. On the other hand, Bill Bottrell would always have his say. He would listen and orchestrate things, and he'd give Sheryl a hard time about singing bluesy. That would annoy him more than me swinging a guitar pattern or playing a bluesy solo. I thought it was crazy. You know, the album was done, and that was another thing altogether."

To this day, Sheryl's former colleagues in TMC have a real problem with this attitude. Indeed, the live band's failure, in their opinion, to do justice to the music is one of the issues which they do all agree upon, and none of them has any qualms about pointing out the shortcomings.

"I went out on tour and I rode with them in the Winnebago, and it threw me entirely when Sheryl didn't want me there because I was commenting on her performances," says Bottrell. "It was me just wanting to help her and the music. I didn't have a problem with the fact that the record company was going to market her as a singer-songwriter. It became a problem later. No, I thought that was the right way to do it, and every way they would let me support that I did. However, I think they waffled between wanting me to go crawl in a pit and stay out of sight, and 'Well, okay, come help.'"

Having sat in for one number when the tour group's original lineup played Boulder, Colorado, back in late August, Dave Baerwald then attended a few of the other gigs. He now regrets this.

"I went to one at the Hard Rock, and it was a really appalling band," he says. "I got really drunk, I'm afraid, and I was watching the guitar player doing all of these blues licks and the drummer twirling his sticks and Sheryl just standing there like a shot dog, and I was thinking, 'God, this is fucking horrible.' All of the A&M corpo guys were going, 'Isn't this marvelous? Isn't this marvelous?' because we were selling records and that's what everybody was thinking about. But I was thinking, 'This is not marvelous. This is a disgrace.'

"You know, it had taken us—especially Bill—a long time to find that sound, and then to hear it turn into this less-than-adequate bar band was pretty horrible. So, I said something about it and Sheryl got really upset. In her defense, she had a tiny budget and a lot of ground to cover. If she had actually hired all good musicians, she wouldn't have been able to stay on the road like she did, and that was how she broke that record, just by touring forever. It took a long time, against all odds, and against all bettors."

Still, while the TMC guys had a uniformly negative view of the stage act, Todd Wolfe believes that any musical problems were not of the live band's making. What's more, he asserts that a couple of months into the first tour, he and his colleagues felt vindicated by the positive audience reaction to their performances.

"There were different agendas and different views," he says. "Sheryl wanted us to put our own interpretation on the music, and of course Bill Bottrell didn't want that, but you can't have it both ways. Aside from Scott Bryan, none of us in the band were session musicians; I'll admit, I'm not the kind of guy you want if you're trying to reproduce this, that, or the other. So, if Bill really wanted the shows to sound like the album, he and the other guys should have gone out and done them. Instead, we were getting shot down by them, and it's pretty sad that there was all this bad blood.

"When that first album came out, I had a lot of people ask me, 'Can she really sing?' and I can understand that, because on the record Sheryl didn't sound like somebody who was a backup singer for Michael Jackson and Don Henley. She sounded like this quirky artist who had her own little thing going on. However, my background is bluesy rock, so that came out when we played live, and she would sing that way. She would belt it more and sing a bit bluesier, and that's why I think we built something during those years.

"People would say, 'Yeah, I love the record, but man, this band rocks!' You know, it was a good album but not a rocking album, and we would rock a lot harder. Sheryl's voice would get a little bit bluesy, and I always thought that was great, but she fought this and Bill fought it. I guess the TMC guys wanted her to be something different, and she wanted to be something different as well. Still, once this unit with Tad Wadhams [on bass] and Wally Ingram [on drums] really started becoming a band, they could say all they'd want, but we were up on our own legs and taking it somewhere else.

"I remember somebody from the label who hadn't heard the live band coming down in the early days when we were in Colorado, and he was like 'Whoa!' because it rocked and Sheryl would sing her ass off. People were always moved by that, and she definitely went with it for a while. We were all like 'Yeah! Let's go! Let's go out and rock!' and we'd always get a good response. The only people who didn't give us a good response were the Tuesday Night Music Club."

This was for a good reason, and one that neither the touring band nor the A&M execs were ever really aware of, because in the final analysis it actually had very little to do with musical ability, a too-bluesy voice, or out-of-tune instruments. Instead, it had everything to do with artistic intent, the creative vision of one man, and that man, Bill Bottrell, watching his dream, the culmination of many years' work, study, and ambition, unravel in steady installments from the moment he delivered the *Tuesday Night Music Club* album through to hearing the material performed in concert.

"It was about 'What game are we in?'" Bottrell explains. "You know, 'Into which ring have we thrown our hats?' The ring our hats were in was the cutting edge of pop music. I'd spent eight years or so trying to play in that ring. From Jeff Lynne in 1980 on, I was hooked. It was the most exciting career I could imagine. I would fail and learn, fail and learn. I wanted to work with the best, and I did.

"You must understand, this is a craft which is time-specific. Highly transitory, very delicate, like trying to spot new particles in physics, and getting them named after you; defining the Zeitgeist, and receiving the power it has to offer. It has almost nothing to do with music. It's more like surfing. Catching the waves of Zeitgeist—there's a feeling when you're in the tube. I spent years waiting for the right wave, my wave, positioning myself, preparing everything. Nirvana had come and gone, Depeche Mode were still on the charts, women were nowhere in sight, the cutting edge was populated by electro-noise bands like Tool and Nine Inch Nails, lyrics were either shocking or high-school poetry, the guitar was a thing of the past. Everything had a scary, lo-fi, Japanese reverb quality. It was still the '80s in 1992.

"The boys of TMC deferred to me because they, too, were into Zeitgeist surfing, and in that area I was the most experienced and the most gifted. They could feel me positioning us, testing, trying. The construction of Toad Hall, the Wire Train and *Triage* albums, were all part of the process, like a slot machine coming up with occasional sevens, though it was accepted that the wave just wasn't there. I'd been a famous player in this field for a decade, and I'd caught a big wave in 1989 with Michael Jackson. I'd used guitars and samplers and loose, free vocals to create his biggest number one hit ever, a sound he'd never made before."

The song Bottrell is referring to is "Black Or White," which equaled the success of Jackson's "Beat It." Nevertheless, by the time of the *Tuesday Night Music Club* project, Bill and his TMC collaborators were focused on catching the Great Musical Wave as well as producing a hit record. It was, in short, a quest to discover and draw on other powers from within the aforementioned tube.

"Sheryl's singing and political ability completed our position," Bill continues. "She was indispensable. But she didn't know any of us were surfing, even though I tried to teach her. Therefore, when Sheryl cut me off the project, I knew I had a problem. She was playing the wrong game! Still, I needed to guide her until she 'got it.' When I saw Sheryl's band live, it was all too clear they weren't even in the game. They were simply playing rock and roll music. Good, bad, it didn't matter.

"L.A. is the Zeitgeist-surfing capital. When Sheryl came to town under triumphant circumstances to play the House of Blues [on October 28, 1994], it was mayhem. Everyone was there. Everyone wanted in. They needed to check it out. I stood on the balcony and watched the buzzing crowd and felt the excitement before she came on, but then it took two songs for that audience to turn from the stage and start talking and ordering drinks. They knew. She was merely a rocker-chick, and I felt the universe flip. My work of craft, my statement on Zeitgeist, my wave, my attempt to harness power in the name of purity, in the name of—ironically—music, became, within seven minutes, un-hip."

"This nails it for me," says Dan Schwartz. "It gets to the essence of everything I felt and why I didn't want to continue."

"Sheryl would eventually learn the craft, sometime between my quitting her second record and the release of 'If It Makes You Happy,'" adds Bottrell. "A nice ride!"

The problem was, while Sheryl may have comprised the indispensable final part to the TMC equation, from the very start of the project she, Bill, and the record company were operating at cross-purposes. Utilizing the contributions of some like-minded musicians, Bill had continued on his voyage of discovery to the point where the *Tuesday Night Music Club* album was the logical next step, yet Sheryl hadn't been a part of that evolutionary process. She came in cold, without a sense of direction but with a very definite purpose—to turn her own career around, which is the sole reason why A&M asked Bill to produce her record. To that end, she was fully committed to the sessions, but there was little chance that, during the course of a few months, she'd truly buy into a philosophy that had never been hers in the first place.

Still, this was by no means the only issue. When Sheryl and her band hit the road in the late summer of 1993, there were already plenty of hurt feelings and struggling egos, and the troubles were quickly exacerbated by events surrounding the filming of her first video. The promo for "Run, Baby, Run" would include shots of Sheryl performing with her band. The question was, who'd be in that band?

Initially, Sheryl asked the same TMC guys who had played at the Coach House—Bill Bottrell, Kevin Gilbert, and Dan Schwartz—to don sharp clothes and turn up at the production offices on Fairfax Avenue, where they were scheduled to meet the video's director, David Cameron.[1] This they did, even though Dan's future wife Elin, a wardrobe stylist, ran into the video's stylist the day before and saw her picking costumes for professional actors.

"The director didn't show at the meeting," Dan recalls. "He simply sent his flunky to take our pictures. Afterwards, when we got out into the parking lot, Bill said to Kevin and me, 'Something's funny here. They don't put people like us in videos.' Well, the next day I got a call to book me for the video, then a few hours later the cancellation call came in, and that night I got a call about it from Sheryl. I got less than twenty-four hours' notice, so I told them, 'Well, fine, but you've booked me for this, so you've got to pay me.' I happened to know that the actors had already been picked, so why even go through with this?

"We all had a huge investment in the album. We all wanted it to be successful, and without those videos it never would have been. However, what are the videos? They're

---

[1] *The "Run, Baby, Run" video would subsequently be reshot by David Hogan and released in April 1994, incorporating just a small amount of the David Cameron footage.*

what we did, together with somebody else's images. They had nothing to do with the band. Sheryl's success was strictly tied to putting images of her to us playing. It wasn't rock 'n' roll, it was the gesture of rock 'n' roll. There's this perverse notion—and this is not Sheryl's fault, this is Sheryl's choice—about being one of the ascendant pop consumable items of the '90s. There's a whole level at which you simply have to play the game, and what is the game? The game is full of gesture. It's like the director of the video for 'Run, Baby, Run'—'What do the musicians who make that record look like?' Well, they evidently don't look like *me*. I'm actually one of those people, but that doesn't fit in with the marketing. I think Sheryl was pushing for more reality and asking for us to be in the video, but I remember hearing that the director wanted the band to look like the Allman Brothers on the cover of *Live at the Fillmore East*."

Bill Bottrell's take is slightly different. "You couldn't have orchestrated things better if you wanted to start a war," he says. "I think I know what the overall motivation was regarding Sheryl, Al Cafaro, David Anderle, and these guys. It was 'They have to go away. They've got to shut up and they've got to stop existing for a couple of years while we promote this record.' It was a lot to ask of them, and the video episode was just a passive-aggressive way of achieving the same thing."

Anderle states that he never knew about the Tuesday Night Music Club concept—about the collective nature of the work, or Bottrell's vision of an ongoing project that would produce further records, featuring varying permutations of the same artists under his own direction—until after the album had been delivered. As far as the label was concerned, Bill had simply been hired to produce an album for A&M artist Sheryl Crow, and to that end several musicians had been recruited to perform as the band. When Anderle learned otherwise, he suddenly found himself dealing with a sticky situation—Bill had already experienced Sheryl telling him that the album was solely her baby, and the record company was now doing the same thing.

"I was so impressed with what Bill had done," Anderle insists, "and so happy that he'd saved my ass! Coming in about $7,000 over the $200,000, he'd done an amazing job, and I therefore called him after the record had been delivered to see if we could meet and work out some sort of a production deal. At the same time, he'd been on the lot, having plenty of meetings with people in other departments, and they'd been calling me and saying, 'Bill Bottrell is the producer. Why is he in my office talking about the artwork?' So, I had also called him in to talk about that, and I said, 'I don't know if you should be doing this,' and I think he was very confused. Then he explained to me that the Tuesday Night Music Club thing was his concept, and that he saw this as being his idea and his record, with Sheryl as the lead singer, and I went, 'Oh, my God! I had no idea!' I remember just sitting there with my mouth open thinking, 'Oh my God, do we have a problem!'

"I totally understood why Bill was so upset. As far as I knew, the album had been named by Sheryl. It came in as *Tuesday Night Music Club* and that made sense to me. However, this was where the trouble happened, and everything from that point on went downhill. We, the entire A&M crew, were focused on our artist, Sheryl Crow.

Until Bill told me about it in my office, no one had the slightest idea that this was anything other than Sheryl's album, and everything we did was based on that assumption. When I told Al Cafaro, he was shocked too, because we couldn't figure out what was going on with Bill.

"I hate the Bill Bottrell part of the story, because it was such a misunderstanding. For my part, maybe if I had been in the studio more I would have seen what was going on, but until Bill explained things to me in my office that day.... I'm surprised I didn't break my jaw, it fell so far. I was so taken with what he told me, I was shocked. I just hired a guy to make a record, and he made a great record.... He thought he'd made *his* record! And I remember saying to him, 'Man, we didn't sign you! We signed Sheryl. It's her record. I understand your problem but you've got to get over it.' In fact, I even tried to find out if we could change the title of the album. I'm telling you, I felt bad for Bill, because I know what that's like. That's his dream, and he thought he had it. I don't recall if I ran the idea of changing the title by Sheryl. I may have run it by whoever was managing her at the time."

Bottrell contends that this recollection is way off base—that he and Anderle met more than once, that their initial discussion related to the producer's dealings with Sheryl, and that the A&R chief wasn't all that supportive.

"The whole 'jaw-dropping' thing is totally false," Bottrell insists. "There were no jaws dropping. There were two meetings with David Anderle after the album was turned in. The first one was at his office, soon after the debacle surrounding the Coach House and Roxy shows. I went to him, as the guy who had hired me, and I tried to explain why I needed to stay involved in the project. I wanted him to support me. Sheryl was going to the label, telling everybody I was getting in the way, and they took her at face value, having no way of knowing what an insidious smear campaign she was waging. I explained this to Anderle. I said, 'She is too inexperienced to run her own band and show.' I said, 'She needs me,' but he settled back in his big office chair, raised both hands over his head, and said, 'I can't help you.'

"The second meeting with David was much later, probably after success was in the bag. We met at Farfalla, a restaurant down the street. I wanted to pitch the idea of A&M signing the Tuesday Night Music Club. This had nothing to do with Sheryl. He was very cold the whole time and non-committal. He said he would take it up with Cafaro. When I heard nothing back after several weeks, I called. He said he still hadn't talked to Cafaro. A couple more months went by and this time he told me I had to wait because Cafaro went off to Harvard Business School for a couple of months. Probably nine months after our initial meeting I called again and he said, 'Okay, let's do a deal. But there's one condition: you have to fire your lawyer and use ours.' Obviously, that wasn't an option."

Bottrell also asserts that, from day one, he never had any misconceptions that he was making a Sheryl Crow album. In fact, he says, he'd encouraged A&M to promote it as a singer-songwriter's record, but what he'd never expected from either her or the label was the extent to which they subsequently acted upon this, pushing everyone else out of the picture.

"There was no way I ever intimated that the album was anything but a solo album," Bottrell maintains. "What does it matter who named it? I named it in an attempt to increase the profile of my band within an atmosphere of complete war. It was a defensive move. I was very surprised Sheryl accepted the suggestion, given the climate of all-out battle.

"I'd had a conversation with David Anderle six to eight weeks into this project, when there were three or four songs down on tape. I said, 'We're making what sounds like a singer-songwriter album, and you have to promote this as a singer-songwriter album to the public, but in fact we're all writing and it isn't really that kind of album,' and that's exactly what they did and they did it with a vengeance. They needed her to be a singer-songwriter to her fans, and she needed to be a singer-songwriter to her fans, and she needed to live up to lines about being born in November of 1963, on the day Aldous Huxley died, but she couldn't fucking live up to that!

"However, as Sheryl's proved on her albums since then, she does have the goods to be a great singer-songwriter. Creatively, song-wise, and vocal-wise, she was totally lost when she walked in through my doors, but she learned a lot during the year I worked with her and she took that and ran with it. You know, L.A. is just crawling with people who are like her when she first met us, which is not to say they don't all have the potential to be great singer-songwriters. They do, I suppose. Things can be learned. You're not just born with it, and I don't think there are any geniuses."

Kevin Gilbert was the next to vent his anger. Depressed over the unraveling of his relationship with Sheryl, and resentful of all the attention she was getting in comparison to his own lack of recognition as a solo artist, Kevin went out of his way to stress that *Tuesday Night Music Club* wasn't her album.

"Kevin was the kind of guy who, as long as he was in control, things were okay," says Patrick Rains, an artist manager who befriended Gilbert in late 1992 and signed him to his small PRA Records label. "When he wasn't, they always got rocky. He was a very troubled guy who felt that life hadn't dealt him a fair hand, and as Sheryl's record finally started to click, that seemed to be the thing that finally flipped Kevin over to the other side."

As Sheryl became more and more involved with her career, she had physically less time to spend with Kevin and emotionally less time to invest in his concerns. By the end of 1993, their volatile relationship was basically over, yet their real troubles were just about to begin.

"Because of his experiences, getting burned on some prior projects, Kevin was always wary about being exploited and not credited," says a close friend and associate who wishes to remain anonymous. "He was extraordinarily worried about that happening with TMC. He was a very sweet guy, but Kevin had a big ego, and rightfully so. Then again, he wasn't crazy on how he perceived Sheryl being manufactured and packaged as a star. That definitely bugged him, especially as everything appeared to be flowing so smoothly while his own solo record had stalled, and it also wasn't helped by the fact that, as soon as their relationship was over, she became romantically involved with [an artist development/marketing executive] at A&M. Kevin was kind of aghast."

Accordingly, when Sheryl appeared to be taking credit for the writing of "Leaving Las Vegas" during her debut appearance on *The Late Show with David Letterman* on March 21, 1994, it was like the red rag to the bull. Having performed the number, she sat down with the host for the obligatory two-minute interview that closes out the show: "Hey, great song! What's it about?" That kind of thing. In this case, Letterman asked if "Leaving Las Vegas" was autobiographical. "Yes," came the answer, before Sheryl then compounded the white lie by saying, "I've never been to Las Vegas. I wrote it about Los Angeles. It's really metaphorical."

"As soon as I said the word 'yes' I was doomed," Sheryl later told *Rolling Stone*. That she was, at least with regard to a couple of people who were watching the show. Gilbert, for one, went ballistic, calling Sheryl on the phone to rant about what he considered to be grand deception and a sure sign of her ingratitude for all that he'd done. It was, in short, a complete overreaction to a fairly innocuous event.

"It went by me," says Bill Bottrell, who played guitar and sang backup on the Letterman show. "I was as nervous as she was, thinking 'Oh, what's she gonna say?' and it went by. However, that moment sort of summed up the entire two years, before Sheryl was huge, before the album started selling. It summed up her and everybody's motivation at the company to pass her off as the singer-songwriter who did this work."

"She slipped up, and then it was just spin, spin, spin, spin, spin," agrees Dan Schwartz. "Nobody was willing to say, 'Get off her back!' It was her first national appearance and she was nervous. I didn't have an issue with it."

Nevertheless, another person who did have a major problem with Sheryl's appearance on *The Late Show with David Letterman* was John O'Brien. The deeply troubled author, whose book title had been used for that of the song "Leaving Las Vegas," had asked for an acknowledgment in the album credits, but despite requests made on his behalf by David Baerwald, that never happened. Now, tanked to the gills, sitting in a bar-restaurant called Hal's near his home in Venice Beach, O'Brien saw the TV broadcast and flew into a rage. Baerwald, who also frequented Hal's, later heard about this from the bartender: "John was in here, flipping out over some TV show. He went completely insane."

The next day, O'Brien was arrested for drunk driving. His father drove him to Baerwald's house, also in Venice, where he pounded on the door. Baerwald, who divided his time between two homes, wasn't there, so O'Brien left him a rambling, bile-filled phone message and went on a prolonged bender which ended on April 11, two weeks after the film version of *Leaving Las Vegas* went into production. That day, John O'Brien turned a gun on himself and ended a life long on despair.

"I don't think anything at all having to do with this Sheryl Crow business was even one block in the foundation of his suicide," O'Brien's father later told *Rolling Stone*, while John's sister described "the problems that drove him toward the end" as "a long, long bloody trip."

By the time that David Baerwald checked his phone messages, it was too late to call John O'Brien back. "I turned on the machine," David recalls, "and there was John saying, 'You sonofabitch! You sold me out, you bastard! I can't believe you sided with these Hollywood creeps! You of all people! Blah, blah, blah, blah, blah....' I was thinking, 'Whoa, John, relax man,' and I tried calling him back, but he'd already killed himself. All I knew at the time was that he wasn't answering his phone.

"I'd seen Sheryl not that long before in Colorado. I called her up and said, 'Sheryl, listen, you can't do this kind of shit to these civilians. It's just wrong. The guy shot himself.' I hadn't seen the Letterman show, so I wasn't exactly sure what had gone down, but that's when she said, 'Maybe you should talk to my attorney.' I said, 'What? What do you mean? Call him about what? What are you talking about?' She was cold as ice. I was actually at my mom's house, I was sitting on her porch, and I just put the phone down and went, 'Wow! This is something else!'

"Then, the day of John's funeral, I was driving down the road and 'Leaving Las Vegas' was on the radio. There was this little blurb with Sheryl lasciviously saying, 'Hi, this is Sheryl Crow! I won't be leaving Las Vegas until you come to the Hard Rock Hotel & Casino....' It was the day of his fucking funeral, and I was thinking, 'Oh man, this is vile! This is so fucking disgusting! This is just gross!' You know, 'What the hell is this about? Are you some kind of stripper?'"

In her 2002 interview for VH1's *Behind the Music*, Sheryl asserted that she was actually very upset by John O'Brien's death. "I still have trouble with the song, because I know that somebody out there killed himself because of how bad his world was," she said. "It kills me still. It really bums me out."

This comment doesn't convey any awareness of the real reason for Baerwald's anger, which pertained to his earlier request for his friend's name to be included among the album credits. Prior to the record's release, he insists, he'd stated this in writing; there should be something along the lines of "a very special thanks to John O'Brien."

"That was all John wanted," Baerwald explains. "He didn't want money, he just wanted recognition."

However, when the album hit the stores, O'Brien bought a copy and immediately noted that there was no "thank you," and no mention of either him or his book.

"He called me all hurt, as he should have been," Baerwald remembers. "So, I said, 'Uh, let me look into it,' but I had a sinking feeling. I called Anderle and said, 'Hey listen, you've got to put this goddamn credit on the record. It's part of the deal.' He went, 'Oh yeah, no problem, Dave. It was just an oversight. It'll go on the next pressing...' and this is where I get mad at myself, because I knew he was lying to me. I mean, I asked him, he said he was going to do it, and the guilt I have is that I knew he wasn't going to do it. But what could I do? This was one of the top guys at the label, and he already thought I was a nutcase anyway. They were already pissed at me just because I had spoiled a promising pop career by turning into such a raving conspiracy-minded lunatic. Still, instead of calling him up, I should have gone and jumped up and down on Anderle's desk."

In 1996, David Baerwald would vent his anger about John O'Brien's death in an article that he'd write for the *L.A. Weekly*. This, in turn, would lead to media reports that Baerwald had, by implication, suggested that Sheryl was in part responsible for the suicide—another example of how she was being annihilated by her bitter former colleagues in TMC. Untrue.

In fact, after briefly describing his friendship with O'Brien, the novelist's drinking problem, how the song "Leaving Las Vegas" was conceived, and why O'Brien died angry at both him and Sheryl, Baerwald concluded by stating: "Life goes on. And now they made a movie out of it. Cool. I hope it's a better memorial than that goddamned song. I'm not saying that John wasn't hell-bent on suicide from the first day I knew him, or that I or anyone is responsible for his death. He just didn't have to go away mad. Not at me."

"Hardly anyone saw that article," Baerwald asserts. "Basically, there was all of this hoopla about 'Leaving Las Vegas' and nobody said a goddamn thing about John. It was like he never lived, and that was his big hang-up. He felt like he didn't exist. He just wanted somebody to say, 'Yeah, John, you're in the room! You're there, buddy! I see you!' but that never happened, and so I wrote this article in which I said that, because of Sheryl, John died mad at one of his best friends and left me with that forever. It would have been ridiculous to suggest that she was responsible for his death. She was just trying to promote her record."

By this point it didn't matter. Dave Baerwald had some heated exchanges with both David Anderle and Al Cafaro, and this only served to confirm his reputation as a loose cannon. Not that he cared.

"I guess I was pretty belligerent in those days," he says, "because by then I didn't have much respect for Al Cafaro, and I really resented David Anderle's smug, hypocritical, lying corpo bullshit. He got really, really mad with me, and it's because I wasn't with the program."

Indeed. On one occasion, Baerwald quipped that the next time he saw Anderle it would probably be down the barrel of a shotgun. At the same time, Cafaro wasn't exactly harboring warm feelings towards Baerwald either, especially after being physically shoved by him during one of their encounters.

"I responded to the Baerwald aspect of the whole situation, because I was very conflicted about David," Cafaro admits. "I mean, David is an extraordinarily talented individual; a brilliant guy, absolutely brilliant. His two solo records for us could be just about as good as anything that I've been associated with in the deepest sense of quality. On the other hand, he was just a wacko of a guy, and in my judgement I would say that to his core he felt that it should be him, not Sheryl, because this was a guy who wanted it as badly as she wanted it."

"Bullshit," is Baerwald's terse response. "What I did want was not that. What am I going to do? Sing songs about being a feckless, carefree girl, smiling in the face of adversity? I can't do that. Those lyrics were written specifically with Sheryl in mind, using her experiences and the persona she was developing."

Together with the negative vibes being privately communicated by some of the other members of TMC, this kind of bad blood served to place a big fat target on the band's collective forehead. Then again, hardly helping in this regard was Kevin Gilbert, who by constantly sniping at Sheryl for taking too much credit, was apparently affirming what her defenders assumed was the true motive for everyone's unhappiness.

"Here we were, off and running; 'All I Wanna Do' was a huge record, and then after that we came back with 'Strong Enough' and 'Can't Cry Anymore,' and we were rocking," Al Cafaro recalls. "But then all of this other noise started coming up with the guys who made the record. I was always perplexed by it. To me, Bill Bottrell was the producer of the record, and I thought he did an incredible job. I was very grateful for the job that he had done. I knew that there was an association with everyone and that there was a collaboration, and to me the issue was all about crediting and payment. However, it was always my understanding that we were paying for a Sheryl Crow record. No one ever talked to me about this band called the Tuesday Night Music Club. I've got no reason to slag Bill, but he was a pro, he'd been around, so to some degree it might be disingenuous for him to think that we were going to hear this as a group project.

"There's no question that the creative process is one where the strongest survive. Certainly, in the commercial process the strongest survive. And although music is less collaborative for the most part than other commercial artforms like film and TV, there's still an element of collaboration in it, and at the end of the day I do come back to the adage that the only way to keep score is credits and money. That's really how I always choose to deal with it. You know, 'Were you credited? Did you get paid?' Well, you know what, if you were credited and you got paid, I don't know what you can really complain about. I can understand that you might personally have a problem with it, but to say to a third party that you were wronged doesn't seem right."

"We were never bitter about the credit or the money," counters Dan Schwartz. "Never in private, never when we were working together as TMC, was there ever any grousing towards Sheryl about insufficient credit or insufficient money. The crux of the matter has to do with what's important in life. That's where the essential division is. I saw this as a friendship, as a musical collaboration, as something that was life-enriching, as well as something that might earn us money as musicians, but what I then saw was the emphasis change completely so that all it was about was creating the celebrity who can be marketed. To that end, the real partners were the record company, which was interested in the money, and Sheryl, who was interested in the celebrity and the success."

Not too surprisingly, Al Cafaro has a different outlook on the commercialism, citing that it simply reflected the process of a record company trying to fulfill the potential of a brilliant record.

"It seems to me that what you want to do is get into a place where you expose as much of the art—and I will call it art, because that's what I believe it is—to as many people as you can, in a forthright, responsible fashion," Al explains. "If you go for the easy way first, you might not get to the nuances, but by rolling it out properly—and this wasn't as consciously brilliant as some people would like to make it seem, it was a process of discovery—we got people to hear a lot of this record. Having said that, I always saw the Sheryl who wanted to be huge. I saw her as intrinsically musical, and I saw her as a star. So, I will give the guys their due, in that record companies want stars, absolutely, and we wanted Sheryl to step up and deliver."

This she certainly did, although Dan Schwartz maintains that what he and some of his colleagues found unacceptable was the manner in which the delivery took place.

"*Tuesday Night Music Club* was a great record," he says, "and there should have been no problem with the truth of how it was made, except for the ego that ties in with the belief that after Dylan and The Beatles it was no longer cool for an artist to not be a writer. Here was this album of songs based around Sheryl, very little of it written by her but some of it written with her, and she provided a great voice on these great tracks. We were all playing as good as we could play, in an intrinsically human style, and she was singing beautifully, but somehow that was not enough. It was 'I have to be the sole creator, I have to be the creative mind behind it,' and that was a psychological problem. Now, whether that was a psychological problem coming from Sheryl or whether it was a fear coming from the likes of Al Cafaro, David Anderle, and [publicist] Diana Baron, I don't know."

David Baerwald, like Dan Schwartz, makes it clear that any anger on his part had nothing to do with songwriting credits or payment. In fact, at a time when grunge was still at the rock forefront, he didn't expect the TMC record to do all that well.

"I thought it was a really good record that would probably sell 300,000 copies to people who missed the '70s," he remarks. "I had no idea it was going to turn into this huge thing. I was used to making records that flopped no matter who wrote what, so I could care less about the credits, but Bill said, 'You know, we've got to give Sheryl publishing on songs because she's so in debt to A&M for the Hugh Padgham record. She's going to need tour support and all that stuff, and she's not going to be able to support herself if there's no publishing.' So I was like, 'Sure, what the hell?' I mean, whatever. After all, it was her energy. We were doing this and that, throwing words around, and Bill was fixing everything we did anyway, so it wasn't a big deal.[2]

"When I finally realized that this was going to be a record, I thought, 'We shouldn't be credited as writers, because it's just going to look like Sheryl's some puppet, and that's foolish.' To this day I really think we should have been credited for the purpose of royalties, but not on the album credits. I think it would have been a lot cleaner, there would have been far fewer public suspicions, and the record company would have been a lot less paranoid. If it had said, 'Produced by Bill Bottrell. All songs by Sheryl Crow. Thanks to John O'Brien and Wyn Cooper,' and if the royalty checks had been the sole representation of the truth, none of this would have ever happened. I wish we'd done that. I mean, like Bill said, you don't see Bill Casey running up on stage, saying, 'Hey, I wrote

---

[2] On VH1's Behind the Music, Sheryl stated, "I made the same money on that record that everybody else did, so my karma's clean." However, sales and publishing royalties were not distributed equally. Instead, Bill Bottrell ensured that on a song credited to multiple writers the percentages were commensurate with their respective contributions, or even weighted in Sheryl's favor as an incentive for her to sell the record and repay her debt to A&M.

that speech for Ronald Reagan!' What kind of idiot does that? Casey and Reagan are on the same team. They understand their positions."

Unfortunately, one person who apparently didn't understand his own position was Kevin Gilbert, who found it difficult to avoid or comprehend Sheryl's celebrity in the form of TV appearances, press interviews, or even a giant billboard high above the Sunset Strip. "How can she be hailed as the 'female Van Morrison of the '90s' when she's only written a small percentage of the songs?" he'd demand of anyone who took the time to listen. What he evidently couldn't—or wouldn't—grasp was the fact that, when TV producers are being pitched about why they should feature an artist on their current affairs show, they don't usually care about who the songwriters are.

Kevin had been instrumental in championing Sheryl's cause, introducing her to the Tuesday Night Music Club, and therefore helping her on the road to success. However, it was unrealistic for him to expect her to acknowledge this in public, even if in private she yearned for his approval—for an approval that was never forthcoming, because Kevin wasn't exactly free with the compliments. It was an unhealthy situation, and one that became decidedly unpleasant when he and Sheryl started to take phoned and faxed swipes at one another.

"While we were doing this tiny little tour to promote [his solo album] *Thud* in 1995, Kevin did a radio show in L.A.," recalls his aforementioned anonymous friend and business associate. "They were talking about how great TMC was doing, and how great he must be doing, having helped write a bunch of the songs, and Kevin said, 'Well, I haven't seen a dime yet.' It wasn't like, 'Oh, I'm being ripped off,' it was just that he hadn't been paid yet, but Sheryl went ballistic. She somehow tracked us down to a Best Western on the outskirts of Seattle and sent a fax along the lines of 'I heard that radio show where you said that I'm ripping you off! I'm gonna sue you! You can't say these kinds of things!'

"It just got really bad, and then there was the relationship stuff that I'd hear in the form of phone messages left at his studio. She'd leave about twenty messages and there'd be ten hang-ups on the machine. It was really ridiculous, and it got to be a joke: 'Oh, Sheryl's in town.' At the same time, I can't tell if Kevin was calling Sheryl a zillion times, because he never did it around me. For that matter, he probably wouldn't do it around me or anybody else."

Dan Schwartz points out that following a talk with Kevin after the *Letterman* show about where things appeared to be heading, they never discussed his problems with Sheryl again. However, in the eyes of numerous others, Kevin continued to wear his heart firmly on his sleeve, and he couldn't dispense with his anger over feeling used and abused by his ex-girlfriend. At times it was even as if he was haunted by Sheryl—when hundreds of crows descended on Kevin's Lawnmower & Garden Supplies studio and started tearing the roof off, manager Jon Rubin and engineer Garry Creiman had to disperse the birds by shooting at them with pellet guns. On a bathroom wall at the same studio, a black-and-white photo of Sheryl was superimposed with text that, while clearly a joke, still gave a fair indication of where Kevin was at:

Have Some Fun With
SHERYL CROW!

1. Bundle her into a sack with several starving ferrets and half a dozen bricks, then throw it in the canal!

2. Snatch her handbag off her and lob it into the tiger enclosure at Aspinall's private zoo, so that she gets mauled to death trying to get it back!

3. Steal a gnome from her garden, then tour with it all around the world, sending letters to her affecting to be from the gnome bragging about what a good time he's having, with photos enclosed of the little fellow in a variety of exotic locations wearing cool shades!

4. Hire a helicopter and circle low around her house in the early hours of the morning, playing "All I Wanna Do Is Have Some Fun" at full blast on repeat mode!

5. Affect a stutter and try to sell her double-glazing over the phone. Remember—be persistent!

6. Tie her to a tree and throw fresh cow pats at her!

7. Break into her house, commit suicide in her bath and make it look like murder!

8. Study the Koran for several years, convert to the Islamic faith, rise through the clerical ranks until you become Ayatollah, then declare a fatwah on Sheryl Crow on account of certain anti-Muslim sentiments you have perceived on her latest album, forcing her to spend the rest of her life in hiding from murderous extremists!

Similarly caring statements about Sheryl would also make their way into the lyrics of a couple of Kevin's songs. In the 1994 composition "Leaving Miss Broadway," posthumously included on the album *Live at the Troubadour,* he can be heard singing about "the sexual harassment that follows you around," serving as a means "to clear the deck for some new prospect that you've found." While in the same number he also mentions seeing this person on TV, taking credit for his work, Kevin actually refers to Sheryl by name in a track on *The Shaming of the True,* the posthumously released rock-opera album that he was working on at the time of his 1996 death. As one of the characters in the ironically titled "Fun," she is depicted at a party, failing in her quest to have sex with any of the L.A. Lakers after they hear that she's already slept with an AIDS patient.

Feel-good music this was not, even if Kevin may have excised these lyrics had he lived to record a finished version. Meanwhile, after the TMC project received five Grammy nominations in January 1995, he and his new girlfriend, playwright Cintra Wilson, turned up at the subsequent awards ceremony in nineteenth-century funeral regalia.

"He was angry about how much credit Sheryl was getting for the record, but he didn't like that record!" exclaims David Baerwald. "He didn't like the music. He thought it was candy-assed, so that's bullshit, and that's just not grown up. By the time we finished that record everybody knew what this thing was. We had Sheryl, who was going to kiss babies. You wanna do that? I don't wanna do that. I don't want to get up at six in the morning and go trade air-kisses with some morning-TV host. I'm not gonna do that and Kevin wouldn't have done that either. She was willing to do that, and more power to her, 'cause sometimes that's what you have to do."

In his 2001 interview with Wayne Perez, Brian MacLeod expressed a similar opinion regarding Kevin's bitterness towards Sheryl for not according TMC enough recognition.

"I said, 'What do you expect?'" Brian recalled. "'Madonna doesn't talk about [co-writer/co-producer] Pat Leonard, but he's making all the money.' That's how I saw it. 'Wow, I got publishing on a record. I don't care if she goes out and kisses babies and says she wrote on everything and played drums on the record. I still get the check in the mail. She's better looking than me. Better to see her on Letterman's couch than me.'…That's why, if you notice, I'm on the second record [1996's *Sheryl Crow*] and nobody else is. I felt bad for her and Kevin breaking up. Kevin was one of my closest friends, so I was bummed out about that. But I wasn't bummed out about her promoting the record."

On March 1, 1995, Sheryl was a triple winner at the 37th Annual Grammy Awards, scooping up the prizes for Best New Artist and Best Female Pop Vocal on "All I Wanna Do," which itself was named Record of the Year. Nevertheless, the celebrations were tinged with no small degree of tension.

"Bill went up for the 'Record of the Year' award, talked about the band, and took over as if it was his thing and not Sheryl's award," David Anderle recalls. "That pissed off a lot of people. I, too, was angry at Bottrell for doing what he did, but I understood where he was coming from. I had hoped that it would work out nicer, but I also understood how he was very proud of that record."

"I certainly had no interest in humiliating Bottrell, and that was for a lot of reasons," adds Al Cafaro. "I mean, I wanted Sheryl to do the next record with Bill. He did an amazing job, and that's why another part of me was sad about all this—that Bill couldn't enjoy it, and I'm not faulting him for this. I felt bad for Bill. I really did. The other guys I didn't know at all, except for Baerwald, and Baerwald I wanted to strangle! No question about it, and I said it to David. He showed up to accept the Grammy, in his bad fuckin' suit and tie, and I busted his balls that night!"

"He's right," Baerwald agrees. "It *was* a lousy suit."

According to a July 1 feature by Giles Whittell in the *Times* of London, A&M's head of Artist Relations, Bob Garcia, stood outside the label's neo-Tudor HQ, welcoming guests to a post-show party, and when asked why he thought Sheryl Crow had managed to make such a successful record with the Tuesday Night Music Club following the shelving of her first effort, Garcia replied that the other TMC members "happened to be very wonderful hanger-outers, that's all."

Things would continue to get worse. On Saturday morning, May 18, 1996, Kevin Gilbert was found dead in his Eagle Rock home, just north of Los Angeles, by friend and manager Jon Rubin. Wearing a black hood and skirt, his head resting on a leather strap chained to the headboard of his bed, Gilbert had succumbed to autoerotic asphyxiation, depriving himself of oxygen while heightening the feeling of orgasm. Whether this was misadventure or suicide would remain open to question. At Kevin's funeral service, his brother would recall how, from early childhood, Kevin had always lived on the edge, always pushed the envelope. This time he'd pushed it too far. He was just twenty-nine.

Immediately there were articles in the press in which the usual variety of "sources" speculated that it was depression over the falling-out with Sheryl that led to Kevin's demise. However, nobody who actually knew him—not even Cintra Wilson, who turned on Sheryl at the memorial service and growled "Run, baby, run,"—would lend any credence to the salacious gossip.

"For Kevin the glass was always half-empty," says Patrick Rains. "He was a brilliant musician, very talented, but a very, very dark individual, and it's in his music. He himself would admit that he was manic-depressive, and during the time that I was associated with him he started taking some anti-depressants. He would go from one extreme to the other."

Sheryl herself wasn't surprised by Kevin's death. "As long as I've known him, he's struggled with life, as if every single event in life was out to bring him down or trip him up," she told *Rolling Stone* a few months later, while in the November '99 issue of *Playboy* she described how she "loved Kevin, but he was a really unhappy person. He was unhappy when I was with him, and nothing I did made him any happier. I've never seen anyone more at odds with the universe than he was—not even me. Kevin's death was a colossal waste of a young and talented mind, but he just wasn't able to help himself. I knew exactly what he was going through, because I've gone through that myself. I was a good Missouri girl, raised in the Bible Belt, and all I wanted to do for a long time was just end it all. If I couldn't get a record deal, if the industry disillusioned me, if I felt unhappy, well, then I just wanted to kill myself. It's not really that you want to kill yourself, though, and I don't think that Kevin wanted to kill himself when he died. You just want to get rid of what's making you so sad. It took five years of therapy for me to stop making the same stupid mistakes and find a strong identity. Kevin never got to that point."

Sheryl was accompanied by "Solidify" co-lyricist Kevin Hunter to the memorial gathering at Bill Bottrell's house. There she spoke cordially with Dan Schwartz and David Baerwald, before running into Cintra Wilson, who was sitting next to Brian MacLeod.

"I felt really bad about that," says Baerwald. "It kind of went by before I even caught it. We were all kind of sitting around the table being unbelievably depressed, and Sheryl came over and she was upset. However, Cintra—who couldn't fucking stand Sheryl, she hated her guts—just started yelling at her, and Sheryl took off. I remember thinking at the time, 'That's pretty harsh.'"

"The whole situation was sick," adds Dan Schwartz. "Kevin's parents were there along with Kevin's friends, Kevin's fans, and people who didn't even like Kevin, and then over on the other side of Bill's house there were all of these business people who had no regard for Kevin, and they were doing business! They were schmoozing with each other and doing deals at Kevin's fucking wake!"

What's more, Gilbert's death would continue to be exploited, and his name abused, in a number of newspaper and magazine articles. One of these, written by Joel Selvin for the September 22, 1996, edition of the *San Francisco Chronicle*, used his interviews with Bottrell, Baerwald, MacLeod, and Schwartz—all taken down in shorthand—to help paint a picture of a tragic figure and his ungrateful protégée. As paraphrased by Selvin, Kevin and his "Tuesday night cohorts" described Sheryl as "a marginally talented singer who exploited his skills and theirs in a ruthless grab for success."

"Everybody was equal except Sheryl," Baerwald was quoted as saying. "She wasn't one of us. We helped her make a record."

"I add Sheryl Crow to a long list of people in Hollywood who told me they were my friend until they got what they wanted from me," was one of Dan Schwartz's alleged contributions.

"I thought Joel Selvin had come here to talk to me about Kevin, but he was trying to talk to me about Sheryl," Schwartz now explains. "At the end of the interview he said, 'Well, you don't seem angry at Sheryl,' and I said, 'No, I'm only angry at myself for believing she was my friend.' About a week later, I was listening to the radio and heard Linda Perry, who all of us TMC guys agreed we loved. We'd worked on Linda's album [*In Flight*], and now she was on the radio taking credit for everything. I immediately called Joel and said, 'Here's Linda doing exactly what you've accused Sheryl of doing. You can't have it both ways.' I was defending Sheryl, but Joel took my statement and twisted it."

"That guy should be writing for the *National Enquirer*, or for porno movies," adds Dave Baerwald. "Selvin came to me and said, 'I want to do a piece about this brilliant Bay Area musician, Kevin Gilbert,' and I said, 'Yeah, you're right. He was a brilliant fucking musician.' But then he totally misquoted everybody all over the place, including me saying, 'Everybody was equal except Sheryl. She wasn't one of us.' It made all of us sound like the biggest pricks and liars. I called him on it; I wrote him an angry letter, and that was the last I heard of it."

In shaping his article about Kevin Gilbert, Selvin was able to make it appear as if the surviving TMC members were retaliating against Sheryl for a piece by Melinda Newman that had appeared in *Billboard* magazine that August, just prior to the release of Sheryl's second album. Newman reported that Sheryl felt "the very people who had helped push her up the mountain were only too eager to throw her off the top," and quoted her as saying, "There were guys in the group who were feeling bitter about the record doing so well. There's only two of them that struck out at me, [but] I wasn't prepared for it…. Maybe I should have called [the record] something else. I was completely devastated by people's attitudes [toward] it. I'm still not over it."

"My advice to Sheryl was not to let criticism—particularly criticism that comes from a very petty place—get to her," Al Cafaro stated in the same article. Battle lines had been drawn, and while both sides were trading shots, neither appeared to have—or was evidently interested in having—a proper understanding of the other's concerns. At the same time, not only did the record company have bigger guns in its arsenal, but the TMC guys weren't even a cohesive unit. Each had his own gripes; some went public with them and others didn't. Consequently, in a tit-for-tat scrap, they sustained far more damage, not least because it was easy for the press, the public, and Sheryl's supporters to believe that her erstwhile collaborators were simply acting out of jealousy and resentment.

"A few of these folks have even implied that Crow was somehow a factor in the deaths of O'Brien and Sheryl's short-term beau Gilbert," stated a November 30, 1996, *Billboard* editorial titled "Sheryl Crow's Winding Road." "Fans seeing these odd diatribes in assorted U.S. and U.K. publications could be forgiven for wondering if they'd stumbled upon a Hollywood enclave of the He-Man Woman-Haters Club."

Meanwhile, the fact that the truly bad blood between Sheryl and her former colleagues was spilled just before and after the release of her follow-up to *Tuesday Night Music Club* left them with the distinct impression that this was not only a case of damage control, but also a means of actually publicizing the new record.

"I don't know who was the mastermind behind what I refer to as 'marketing the second album on our backs,'" says Dan Schwartz, "but on the face of it this was down to Al Cafaro and Sheryl. You know, 'Why isn't Sheryl working with TMC? Because they're greedy, they're bitter over who got the credit, they're assholes....' The fact of it is, by that time TMC would not have welcomed her back. I mean, you can take all the credit you want—that's normal—but you don't have to be dissing us in the process.

"People behaved so badly. My God, they were attacking Kevin after he was dead, and yeah, Kevin was not a perfect human being. I had fights with him all the time—sometimes we were really good friends, sometimes we weren't—but for Chrissakes he's dead, leave him the fuck alone! Slagging off Kevin Gilbert, who's dead, just to push more units of Sheryl Crow product—that is morally offensive. What I'm expressing is not bitterness, it's about what choices you make in life.

"At the time of Sheryl's second album, there was a reference by Chris Willman in the *L.A. Times* to her being unfairly dissed. I called him up and said, 'If you're going to say this stuff about us, why don't you talk to us?' and his response was, 'Well, Diana Baron, the head of Publicity at A&M, is a good friend of mine. It would never occur to me that she's lied.' So, here we have the *L.A. Times*, in its role as the local paper of record for the entertainment industry, getting lines fed by the head of PR at A&M Records, and the journalist never bothers to call up anybody from TMC and say, 'Look, what's your side of the story?' Sheryl's backers evidently felt that there was a need to constantly create spin around her, but there was no need! The truth was totally fine, so the fault was down to either Sheryl's psychology or A&M's fear of not sufficiently perpetrating the myth of the singer-songwriter."

Interestingly, *L.A. Times* and *Entertainment Weekly* contributor Chris Willman had even popped up in the previously mentioned TMC-related article by Giles Whittell in the *Times* of London. Described as a "seasoned observer of the L.A. music scene" who thought that the TMC guys were "suffering from simple sour grapes," Willman had been quoted as saying "Worse shaftings have happened. Maybe they expected too much."

When asked whether, in defending his artist against what appeared to be a series of attacks in the press, Al Cafaro opted to crush the offenders by retaliating with bigger guns and orchestrating a press campaign against TMC, the former A&M CEO can't recall specific examples. On the other hand, he doesn't deny the possibility:

"I would say absolutely that I would've been very aggressive about 'Hey, wait a second….' I probably would have asked David [Anderle], 'What's the fuckin' problem here?' You know, 'Bottrell produced the record, he got paid for the record. The guys who were on the record got credited and got paid. What the fuck is the problem? I mean, if there's a problem, fuck 'em!' And I'm absolutely certain I would have said that. Now, I wouldn't have said, 'Fuck these guys! Go get 'em!' but I absolutely would have said, 'Shit, we've got to defend Sheryl. If people are going after her, we've got to be there for her.' Everything about me, my instincts, would have been to defend the artist.

"I would like to think that there would have been a line beyond which we wouldn't have crossed. I guess whatever was written speaks for itself in that respect, but it was written by other people. It did seem monolithic at times, referring to Kevin Gilbert's death and so on. Whether or not it was shoddy journalism, I'm sure it contributed to the controversy. However, I believe that relationships are complex and I don't believe that there's only one view of the world, and I wish all of the guys nothing but the best, because at the end of the day they really did contribute to something that was very special."

Nevertheless, the man who played the biggest and most vital role in this regard, Bill Bottrell, now rejects any notion of a collective Tuesday Night Music Club entity. Several people did work together on the album, but they only did so for a very short time, their contributions differed, and their recollections are varied…all of which brings us back to *Rashomon*.

"People keep saying 'They,' but there is no 'They,'" Bottrell asserts. "There was Kevin, who was a jilted lover and felt abused; there was Baerwald, who had betrayed his friend and needed to put the blame somewhere else and tried to put it on Sheryl; there is a different story with each person, and there is no 'They.' The only time there was a 'They' was this two-month window when there was a slight chance that we might have been the band to go out on tour with her. That was a perfectly legitimate little back-and-forth play, and that was the only time it was 'They.' There is no 'They.'"

Instead, there were a bunch of I's: Bill Bottrell and Dan Schwartz were aggrieved by how Sheryl turned her back on the TMC ideals once she took delivery of the album, as well as the manner in which she was marketed as a singer-songwriter to the exclusion of everyone else; Schwartz was disappointed that Sheryl wasn't the kind of friend that he'd assumed her to be; Kevin Gilbert, hurt and angry over the demise of his relationship with Sheryl, resented her success and the credit that she was accorded for the album; and, following John O'Brien's death, Dave Baerwald was mad at the label for not affording the writer his requested credit, at himself for not ensuring that this happened, and at Sheryl for what he considered to be her unsympathetic attitude.

Partly shocked by the anger being leveled at her, partly unreceptive to the criticism, Sheryl mostly caught grief from Kevin, who was unrelenting in his insistence that the *Tuesday Night Music Club* album had little to do with her. When this was relayed to management, Sheryl's friends, and the record-company execs, it tied in with a general assumption that payment and credits were the common problem; everyone within TMC got tarred with the same brush, and the spin doctors were stirred into action. A case of eyes closed, guns blazing, in all directions.

"That was a total baptism by fire for me," Sheryl remarked on VH1's *Behind the Music*. "I was changed after that. I was really, really changed.... When I went out and faced my audiences, I felt very on guard. I didn't want to get too close to anybody, I didn't want to make contact, and I felt in a weird way like the world had changed towards me."

"In the climate that developed, I have never been allowed to say—or been asked the proper questions that would allow me to express—how talented I think Sheryl is and how good she is," states Bill Bottrell, who relocated to Northern California in the wake of the TMC fallout. "There could have been an appropriately viable and truthful and reputable myth created around her that would have expressed exactly who she is, instead of her getting so stressed trying to live up to one that doesn't express who she is. She would have been just as admired as an artist, because she is an admired artist, but the way they worked it—and perhaps, from its humble beginnings, the way I worked it, although I never intended it to turn out this way—meant that she has to live up to things that she doesn't want to live up to.

"What I learned from that experience is to not go searching for a new artist to make records and try to start a career. I mean, having gone through that, I tell you, the super-stars were a pleasure! At least with Madonna and Michael you know where everybody stands and why. Everybody's earned their position and you fit in a spot. The way I did it with new artists, with this sort of cooperative let's-all-share approach, didn't work at all, and hopefully I've learned that lesson."

"It just about killed all of us," David Baerwald concludes. "Even Bill, who was a really well-established guy. I mean, forget about me. It's like when all this stuff went down, someone asked me, 'What do you do after this?' and I said, 'I don't know. What does a gunshot mule do? You just bleed, that's what you do.' For me, I always loved hearing Sheryl sing, and I wish to God all of that other shit hadn't gone down."

# CHAPTER ELEVEN

# *Strong Enough*

During the twelve-month period that began in September 1994, Sheryl had more on her mind than just the bad vibes and angry words that were flying back and forth between her and several members of TMC. For one thing, she had to deal with a packed schedule of publicity and concert assignments; for another, she had to find the time and the way to get together with Bill Bottrell and start work on a follow-up to the multiplatinum *Tuesday Night Music Club* album.

That year, the record sold in the region of three million copies domestically (the current figure is about 4.37 million, and more than nine million worldwide), and Sheryl set off on a fall tour of the U.S. in order to capitalize on this success as well as that of "All I Wanna Do." Again building on her following without just playing the major markets, she and her band performed at venues that ranged from an audience capacity of 840 at the Varsity Theater in Baton Rouge, Louisiana, to one of 5,000 at the Aragon Ballroom in Chicago. The public response was uniformly good.

"Detroit broke big and Chicago broke really big for her," says booking agent John Marx. "Atlanta was a good market, Dallas was a good market, New York was a great market. With alternative music reigning at that point, and with the type of music that Sheryl was performing, it was important not to package her with Jackson Browne and Kenny Loggins and those kinds of people, because then alternative radio wouldn't have touched her.

"We always tried to frame Sheryl with more cutting-edge artists. Even in the beginning, she'd worked with The BoDeans and with Big Head Todd and the Monsters, who were a hippie band at that point. A&M was very, very sensitive to the way we were booking her. Larry Weintraub was the voice for the company back then, and he and Jim Guerinot were very careful in terms of making sure that we stayed online with this and didn't package Sheryl with older acts."

Nevertheless, in front of more than 65,000 people at the Rose Bowl in Pasadena on Saturday, October 8, Sheryl did make the most of an opportunity to open for The Eagles. Then, in New York on October 18, 19, and 20, she supported Bob Dylan at the Roseland Ballroom, before performing "Live With Me" alongside the Rolling Stones during a show at Miami's Joe Robbie Stadium that was broadcast worldwide via pay-per-view on November 25.

"Sheryl really wanted to work with Bob," Marx comments. "By that time she'd already become established, so it was okay for her to appear with him and with The Eagles. After all, The Eagles were a huge band and it was their first comeback tour, so the dates that she did with them were important. Sheryl had already been receiving play on alternative radio, and the shape of who she was as an artist had already started to take form at that point."

Not that everyone who paid to see her was necessarily interested in Sheryl's artistic shape. "All the way through my set I had a guy yelling, 'Take your top off! Show us your tits,'" she recalled about one of the Dylan gigs in a 1999 interview with *Maxim* magazine. "You don't expect that from a Bob Dylan audience!"

One way or another, Sheryl was getting noticed. Touring, press interviews, and radio appearances were all helping to raise her profile, and another major aid was the healthy amount of rotational play that her videos were afforded on MTV and VH1. The symbiotic relationship between Sheryl's records and videos really helped establish her name, and in this regard she certainly caught a break when, in September 1994, Wayne Isaak quit his job as A&M's Executive Vice President of East Coast operations to become Senior Vice President of Music and Talent at VH1.

A middle-of-the-road MTV offshoot, VH1 was in the process of overhauling its image and targeting a different audience from that which had previously tuned in to watch the likes of Kenny G, Michael Bolton, and Anita Baker. Ratings for the music programming had been in decline, and a nightly comedy hour didn't help—it was as if viewers were being told, "We're a music channel, but here's some comedy to keep you going!" Something needed to be done, and when John Sykes rejoined MTV Networks as its president, it was with a view to making VH1 more relevant as well as more fun to watch; to go for a more active, adult-contemporary music audience that enjoyed the hard-rock sounds of bands such as Stone Temple Pilots together with the R&B-flavored pop of an artist like Des'ree. To this end, Sheryl Crow would be a perfect fit, helping to open up a new landscape, a new environment that separated itself from the grunge, rap, hip-hop, and extreme alternative that teenagers were into at the time.

"I was saying to myself, 'Look, this 25-to-35-year-old audience that we're gonna shoot for, they're gonna be looking for some music that's kind of theirs,'" Wayne Isaak recalls. "As a result, I pushed to get behind Sheryl Crow, Hootie and the Blowfish, Blues Traveler, and eventually Jewel, Joan Osborne, and people like that. These made sense. They were great younger artists, they were in their late twenties, early thirties, and they played music that had contemporary production qualities while harking back to some great rock 'n' roll.

"When I unofficially started working for VH1 that August, we decided to have this celebrity golf event, and we wanted to have a concert, so we just decided to get our young up-and-coming artists. We booked Sheryl, who was the brightest—she was the headliner—but we also added Hootie and the Blowfish, who were really good, and Toad the Wet Sprocket. At any rate, that's where we were headed, and we were also still willing to play the classic rock—The Who, the Stones, and so on. We wanted to entertain a mid-twenties to mid-thirties audience with music that was really up their alley.

"VH1 was certainly into Sheryl, and I came in and flipped the switch on her. We pushed, and she made a lot of fans. John Sykes liked her from the get-go. It wasn't even really much of a decision at that point, and she was one of our first choices as 'Artist of the Month.' We wanted to put the image out there that 'Hey, we do help break new music, we do have new artists on the channel, and this is an artist that you're gonna love if you're twenty-something or thirty-something. You're gonna love Sheryl Crow.' That's how we used it at that point. We got her to do some things, some interviews, and we did a half-hour show with her. 'Artist of the Month' isn't a given. It's a strategic weapon, if you will, or a tool that we'd use to image the channel and highlight an artist."

In both respects, it worked. Sheryl's popularity soared in line with VH1's ratings, and this was boosted by some very astute planning on the part of her manager, Scooter Weintraub, and her booking agent, John Marx. Basically, from 1994 through early 1999, Sheryl's headlining concerts would mostly be staged at venues with an audience capacity of just a few thousand people—to date, she's never headlined an arena tour. Yet, she would consistently appear at very high-profile events—Woodstock II in 1994, the Lilith Fair tour of 1997, and numerous other multi-star tribute and benefit concerts that were aired on TV—where she'd share the stage with superstar artists who certainly did head-line arena or stadium concerts. In 2001, Sheryl would even be on the bill of *Rock in Rio III,* which would attract a worldwide television audience of around one billion people.

Fame by association. It was a sharp move, and one that would help ensure that Sheryl's concert audiences would continue to grow even when the sales of her subse-quent albums wouldn't match those of their predecessors.

"We've always underplayed Sheryl for almost every show she's done since getting out of the saloon-type venues," says Marx. "We've never tried to overreach, and as a result of that her shows have always been full to capacity. By putting on a great show and playing sold-out shows, you keep making those forward strides. Otherwise, you'll try to bite off too much and end up with patrons sitting in venues that are half-full, feeling they're at an event that maybe isn't as cool as they thought. It sends a signal, whether they're conscious of it or not, so when we could have played the Universal Amphitheater, we did three nights at the Pantages. Whatever we do, it's always to create a hot ticket, and we try to look for those events that are going to have national or worldwide coverage. We only did two shows on the first Lilith tour, but Sheryl got a lot of attention out of that. She was on the front page of *People* magazine, and people thought she did the whole tour."

This strategy was still in its early stages back at the tail end of 1994, but Sheryl's star was truly on the rise, even if she had trouble securing a long-term bass player for her touring band. After the quick departures of Eric Hotter and Anders Rundblad, the live outfit appeared to hit its stride once Tad Wadhams joined the lineup. But then, following a New Year's Eve date on the Hawaiian island of Maui, Wadhams was ousted for what guitarist Todd Wolfe tactfully describes as "a little too much of that rock 'n' roll behavior," and thus the bass-player merry-go-round continued to turn.

"Tad had got a little wild and things were starting to get a bit messy," says Todd. "I remember it being a little rough around the edges, and Sheryl wasn't too pleased about that. A few of the gigs had been a bit up and down, but it was kind of tough for all of us, because we really felt that it had become a band."

Wadhams's replacement, Jennifer Condos, came with a recommendation from Don Henley after she'd played bass in his live band. On January 20 and 27 of 1995, Condos performed with Sheryl's road outfit in both Ventura, California, and Park City, Utah, before they reunited the following month to tape an appearance on MTV's *Unplugged*. Filmed at the Brooklyn Academy of Music on Wednesday, February 15, the *Unplugged* performance was preceded by four days of rehearsals at the SIR Studios facility in New York City. Bill Bottrell was there to help with the material, and once again the band members felt the pressure, although for various reasons.

"At that point Sheryl wanted Scott Bryan and I to learn pedal steel, because we were only playing slide guitar to mimic some of the pedal steel lines that were on songs like 'All I Wanna Do' and 'Strong Enough,'" remembers Todd Wolfe. "In the 'All I Wanna Do' video I was the guy sitting behind the pedal steel, and when we did TV shows—usually in Europe—they'd want us to just play to the record. Well, I didn't know anything about a pedal steel guitar, so I'd be wanking around on it, sliding the bar and going 'Yeah!' and everyone would say, 'That's good, that's good.' Then, when I actually learned the parts, I realized your hand doesn't really do a whole lot. It doesn't move around in a lot of different ways while you're doing pedals and kicks, and so at that point I got reprimanded more for not making it look as exciting as I'd done on TV!

"Anyway, I had to learn the pedal steel for 'All I Wanna Do' and 'Strong Enough,' and Scott had to learn it for a couple of more difficult songs, so that was a very tough time. We were making this transition, and then during rehearsals for *Unplugged* Bill Bottrell was there to really help us get it down. This was the last time we ever got the treatment from him, and I don't think it helped matters. It created a lot more tension while we were trying to change the band around. In fact, I questioned if I should even be there. I was thinking of just leaving, because perhaps there'd be somebody much more suitable to do this than myself. So, we had some tough rehearsals, but luckily we pulled it off."

A positive result of the *Unplugged* rehearsals was a new, Bottrell-contrived version of "All I Wanna Do," incorporating a slower tempo and an altogether more laid-back feel than on the record. This worked so well that after performing it on the show, the band stuck with this arrangement for the subsequent concert tour.

"It was really cool," comments Todd Wolfe. "Bill had probably thought, 'Okay, this is what I have to work with; let's see if we can get them to do something.' I remember coming up with my own guitar lick, and we all came up with a little bit of something, and what we ended up with was this vibey song that was the total opposite of how people usually heard 'All I Wanna Do.' Wally played the djembe instead of drums, I played this very atmospheric tremolo type of guitar, and Sheryl would sing it almost like a beatnik reciting poetry, laying across a big old chair with her legs over the arms. The whole thing was slow, smoky, and casual; a case of Bill coming in and producing the live band to do something different instead of trying to recreate what they did on the album."

A couple of months earlier, Sheryl had spent three weeks at Toad Hall, working with Bill on her next album, and they had done the same during January. Also present at the sessions were guitarist Jeff Trott, drummer Brian MacLeod, and on one occasion,

Todd Wolfe. "I'm very comfortable with Bill, and I think that's why Sheryl thought working with me would be okay," says Trott, who'd been in the lineup of roots-rock singer/composer Pete Droge's band when it opened for Sheryl on several live dates. However, given all of the bad blood that had flowed—and was continuing to flow—between Sheryl and her producer, there were tensions right from the start, and it seemed like only a matter of time before the lid would blow off the pressure cooker.

"After the incident at Ben Franks I could never quite get along with Sheryl," Bill explains. "We tried, and we tried real hard. I was making no demands to work with the group that had made the first album. When we started, she said, 'I don't want that TMC vibe or any of those guys, but I'll take Jeff and Brian,' so I said, 'Okay,' and the four of us started working. I was up for that, because I knew the trouble the other guys had caused. We wrote lots of songs working with Jeff and Brian, and on the surface there were no tensions, but underneath there were. I mean, I didn't like myself for being there, but I was trying to play along. I have a history of setting something up, not exploiting it, passing it by, and going on to the next thing, but I didn't want to do that. I wanted to do the second album."

Unfortunately for Bottrell, the December '94 and January '95 collaborations at Toad Hall revealed a Sheryl who, emboldened by her success, was far more assertive than the compliant artist of the *Tuesday Night Music Club* sessions. No longer was she the willing novice who was grateful to be featured on Bill's type of record. Instead, she was intent on largely retaining the direction that he'd provided her with, while also adjusting it to more closely conform to her own tastes and self-image.

"Comments from Scooter Weintraub like 'Well, you know, we really want this to be more alternative-sounding,' amounted to the last thing I wanted to do," Bill explains. "I guess by 'alternative-sounding' they meant grungy guitars, Jeff Trott, and what came out on that video for 'If It Makes You Happy'; a harder look and a harder sound. That wasn't my interest, and so why they would want me to produce the new record beats me. You know, there were plenty of guys who were doing that at the time. Anyway, there was a lot of disrespect coming from the label, and in fact one time when Sheryl and I were in the studio I sent her home. I said, 'Get out of here until this is sorted out!' In the end, we had a meeting and essentially I promised to just do it and make it easy on everybody.

"I was getting shafted by A&M. They were at about three million [units] on the first album, selling lots of records, and they brought me into Al Cafaro's office and said, 'Okay, man, second album, right?' I said, 'Well, yeah, I want to do it.' They said, 'You won't get any trouble from us this time.' I'd had all of these legal and money hassles with them on the previous record, trying to make it for $150,000 and not getting paid. In the end I'd still spent lots of my own money on it, because it was an all-in deal and I only had $150,000 to get us through the year. Anyway, this time around they said, 'You'll get no problem from us,' but when it came time a few months later to do the second album, the legal department's insensitivity and disrespect were terrible.

"I didn't want anything other than the same as I'd got for the first album, essentially, but they were just treating me like shit and I felt like it was coming from Sheryl. She now had more power than ever, and I felt that she was changing things as we went and they were responding to it, contrary to what they'd told me in their office. What they were doing was changing the framework to where she had more creative power, and they wanted to put it in writing. That's never been done with any contract I've been a part of, and it wasn't sitting right with me."

A&M's then-head of A&R, David Anderle, maintains that he wasn't a party to any such finagling.

"That must have been between Scooter and the business affairs people," he surmises. "I didn't know anything about it. We wanted Bill Bottrell to be the producer of the next record, because he'd had so much success with the first record. I'm old-school music business, and I always think that if a cat helps you to do it the first time, then he should get a crack at the second time. We were pushing for that, but we also knew what the problems were. We knew that there were personality problems here, so what do you do? You hope that the personality problems will play out, you hope that people can get above all that, and you hope that they can see the benefit of the creative thing that can happen. Sheryl appeared to go along with it and she had some ideas, but then she has a million ideas for everything anyway."

Part of the problem was that Sheryl's ideas didn't necessarily tally with Bill's, and the fact that he was being contractually asked to conform to her parameters left him with the distinct impression that she was trying to maneuver herself into the producer's chair. David Anderle confirms this.

"She was," he states. "I was insistent with Sheryl that Bill should be the producer. I knew all along she didn't want to do it with him, but initially when she said she wanted to produce her own record I fought her on it. I said, 'You've got to work with Bill again.' I mean, she was hinting; 'I could do it, I could do it.' Being a producer myself, I always felt that if a producer produces a hit record, he automatically gets the next shot."

It was amid this charged, uneasy atmosphere that initial sessions for the *Sheryl Crow* album took place, and, remarkably, several good songs did get written. Three of these—"Maybe Angels," "Oh Marie," and "Hard To Make A Stand"—would make it onto the finished record, although not the original recordings.

"The stuff that we did worked amazingly considering she didn't like me much and I didn't like her much," says Bottrell. "It was two professionals gritting their teeth and sitting down and getting on with it, and it wasn't that bad, because our minds were on the music and the music was coming out well."

As a result of the troubles that were to follow, Bill would hold onto the tapes and the Toad Hall recordings would never be released, including a Crow/Trott composition titled "You Want More" that would be ditched and subsequently covered by Holly Cole on her 1997 album *Dark Dear Heart*.

"Our original recording was really, really beautiful," Jeff Trott recalls. "It had pedal steel and a ton of Sheryl's voice, along with a bunch of airy, multi-layered harmonies along the lines of 10cc's 'I'm Not In Love' and Pink Floyd. I came up with the chord progression and some lyrics, and then Bill took charge of the production and did most of the work on that song, and it sounded really great. However, he paid for the tape and it was his studio, and so when he and Sheryl had their big falling-out the recording stayed with him.

"Sheryl's attitude was, 'If he's going to be that way then fuck the song. Who cares?' But it was really a bummer, because we had a DAT copy of it, and later on when we were going through some of the songs that we'd recorded, we listened to that song and we went, 'Oh man, if there was a way to have that on the record it would just be so amazing.' It wasn't a big song or a big commercial hit or anything like that, but it had beauty written all over it. It was the most beautiful-sounding song I can remember, and it's just such a shame."

Unlike "You Want More," the Crow/Trott/Bottrell composition "Oh Marie" would make it onto the album, although with Steve Donnelly's guitar in place of Jeff's, and drumming by Pete Thomas rather than Brian MacLeod—Donnelly and Thomas have also played together on recordings by Elvis Costello, Suzanne Vega, and Bonnie Raitt.

"That was the one song that I co-wrote but didn't play on," Jeff remarks. "My involvement was that I brought the chord progression into the studio, and then Sheryl just started sketching in some lyrics and ended up working on the song with Bill. Again, after the bust-up, Bill wouldn't release the tape, but I prefer the original recording, not only because I played on it, but also because it had more snap. It was more like a Badfinger song."

"Maybe Angels," destined for pole position on the *Sheryl Crow* album, was composed by Sheryl and Bill as an allusion to personal beliefs and the search for spirituality. "There's got to be something bigger than us," Sheryl would comment in an A&M-contrived interview that was included in the album's press package. "God, aliens, John Lennon, whatever." Meanwhile, at around the same time that Sheryl and Bill wrote "Maybe Angels," they also collaborated with Todd Wolfe and Scott Bryan on "Hard To Make A Stand," a standout number that focuses on a cross-dressing older man who Sheryl encountered at a coffee shop near Toad Hall.

In the aforementioned A&M interview, she described this character as "a really strange-looking guy. Maybe a little demented, I'm not sure, or maybe highly intelligent. But he'd always give you a flower and talk to you at length, and generally it didn't make too much sense. He called himself Miss Creation. He kind of hung around the coffee shop, and one day he wasn't there—they had asked him to leave—and he had slipped a note under the door saying, 'If I'm not here, you're not here.' That was just kind of his way of thinking—I guess it's kind of existential. I just thought it was interesting. There are people in the world every day who are striving to figure out who they are and why."

Musically, "Hard To Make A Stand" opened with a Todd Wolfe guitar riff while Scott Bryan played bass, Bill Bottrell played an acoustic guitar, and Sheryl switched between an acoustic and keyboards.

"I pretty much wrote all the chords," says Todd. "Bill came up with a chord on one of the changes, and the lyrical content I thought was Sheryl's, although Bill apparently gave her some ideas for it. Later on, we got into some stupid crap about how that song should be split."

Later on, in fact, there would be a lot of crap, not involving Todd Wolfe, but between Sheryl and Bill. However, before any of that took place, before the fallout with TMC went nuclear, and before she temporarily revamped her image to match a harder, more acerbic sound, the Sheryl who appeared on TV and in front of concert audiences was very much the fresh-faced, flowing-haired, golden-girl-next-door; the soft-spoken native of a small town down South, who remained close to family and friends, and who took her burgeoning fame in stride.

This was also the Sheryl who the aforementioned family and friends truly knew, far removed from the hard-nosed, self-serving traits that had been perceived by her professional adversaries. When a friend's parent was ill, Sheryl would be the first to make a telephone call, from wherever she was in the world. When an old acquaintance in Kennett couldn't afford costly medical treatment, Sheryl took charge of the situation with no desire for this to ever be publicized. And when she commenced a new concert tour on February 20, 1995, she made sure that the first date was at her alma mater, the University of Missouri in Columbia.

"She performed at the Jesse Hall Auditorium here on campus, and they threw out the red carpet and laid on a huge party for her," remembers Sheryl's former piano teacher, Ray Herbert. "It's amazing how, when somebody becomes very famous, the upper administration says, 'Oh, my God, she was our music student!'"

Prior to this, Herbert had been surprised by Sheryl's persona when he saw her on television. "I didn't remember her being that extroverted," he says, while the girlfriends who'd known Sheryl during her formative years initially didn't recognize her singing voice. "As I recall, she was a classically trained soprano, and so the hardest thing was hearing this new, raspier version," remarks Debbie Welsh. "That's not the voice I remember. It has a different tone and a different pitch from what I was used to hearing, and it took me a long time to appreciate it."

Debbie was among thirteen close relatives and friends who Sheryl ensured were in Los Angeles on March 1, 1995, when she attended her first Grammy Awards show. "It was like the Beverly Hillbillies coming to Hollywood," Sheryl recalled in her 2002 interview for VH1's *Behind the Music*.

At the Shrine Auditorium to see her win three of the top prizes were parents Wendell and Bernice, brother Steven, sisters Karen and Kathy, and even Sheryl's eighty-three-year-old grandmother, all of whom were accompanied by Judy Stakee. In a different part of the venue, Sheryl sat alongside Scooter and her boyfriend, Joe Blake, a screenwriter and film producer whom she'd met while making the "Leaving Las Vegas" video.

"We got there at around one o'clock, and by six o'clock we were in our seats, which were positioned a little way back," Judy recalls. "However, when it got towards the end of the show and the award for 'Record of the Year,' Sheryl kicked Scooter and Joe out of their seats so that her parents could come and sit with her. Then, afterwards, we had two limos to cart everybody to the party, but nobody would separate, so we all got in one limo."

"The vacant limo followed us all night long," adds Brian Mitchell, one of the Kennett friends who'd flown into town. "That may be the epitome of Sheryl and how she values those around her."

"She couldn't actually get us into the Grammys event, so we got ourselves dolled up, we went out for this wonderful dinner, and then we were allowed to go to the after-show party," says Debbie Welsh. "We took a limousine there, and when we arrived, a photographer came up to us and said, 'Oh, you must be the friends who we were told were coming.' I was thinking, 'Do we really look that much like we just got off the turnip truck?'"

Always in close contact with her family, Sheryl had enjoyed less communication with her childhood friends while focusing on her career during the late '80s and early '90s. However, once that career was up and running, she kept in touch more regularly.

"She had control of her life and she was more confident," Welsh comments. "She had her mind set on what she wanted her career path to be, how she wanted to be handled, and she did it. She had a game plan. One thing about people from Kennett is that those who are successful and make it in the outside world are driven. They have to be aggressive to leave and succeed like Sheryl."

"Sheryl's always been very sweet, kind, fun to be around," adds Carlotta Tarver. "It's so nice how she hasn't changed. She and the performer are two different people."

During the weeks following her Grammy success, that performer continued touring while her album peaked at No. 3 on The Billboard 200. Nevertheless, by the summer Sheryl once again had to find a bass player for her touring band. Through the first half of 1995, Jennifer Condos had filled the role on a tour of the U.S., Japan, Australia, New Zealand, Singapore, and Europe, where Sheryl opened for Joe Cocker. However, it wasn't a good fit.

"Jennifer would learn everything note for note, but we were still experimenting," Todd Wolfe explains. "You know, we'd jam without counting the bars before going to a solo. It was like 'Let's just feel it, and we'll know when we want to break into this next part,' but I don't think that's Jennifer's forte, and she also felt like an outsider. She was the one new member in this band, and on top of that she was female. We thought that would work with Sheryl, but Sheryl reacted the same way as us, like there was an outsider within this old family."

Jennifer Condos was subsequently replaced by Spencer Campbell, who'd known Sheryl since they performed on the road with Toy Matinee back in 1991. Campbell would play with Sheryl's band from the 1995 summer outdoor festivals and opening for Elton John in South America that November, through to a small gig in Beverly Hills the following May. Then he, too, would succumb to "outsider" syndrome. Still, the touring experience proved invaluable to Sheryl, who had come a long way since her solo debut at a small St. Louis club back in July 1993.

"She became more confident on stage, as well as a little more consistent and a little bit more professional," recalls Todd Wolfe. "She learned how to work a crowd a bit better, and I think that was partly because the band became a little more efficient at playing in a way that would make her comfortable.

"For Sheryl, I think performing live is easier than the creative process. I mean, she's definitely a great keyboard player and she's definitely a great vocalist, especially backup. I've watched her work in the studio—she's sung backup on some of my stuff—and she'll just hear the parts in her head. Backup vocals are the quickest thing that she'll do on any record; she'll knock them out and nail the parts. However, with the creative process she's always hard on herself. She'll go, 'No, I don't like that,' and redo a song or strip it back down, and that's probably because she's a perfectionist."

Not that perfectionism was obstructing the creative process when Sheryl and Bill Bottrell tried to work on her new album. Rather, it was their largely unspoken mutual antipathy that got in the way, and this was exacerbated when, in the spring of 1995, Sheryl decided to explore an alternative route by recruiting Jeff Trott, Brian MacLeod, and engineer Blair Lamb for a songwriting session at MacLeod's cabin in the Gold Country region of Northern California. Back at Toad Hall, Bottrell had been regrouping TMC for a new project, and in that regard this episode was one of the straws that broke the camel's back.

"We were supposed to get together to make another album," he explains. "We'd waited at least two years for a time when everybody could do it—Brian kept going out on tour, David did a David & David album that got scrapped, and finally everybody was available. We were going to have our band and make our record without Sheryl, and we spent a couple of weeks on it. But on about week three I got a call from Brian saying, 'Jeff, Blair Lamb, and I are up here at the cabin and we're making Sheryl's new album.' Well, they couldn't have invented a greater way to break up the band, and it did. It seems like I spent the decade of the '90s trying to do a Tuesday Night Music Club project and having it very cleverly cut up. Of course, none of those tapes were ever used.

"I could've got another drummer in, but I didn't want to. Those guys were the guys I'd met for the previous ten years, and I wanted to use them. That's why they were there on the Sheryl Crow album, that's why I invited them into my studio to record for their respective projects and bands. It didn't occur to me to do the project without Brian, but I'd be exaggerating if I said that was the only incident that broke up the band, because it wasn't. I mean, it subsequently turned out that David Baerwald was signed and keeping that from us! That whole decade, for me, was just *Bonfire of the Vanities*."

"Hogwash," retorts Baerwald. "Bill, Dan, and I went out to [actor Kevin Costner's Twin Palms] restaurant in Pasadena and we talked about it. I had real misgivings about how we were going to pull this thing together, and I needed a job. It was just too fragmented. We needed a front person."

"Bill tried to keep it going," Brian MacLeod confirmed in his 2001 interview with Wayne Perez. "We almost signed this multi-million dollar deal with Apple Computers to be their first online band…the Internet was a baby, it was a fetus. [The executives] were flying down. Literally, we were each going to get almost a million. Somehow it exploded. One reason: Baerwald wanted to go do a solo deal, he didn't want to be part of a band. Then Bill got pissed because he thought Kevin and I were too cynical and dark. It was just this weird explosion and so TMC dissolved and we were like 'Whoa, what happened? We want to keep going.'"

"There's a picture of us at around that time, and we look wiped out," Baerwald continues. "Kevin looks like somebody's just sandbagged him and Dan looks like Trotsky…Trotsky in Mexico with an axe in the back of his head. We were not in good shape. It was a very dysfunctional family."

Not that things were totally healthy up at the cabin, where an 8-track setup had been assembled courtesy of a small budget supplied by Sheryl. Bill may have viewed this as a divisive ploy, but as things turned out, the writing session only lasted a week.

"It was close to 110 degrees and there was no air conditioning," says Jeff Trott. "Added to that, we were partying pretty well and things kind of got a little bit intense between Sheryl and Brian. She was dealing with the Tuesday Night Music Club situation, and although she mostly got along with Brian, who was a little less egotistical about the whole thing, there was quite a bit of tension between them."

Still, for all this, it appears that Sheryl hadn't yet given up hope of patching things up with her already-former colleagues. Following the "cabin incident," there were more TMC gatherings at Toad Hall, and during one of the sessions the band members learned that Sheryl had left a message on Bill's answering machine, stating that she was thinking of coming along.

"Everybody was going, 'Oh my God, no! What is she thinking?'" Dan Schwartz recalls. "The general agenda was to leave before she showed up, but first we jammed and came up with a song: 'Here she comes, here she comes, here she comes, here she comes, here she comes, here she comes, so RUN!' It was one of those true instances of everybody getting it together. Then we got the hell out of there."

Meanwhile, when Jeff Trott didn't hear from Sheryl for several weeks, he assumed that the week spent at Brian MacLeod's cabin had been a waste of time.

"We'd got, like, five songs together, and I was thinking, 'Nah, she didn't like them,'" Jeff says. "However, as it turned out, three of the songs that we wrote up there were 'If It Makes You Happy,' 'A Change,' and 'Everyday Is A Winding Road,' so it wasn't a bust!"

True enough, yet what was a bust at this stage was the irreparably damaged relationship between Sheryl and Bill, who were like a couple headed for divorce, trying to remain cordial for the sake of the kid (in this case, a new album). More than two years of pent-up anger were eating away at Bill, not least that relating to how he perceived himself being treated by Sheryl and the label. When she suggested getting away from the bad vibes of Toad Hall by switching to the neutral ground of New Orleans, he went along with this. However, the flame was nearing the end of the fuse, and on the second day at producer Daniel Lanois's Kingsway Studio there was the inevitable explosion.

"I felt on day one in New Orleans that not only did Sheryl want a neutral zone, but that she was now going to make a creative power play against me," says Bill. "It's her right to do that as the artist, but it's also my right to not want to do it. You know, I was about 45 years old at that point and I'd seen it all. So, if I didn't want to write a certain kind of song for a certain kind of artist, I didn't have to. There was no contract, and I knew where I stood—after all of this, I was being auditioned."

At one point, while Sheryl and Bill were in the Kingsway control room, Trina Shoemaker walked in to retrieve some DAT tapes from a storage compartment behind the console. Two months earlier, Trina had quit as the studio's Chief Engineer, but as she was friendly with the manager and still had some gear there, she would drop in from time to time. When she passed through the control room, Trina noticed that Bill had a drink perched on the ebony frame of the API board, and so she mentioned that the house rules didn't allow this. Then she exited. All in all, Bill was convinced that he shouldn't be there.

"Ironically, what finally pissed me off was Brian MacLeod showing up drunk," he says. "We went out to the local café and ate some dinner, and I couldn't sit there and listen to him. It was him showing up, amid the context of sort of being set up, that pissed me off. I mean, I knew he was showing up, but when I saw him and pictured having to work with him after what had gone down with the phone call from the cabin, I got drunk myself and I said, 'I'm not doing this.'

"It ended with a slanging match between Sheryl and me on the street outside the studio, and me saying, 'I quit!' I don't remember the details, but essentially it was the pent-up stuff between two people with four years of intense history. I exploded and then she exploded back, but I just wanted to leave, and I wanted to leave quick. I knew exactly what I was doing, and I never looked back. I never even heard her second or third albums except for what I heard on the radio. I didn't care. My whole ideal of the first album was anti-postmodernism…if she wanted to make a postmodern statement and an album that was more punk, that was fine, but that's not what I do."

When Bill walked, he essentially left Sheryl high and dry in New Orleans. However, if she felt any sense of panic as a result of suddenly losing her creative mentor, this was tempered by the long-desired and now-glaring opportunity to take sole possession of the producer's chair. Indeed, Sheryl later acknowledged as much in an interview with the *Toronto Sun*.

"I went into the studio feeling really raw, and I wanted that to be captured on tape," she recalled. "And I got very lucky in that the very first day Bill, my producer, left, and I think that was the beginning of a new period for me of just saying, 'I know what I'm doing. I'm going to do it on my own.'"

About six hours after she'd encountered Sheryl and Bill in the control room, Trina Shoemaker received a call from the manager at Kingsway. "You've got to get down here!" she was told. "Sheryl Crow's producer has just left and her manager's asking if there's an engineer who can at least run this room tonight until she can get her people out from L.A.…."

Trina knew the facility inside out, and she also happened to be familiar with the L.A. scene. Having spent most of the '80s performing there as a musician, working in record stores and at record companies, and hanging out in studios, Trina had ended the decade by becoming a full-time assistant engineer at a small 16-track facility named Dominion Sound. As such, she was one of the few women in this field, and she soon discovered why when she attempted to get work elsewhere—"Girls don't do this" was the attitude of West Coast studio managers. Depressed yet undeterred, Trina relocated to New Orleans on a romantic notion, and this appeared to pay off when she secured employment at a studio called Ultrasonic…as a cleaner. Almost immediately, the house engineer invited her to assist on a session with local artist Clarence "Gatemouth" Brown, and thereafter she worked at various nearby facilities, including Kingsway.

Now here she was, struggling to make a living as a freelancer, and a money-making opportunity had fallen into her lap. Trina wasn't about to turn it down, but first she had to talk on the phone with Scooter Weintraub and explain that, as she no longer worked in-house, she'd need to be paid separately. Scooter agreed.

"Sheryl was freaky that night," Trina recalls. "She was absolutely traumatized, shouting, 'This goddamn Wurlitzer doesn't work!' and 'Why are we even down here?' I said, 'Hey look, you know what, I quit this studio because I worked under someone who yelled at me all the time. I can't take that anymore. Let's just be cool. I'm here, I'll record you tonight. I don't know what happened with your guy, I don't even really know who you are, but I do know that you're an artist who needs an engineer tonight.' Sheryl and I didn't start off on the greatest footing, because I was thinking, 'Another mean and angry musician? I'm not into this. I'll record you tonight because I'm broke and I need some dough, but that's it.' Well, within a few hours she calmed down."

The next day, the phone lines were buzzing between Kingsway, Scooter's office, and the executive suites at A&M. Given all of the daggers that Sheryl and Bill had been throwing at one another, David Anderle was philosophical about closing the book on their collaboration, and he also wasn't surprised when Sheryl asked if she could try to produce herself. Anderle agreed, and he immediately called Al Cafaro to reassure him that everything would work out fine.

"David presented this to me as a *fait accompli,* so he should get a lot of credit for that," Al states. "You're never interested in an artist self-producing. You never sit there and go, 'Oh, that's a wonderful idea!' There were other times later in my run at A&M when I fortunately had some success letting people do that, but it wasn't like it was a natural instinct. You know, 'We're going to sign you and you're gonna produce your record.' Still, in that respect, how will artists ever produce their own record? They're going to have to fight for it, and they're going to have to do what the record company wants…until it doesn't work. If truth be told, we weren't keen on Sheryl producing her next record—it's not what you do—and when Bill walked I was marginally more concerned than David. He and I were completely in sync on so much that we did, but I absolutely would say that David reassured me that she could make this work."

"I knew she would," Anderle asserts. "You know why? Because she wasn't going to stop until it was right. Now, that may take forever, but Sheryl doesn't want to fail. Sheryl is not about failing. It wasn't difficult for me to say okay to her producing herself. At this point she'd already exhibited that she knew how to write; she's a great musician, she's tenacious, so really what were we going to find out? We'd find out once she got into a control room whether or not she understood the control room, because she understood everything else and the demos were really good.

"When I first produced records I didn't know anything about what I was doing, and so I figured that if I could learn how to do it then probably she could, too. It's a matter of having really good musicians and a really good engineer, as well as an A&R guy who can help, and that's basically what happened. I knew that Sheryl is smart enough to know that, if she needs help, she'll get it. Ultimately she wants to win, and she ain't no dummy, this girl, so she's not going to sit there and hammer away at something if it's not right. That's what you bet on. You bet on that kind of talent, you bet on people who want to win."

On the second day of recording, Jeff Trott had received a call from Sheryl asking him to immediately join her, Bill, and Brian in New Orleans. By the time Jeff arrived, Bill was gone.

"She ran up to me and said, 'Oh, it's just gone really horribly wrong!'" Jeff recalls. "She was like 'What are we going to do?' I said, 'Well, let's get in and start writing and recording,' so that's what we did."

On the night when she first produced herself at Kingsway Studio, Sheryl didn't notice Trina Shoemaker setting up microphones and arranging to bring in a Wurlitzer, a Hammond B3, and other rental gear from Nashville. What's more, Sheryl also didn't realize that the engineer was rolling tape from the moment she and Jeff began writing.

"I went through about six reels of tape while they worked," Trina remembers, "and then at around two o'clock in the morning Sheryl said, 'We need to start rolling tape because this is turning into a song.' I said, 'Sheryl, we already have that,' and I could see a click in her eye. She said, 'You're pretty cool! I like the fact that you just record and don't talk.' I had the very first writing moment down on multitrack, and that was the take that ended up being used."

The song that Sheryl composed that night was "Home," a country lament with beautiful, world-weary lyrics that mostly came to her as she was singing into the mic. Playing bass while Jeff Trott and Brian MacLeod were having little success working on another number, Sheryl began singing "Home" and the three of them fell in together.

"We tried to record it a few times later, and it just never had the initial spirit," Sheryl told David Wild during their 2002 interview for *Musicians*. "It was just one of those unusual songs that wrote itself."

Then and there, a seemingly chaotic situation was turned on its head. During her first few hours of autonomy, and with inspiration that materialized out of nowhere, Sheryl had unwittingly accomplished her maiden solo production. Sure, the song structure and musical arrangement were fairly straightforward, but the results were laudable, and from here she would pick up the pieces and, with the aid of her fellow musicians and an innovative engineer, start learning a new craft as she went along.

"We felt like, 'Hey, we so totally don't have anything to lose, because nobody is betting on us,'" Sheryl recalled on VH1's *Behind the Music*. "'We are such dark horses that even if we get near the finish line, we're going to slap ourselves on the back.'"

"She had every intention of proving herself to the world," adds Trina Shoemaker.

And prove herself she would. Once again, for Sheryl Crow, there was nothing like a challenge.

# CHAPTER TWELVE

# *Redemption in the Big Easy*

"New Orleens," "New Orleeyans," "Noo Orl'ns," "N'Awl'ns." However you want to pronounce its name, the home of Dixieland jazz is one of America's most unique and exotic cities, where the French heritage serves as a backdrop to a cultural potpourri of African, Spanish, and Caribbean influences, and where the land nestled between Lake Pontchartrain, Lake Borgne, and the Mississippi is so low that residents' graves are constructed above ground.

Nicknamed the "Crescent City" because of the river-etched curve around its southern end, as well as the "Big Easy" in reference to its slow pace and sometimes-slack morals, New Orleans is as famed for its voodoo, vampires, and ghosts as it is for Mardi Gras, ceiling fans, wrought-iron gates, great music, and spicy food. Indeed, while the old bordellos and gambling houses of the French Quarter have been superseded by Cajun restaurants, bars, clubs, and strip joints, this and the adjacent neighborhoods are replete with walk-ups, shotgun shacks, and southern mansions that reputedly play host to a ghoulish array of lost souls: the Myrtles, the Delta Queen, the Octoroon Mistress, the Creole Lady.... Not for nothing is New Orleans also known as "America's Most Haunted City."

One property that perfectly suits this image is the sprawling, rustic manor on Esplanade Avenue, just a few blocks north of the Quarter, which was purchased by producer Daniel Lanois in 1989 and converted into Kingsway Studio. Incorporating a console within its open-plan recording area (as was the case at Toad Hall), the facility provided the ideal environment for Sheryl and her fellow musicians to play together as a band, while it was also conveniently located for them to draw songwriting inspiration from various local attractions.

"During the two months we camped out there we did all sorts of stuff," says Jeff Trott. "We went to strip joints and cemeteries and we experienced a lot of things, soaking in the local atmosphere. I mean, New Orleans is just full of atmosphere. If you can't write a song there you don't have a chance."

One of the strip clubs that Jeff and Sheryl visited was Maiden Voyage, whose name was the original title of the song "Sweet Rosalyn." Located at 225 Bourbon Street, in the heart of the city's red-light district, this place is hard to miss, not least because of a giant-sized tropical fish tank that bulges out of its front wall. To the left sits a hostess, while behind her, blocking the door, are the obligatory gorillas in penguin suits; a trio of peacefully threatening-looking guys, sporting tuxedoes and hot-pink bow ties. On the inside, the businessmen, tourists, and locals are treated to a tropical island theme, where topless dancers move around palm trees and cylindrical lava lamps. Fiji on the bayou. It's an intriguing concept.

"We were trying to get some song ideas, and I'd been reading a magazine article about this typical American housewife who decided to change her life by becoming a stripper," Jeff explains. "She got into bondage and all that stuff, and in describing this woman one of the lines from the article was 'At this point in her life she had been known to slap leather.' This lent itself to the first line of 'Sweet Rosalyn,' and we then thought, 'Well, let's go to this strip joint and take in the ambience,' because Sheryl would take off on those ideas and run with them."

"When I wrote 'Sweet Rosalyn,' it was exactly about what was going on in my life at that time," Sheryl told the *Chicago Tribune* in April 1999. "I wasn't stripping physically, but metaphorically I felt like I was stripping because the press had gone really negative. All these things in the songs were metaphors for what was going on in my personal life. There was some masking going on there, but I love writing in a lot of different mediums: short stories, poetry."

As their partnership developed, both Sheryl and Jeff quickly discovered that, whereas his main compositional talent relates to instigating songs, hers lays in taking a good idea and turning it into a great one. It is, in short, the perfect chemistry, and during many of the sessions for the *Sheryl Crow* album Trina Shoemaker helped them to realize their ideas.

"More than twenty-five songs were written and cut for the *Sheryl Crow* record, and while all of this was going on, Sheryl was also trying to learn how to produce herself," Trina recalls. "As a result, there were a lot of roads that we went down that some people would have considered to be huge wastes of time and money. We, on the other hand, regarded it as the means of her finding out what the record should be and how she could make it great.

"For example, during the first few days of recording, we worked on a song that never ended up making it onto the album. It was real interesting, it had a vibe, and it was potentially going to be pretty cool. There was this great drum part on it, some cool guitar, Sheryl played this really weird, eclectic bass line and sang some interesting lyrics, and we spent weeks on that song. I'd say, 'This bass is out of tune,' and she'd say, 'Oh, well, we want that exact bass line.' 'Okay, let's play it again.' 'No, I can't play it again. Can you pitch-shift it?' 'Well, Sheryl, it's gonna be really hard to pitch-shift a whole bass line.' 'Yeah, but if I play it again, it'll lose the vibe.' 'Okay, then I'll try to pitch-shift it.' So, that took me, like, a hundred years, and then she said, 'That still sounds out of tune,' to which I replied, 'Well, it always is going to be out of tune because it's essentially…out of tune!' 'I hate this song!' 'Okay, me too. Let's move on.'

"A week later that song reappeared, and so we spent a lot of time on material that we both sort of knew was not going to be on her record, but she just wanted to wrestle the mother to the ground anyway. She needed to make the point to herself, if only to find out why the song wouldn't jell in the studio. In that way, she was learning, and so I would go there with her even if I perhaps should have said, 'You know what, this is a waste of time. It will not work technically. I cannot pitch-shift an entire bass line.' Basically, we would try everything, and in that way she would know that, when she'd have to say that a song was off the record because she couldn't make it work, we'd left no stone unturned."

In Marc Woodworth's book *Solo: Women Singer-Songwriters in Their Own Words*, Sheryl likened the working relationship between her and Trina to "a couple of middle-aged cooks in a Southern kitchen, sharing a really crazy recipe and putting it all together." Indeed, she asserted that the female dynamic played a significant role in putting her at ease during her solo debut as a producer. "I don't always enjoy the sexual tension that gets in the way when creating with a man," Sheryl stated. "It was a real joy to work with Trina, not only because there was that common language and understanding, but no sexual tension and no problems with ego. I've never met someone so willing to abandon what she knew, to be able to say, 'I know you like the sound of Keith's guitar on "Gimme Shelter," and this is the way that Jimmy Miller recorded it, but if you really want it to sound wild, then let me try it this way.' She abandoned everything that engineers grow up learning. I owe a lot to her for the way the record sounds."

Trina Shoemaker's open-minded attitude gave Sheryl free rein to find her feet as a producer, while the engineer's technical virtuosity also enabled them to come up with some interesting sounds—"Maybe Angels" opens the album in unconventional style, thanks to a grungy loop, Jeff Trott's distorted guitar, and a clanging shovel. Still, not everybody was crazy about the results, including one of Jeff's musical acquaintances, bass-player and rock-fusion maestro George Porter, Jr., who happened to live a short distance from Kingsway.

"I wanted him to play on this funk track, 'Maybe Angels,' but it didn't work out," says Jeff. "I was like, 'Wait a minute, you're the groovemaster guy,' but he didn't like the song. It has the banging of a shovel on the intro, and he hated that. He said, 'There's something wrong with this track. There's this weird sound, I can't figure it out. It just irritates me.' He just didn't like playing the song. He was going, 'I don't know what that sound is,' and we'd say, 'It's a shovel!' 'Why is there a shovel on this song?' He had a really difficult time."

George Porter, Jr., wasn't the only one who had a problem. Trina Shoemaker, trying to deal with constantly evolving, loop-driven material, as well as a drum kit that was set up on a small piece of marble flooring next to the console, would either have to mike the drums so that they had a large, roomy sound, or build a small foam hut over the entire kit to make it as dead as possible. It all depended on the nature of the tape loop.

"Sheryl came to the studio with several loops already created, and three or four of these made it onto the record," Trina explains. "Her whole notion was super-live yet super-dead, super-funky yet super-pop, while also loop-driven, and at first that dichotomy appeared to be impossible, but she pulled it off. That's when I thought, 'Wow, she knows what she wants! Just follow her and go there with her.' It was by trying a million things that didn't work that we arrived at this one perfect dichotomy, like 'Maybe Angels,' which sounds completely live but is, in fact, a loop.

"In telling me that she needed a loop, Sheryl said, 'The loop cannot swing, but I want to swing over the top of it.' You try doing that! We'd work on a load of different rhythms and she'd be saying, 'No, the loop is swinging! Can't you hear that?' 'Uh, no.' 'Well, it is, because I can't swing if *it* swings!' So, finally we came up with a loop pattern that had just enough of a swing in it to create the illusion of swing, and which she could also swing the instruments over. It started with Brian MacLeod playing a drum groove and also hitting something metallic to give a ringing sound, which was then mixed into the normal, dry, organic loop which I created. The result doesn't sound as if it swings, but it actually does, and that's what makes that song so groovy."

The mid-tempo number "A Change," full of organ stabs and bluesy guitar riffs, was originally conceived at the MacLeod cabin, with a rhythm track consisting of composers Brian, Sheryl, and Jeff clapping and stomping on a wooden box. This ended up on the finished recording, supplemented by real drums, yet the number wasn't completed until the sessions switched to New Orleans.

"I wrote [this] song about people just not being able to handle life, you know, as a day-to-day experience," Sheryl later stated in the A&M publicity blurb that was issued to coincide with the album's release. "It's a barrage of conscious stream, day-to-day vignettes that everyone will experience."

In a 1999 interview with *Playboy* magazine, Sheryl also explained that the Prophet lo-fi pioneer mentioned in the song is Joe Meek, the ground-breaking independent record producer who created hits such as The Tornadoes' "Telstar" in his tiny home studio, located above a shop in North London.

"I had read a couple of articles about the reissue of the Joe Meek collection," Sheryl recounted. "Joe Meek was a really lo-fi music producer in the early Sixties. He was producing music in his apartment, recording drums in the kitchen and vocals in his bathroom. He eventually went crazy. He shot his landlady, then went and shot himself. He was really a loon, and that's what the song is about."

"We had it in our minds that we were going to write three verses, each focusing on a different person we knew," adds Jeff Trott. "The first verse is kind of about Bill Bottrell, the second verse is sort of about Madonna, and the third one is more or less about Sheryl. Basically, we just got some idea, she had some lines, and then Brian and I added our own little bits. Like I added the line about wearing fake fur on the inside. We collectively just wrote lines down on pieces of paper, threw them into a hat, and drew them out, and so of course they didn't come out perfectly, but we'd kind of reshape them from there.

"You have to play a lot of games when you're writing with other people in order to distract yourself from the consciousness of writing, because it's very difficult to co-compose songs. A lot of it has to do with the combination of people—there are certain people who will supply the missing ending—and it's also a question of trust. You really have to trust the other person insofar as his or her judgement is good, and you also have to trust them so that you can make an ass of yourself in front of them. Because with some of the best ideas that you get, you really have to lose your inhibitions and be able to say things that are sometimes very painful.

"You can't come out of the hatch just writing something that's absolutely brilliant," Jeff continues. "That rarely happens right off the bat. A lot of it is real craft, there's a lot of tweaking, and it's a case of edit and edit and edit until it's like, 'Okay, wait a minute, I have to find a better word that's not so flat. I need something that pops.' Sometimes you can get so oblique that you lose the message, so you have to find a way of making something that is both poetic and also cuts through the crap.

"With Sheryl and I, there's no real set method to writing. We just get together and start talking and hanging out, drinking a couple of beers, maybe playing cover songs, and generally listening to music. Someone will sit down at a harmonium and start droning some kind of melody, and basically it's weird, because it's so random most of the time. I mean, when someone else is inspired by what you're doing, he or she will join in and perhaps take it somewhere, and that happens a lot with us. I'll be strumming something and she'll say, 'What's that? Is that a song?' I'll say, 'No, I'm just playing,' and she'll say, 'Well, keep playing that.' Then she might come up with the melody. On the other hand, there are times when we'll sit around and say, 'Okay, what are we going to write about? Is it going to have any characters in it?' That might mean getting out the magazines and finding something that's going to stick. Once things start sticking you then know what direction you're heading in."

Up until the mid-'60s, the most successful songwriting partnerships usually consisted of lyricists and tunesmiths who didn't stray far from their specialized crafts; teams such as George and Ira Gershwin, Sammy Cahn and Jimmy Van Heusen, Richard Rodgers and Oscar Hammerstein, Gerry Goffin and Carole King. Since then, however, the lines have been blurred by people performing both roles, and the result is often an imbalance in terms of the collaborative contributions and, for the listeners, a difficulty in ascertaining precisely who did what. In this regard, the Crow/Trott partnership is no exception. Some of their efforts amount to a fairly even split, while others comprise a song mostly written by one party and then embellished by the other. "If It Makes You Happy" is a case in point.

As the lead-off single on the *Sheryl Crow* album, this would be perceived as Sheryl's riposte to her critics both within and without the Tuesday Night Music Club; an angry woman giving the finger to her adversaries. However, despite the sullen-aggressive attitude and air of fuck-you catharsis, the words clearly allude to a troubled romance, and this is because the song, as originally conceived both musically and lyrically by Jeff Trott, centered on him trying to figure out where he'd gone wrong—and how to ease the pain—after breaking up with a girlfriend.

"I was just trying to make myself happy by speaking to lost love," he explains. "It was a song that I'd worked on while I was in Pete Droge's band, before I had even hooked up with Sheryl, but it was kind of unfinished. I had lyrics, the melody, and the chord progression. The first verse, about putting on a poncho and playing for mosquitoes, referred to a tour that my former band, Wire Train, did with Bob Dylan for several months in 1990. We were playing in Hannibal, Missouri, which is right on the banks of the Mississippi, and it was sweltering hot. At nine o'clock in the evening it would still be about 110 degrees and something crazy like 90 percent humidity, and there were mosquitoes everywhere. I remember going to the microphone to sing and getting a whole mouthful of them, and I'd be spitting them out. So, that's where those lyrics came from. There again, the part about derailing your own train was a reference to the end of Wire Train, and so for me that song was really a collection of thoughts and images relating to experiences on the road."

When Jeff first played Sheryl the song at the MacLeod cabin, she was taken not only by the melody, but by a feel that she could instantly identify with—"I'm standing up for who I am." Originally written in the key of E, "If It Makes You Happy" was transposed to G in order to fit Sheryl's voice.

"She related to that song and was able to carry it to where it really needed to be, to a place that it would never otherwise reach, because for her I think it represented some kind of triumph over trying to prove herself," Jeff says. "The original idea was mine, but she took it and made it her own, and I think it was this number that really brought us together in terms of being able to relate. She changed some words, wrote the second verse, and strengthened the melody in a way that only a great singer can. Sheryl has this ability to take these germs of ideas and really make them explode. She's got a way of being able to communicate, and that in itself is invaluable. One of her best assets is that she's really believable, because when she likes a song she believes in it and her performance is totally convincing."

In the aforementioned A&M press release, Sheryl explained that "If It Makes You Happy" tapped into "a credo that I have, that if you're in the moment and you can find some joy in that, it just can't be that bad. You've got to make the best of your situation and not always be looking past the moment, because then you'll miss out on what life is. That's been a battle for me, always has been. Having a little levity has been my real challenge."

Aside from a strident opening guitar riff, the attention-grabbing aspect to "If It Makes You Happy" is Sheryl's switch from the bottom of her vocal range on the verses to a searing, high-impact delivery for the chorus. Right there is the rush, the magic that hooks the listener, yet the song underwent several different arrangements before it delivered the knockout punch.

"It started off as a twangy, David Lynch-esque sort of thing," remembers Jeff Trott. "Then, when we were first fleshing it out and trying to find the right key for Sheryl to sing in, we played it like punk rock—really fast—as well as country and funky. You know, you get a song and put clothes on it to see what looks good and what doesn't, and usually when you find the right one it's pretty obvious. With that song it was real obvious.

"When we were fleshing it out up at the cabin and getting it to work, I think we had a clue that it was a really, really good song. Then, when we started recording it properly at Kingsway, some people staying in an apartment next door to the studio kept hearing it; we walked by them one time, and one of them said, 'You know that song

"Happy" you've been playing a lot? We really love it! It's really great!' Soon, whenever people heard it they'd say they just couldn't get it out of their heads, and so we started to realize how important the song was."

So did Trina Shoemaker, who was witness to positive feedback from another Kingsway neighbor: "Ruth Bodenheimer, a very respectable lady who's daughter is a senator and who owns a mansion across the street, came over and knocked on the door. She was like 'I just want to say this "If It Makes You Happy" song that I'm hearing out of the front of the house…well, it does make me happy.' She didn't realize that it's actually not an uplifting song."

"I became really conscious of how much it meant, and I was overwhelmed by that," Jeff Trott continues. "I spent an entire day working on the guitars. I played that song in open E tuning and the song is in G, so I had to barre chord it. Trying to play barre chords low on the neck through the whole song and making it really tight was very, very laborious. My hand turned into this marble claw and practically fell off. However, after spending all of this time on the song, I finally got it sounding really great. I wanted to get absolutely the biggest intro possible, and all the time Sheryl was kind of kicking me in the ass like 'You know how great this is going to be. This is your time to make history.' We were just pumping each other up. Still, the silly thing is, after going through all of that labor, when we started rehearsing to go on the road with that song, I discovered that I could have just had it in open G. All I would have needed to do is play all of the strings open and then just add the little [descending] riff. A child could play it, yet I'd worked it out in open E and got carpal tunnel for my efforts!"

While the bass on "If It Makes You Happy" was played by noted session man Dan Rothchild (the son of legendary Doors producer Paul Rothchild), the recently self-taught Sheryl fulfilled this role on many—though not all—of the other tracks. As had previously been the case with her touring band, throughout the *Sheryl Crow* project the artist-producer experienced no small degree of difficulty trying to attain the desired bass sound, yet both she and the engineer were convinced that this was down to the instruments, not the players.

"For some reason we were plagued with bass problems," Trina Shoemaker confirms. "None of the instruments sounded good. It would be like, 'Hey, we've found this $8 billion old gold-plated Fender. I'm sure it'll sound great.' But then, when we'd plug it in, it would sound like crap! It seemed like every person in the world with an expensive bass was cruising by the studio—'Hey, I heard Sheryl Crow needs a bass'—but we just seemed to end up with these dorky basses, none of which sounded good, aside from a few exceptions such as the brand-new Precision which Dan Rothchild showed up with. That sounded great."

The second track to be released as a single off the *Sheryl Crow* album would be the Crow/Trott/MacLeod composition "Everyday Is A Winding Road," a funky number driven by a pumping slide guitar, with offbeat lyrics that relay Sheryl's struggle to find herself while swimming in a sea of anarchy. Unfortunately, during the early stages of its development, the song itself appeared to be drowning in a sea of overkill.

"'Everyday Is A Winding Road' basically started off with the rhythm-guitar riff, not the slide guitar, and it was something really simple," Jeff explains. "Well, we worked on that song, and I tell you, I must have overdubbed thirty instruments on there to make it work, and it was just the biggest piece of you-know-what. It was so bad. I went nuts on it—'Okay, bagpipes. Oh no, here we go....' We were really finished once the bagpipes went on there."

Consequently, when songwriter/guitarist Robbie Robertson called Sheryl to ask if she could provide a song for the *Phenomenon* movie soundtrack that he was executive producing, she was more than happy to offer "Everyday Is A Winding Road." A case of "Let's get this song out of here!" Jeff agreed. However, on receiving their rough mix, Robertson's response was to approve the number while asking them to remix it with fewer instruments. Sheryl, Jeff, and Brian didn't realize it at the time, but by obliging this request they were unwittingly rethinking the entire song; the initial result was a stripped-down version that retained just the rhythm guitar and drum groove from the original recording.

"The bass wasn't really happening," says Jeff. "There happened to be a Minimoog synthesizer at the studio and I thought, 'You know, the Moog's a really great-sounding bass instrument.' Now, with the guitar I can do a lot of things, but at that time my keyboard playing was very, very basic, so I played a fairly straightforward bass line on the Moog and all of a sudden the song became funkier and started to take on an interesting character. Sheryl was saying, 'Well, why don't you now put some slide or something on it?' because one of the things that she likes about my playing is my slide guitar work. I don't play it like 'Blind Melon Griffin,' but more in between George Harrison and whoever. So, I played that crazy slide part, and I got this really weird tone in the studio that was overly compressed. It felt like I was playing a rubber band and I was going, 'Sheryl, check this out! It sounds like elastic or something!' I wasn't even looking down at the guitar, but the riff just sort of developed from this weird sound."

Thereafter, "Everyday Is A Winding Road" was reassembled with the addition of acoustic guitars and percussion, and the end product was so appealing that its creators suddenly weren't so sure about lending it to a movie.

"To me, that song is the quintessential Sheryl Crow," remarks Jeff. "It's not afraid of exploring the sorts of things that seem normal but which really have a kind of dark, creepy side to them. Sheryl likes to write about the ordinary guy while also exposing the interior a little bit, going under the floorboards. A large part of the collaboration between her and I is one person seeing the potential in a song and pushing it to the next step. It may take a mailman or whoever to say, 'Oh, that's a really dumb song,' and then we'll think, 'Ooh, maybe we have something....'"

In America, the "Everyday Is A Winding Road" single would be supplemented by "Sad Sad World," a Crow/Trott/MacLeod composition that also appeared on the special "Signature Tour Edition" of the *Sheryl Crow* album in the U.K., as well as on various releases in Europe and the Far East. A plaintive country dirge featuring Sheryl's pedal steel playing, it conveys her unexpressed feelings in the wake of Kevin Gilbert's death: mourning his loss while castigating herself for letting him down. Unable to gain Kevin's approval while he was alive, Sheryl now knew that possibility was off the radar screen. "Sad Sad World" served as her footnote to the Crow/Gilbert relationship.

In "The Book," the singer rues the discovery of a novel written by a former lover that documents the details of their relationship. A dark and moody song with a naturalistic vocal but a cheesy Wurlitzer solo, the material draws on the atmosphere of New Orleans.

"They're so into music there that even a death march is one of the most beautiful, intriguing things to hear," says Jeff Trott. "'The Book' is basically a major-to-minor chord progression, and that is such a beautiful sound. It's very intriguing."

Altogether more intriguing was the situation that Sheryl found herself in thanks to a misassumption that she and Jeff made when deciding to have the number orchestrated. Having fallen in love with the darkly Southern arrangement on the old Bobbie Gentry hit, "Ode To Billie Joe," they both thought it would be a great idea to have the person who orchestrated that song do the same for "The Book." No matter that their cassette copy of "Ode To Billie Joe" didn't list the orchestrator, they were pretty sure who it was… you know, that guy who did all of the string stuff back in the mid-to-late '60s. What's his name? Van Dyke Parks. Yeah, that's it! Talk about *Spinal Tap*….

Sheryl contacted the accomplished composer/producer/arranger/musician at his home in L.A. and, without asking any questions, stated that she'd really like him to adorn "The Book" with an orchestration similar to that on "Ode To Billie Joe." Van Dyke was enthused. He, too, thought that "Ode To Billie Joe" was a great song, so Sheryl sent him a DAT copy of "The Book" and he set about working on it. However, when the DAT came back, the added piano orchestration wasn't so much dark and evil as a little too precious, a little too pretty. It was lilting rather than haunting, so Sheryl phoned Van Dyke and emphasized that she wanted something more along the lines of Mahler's "Funeral March." Van Dyke wasn't fazed. He'd take another listen to "Ode To Billie Joe" and get it right. Oh yeah, he really loved that song….

"We didn't hear back from him for quite some time," Jeff Trott remembers, "and then he called Sheryl and said, 'Okay, this is the most brilliant string arrangement I have ever done.' We were like, 'Oh, great, great! He got it! Is it dark?' and he was going, 'Oh yeah, yeah.' Well, a few months later we were in L.A., finishing up the record, and Sheryl called me and said, 'Hey, you wanna come down to the Capitol Records studios? We're gonna cut the strings for 'The Book' and Van Dyke has got the arrangement. I'm not sure what it sounds like because I haven't heard it, so I'm hoping he changed what he had before.' I was like, 'Well, he's a pro, y'know. How much are you paying for this?' and she said it was about $40,000. I'm thinking, 'Well, it's got to be good, right? I mean, if it costs a lot of money isn't it always good?'"

This story keeps getting better, or worse, depending on one's involvement. At the studio, everyone was keyed up: Van Dyke, his family and friends, the A&M execs, and Sheryl and Jeff, neither of whom had heard one of their songs embellished by an eighty-piece orchestra before. The excitement was building. Then it was time for lift-off.

"They started the song, the orchestra came in, and at first it kind of sounded pretty cool," Jeff recalls. "But then it just got frillier and frillier, and flowers seemed to be popping out all over the place. Sheryl grabbed my left arm and squeezed so hard, and I was thinking, 'Now, is she really excited and really happy, or is she furious?' Because in my mind I was shrieking in horror and almost ready to cry, going, 'Oh my God, this is horrible! This is so awful-sounding, I'm embarrassed! I want to shit my pants!' and I was hoping that she felt the same way. I was thinking, 'She can't be liking this! She just can't be!' Anyway, they finished it and Sheryl said, 'Um, I want to change a few things on this.' So, we looked at the score and she said, 'This over here—can you guys maybe not do so many of those waterfall-type things?'

"Well, now there is dead silence. I mean, after the orchestra had played, all of these execs and important people had been high-fiving each other like 'This is the greatest thing ever! Oh, my God!' and now I'm thinking they're going to start crying. It was really embarrassing, but Sheryl looked at me and I instantly knew that she was on the same page as I was. Like we were both ready to run out of that studio and go down to [Hollywood restaurant] Musso & Frank's and drink a couple of stiff ones. Instead, she looked over at Van Dyke and said, 'Hey, you didn't change anything, did you?' and he was like, 'Oh yeah, yeah, I made the changes,' to which she said, 'Well, it sounds exactly like it did before.' 'Yeah, well, it'll be great,' he said. 'I mean, this is like one of the best things I've ever done,' and then he looked over at me and he said, 'You should be proud!' I was thinking, 'I *know* I *should* be!'

"We were trying to be polite, but Sheryl said, 'We've got to get out of here. You know, I just lost $40,000 and I feel horrible.' So, we went down the block to Musso & Frank's, and we had a couple of martinis, and I was sitting there going, 'I can't believe this! Where did we go wrong? We got the wrong guy. Van Dyke Parks—didn't he do stuff with The Beach Boys and on and on?' Sheryl said, 'I don't know what he's done really. I mean, he did U2....' At that point, in walked Van Dyke and his family. He sat down and he was like, 'Oh, yeah! I wanna have a drink!' He then repeated, 'This is one of the best things I've ever done,' and he said it over and over again, at which point Sheryl just looked at him and went, 'Well, you can put it on your record. I can't use it.' His reaction was along the lines of 'Well, I think it's great.' It was just one of those really sad, sad situations."

If Sheryl had done even a little investigating, she'd have discovered that Jimmie Haskell was the orchestrator of "Ode To Billie Joe." No one had bothered to ask Van Dyke Parks about this. He'd just agreed that it was a great song.

"Sheryl always kept talking about how she wanted these string parts to be like the ones on 'Ode To Billie Joe,'" confirms David Anderle, who was among the execs who attended the orchestral session. "Fine. And then she called and said, 'I'd like to have Van Dyke Parks.' She didn't say anything about 'Ode To Billie Joe,' she just said she wanted Van Dyke, and I said, 'Really? Van Dyke?' I thought, 'Okay. Sheryl wants to do something a little offbeat. Why not? It makes sense to me.' She just wanted Van Dyke to do the introduction. I thought, 'Oh great, this is going to be fun!' I'd signed Van Dyke to his first contract at MGM and then I'd managed him for a year, so I called Van out of nowhere—we hadn't talked for years—and talking to him on the phone I was thinking, 'Oh, my God! She must have something in mind. She must have heard something that he did; maybe a Randy Newman-ish kind of thing.'

"At the session, I saw Van and his wife, and he said, 'Davey, I'm really having a great time.' I'm watching Van, and I know he is having a great time. The musicians are coming in afterwards, listening, and going, 'This is a great song, Sheryl. Van, you've outdone yourself!' And I'm looking at Sheryl and I know it ain't happening with her, and I don't get it. So, then she says, 'Can I talk to you in the other room?' I said, 'Yes,' and we went in another studio and she said, 'What's going on?' I said, 'What's going on? Haven't you guys met? Haven't you talked about the song?' 'Well, yeah, we talked on the phone...but this isn't "Ode To Billie Joe."' and I said, 'Well, no, it's Van Dyke Parks.' The end result is that we bagged his arrangement."

Noted roots experimentalists Mitchell Froom and Tchad Blake were hired during the latter stages of the *Sheryl Crow* project—Froom as a consultant, Blake as an engineer. From Los Lobos and American Music Club to Froom's wife Suzanne Vega, the pair had forged a reputation for distorted textures, reverbed vocals, and junkyard percussion, and it was they who now replaced Van Dyke Parks's arrangement for "The Book" with phasey, funky funeral horns.

"I think they nailed it pretty well," remarks Jeff Trott. "Obviously, we had hoped that it would turn out like 'Ode To Billie Joe' and it hadn't, but at least this was kind of dark. They really got the point, so hats off to those guys. Both of them are geniuses. I'm just so lucky to be in their company, because they break a lot of ground in terms of recording. I even hear people who are influenced by Tchad Blake now; I hear these recordings and everyone's using distortion pedals on drum boxes and loops."

In addition to Tchad Blake, who also mixed the album, there was engineering by Blair Lamb and Bob Salcedo on the tracks that didn't feature Trina Shoemaker's involvement—"Superstar," "Redemption Day," "Ordinary Morning," and "Hard To Make A Stand," which were all recorded at either Sunset Sound in L.A. or Electric Ladyland in New York. It was in conjunction with these varied contributions, influences, and environments—especially the crucial, barely mentioned input of Froom and Blake—that Sheryl blended strange sounds and pop-culture references with the roots-rock sensibilities of the *Tuesday Night Music Club* record to produce a musically eclectic, postmodern album.

Nevertheless, in light of all that had gone down between her and the other members of TMC, this woman who'd worked so long and so hard to achieve fame was now beginning to question its worth. Hereafter, Sheryl's public pronouncements on celebrity would combine appreciation with skepticism, even though the vigorous manner in which she'd continue to pursue her career and accompanying social life would ensure her constant presence in the media spotlight.

"I've always had this fascination with the way media creates heroes and overnight successes and then just drops them," Sheryl commented in her new album's accompanying publicity release, while describing how the song "Superstar" was inspired by the feel of John Fante's *Ask the Dust*, a semi-autobiographical novel about a writer's struggle to make it in L.A. "Right now, we as a nation have such a fascination with stardom. It's a growing illness that this nation has. Maybe the world. It's a really discouraging pattern that we're in. That's what this song is about, though it's kind of poking fun at it—the transparency of it all."

"Superstar" was born as a result of Jeff Trott's preferred method of quietly playing late-night song ideas into a small Realistic cassette recorder when staying in a hotel and not wanting to wake anyone up. In this case, he contrived a Temptations-style riff, and then added a fuzztone guitar at the studio the next morning.

"I used this little Danelectro amp with an old MXR fuzztone, and I also had this slightly glam-rock thing going on, but it was a hard song to play live," Jeff explains. "I think we played it live maybe three times, and it never worked. We either couldn't get the groove right or something else would be problematic. I don't think it's one of the stronger songs on that record. You know, it's a different side of Sheryl, and I'm by no means embarrassed by it. The idea was great to begin with. Sometimes the songs that are fun to play live you tend to think of as the really good songs. It doesn't necessarily mean that the recorded version is bad, but you just never know how it's going to translate to the live thing.

"For a long time we had this idea, 'Well, don't worry about it. We'll figure out how to play it later.' 'Yeah, but what about the bagpipes....' In reality it shouldn't be a consideration, but the funny thing is that when you're on the road and thinking about when you're going to start recording again or start writing, you always think, 'My God, I'm going to write something that is just gonna be fun to play on the road.' For instance, 'If It Makes You Happy' is one of the most enjoyable songs to play—for me as a guitar player, just playing the intro chords to that is such a triumphant thing. I feel like I'm sounding the fanfare at some great event. I mean, I hate to be tooting my own horn here, but I'm sure it's like the same kind of feeling that Keith Richards has when he starts up 'Satisfaction.' God, you know, that is such a recognizable intro, and it shows you how important those intros are, serving as the signal to what's coming."

"Hard To Make A Stand," one of the songs originally worked on at Toad Hall, would be included on the U.S. release of the *Sheryl Crow* album in a version featuring Sheryl on vocals, bass, acoustic guitar, and organ; Steve Donnelly on electric guitar; and Pete Thomas on drums. However, this is a rerecording of the altogether gentler, more country-tinged "alternate version" that appears on the album as released in Europe, Hong Kong, Thailand, China, and Australia, as well as the U.K. "Special Edition."

Recorded at Electric Ladyland, this basically showcased the old touring lineup: Sheryl on vocals, acoustic guitar, and organ; Todd Wolfe on electric guitar; Tad Wadhams on bass; and Wally Ingram on drums and djembe. Twenty-three seconds longer than its counterpart, the "alternate version" stands on its own merits.

"To this day I prefer the original, but I guess Tchad Blake and Mitchell Froom didn't like it, and maybe Sheryl didn't like it either," says Todd Wolfe. "To me, it sounded more like Sheryl, whereas the one that's on the record sounds as if Froom and Blake are trying for something. I hate the guitar sound. They might have been trying for a Stones feel, but it sounds more like a Lou Reed guitar to me and I never liked the tone."

In fact, the song borrows its guitar riffs from the Velvet Underground's "Sweet Jane" and its feel from the Stones' "Tumbling Dice." "Love Is A Good Thing," also recorded at Electric Ladyland, and featuring Sheryl's music and Tad Wadhams's lyrics, causes Todd similar consternation.

"That was in the live set every night, and it was a rock anthem," he asserts. "Sheryl did this primal scream thing in the break and it would always get the crowd going. People didn't know what the song was, the second album wasn't out yet, but for me it was a big disappointment when we got into the studio because Sheryl didn't want us to play it like that. I was like 'Why?' and she said, 'It's been done like that,' to which I said, 'Well, not on record it hasn't.' If you listen to the version played at Woodstock, it just rocks, and to have a song that you wrote on the road become a mainstay in the set but not make use of that is, I think, a little bit crazy."

In its subsequently funkier, less anthemic form, the recording of "Love Is A Good Thing" still attracted plenty of attention when the *Sheryl Crow* album was released, although this was due to its lyrical content rather than the reasons that Todd Wolfe had envisaged. At the same time, it's interesting to note that, in line with Bill Bottrell's concerns regarding her live performances, Sheryl also refrained from imbuing the record with an overtly rocking or bluesy feel once she took hold of the production reins. She was not without her advisors, however: Mitchell Froom, as well as a supporter from way back.

"Just as with the Hugh Padgham record, Don Henley had something to say about the *Sheryl Crow* album, too," remembers David Anderle. "In fact, he had even more to say about that since she was basically on her own. She possibly went to him even more at that point, and I had no problem with it."

Al Cafaro, on the other hand, found himself in a quandary when Sheryl first played him some of the tracks at a studio in the San Fernando Valley. By this time, A&M had been on a hot run with albums by the likes of Sting, Bryan Adams, Soundgarden, Extreme, Blues Traveler, and The Gin Blossoms, and Cafaro felt comfortable and qualified to be honest in his opinions. What's more, he felt it was his responsibility, as Sting had discovered when his album *Ten Summoner's Tales* had come in for some pointed criticisms from the company boss. Still, when Al listened to some rough mixes of tracks such as "Maybe Angels," "A Change," and "Hard To Make A Stand," he wasn't sure what to make of Sheryl's work-in-progress.

"'Maybe Angels,' with its grungy, grinding opening sounds, was really symptomatic of how that whole session went," he recalls. "I remember saying to myself, 'I just don't know, I just don't know.' I think it was complicated by the fact that Sheryl was self-producing. It tapped into some of my fears, and also what I was hearing was very rough. None of it had been finished. I distinctly remember leaving without giving her any real feedback, and that was because I honestly didn't know how I felt about it. I must have said something, but in all honesty I don't recall giving her anything to hold onto.

"I'm sure, frankly, that despite all my protestations to the contrary, I was listening for the hits. My ears were colored by 'Where is my Sheryl Crow smash follow-up?' I'm sure that I was guilty of the things that I would hate to be guilty of, and towards that end, rather than say 'I'm afraid we don't have any hits,' or 'Where is the hit?' I chose to say nothing. I think I might have said, 'I need to absorb this,' or 'I need to get some perspective on this'—it would have been something along those lines—but I definitely didn't say 'Sounds great!' I wasn't going to do that, particularly to her, because she would have known. At that point we knew each other pretty well, but I still regret not saying something. I think it hurt her, I think it freaked her out, and that was certainly not what I wanted to do. I don't believe that artists work well out of fear, but on the other hand I felt really obliged to not mislead her.

"I guess part of me would like to say that, even though it was really rough, I could hear the potential, but that wouldn't be true. Instead, I walked out to my car and I remember being a little bit more forthright with Scooter, saying, 'Geez, it sounds like she might have some stuff, but I just don't know!' Because we needed to have a great record. She was our star. However, that's the kind of thing artists have to navigate, and given that, I think it's extraordinary that any artist can persevere. It's remarkable to me, although I'm not saying that about Sheryl, because she had to believe that she could do it, then she had to get to do it, and then she had to play it to someone who she knew loved her for every reason—you know, loved her as a person, loved her as an artist, and loved her as a meal ticket. And then to not get that positive reinforcement is tough shit, man. That's really tough."

Al Cafaro wasn't panicked when he walked away from the studio, he was confused, and he communicated his concern to David Anderle. At the same time, whether or not Al's apparent indifference galvanized Sheryl, his subsequent reaction when he heard the finished record in Dave Collins's mastering suite at A&M was all that she could have hoped for.

"It blew my mind," Cafaro asserts. "I think hearing something for the first time, in its rough form, is always a bit of a challenge. You know, as much as we all want to say we can hear it rough, there are times when we just don't, and so I think my subsequent reaction was down to a combination of the other songs that I heard, and hearing something that was properly mixed and finished. I mean, by this point we're talking about global expectations, but I will say that when I heard the record that day with Dave Collins mastering—and with Sheryl there—it was just like a flower opening up. As the first track, "Maybe Angels" does throw you, but I went with it, and when I heard the record in its entirety I knew that we were going to be fine. I knew that she had a great record, and 'Redemption Day' flipped me out."

A folk protest song, "Redemption Day" was the last number that Sheryl wrote for the album, following a USO trip that she made at the request of First Lady Hillary Rodham Clinton in March 1996. As the recording sessions began to wind down, Sheryl flew to the U.S. Army base in Baumholder, Germany, and then on to the Bosnian town of Tuzla, where she performed acoustic sets for the troops. Struck by the sight of smoking villages and armed looters in the war-torn region, Sheryl sat down in front of her computer after returning from the former Yugoslavia and wrote "Redemption Day" in a single eight-minute burst.

"The experience was unlike any other I've had writing a song," she recalled in Marc Woodworth's *Solo: Women Singer-Songwriters in Their Own Words*. "For me, using such a structured form and writing such verbose lyrics, elements very typical of early Bob Dylan and protest songs from the folk tradition, is unusual, but that's what came out.... After going to Bosnia, seeing what was happening in Rwanda on TV, and then watching the elections in Bosnia on CNN, I was disturbed by the fact that we watch from a safe distance, without any emotion, the same transgressions going down again and again. It shouldn't be like watching *Sophie's Choice* and thinking, 'At least it's a movie.' You can't do that when you know that what you're seeing is going on at that moment. 'Redemption Day' was my response to that recognition, and even though it's very different from anything else on the record, I felt it deserved to be heard."

That it did. Sheryl recorded the song during the last week of April, and when Al Cafaro heard it his belief in Sheryl's talent was reaffirmed.

"For me, 'Redemption Day' embodied the extraordinary artistry that she represents," he says. "I also loved 'Hard To Make A Stand' and 'Sweet Rosalyn,' while 'If It Makes You Happy' was, sure as could be, a song that was going to go over big on the radio. We had to go with that as the first single. We had the world waiting. It was clear to me that the three singles—'If It Makes You Happy,' 'Everyday Is A Winding Road,' and 'Home'— could drive this record. I was almost overcome with how happy I was."

Nevertheless, according to David Anderle, the approval of others isn't necessarily enough to satisfy Sheryl Crow. On the contrary, praise for her work is often greeted with a dismissive, self-effacing attitude that serves to puncture the moment, and while this may be a sign of her perfectionism, it can also be gratuitous.

"She has a hard time accepting compliments or accepting goodness," Anderle states. "Somehow she has to turn it around a little bit. On the second album, I went with her down to Sunset Sound to listen to all of the stuff she had, and I remember a couple of times I would hear a track and say, 'Man, is that you playing bass on this?' and she'd say, 'Yeah,' and I'd say, 'That's a great fucking bass line!' She'd say, 'Nah, that's nothing. I'm gonna have a real bass player come in and play.' Okay. Then we'd listen to another thing and I'd say, 'That vocal is really great.' 'No, it's just a work vocal. I'm gonna have to go back and redo it.' Finally I said, 'You know, Sheryl, you make somebody feel real bad about their perception of your work! It would just seem easier to me to not say anything, except I can't because your stuff knocks me out! And when it doesn't it doesn't.' She has a real hard time just saying, 'Great, thanks,' except she will at a certain time say, 'Yes, it's mine,' so there's also that part of her that is very aware of what she can do and what she is doing."

At the 46th annual BMI Awards in Beverly Hills in May of 1998, Sheryl and Jeff Trott's collaborative work on her 1996 album would earn them the prize for Songwriter of the Year, shared with Babyface and R. Kelly. Each of the prizewinners had three of the seventy-three songs recognized by BMI as the most performed of 1997.

Back in 1996, meanwhile, with a new album in the bag, and a harder, more defiant attitude to convey, it was time for Sheryl to undergo an image makeover. This was achieved courtesy of her own ideas, in conjunction with those of the A&M crew led by Jeri Heiden, who was Rich Frankel's replacement as Senior VP of Creative Services. Gone was the happy-go-lucky neo-hippie with a head full of curls, replaced by a sullen vamp with heavy lipstick, death-warmed-over mascara, and straight, streaked hair—strung-out, a living corpse, heroin chic.

At least, that's how she appeared on the cover of her eponymously titled album—another sign of self-assertion, even though her shelved record had also been called *Sheryl Crow*.

"I should have just called it 'Reaction,'" she'd tell *Entertainment Weekly* a couple of years later. "It was a reaction to the really fast climb that I had for about a year, and then it was a reaction to people's reaction to that—which was very negative in the press. Compound that with the fact that I'd been doing nothing but play for two and a half years in a row, and by the time I got in the studio I was like a tightly wound spring."

The image was toned down only slightly for the "If It Makes You Happy" video. Directed by Keir McFarlane, this featured Sheryl as a miniskirted attraction in the "Endangered Species" exhibit of a zoo, where it appears that the other animals have already paid a visit to the local taxidermist.

"Sheryl was a little bit leery of Keir's idea, but she really liked his [sample work] reel and she wanted to do something different," says Randy Sosin, who, as the record company's Vice President of Music Video Production, met with the artists, talked about what they wanted to do, and assigned the appropriate director. "She got on the phone with Keir and they talked a lot about what would be going on. In the end, we spent about $400,000 on the video, which by today's standards isn't that much money, but back then was quite a lot.... You really base it on how many units you're gonna ship. It's part of your marketing budget, so if you're shipping a lot of records you spend more on the video. We knew we'd do well on that record."

In other words, the "If It Makes You Happy" video cost about twice as much to produce as the *Tuesday Night Music Club* album. Given the projected returns, this was fine, so long as everybody was happy with the results. Unfortunately, some weren't.

"I'll never forget when we showed that video for the first time at the company," says Al Cafaro. "There were people who absolutely thought it was the worst thing Sheryl could do; that her lips were too prevalent, that it was too sexual, too hard, she wasn't warm enough, that alternative radio stations would hate the image. I encouraged people to speak their minds and I would ultimately try not judge them for it, but I remember at some point just saying, 'Fuck you! Get the fuck outta here!' Talk about over-thinking....

"To me, it was so interesting to see it in the context of expectations and the artistic process, and how difficult it is to take chances, and how you can be slaughtered for taking chances, even when what you do is ultimately good. It really spelled that out to me, because to have her pull that video off was not an easy thing. That wasn't a fun shoot. I think Sheryl liked the video more than the others that she'd done, but it was a tough thing to shoot because it had a lot of revealing stuff in there. I mean, you look at that video and see the way she was dressed, and the physicality and the beauty and the sexuality of it, as well as all of that edge…. That's her! A lot of her is there!"

Indeed, unlike other female rock stars, such as Cher or Madonna, Sheryl has never felt all that comfortable about adopting a new look or redefining her persona.

"It's been really difficult for me to play the game with fashion and with imaging," she conceded in some outtake interview footage from VH1's *Behind the Music*. "I don't handle it well. I mean, it's obvious. If you look through my long history of kind of pseudo image changes and stuff, they were all experimental according to my moods. Like the artwork on the second record was a person that didn't want to be that person anymore…I was abandoning everything that had been me before that: jeans and vintage clothes and 'Hey, how ya doin'?' Y'know, 'Yeah, I'll tell you anything in an interview.' I was so like 'Let me get as far away from that as I can….'

"Imaging's so much of it now. It's such a big part of being a celebrity or whatever, and I just haven't really cared that much about it…. I've always just put on clothes that made me feel good or that expressed who I was, and as soon as you start wearing high-fashion things it's like 'Oh, now she thinks she's this and that.' It's all up for interpretation, and you just have to sort of think about it all the time, and I've been really lazy about that. I've been really lazy about, like, 'Okay, what is it going to mean if I wear this?' I haven't really cared that much about it…."

Regardless, Sheryl did care about it when striking out on her own at the time of her second record, and the effort paid off. Released on September 3, 1996, "If It Makes You Happy" spent 27 weeks on The Billboard Hot 100 singles chart, peaking at No. 10 and selling about 504,000 copies (2,000 less than "All I Wanna Do"). The *Sheryl Crow* album, released on September 24, sold 79,000 copies during its first week to enter and peak at No. 6 on The Billboard 200, where it would spend 63 weeks. Still, it didn't get there without an initial spot of drama that undeniably put a dent in the sales figures, even if the related publicity partly compensated for this.

On the track "Love Is A Good Thing," the opening line features Sheryl sniping at the sales policy of America's largest retail chain Wal-Mart, by claiming that children kill each other with the guns they buy there. When visiting one of these stores while on the road in Albuquerque, Sheryl had been shocked to see semi-automatic rifles and "dum-dum" bullets being sold next to the children's toy department. Wal-Mart, of course, is the same store that has swallowed up much of the local business in Sheryl's hometown of Kennett, where, as in many other rural areas, it is *the* dominant record outlet. On an annual basis, the Arkansas-based chain accounts for around $50 million in record sales nationwide, roughly one-twelfth of the total market.

In 1996, guns were a touchy subject for the company, which had been sued three times during the previous four years as a result of weaponry it had sold being linked to crimes. One of these cases involved the bullets used by a pair of minors to kill a man. Wal-Mart had made efforts to tighten up its sales practices, but when advance copies of *Sheryl Crow* were circulated at the start of September and the lyrics of "Love Is A Good Thing" came to light, the fur began to fly. If Sheryl didn't edit the offending line—

or else omit the song from the album—then Wal-Mart would refuse to stock it. Sheryl wouldn't budge, so the company followed through on its threat.

"Wal-Mart believes this is an unfair, untrue, and totally irresponsible comment," said company spokesman Dale Ingram, while pointing out that the sale of guns to minors was strictly prohibited at its stores.

In a published statement, Al Cafaro fired back that Wal-Mart was choosing "guns over music.... Every day in America, children are dying by guns bought legally. This is a fact.... Sheryl's responsibility as an artist is to reveal the truth, and it is our responsibility as a record company to defend her ability to do so.... I believe that Wal-Mart's decision is wrong, very wrong."

This was the first time that the discount chain had banned a record for mentioning its name in a negative context, but not the first time that it had tried to strong-arm a record company into changing its product. In 1993, Wal-Mart had demanded that Geffen reissue Nirvana's *In Utero* so that the track "Rape Me" would be nonsensically listed on the album sleeve as "Wait Me," and there were also numerous examples of the store carrying sanitized hip-hop CDs. With this kind of sway over the marketing, distribution, and consumption of product, the likes of Wal-Mart play a major role in how music is sold in the United States as well as what many Americans actually get to hear.

The ban on Sheryl's record amounted to an estimated 400,000 fewer sales, yet A&M stood firmly behind its artist, who suddenly assumed the mantle of someone who wasn't afraid to speak out on hot issues. "It just seemed like a strange position to take, to not step up to the plate and take responsibility, but, instead, to ban my records," Sheryl remarked in a February 2000 interview with *The Dartmouth*, the in-house newspaper of Dartmouth College in Hanover, New Hampshire. "And they really had an opportunity to rise to the occasion and make a great, altruistic statement, but chose not to."

Wal-Mart did subsequently change its policy so that guns and ammunition would only be sold via catalogues. Meanwhile, back in September of 1996, neither Sheryl or A&M were averse to how all of the publicity generated by the Wal-Mart controversy neatly coincided with their album's release. In certain areas, local radio stations even took to distributing the record in Wal-Mart parking lots. To date, U.S. sales of *Sheryl Crow* stand at more than 2.36 million copies, while the worldwide figure is in excess of four million.

Amid all the hubbub, the album drew favorable reviews from most music critics. "The lyrics seem grittier and more intimate," stated *Rolling Stone*. "The craftsmanship is strong and self assured...her voice is warm and raspy sweet."

*Spin* alluded to the album's "bigger beats and dirtier guitar/keyboard effects.... Nothing extreme, perhaps, but almost psychedelic when joined to big mainstream melodies.... It just sounds gorgeous, and current...pop musicians will be learning from it for years to come."

*Q* described the record as "radio-friendly, not too self-important, light on its feet, sometimes too ready to disclaim any serious intent," while *Billboard* considered the self-titled collection to be "as consistently appealing as it is adventurous. The quality and breadth of the material is impressive.... A multitalented songwriter and performer who dug deep and pulled up music that speaks from the soul. Worth the wait."

"Crow doesn't expose that much of herself on *Sheryl Crow*—she's an emotional centrist," asserted *Entertainment Weekly*. "But at the very least, she's building a bridge to a lasting career."

That she was, and she was also shutting a door on the recent past. Sheryl's sophomore effort, which was musically more eclectic but also more consistent in terms of quality than her previous record, served to establish her in the public eye as both the creator of her music and the architect of her own success.

"For me, getting the record done was just a joyous experience," she told David Wild during their 2002 interview for *Musicians*. "When I listened to it, I felt like every single emotion that I'd had when I went in to make the record was completely indexed...it was all captured, and it was the best record that I could make at that time."

Sheryl Crow had caught the wave, and, musically, things would just continue to get better.

# CHAPTER THIRTEEN

# Global Concerns

In the early summer of 1996, a few months before the release of her sophomore album, Sheryl assembled a new band to go out on the road. Only Roy Scott Bryan was retained from the previous lineup, to play keyboards, percussion, and pedal steel, while Bay Area session man Jim Bogios was recruited on drums, along with former Jellyfish bassist/vocalist Tim Smith and Jeff Trott on guitar. Todd Wolfe initially found himself out in the cold, but after a July 4 concert in front of 85,000 people at the Fair St. Louis, he was invited to rejoin the band and supplement Trott's rock riffs with his own blues licks.

Sheryl herself shifted between guitar, bass, keyboards, and accordion for a number of North American dates through the end of October. During one of these gigs, at the 220-capacity Viper Room in Los Angeles on October 11, Eric Clapton sat in with Sheryl and her band, playing on Willie Dixon's "I Can't Quit You Baby" as well as "The Na-Na Song." This, in turn, fueled media reports about Sheryl's then-current relationship with the guitar legend, whom she'd known for several years but only recently started dating. The gossip had really begun to spread that June, when the two of them performed "Run, Baby, Run" at the *Pavarotti & Friends* War Child benefit concert in Modena, Italy. There, Sheryl also raised a few eyebrows by employing a soprano voice to duet with the opera star on "Là Ci Darem La Mano," from Mozart's *Don Giovanni*. Those who knew Sheryl from way back weren't overly surprised—this was how they remembered her singing at Kennett High and the University of Missouri.

The Crow/Clapton romance would be declared kaput in early March of the following year, yet their friendship would remain intact while Sheryl next satisfied the gossipmongers courtesy of her liaison with Jakob Dylan, son of Bob and lead singer with The Wallflowers. In February of 1997, The Wallflowers opened for Sheryl at a number of U.S. dates; during the last of these, at the Palace Theater in Albany, New York, she again revisited her youth by walking onstage dressed as a baton-twirling cheerleader while Jakob sang his group's Grammy-nominated hit, "6th Avenue Heartache." Later in the evening, he partly returned the favor by running across the stage while Sheryl performed "The Na-Na Song," before the show closed out with a jam session featuring both bands covering material by The Beatles, the Stones, and the Velvet Underground.

For some, the sight of Jakob and Sheryl sharing the microphone and trading verses on "The Night They Drove Old Dixie Down" and "The Weight" evoked memories of Bob Dylan's 1960s collaborations with Joan Baez. In fact, on April 10, Jakob and Sheryl even shared the stage with Levon Helm, one of Bob's former colleagues in The Band, when they appeared with Steve Winwood, Emmylou Harris, James Taylor, Stevie Wonder,

Celine Dion, and The Artist then Formerly Known as Prince at the Universal Amphitheater in L.A. for the fourth annual *VH1 Honors* show. This was in support of music education, a cause dear to Sheryl's heart.

"I was a music teacher in the St. Louis school system," she informed reporters backstage at the concert, which raised over $150,000 to help maintain the music programs of public schools in both Los Angeles and New York. "During the short time that I was there, I saw the music budget getting whittled away. I thought, and still think, that it is a travesty, so being a part of tonight is very important to me."

The Wallflowers alternated with California rock band Dishwalla as the opening act on Sheryl's thirty-eight-city North American tour that ran from January 30 to April 4 of 1997. In May there were trips to Australia, Thailand, Singapore, and Japan; June took the band back to Europe, which it had visited the previous November; and then from July through October there was another tour of the U.S., including a half-dozen dates opening for The Rolling Stones. It was a packed schedule, interspersed with the usual radio and TV appearances, as well as numerous awards shows and charity engagements.

On February 24, Sheryl turned up at the Brit Awards show in London to collect her prize for Best International Singer, and thanked all-conquering British quintet, the Spice Girls, "for not being in my category." On the twenty-fifth, she was in New York City to receive the Patrick Lippert Award for encouraging young people to vote (during a year when, ironically, voter turnout had been at its lowest in decades), and then the following night she was at Madison Square Garden for the 39th annual Grammy Awards ceremony. There, "If It Makes You Happy" scooped up the prize for Best Female Rock Vocal Performance, while *Sheryl Crow* won for Best Rock Album. A total of four awards at three events on consecutive nights—not a bad haul.

The summer '97 North American tour, which included some all-female, multi-celeb Lilith Fair dates in addition to support by Michael Penn and southern rockers Wilco, was sponsored by Tommy Hilfiger. Not surprisingly, Hilfiger designed Sheryl's stage outfits, as well as a t-shirt that was sold to raise funds for research into breast cancer, a disease that had claimed the life of her grandmother. This was the upside to the ever more prevalent use of rock music to hype consumer goods, for by now Sheryl was applying herself to some worthy causes—that summer and fall, she performed at benefit gigs in aid of rape support centers, Planned Parenthood, and the fights against breast cancer and multiple sclerosis. Success may have lessened the need for her to undertake as many meet 'n' greets and personal appearances as before, but the overall workload— some of it self-imposed—was still extremely heavy.

"These people work very, very hard; much harder than most people imagine," says Al Cafaro. "When they're out of cycle it's a different story, but at that point they're worrying if they're ever going to be able to write again. That's the only time when they're not working, whereas once they get in the cycle, man, they work. The machine expects it, and when I say the machine, I don't necessarily mean the record company machine, but the press, the media—they expect it."

Also on the schedule during 1996 and 1997 was one of Sheryl's traditionally less anticipated tasks, the making of promotional videos, even though the *Sheryl Crow* project saw some of her most creative, successful, and ultimately gratifying experiences in this regard. Most notable, following the earthy persona and in-your-face attitude of "If It Makes You Happy," were the more understated but equally powerful black-and-white promos for "Everyday Is A Winding Road" and "Home."

The "Everyday" video, directed by Peggy Sirota and featuring a dowdily dressed Sheryl, was a sepia-toned tapestry of wonderfully filmed images and superb cut-to-the-beat editing. Shot in New York City in October '96, it tied in with Sheryl's relocation there from the studio scene of Los Angeles; initially living near the intersection of Greenwich Avenue and Bank Street in the West Village, she'd subsequently buy a loft in NoHo, the downtown area just north of Houston Street.

"I find that in New York I'm out all the time, whether I have plans or not," she told E! Online. "I'm constantly meeting people and doing things. I'm constantly seeing people play, which I don't ever do in L.A., where you just sit at home waiting for someone to call."

Unlike some of her previous efforts, the completed "Everyday" video pleased Sheryl, and the same could also be said for the altogether different "Home" promo, which was shot at a country fair in Hemet, California, southeast of Los Angeles. Directed by Samuel Bayer, this slice of Americana featured an assortment of natural, largely unglamorous-looking people in a rural setting—folks with crooked teeth and hard, weathered faces, whose physical imperfections were juxtaposed with the bodily attributes of Ms. Sheryl Crow in her babydoll negligée and cowboy boots. Reverting to her softer, tousled-hair image, Sheryl had never looked better.

"Sheryl loved that video," confirms Randy Sosin, then A&M's Vice President of Music Video Production. "She spent four days in Hemet and worked her ass off. It was Sam Bayer's idea to shoot it at a country fair. We weren't going back to Missouri, but Sheryl wanted it to look like where she grew up, with country fairs and real people. Sam got real-life portraitures of people, along the lines of [photographer] Sally Mann, and he included some interviews in the video. Sheryl was such a good sport. Y'know, the last day she stood there in her dress and we splashed her with this mud from a truck driving past. To get splashed like that in front of everybody is not a glamour thing, but she did it, she loved it."

Everyone appeared to agree that "Home" was Sheryl's best video yet; everyone, that is, except the execs over at MTV and VH1, who weren't exactly enamored with the shocking dearth of beautiful people.

"'Home' was nearly brilliant," comments Wayne Isaak, who was VH1's Executive Vice President of Music. "You see, from the marketing perspective, they spent too much time on the ugliness. They spent too much time on the kid with bad teeth and all the circus stuff on the side. I don't mean to be inhuman, but I thought they could have had more Sheryl in it. I don't know that Sheryl has ever looked that good in a video. Her makeup, her clothing…I would have liked to see a little more Sheryl and just a little less of the freak show.

"Those are just little comments I gave to the record company, and everybody looked at me like 'What are you talking about?' My good friends at A&M, who I used to work closely with, were appalled I would say that, but I think it's an important thing. Videos are marketing tools first and foremost, and secondly they should be artistic endeavors, and they are, but if you can combine those two purposes—like Madonna does consistently, and like The Foo Fighters, who consistently make the best videos—that's really the key."

Al Cafaro fully understands Wayne Isaak's point, but he still doesn't see how this applies to "Home," which he describes as "a killer video."

"To me it was a piece of art," Cafaro asserts, "and because of that I was so distressed at the response to it. You know, there are times when directors put things in videos that are gratuitous and stupid—'Why do we need to see an octogenarian there?'—but that video was so real. It embodied the song to me."

Despite Wayne Isaak's "little comments" regarding the promo, he states that networks such as VH1 generally aren't involved in the artistic decision-making beyond being consulted, for instance, on how many film clips should be included in a movie-related video, or whether live performance footage should be shown in black-and-white or color.

"Every now and then somebody would say, 'I've got an idea and what do you think of this?' but that didn't happen very much, and frankly I'm glad that it didn't," Isaak remarks. "I mean, if I'd have said 'You should go for that, you should do it,' and they did it and it wasn't very good, or the song was a dog, then we'd have been kind of stuck custom-ordering it."

"You just cannot tell how the likes of MTV and VH1 are going to react," adds Randy Sosin. "Sometimes you do the art thing and they love it, and sometimes you do it and it's not what they want from that artist. When we produce videos, we won't do anything that's so offensive it'll never get played, but we also can't let MTV tell us what to do, because they'll just water it down. Ultimately they do water it down! Still, although the cable networks don't have control or the ultimate say, we wouldn't make a heavy metal Sheryl Crow video that would have them going 'Aagh!'…unless that was our whole marketing plan and there was some bigger game."

On June 28, 1997, prior to a gig at London's Royal Albert Hall, Sheryl met with the producers of the upcoming James Bond movie, *Tomorrow Never Dies*, who wanted her to write and perform the film's title track. Sheryl took the assignment, and under pressure to come up with something at short notice, she initially turned to Jeff Trott and asked him if he had any Bondish-sounding tunes stored away.

"We fooled around with some ideas, and then it was like 'Well, I need to come up with something that has an orchestration,'" Jeff recalls. "It was such a monumental task, and although I can do orchestrations, I'm not able to sit down with an orchestra and write out arrangements for the players. Sheryl needed someone who could do that fast, so she got Mitchell Froom, and within a few days he was able to knock something out. That was a good move, and actually I was a little bit relieved. I mean, if I'd had a couple of months to work on it I would have accepted the challenge, but it was too short a time for me to come up with the goods."

Froom's work paid off; "Tomorrow Never Dies" would earn a Golden Globe nomination for Best Original Song in a Motion Picture.

"I loved doing that," Sheryl told *Musician* magazine in April 1999. "It was an interesting experience in that it was a James Bond movie, so you not only have the luxury of getting to step outside your genre, but you have the legacy of these great songs that have come before and the great tradition of James Bond the spy. So, the direction we headed in was to create something that was reminiscent of early James Bond."

Mission accomplished. Singing in an uncharacteristically smooth manner about the requisite martinis, girls, guns, and murder, Sheryl delved into Sheena Easton territory on a formulaic song that combined trademark Bond guitar twang with elements of the *Perry Mason* theme tune. Then she slipped out of the all-black getup that she wore for the typically eye-catching video (directed by Daniel Kleinman), and while the record company was dealing with the promotion of her latest album, Sheryl started to think about the production of her next record.

Initially, she planned to do this on the road, utilizing the combination of vintage and state-of-the-art equipment that she'd begun to purchase as an alternative to spending money in a commercial studio. In the long run, this would prove to be far more cost-effective, especially as Sheryl could write and demo material whenever she felt like it without having to watch the clock. All she was missing was a mixing board and 24-track machine, and so after the *Sheryl Crow* tour ended in October '97, taking advice from engineer Blair Lamb, she invested in a custom Neve broadcast console and Studer 24-track. Now the question was, where to put all of the gear?

First, she intended to house it in her loft residence, but this idea was shelved when it was pointed out that the co-op board would never stand for any noise emanating from a recording setup within its building. Then Mitchell Froom told Sheryl about a facility adjacent to the one where he'd produced the *Cool Down Time* album of former Del Fuegos frontman Dan Zanes. Globe Studios, located at 416 West 13th Street, in the heart of Manhattan's meatpacking district, had been opened in 1994 by musician and film composer Bob FitzSimons. Occupying a suite within the vintage former Colliers Building constructed by Jacob Astor in 1901, the studio needed reequipping, but FitzSimons didn't have the necessary funds. Therefore, when he and Sheryl were introduced to one another by Mitchell Froom, they quickly shook hands on a mutually profitable deal.

In return for eight weeks of session time, Sheryl's quarter-million dollars' worth of gear would spend a year at Globe, to be used by any number of commercial clients. Thus, her new project would incur hardly any studio fees, while Globe would benefit from the use of Sheryl's equipment. For both parties the deal made perfect sense, even though eight weeks of studio time effectively turned into four months; the installation began around Thanksgiving of 1997, but it wasn't until the following February that Sheryl was ready to commence work. Still, Bob FitzSimons wasn't complaining. The publicity generated by playing host to the recording of her latest album would more than make up for the lost time, while Sheryl herself appreciated having to travel only five blocks from her home.

"I loved working there," she'd tell the *New York Times* in October 1998. "My studio was across the street from Hogs and Heifers and the Hog Pit, where I could get mashed potatoes and fried chicken any night I wanted. And then you have transvestite hookers everywhere, and Hells Angels, and it was just a cool, cool vibe. If you ever got really hung up in the frustration of trying to get something accomplished in the studio, you could walk out and just be amongst some bizarre energy. It clears your head and gives you some perspective when you walk out in such a strange, frenetic, unpredictable atmosphere."

The reference to "my studio" would later turn into a major source of friction following the project's completion. In the meantime, Sheryl was a hell of a long way from Kennett, Missouri, and she was also in a dark place inside her head, suffering the depression of numerous performance artists who struggle to find their *raison d'être* when they're not on the road. Still, as countless predecessors had already discovered, there's nothing like a spot of misery and introspection to inspire truly heartfelt music, and in Sheryl's case she was motivated to write less as an observer, and more in the first person, about the role that she'd played in the demise of her relationships. Productive melancholia—it proved to be a double-edged sword.

"That's a nice emotion to be able to tap into when you're writing songs," Sheryl remarked during her *New York Times* interview. "But when I'm really miserable, I can't accomplish anything. Part of being miserable for me is that I'm convinced everything I do is terrible. So then you start ripping it apart before you even finish it."

Accordingly, most of the songs that Sheryl initially wrote for the new record didn't make the final cut, and neither did many of her co-compositions with Jeff Trott. Uncertainty, that curse of the artistic psyche, reared its ugly head, and the result was plenty of chopping and changing with regard to song structures and the actual choice of material.

"I had just moved to New York, and I didn't know a lot of people there, and was going through a lonely time," Sheryl told the *Chicago Tribune* in April 1999. "I had just come off the road and was thinking about what I didn't have in my life. I had let my life at home go, my relationships had fallen apart, I lost friends because I had been gone so long. I didn't really have a place I could call home anymore. All that stuff started to wash over me and overwhelm me."

This is where Sheryl was at when she began work on her new record. No longer trying to be one of the beer-and-tequila-drinking guys of the *Tuesday Night Music Club* sessions or the garish-looking rebel of the *Sheryl Crow* album, she wanted to get closer to the core of who she was and how she felt, even if this wasn't a particularly easy thing to do.

"It wasn't a reaction to one relationship," she recalled in a September 1998 interview with *Entertainment Weekly*, "it was a reaction to ten years of relationships that I sped through and didn't even look at. And there was a lot of self-analysis as to who I was in those relationships and why I'm still single and why the only thing in my life for five years has been music. Ten years, really. It was a harsh period."

The room where Sheryl intended to record at Globe Studios didn't exactly ease her inner turmoil. "It was huge, and the sound in there was a disaster," says Trina Shoemaker, who reprised her role as engineer despite the fact that she hadn't been involved in choosing the facility or the equipment. "There was no isolation, so we had to build a drum tent that ended up looking like a homeless shelter in the middle of the room. There were pieces of cardboard and wood, just slathered in baffling, blankets, and curtains. We didn't have enough blankets or curtains or baffling material, and although the drums came out sounding real cool, it was ridiculous. It was like 'Oh my God, that's what your drummer's inside?' and I was saying, 'I know, it looks like a pile over there, but believe me, it won't fall in on you.' So, we made do. I just showed up, hot off a record with Blues Traveler, and I was told, 'This is the equipment, this is the place, let's roll.'

"In my opinion, Sheryl is a naturally great producer, because she's so musical, she's so intuitive. Then again, there's a whole administrative aspect to producing records, and her management takes care of that. In the studio, she doesn't walk around like some producers, with a big, fat notebook containing details of every single song, constantly updating our schedule. None of that goes on with Sheryl. She doesn't produce in that way.

"Sheryl Crow is a wildly gifted musician and a great arranger, but the job of a record producer is more than being a wildly talented musician and a great arranger, and it's also more than being the person who says, 'This part should go here,' and 'I think we've got to get a better take. I don't think it feels right. The drums feel too stiff.' That's musical production. Record production has a lot more to it than that, and Sheryl's growth as a producer hasn't covered all aspects, but musically she's bound to grow because the creative side is her whole life."

While Sheryl utilized a quality cast of road and studio pros for the new album—guitarists Jeff Trott, Todd Wolfe, Wendy Melvoin, Greg Liesz, and Val McCallum; bassists Dan Rothchild and Tim Smith; keyboard player Benmont Tench; violinist Lisa Germano; and drummers Gregg Williams, Dan McCarroll, and Jim Bogios—she combined her writing and production duties with singing and playing bass, keyboards, guitars, harmonica, and percussion.

"I'm a person that kind of obsesses, so that when I get into one instrument that's all I'll play for a while," Sheryl stated in *Musician* magazine. "On this record, playing bass was a really inspiring challenge. So, every time I wrote a song, I either wrote it or tracked it on bass. That just was the instrument I gravitated to. I've been playing acoustic gigs and been playing bass, and I'm getting better and better at that, and then it will probably be something else.... I wrote most of my last record on guitar, but I think writing on bass actually frees you up to think about writing a good melody."

Certainly, the new project didn't lack material, and as had been the case with Sheryl's previous two albums, she made an auspicious start courtesy of a standout number coming together on the very first night; she'd already worked out the acoustic guitar part to the beautiful "Riverwide," and in the studio she then supplemented a melody that was equal parts Indian, Appalachian, and Gaelic, with expressively plaintive lyrics.

"I'm still digesting all the hidden meanings," Sheryl later admitted to *USA Today*, while describing how she drew inspiration from Walt Whitman. "I was touched by one of his poems that made me think about the absence of love in my life. In most of my relationships, I've been the encourager, the caretaker, the edifier, and then I find myself sitting alone late at night more often than I want."

*Riverwide* would be the title of Sheryl's new album until shortly before its release. "The creative process in the studio is so immediate," she stated in her *Chicago Tribune* interview. "I like to pick up an instrument and start playing, so if I'm working on one song and we wind up going down another path, that's when the magic happens. That's how 'Riverwide' came out—I got frustrated and de-tuned my guitar and out came this song."

"It Don't Hurt," a mid-tempo Crow/Trott number about the struggle to move on from—what else?—a failed relationship, was borne of a similar approach. In this case, however, it was Jeff's acoustic 12-string that was de-tuned by his guitar tech as a means of ensuring that the strings didn't snap due to the depressurized environment during a flight. While on tour, Jeff used the guitar to compose in his hotel room, and it was the strange tuning that inspired this particular song.

"I just changed one string so that it was a little more in tune and it formed this really interesting chord," he explains, "and then I started playing this descending riff that sounded kind of spooky. I played the riff for Sheryl and that ended up becoming 'It Don't Hurt.' So, in some ways I suppose I should credit my guitar tech for inadvertently coming up with the tuning. I think it was just B's and E's, and it was really droney.

"'It Don't Hurt' was one of the only songs that we wrote together on the road. You know, it's kind of distracting being on tour, and you don't always get time to write, but that was one song that we managed to come up with. We started playing it live, and it actually went down really well. We thought, 'Maybe this is a little gem.'"

Nevertheless, while more time provided the luxury of mucho experimentation in the studio, this was not necessarily a blessing—some numbers were fairly straightforward to record, yet others, such as "There Goes The Neighborhood," "Am I Getting Through (Part I & II)," and "Members Only," required so much work and reworking that they virtually drove everyone to distraction.

"It was an even split," says Trina Shoemaker. "Half of the songs we struggled for, and half of them just rolled off the tips of Sheryl's fingers and off her band's instruments and right onto tape. 'Am I Getting Through,' 'Members Only,' and 'There Goes The Neighborhood' were loop-based, they were complicated arrangements, they were essentially wall-of-sound-type tracks, and they were traumatic for everyone involved. There was so much layering, from building the loops to getting the harmonies and vocal distortion just right."

The psychedelia-funk Crow/Trott party number "There Goes The Neighborhood" was, in fact, among the first songs to be brewed up in New York at the start of what would come to be known as *The Globe Sessions*. The alternately spooky and celebratory atmosphere of New Orleans had helped kick-start the *Sheryl Crow* album, and now NYC's own idiosyncrasies were serving to do the same for the new record.

"You know, just being in New York, there's so much activity," Jeff Trott remarks. "You're constantly surrounded by people. There are people on the floor below you, people on the floor above you, beside you—it's kind of claustrophobic—and "There Goes The Neighborhood" was initiated by all of this. I had a '50s Les Paul Junior that belongs to Sheryl, and I plugged it into this old Vox AC30 and started trying to get a guitar sound. Sheryl said, 'What is that riff?' and I said, 'I'm just trying to get my guitar sound.' She said, 'Well, that's really good.'

"I got Gregg Williams involved, who lives near me in Portland. Sheryl was looking for a drum programmer—you know, somebody to make loops, to get us going in terms of songwriting. Anyway, he came up with the handclap idea. He loves claps, and so we just kind of developed it. I played the riff and that eventually led into a chord progression. Being in New York and being claustrophobic and never being able to really get a hundred percent sleep at night—I think this inspired Sheryl in a big way.

"We went out on the town a lot. Sometimes you need to blow off some steam, so we'd finish a session kind of late and then go down to this club called Hell, which was this trendy kind of gay bar that basically was the closest thing to us. We'd go in there because it was convenient, and we'd sit there and drink cosmopolitans and just enjoy the night. Summertime in New York, you can just walk around and hang out. No one seems to go to sleep there, so even though it was claustrophobic, I think it produced some real great imagery for Sheryl."

During their last tour, Sheryl and her band had performed covers of Rolling Stones numbers like "The Last Time," "Sway," and "Can't You Hear Me Knocking," and this had left Jeff in a heavy Stones phase, listening to their records, studying the parts. Therefore, when there was a need to build the middle section of "There Goes The Neighborhood," he immediately thought of the vibrant saxophone solo on "Can't You Hear Me Knocking," as performed by the legendary Bobby Keys. "I just totally hear Bobby Keys playing on this," Jeff told Sheryl. "Can we get somebody who kind of plays like him?" As it happened, they were able to go one better—the man himself was in New York for a few days while the Stones took a break during their *Bridges to Babylon* tour, so Keys was asked if he'd play on "There Goes The Neighborhood," and he readily agreed.

"He's such a character," says Jeff. "When he first came in, he had his manager submit a rider that demanded like a case of Corona beer, a tray of sandwiches, some assorted sweet cakes, a bottle of Jack Daniels, a bottle of Cuervo…and this was at ten o'clock in the morning! I mean, come on! I know this is rock 'n' roll, but it's a little early to be drinking, unless you're carrying over from the night before. Anyway, he came in, and he brought the rest of the Rolling Stones horn section—Michael Davis on trombone and Kent Smith on trumpet—and when we played Bobby the song he said, 'Okay, I've got this horn arrangement.' He instantly knew what to play. We were just going, 'Bobby, you do what you do.' Within an hour or two he'd finished the horn track, which is amazing, and then we wanted him to do a solo, kind of like 'Can't You Hear Me Knocking,' which had been the original idea. So, he did that and again he was amazing. He finished at about one o'clock and started drinking some beer, eating sandwiches, and telling some stories, and while we all sat down and had a couple of shots of Cuervo, he proceeded to drink the entire bottle by three o'clock."

At this point, "There Goes The Neighborhood" was in the bag, whereas "Members Only," with its upbeat retro-rock grooves and lyrical swipes at decadence, dance, and

**Sheryl and Scout**
At home with the
orphan dog she
adopted, August 1994.
© *Neal Preston/Corbis*

**March 1, 1995**
The proud winner of
three Grammy Awards
the first time she'd
been nominated.
© *Scott Weiner/Retna*

**The Kennett connection**
At a post-show party,
Sheryl celebrates her
1995 Grammy success
with Carlotta Tarver,
Ann Cash, Debbie Welsh,
and Jo Beth Skaggs.
*Courtesy of Jo Beth Skaggs*

**Monaco, May 3, 1995**
Receiving a World Music Award from Ringo Starr.
© *Schachmes/ Regards/Retna*

**The erstwhile soprano, June 20, 1996**
Performing "Là Ci Darem La Mano" with Luciano Pavarotti at the Parco Novi Sad in Modena, Italy.
© *Corbis Sygma*

**A favorite friend, but definitely no mistake**
With Eric Clapton at an Emporio Armani private party at the Lexington Armory, New York City, September 12, 1996.
© *Bill Davila/Retna*

**Live in London, 1996**
Performing with
Tim Smith and Todd
Wolfe on BBC's Radio
One to promote the
*Sheryl Crow* album.
© *Mick Hutson/Redferns*

**Not one of her preferred chores**
Sheryl takes a break to have body makeup applied during filming of the "Everyday Is A Winding Road" video in New York's Central Park, October 26, 1996.
© *Bill Davila/Retna*

**Sheryl and Sting**
Attending a Rolling Stones concert at the Hard Rock Hotel in Las Vegas, February 15, 1998.
© *Steve Granitz/Retna*

**Playing bass for**
***The Globe Sessions,* 1998**
Although she's most adept at playing keyboards, Sheryl has adopted the bass as one of her instruments of choice.
*Tchad Blake*

**Globe Studios, New York**
At the console with engineer Trina Shoemaker. Drummer Gregg Williams is in the background.
*Tchad Blake*

**Overshadowed by her own image,
May 31, 2000**
Sheryl performs an acoustic set at CNN's
20th Anniversary Celebration in Atlanta.
The show served as a benefit for the
International Campaign to Ban Landmines.
© *Laura Noel/Corbis Sygma*

**If it makes her happy**
Arriving at the 7th
Annual Blockbuster
Entertainment Awards
show in Los Angeles,
April 10, 2001
© *Frank Trapper/*
*Corbis Sygma*

politicians, quickly turned into the song that wouldn't die—the initial victim but ulti-mate beneficiary of Sheryl's pessimism, perfectionism, and tenacity, squeezed and twisted around to meet with her final approval.

"Sheryl just got to the point where she said, 'I don't want it on the record, I hate that song,'" Trina Shoemaker recalls. "Then, when other people really liked it, she went, 'Okay, we'll work on it.' I never thought that song would make the record, yet we kept working on it, we just kept beating it into the ground, until finally it came out great. I don't remember when it got great. I think it got great when I didn't listen to it for a while. Tchad Blake mixed it and I was like, 'Oh, wow! I forgot about that guitar. That's real cool. When did Jeff play that?'

"The whole album was a case of Sheryl constantly carving out her ideas, and us trying to capture them as quickly as they would come out and then form them into something that made sense. She kept saying, 'I don't want to make the same record,' but the process didn't change at all for me. My day felt very much the same. Unlike other projects, where there's a limited budget and things are pretty regimented, with Sheryl there was no such thing as a schedule. I mean, we would stop the sessions when she'd get fed up and want to take some time off or go do a show. Later on, we'd even break down the whole studio [at the Sunset Sound Factory] because she didn't want to pay for the time, and then have to turn around and set it all up again four days later. I was having to match guitar tones—it might still be a Les Paul, but it would be a different Junior, a different Chieftain [amp], a different Memory Man [echo/chorus pedal], and a different guitar player, and I'd have to make it sound like the other track."

Meanwhile, Trina also had to convince Gregg Williams about the need to overdub cymbals onto "Am I Getting Through (Part I & II)," a schizoid piece which takes a headlong dive from meditative ballad into demented rock 'n' roll. Although the drummer was intent on achieving a John Bonham/Led Zeppelin–type sound, Trina finally persuaded him to expand the effect and up the ante.

"There was a lot of high-fiving during the sessions for that song," she says. "Sheryl recorded all the backing vocals in the control room and she just nailed them. She was really laughing because of how magical they sounded, and then there was her funky guitar playing during the third stanza. Moments like that were great."

And so were the other instances when Sheryl displayed her vocal prowess, such as the last-minute retracking of her performance for "Riverwide," which took place just prior to its mix by Tchad Blake.

"She was saying, 'This vocal is ahead,'" Trina Shoemaker remembers. "'No, Sheryl, that's the vocal you sang when you tracked it. It's perfect. It's so real, it's so honest, you'll never beat that.' 'The vocal's ahead.' 'No, it's in the pocket, it feels great.' 'Let me re-sing it right now. I'll sing it in one go. You guys are gonna be amazed.' Sure enough, she got out there and she nailed the vocal on that song. It was just breathtaking. We were all standing in the control room and we applauded when she was done. It was like a show."

"Riverwide" boasts a superb string arrangement by Jimmie Haskell—yes, *the* Jimmie Haskell, who, as Sheryl now knew, wrote the arrangement for "Ode To Billie Joe." In fact, she nearly went Haskell-crazy, employing his talents for several of the new songs, before stripping them back down. Only "Riverwide" and "Am I Getting Through" retained his work.

"When you have orchestra on your songs it's slightly pretentious, so it's a taste thing," Jeff Trott explains. "It's like, 'Well, are we going to make this big statement?' At the time, when we were in the middle of making *The Globe Sessions*, we really wanted to make this big, epic rock record, and we started to do it, but it didn't feel right to Sheryl. She said, 'You know, this doesn't feel homey to me,' so we took out some of the pomp."

Although the main theme of Sheryl's lyrics was pretty depressing, it was also very real, and this provided a firm base for some quality songs. However, about three quarters of the way through the project, it was clear that none of the tracks jumped out as a single, and with this consideration weighing heavily on Sheryl's mind, she decided to lighten the atmosphere by instigating a jam session with an eclectic array of musicians who were in the neighboring studio loft area—keyboardist/producer Mitchell Froom, singer/guitarist Dan Zanes, Bad Company drummer Simon Kirke, and even members of The Ramones, who were working down the hall.

"All of these different types of people from different generations were in this building," Jeff Trott recalls. "Sheryl eventually asked them to come down, but then she said, 'What are we going to jam on?' I said, 'I don't know. Let's do some covers,' and she said, 'Well, I kinda want to record something, but I also don't want to dole out publishing to everyone who walks in and is a part of this thing.' I mean, she and I have an understanding and we recognize each other as writing partners, so we know the boundaries, but the more people you get, the harder it is to get an accurate picture of who did what. You're just kind of in the moment and you're not thinking of keeping track like, 'Okay, well, I wrote the bridge part and I wrote half of that word....' So, Sheryl said, 'Let's come up with a chord progression or something that we can just kind of jam on.' I always have boxes of cassette tapes laying around, containing my little noodle ideas, and I went through them until I found this one chord progression that eventually evolved into 'My Favorite Mistake,' although I had one extra chord in there. We worked on it until we thought it sounded cool, and then we jammed on it with all these guys and it really stood up.

"We also jammed on another idea that sounded like a Herb Alpert song or 'A Taste Of Honey'—the loungey kind of thing—and after that Sheryl was going, 'You know that thing we were jamming on? There's something really good about it, although I don't know what it is and I don't have any words for it yet.' We knew that the actual jam of the song really didn't sound very good—I mean, it was fun playing, but there was a lot of flailing because everyone was just having a good time. So, we decided, 'Well, that chord progression's really good. We should be able to do something with it,' and we started hashing it out and making it sound like it had this dark, bluesy kind of groove to it. At that point, for Sheryl, it started conjuring up this place, this image, and some relationship ideas. I think I know who it is, but...."

A smooth blending of pop and white soul in the Elvis Costello vein, the song would set tongues wagging about the identity of Sheryl's roguish "Favorite Mistake" following its release as the album's lead-off single. Not too surprisingly, Eric Clapton would soon emerge as the prime contender, but another likely candidate had to be Jakob Dylan. True to form, Sheryl was keeping her cards close to her chest.

"Any time I'm seen with another celebrity, it's food for fodder," she said in the November 1999 issue of *Playboy* magazine. "I went on *Letterman* the day Matt Lauer was on, but I didn't even meet him. The next day I was engaged to him in the newspapers. And I can't tell you how many people I know have said, 'It's me, right?' about my songs. I think they want to believe it's them. In reality, very few references are about anyone specifically. 'My Favorite Mistake' is about several people in my life who weren't very good ideas—but not Eric. I've known Eric for over ten years, and I can't look at that relationship as a mistake."

Besides, it's never a bad idea to keep people guessing about lyrical meaning in order to retain interest in a song. While taping an episode of VH1's *Storytellers* in New York on August 20, 1998, Sheryl decided to play it cagey. "I saw this biography on Carly Simon, and there was so much speculation about whether 'You're So Vain' was about Mick Jagger or Warren Beatty," she said when introducing "My Favorite Mistake." "This song really is about the bad relationship that you look back [on] with fondness and you know you'd do all over again, although it was bad from the beginning. So, when asked who this song's really about, I think I'm gonna say Warren Beatty or Mick Jagger."

Jeff Trott has his own ideas as to whom the song is about. However, he also claims to have never asked Sheryl for the answer, as this would betray their mutual trust.

"If I did question her about things like that, she would be self-conscious every time she wrote something," Jeff explains. "I kind of sit back and support whatever it is—I play really hard, trying to come up with cool riffs that will go with it and won't step on the words, and I try to ensure that she can go on this journey and conjure up some of these experiences that are important for her to get out as a writer.

"With 'My Favorite Mistake' she found herself. I came up with the guitar riff that prompted her to realize that she had something bottled up and that it was the right time to express it. As a result, the lyrics came to her very, very quickly. I had nothing to do with writing those lyrics. I was just there to support her and help her get there, and that's the really great journey of collaborative songwriting. You don't know where you're going when you start off, and hopefully you're surprised where you end up. What's more, that doesn't always lead to the most savory place, but you have to go there. You can't hold back, because then you're just going to censor yourself to death and you won't say anything. So, it really is an exercise in tolerance."

"'My Favorite Mistake' went down real easy," confirms Trina Shoemaker. "It was written in a day, we tracked it that night, overdubbed it the next day, and it was done. It was a breeze."

This was all well and good, but for Sheryl, full of doubts and insecurities, the project itself was anything but a breeze. In all, more than forty songs were recorded for the album, and this meant a lot of discarded tracks. These included "Straight To The Moon," a Crow/Trott composition that had originally been titled "The Flag," and which ended up on the *King of the Hill* TV tie-in album, as well as on overseas releases of the "There Goes The Neighborhood" single; "Resuscitation," which was included on the soundtrack to horror flick *The Faculty*, and on *The Globe Sessions* as released outside the U.S.; and numbers such as "The Cheerleader," "Dude" (Jeff Trott's salute to ex–Pink Floyd virtuoso Syd Barrett), and "The Diminished Song" (named courtesy of its diminished chord), which never surfaced in any form whatsoever.[1] The fact was, for Sheryl, the surplus of material didn't necessarily constitute the right material, and during the summer of 1998 she was more than a little depressed.

In early June, citing "exhaustion" and the need to concentrate on her new album, she bowed out of five Lilith Fair shows that she was scheduled to play later that month. "A lot of people say they heard I was on heroin, that I was strung out," Sheryl told *Entertainment Weekly* a few months later. "People love a great story." Nevertheless, before long, she wanted to indefinitely scrap the album, which was already being mixed by Tchad Blake.

"The day I decided not to put my record out, I picked up *USA Today* on an airplane and it was announced that it was coming out with the title *Riverwide* and an August 14 date," Sheryl recalled in the same *Entertainment Weekly* article. "All the way through the airport, I wept. I called my manager and label president and said, 'I can't put it out. I can't face it.'…I couldn't bear for my little brother to hear it. I couldn't bear to discuss it, define what it is, talk about the relationships that motivated it."

In the meantime, Bob Dylan's music publisher offered Sheryl a couple of songs, "Mississippi" and "Girl From The Red River Shore," both of which had failed to make the cut of Dylan's 1997 *Time Out Of Mind* opus. She duly elected to record the former, which he'd discarded due to dissatisfaction with how Daniel Lanois had chosen to produce it, and "Mississippi" quickly turned into one of the standout tracks on Sheryl's still-in-progress album.

"When I heard it, I loved it," she stated during an October 1998 press conference in Milan, Italy. "I thought it might sound like something on *Freewheelin'* or *Highway 61 Revisited*. Very classic Bob Dylan. I felt flattered that he himself had a song that he himself loved and didn't put on his album and thought I might record it."

A country lament with brilliantly illustrative Dylan lyrics, "Mississippi" was treated to an up-tempo, Rolling Thunder–type arrangement, as well as a superb, open-throated

---

[1] *All CD releases of* The Globe Sessions *included an extra, "hidden" track: the funky, unlisted Crow composition "Subway Ride," which expresses exasperation at Congress's and the media's grilling of President Clinton. Another Sheryl solo work, the ballad "Carolina," would make it onto the Japanese release of the album, as well as the soundtrack of the Kevin Costner/Robin Wright Penn movie,* Message in a Bottle. *In 1999, Sheryl's terrific cover of Guns N' Roses' "Sweet Child O' Mine," produced by her and Rick Rubin at Sound City Studios in Van Nuys, Calfornia, and featured on the soundtrack of the Adam Sandler comedy,* Big Daddy, *would be included on U.S. and European rereleases of the* Globe Sessions *album. The track would also be released as a single.*

vocal performance by Sheryl. In 2001, she'd pay homage to the composer by appearing on the song's rerecording for his *Love and Theft* album.

"I just thought it was serendipitous that in that moment of real insecurity about what I'd produced and created, this song filled in the void," she commented in her April 1999 interview with *Musician* magazine.

Dylan had actually called to mention the song on what happened to be Sheryl's birthday back in February of '98. "I was having a bad birthday," she informed David Wild during their 2002 *Musicians* interview. "I was turning 36, and every birthday is about not having [kids]. 'I'm not pregnant. I'm sad.' But [Bob] called [and] he was like, 'Hey, what're ya doin'?' and I said, 'I'm in the studio.' He was asking me what I was working on, and I said, 'It's my birthday.' He was like, 'Oh, it's your birthday,' and I went, 'Yeah,' and he said, 'Well, you don't sound very happy.' I was like, 'Yeah, I wanna have a baby,' and he said, 'Well, let's have a baby!'"

Such a thoughtful, generous guy.... As it happens, "Mississippi" re-energized Sheryl and inspired her to turn the corner on her album. Immediately, she decided to replace two of the weaker songs with a couple of new tracks that, while adding to the record's generally morose sentiments, provided it with greater depth and commercial appeal: "The Difficult Kind" and "Anything But Down." The latter number, setting angry, disconsolate words to a flowing melody and catchy refrain, was destined for release as a single, and accompanying it as a B-side would be "The Difficult Kind," a wistful country ballad with ear-catching chord changes and sophisticated phrasing.

"Mississippi," "The Difficult Kind," and "Anything But Down" served to flesh out Sheryl's best album to date, the record on which she truly found her feet as a singer-songwriter-musician-producer, performing all four roles in a cohesive manner that generated and developed strong, intensely personal material. Hitting her stride, she recorded the latter two tracks in a couple of days, and the result was just a six-week delay in the release of the swiftly recompiled and renamed *Globe Sessions* album...even if the sessions for "Mississippi," "The Difficult Kind," and "Anything But Down" actually took place at the Sunset Sound Factory in L.A.

Basically, Sheryl had already used up her allotted time at Globe Studios, and she was less than happy when Bob FitzSimons informed her that she couldn't return there because the facility had been booked by another client. This signaled the end of friendly relations between the two parties, and things would only get worse when, following the album's release, the facility owner would take major exception to press reports and interviews with Sheryl in which it was implied or stated that the sessions took place at "her studio."

"We tried to get it straightened out, but we couldn't get anywhere with her management," FitzSimons recalls. "Then I got my attorney involved, and Sheryl's attorney said, 'Unless she specifically says, "I own the studio," we don't want to know about it.' It was like, 'Go ahead, sue us. You'll be wasting your time.' You see, it was about making inferences that weren't legally binding; not saying 'I own it,' yet saying everything but that. We finally decided to litigate, and Sheryl called me up. She said, 'Listen, I have no power, no control. People write stuff about me all the time that's not true.' I said, 'Sheryl, I've got all of these articles here. Who are you trying to kid? You're saying this, it's printed. If you haven't, you should be concerned, because they're putting words in your mouth, and even though it's actually making you look good, it's really affecting me in the wrong way.'

"Having had no other projects in here for four months while paying my overheads, I was tapped out. I couldn't afford to advertise, and, thanks to all the press coverage, I wasn't getting any phone calls, because everyone thought it was her private studio. Still, that was Sheryl's out—she had no control over it. About eight months later, I found a transcript of a San Francisco radio show in which she did say that she owned the studio, but by then I'd given up. Besides, if the studio owner sued the client, I'd never have another person walk in here again.

"I don't know who was pulling the strings, but the supposed fact that it was her own studio was all part of the promotion, and it appeared to be spin for the sake of it. You know—first record, big success, Sheryl writes her songs; second record, Sheryl writes her songs and produces them; third record, Sheryl writes her songs and produces them in her own studio which she designed. This was my identity she was taking from me."

During the summer of 1998, Sheryl spent around $1.8 million on a 5,400-square-foot, Spanish-style home in the Hollywood Hills. She'd expressed an interest in the five-bedroom, four-bath 1920s house, with its tower and ornate gardens, shortly after it had been purchased for $900,000 the year before, and she'd kept upping the offers until the owner finally relented. This home would soon house the equipment that Sheryl had left behind at Globe Studios, but in the meantime the switch of location to the Sunset Sound Factory meant that she could record her new songs while monitoring Tchad Blake's mixes of the original material in an adjacent room. Noted mixmaster/engineer/producer Andy Wallace mixed the new material at Soundtracks in New York.[2]

"Sheryl wanted to do the new mixes herself," says David Anderle. "She didn't want Andy Wallace's mixes, then she loved Andy Wallace's mixes, then she didn't, then she did…again, it's part of how she makes music. She's so dependent on absorbing what she perceives as being the best for her music.

"As things went on, Sheryl got more confident; she took more of an upper hand, and the upper hand was there to take. I felt that I didn't need to be there until she asked. I knew that she would play me things when she wanted to, and I knew that she would listen when she heard something that made sense. In some respects, holding her hand would not be beneficial. She is definitely a person who you let run with it, and she's a team player if you're straight with her. She's a girl who does not want to have her butt kissed. She wants to be told the truth, and, even though she'll hate you for it at the time, if you're telling her the truth she'll come back to you."

---

[2] In 2001, the *Globe Sessions* material would quite literally take on new sonic dimensions when David Tickle would accord the album a 6.1 DTS-ES surround-sound remix.

"We were very worried about that record on many, many, many, many, many occasions," adds Trina Shoemaker, whose work on *The Globe Sessions* would earn her a Grammy for Best Engineered Album, Non-Classical at the awards ceremony held at the Shrine Auditorium in Los Angeles in February 1999. "In fact, when my lawyer called me to say, 'You've been nominated for a Grammy,' all I could think was, 'For what?' He was like, 'Well, for Sheryl, obviously,' and I couldn't get my mind around it. I thought, 'Best sounding record? Best engineered record? No way. Not a chance.' So, I was thrilled for her when we got the engineering Grammy, because she bought all that equipment and took a huge risk on recording the album with her own gear in her own setup with the same engineer.

"It took so long to make that record. It was like an eight-month process, and we worked so hard. There was a lot of writing in the studio, so I rarely had the chance to become acquainted with a demo and I had no prep for getting sounds or for where a song was ultimately gonna go. It had only been written a half-hour ago and we were just demoing the track to see if it even floated as a song. So, when we were nominated, I couldn't believe it. I was like, 'No way. That album is so full of mistakes, goofy shit, and poor engineering.' In fact, it wasn't at all. It was just very confusing. We had so many songs going at the same time, all the time; so many rewrites, so many different versions of different songs, so many songs like 'Members Only.'"

*The Globe Sessions* was a difficult gig, but it was also an extremely rewarding one. Sheryl had been a part of the collaborative effort on the *Tuesday Night Music Club* record, and with the *Sheryl Crow* album she'd displayed that she could successfully produce herself. Now, with this latest project, it was clear that, rather than having caught lightning in a bottle, she was growing even stronger as an artist.

"Sheryl's a hard taskmaster because she is so hard on herself," Trina Shoemaker continues. "She demands perfection from herself, she demands super-creativity. There will be no shit writing, there will be no dumb song. She wants for herself the absolute highest standard, and so of course she wants everyone around her to also aspire to that. I certainly do, and that's how come we can work together. I'll sit there for twenty hours until it's perfect. The problem is, Sheryl doesn't need a lot of sleep. She can stay up until five in the morning and then be back in there at ten, whereas I need like eight or nine hours of sleep. It's hard to keep up with her.

"I was hired to do a job, and I wanted very much to please her. I wanted her to like what she was hearing, I wanted her to like her record, and we had words on several occasions where I'd say, 'You've gotta stop saying bad things about the record, because you're hurting the record. Don't say it sounds like shit. It doesn't! You're just unhappy because it's confusing right now. You're trying to write in the studio, and it's hard on ya.' She wanted *Globe Sessions* to be a real tough, real sparse, old-fashioned rock 'n' roll record, but it turned out to be none of those things. It's a new-fashioned rock 'n' roll record. It is not sparse, and while it is tough it is also real gentle."

Released in the U.S. on September 29, 1998, Sheryl's third commercial outing sold over 123,000 copies during its first week, entering and peaking at No. 5 on The

Billboard 200. Each successive album had been faster out of the gate, yet *The Globe Sessions'* total sales figures—currently over 1.86 million copies in the U.S. and around four million worldwide—although very good, nevertheless signaled a downward trend. This was especially true in America (where the album was still certified platinum), indicating a shift in the record-buying demographic. However, it in no way reflected the quality of Sheryl's work, which garnered some of her best reviews to date.

"These tough, knotty, well-made observational songs, sung with sinewy bravado (tinged with tenderness), find a bracing balance between vocal spontaneity and solid song craft," asserted the *New York Times,* while in its four-star review of the album, *Rolling Stone* emphasized that "*The Globe Sessions*...is not a record married to a particular sound or concept.... In the end, it is Crow's singing that unites the record and conveys its passionate thrust."

"The great songs here—and there are plenty—merely emphasise that Crow is a consummate songwriter with a joyous flair for musical invention," stated *Q,* while *Billboard* reached for the superlatives in describing the album as "easily one of the most compelling albums of the year—Crow demonstrates she's every bit as gifted a singer, songwriter, musician, recording artist, and producer as any of her peers. As she has done on all her work to date, Crow manages to dance a fine line between accessibility and adventurism, between street-tough rock heroine and sensitive singer/songwriter.... A landmark album by a talented, consistent artist."

For his part, Al Cafaro heard a hit single when he first listened to "My Favorite Mistake," yet unlike his experience with tracks such as "If It Makes You Happy" and "Everyday Is A Winding Road," his enthusiasm wasn't shared by all at the record company.

"As soon as I heard 'My Favorite Mistake' I knew we had what we needed to launch the record," he says. "However, I was met with a lot of skepticism, and it was a very interesting situation to be in. It was like 'Yeah, that's a fucking smash,' but a lot of people couldn't go there."

The song eventually peaked at No. 20 on the Billboard Hot 100 singles chart. Meanwhile, for the accompanying video, Sheryl returned to Sam Bayer, the director of "Home," with a view to making an inexpensive promo that largely featured the singer-songwriter and her bass guitar.

"She didn't want anyone else in it," says Randy Sosin. "She hates videos with a lot of extra people, and that's what bothered her most about 'If It Makes You Happy.' All of these weird characters kept popping up, and she felt bad for them. Y'know, 'Why are we always showing goofy people in videos?' and then a lot of people gave her shit for 'Home,' saying that she was the only one who looked good. But that's such an unpremeditated thing. It's the director's choice to try to create interesting images. So, for 'My Favorite Mistake' she wanted it to be just her."

To promote the album, A&M employed the new strategy of not only distributing the "My Favorite Mistake" video to TV stations, but also to retail outlets for in-store play. At the same time, VH1 decided to get creative—when the scandal surrounding President Clinton's affair with Monica Lewinsky was at its height, the cable network recut the "My Favorite Mistake" video to include shots of Bill and his erstwhile mistress. Neither Sheryl or the record company had anything to do with that.

"I think it's a real low point in history," Sheryl later told E! Online with regard to the scandal. "It put the country in a bad situation, and I was sick of seeing it in the press. I'm still sick of it. For me, it ruined the Oscars. I got sick of every joke being about politics, Monica Lewinsky, and cigars. I think it's dragged us through the gutter enough."

"Sheryl is good for VH1, and on the *Globe Sessions* album we did really well with her," says Wayne Isaak. "'My Favorite Mistake' tested well, it was a big hit with her audience, and we played it for quite a long time. We played it after it was coming down the pop charts just because it continued to be something our audience liked. There again, I also think that the best song on the album never really got its shot, which was 'The Difficult Kind.' I think in a sense that song was a benchmark for her. It was her best song ever, the most truly connected to Sheryl as a person, to her roots and where she comes from, and I just thought that nothing she'd done to that point could touch it. The performance of that song at Madison Square Garden with Eric Clapton on slide guitar was amazing. It was so good, we took it off that special which we taped for him and made it into a video clip."

The aforementioned multi-star gig, billed as *Eric Clapton and Friends*, took place in New York on June 30, 1999, and was a benefit for the Crossroads Center in Antigua, a non-profit alcohol and drug treatment facility that Clapton himself had founded. By then, Sheryl's tour in support of *The Globe Sessions* was in full swing, yet she'd still found the time while working on her album the previous year to perform at a number of other charitable events. These included a private show for the Dalai Lama to aid the preservation of Tibet's cultural heritage, performed at the Center Stage Theater in Atlanta; and a concert for Don Henley's Walden Woods Foundation, set up to preserve the land around Walden Pond in Concord, Massachusetts, where nineteenth-century essayist, poet, naturalist, and philosopher Henry David Thoreau had lived and worked.

With Sheryl's success came fame, and with fame came opportunity—the opportunity to speak out on topical issues, the opportunity to help those in need and bring attention to special concerns. She didn't pass up the chance. Sheryl's USO trip to Bosnia in March 1996 was just a precursor to the many charitable activities with which she'd become involved during the coming months and years, and to this end she would use her fame to best advantage—to lend her name, her voice, and her actions to causes that need all the assistance they can get, whether they're related to the record industry or to the wider world in general.

"It comes natural to her to try to do something about things that matter," Scooter Weintraub stated on VH1's *Behind the Music*. "It's good that we have people like that."

# CHAPTER FOURTEEN

## *A Change*

*"We cannot seek or attain health, wealth, learning, justice or kindness
in general. Action is always specific, concrete, individualized, unique."*
—John Dewey

With charitable work, results are the bottom line: the assistance provided to people in need, the lives saved, the contribution to making the world a better place. A lot of unheralded time and effort goes into achieving these aims, some of it on the part of celebrities whose names serve as the unrivaled means of raising public awareness about worthy causes. Certainly, events such as benefit concerts can enhance the performers' reputations while helping to promote their latest products, but what's less evident is the altruistic work with which many of these individuals are involved behind the scenes and away from the cameras. Sheryl Crow is a prime example.

"She's been generous in every single way," says Bobby Muller, President of the Vietnam Veterans of America Foundation. "The media interviews that she's agreed to, as well as the performances, have raised us a ton of money to support our projects."

Established in 1979 as a means of promoting support, services, and recognition for the vets, VVAF quickly moved toward a broader agenda that addressed the larger concerns of armed conflict. Today, it operates rehabilitation programs for the disabled in war-affected countries around the world, stemming from its early-'80s initiative to set up clinics for landmine victims. It also leads the campaign against these indiscriminate weapons.

Sheryl, already made aware of the landmine hazard during her 1996 trip to Bosnia, was introduced to VVAF by Emmylou Harris in March 1998, around the time they were recording a duet of "Juanita" for the all-star album *Return of the Grievous Angel: A Tribute to Gram Parsons*. Harris was executive-producing the record, and the proceeds would benefit the VVAF landmines campaign. When Sheryl met Bobby Muller, she immediately expressed her willingness to lend her support. That May, she performed, along with Emmylou, Steve Earle, Mary Chapin Carpenter, and Buddy and Julie Miller, at a VVAF dinner honoring Vermont Senator Patrick Leahy, and in October she was on the bill of a benefit concert in Washington, D.C. In January 2000, Sheryl traveled with Muller to Vietnam and Cambodia, viewing VVAF's rehabilitation programs and witnessing the problems first-hand, and four months later she performed an acoustic concert as the guest and spokesperson of the campaign during CNN's twentieth-anniversary celebrations.

"I think that has affected my music intensely because of the experiences that I have had there and because of what I've been exposed to," she told fan Web site The Waiting Room in 2001.

On the sleeve notes to her *Globe Sessions* album, Sheryl canvassed for contributions to VVAF while pointing out that "every twenty-two minutes, someone is killed or maimed by a landmine; nearly 90% of these victims are civilians."

"Out of all of the artists, Emmy's been our queen, but without a doubt Sheryl's done the biggest lifting," Muller says. "When she traveled with us to Vietnam and Cambodia, she was very, very courageous. One of the things we wanted to show her was a really small community up by the border with Laos, and to get there we had to fly this little five-seater plane. Well, Sheryl's had some friends who were killed in small planes, but she overcame her personal fear and got on that plane, God bless her, to fly to this little village. The fact that she did this to stay with the mission, so to speak, was pretty terrific.

"When we came back, there were some media reports about Sheryl's trip with us, and I wound up getting a letter from Ted Turner and Tom Johnson, the head of CNN, asking me to prevail upon her to play at their twentieth-anniversary concert in Atlanta. If she'd do that, they'd make the show a benefit for the landmines campaign, and call attention to it around the world by way of CNN's affiliates. So, I called Sheryl and told her about this—we'd get a ton of money, we'd get connected to CNN reps around the world, and get a high profile—and she said, 'Okay, let's do it.' That's a perfect example of the kind of steroid that Sheryl Crow can be in terms of pumping up the volume.

"In America, there are over one million non-profit organizations registered—one for every conceivable cause—so there's a lot of competition to get your message heard or get support for your particular efforts. Well, nothing has helped us reach out and get support more than our singer-songwriters, and in that regard Sheryl has helped lead the way. She's not only done landmine benefits, but she's also worked with us with Senator Leahy, a five-term senator who's our godfather in this town [Washington, D.C.]. We connected Sheryl to him, and when she performed the benefit for Leahy it was the hottest ticket at the Democratic National Convention. So, the fact that she's done political outreach, recognizing that the cultivation of political sponsors is critical to getting any campaign advance, shows a political sophistication that, quite frankly, not everybody out there has. Along with being extremely generous, she understands the dynamics of the game. She knows the campaign, she knows the problem, so when the media want to talk to her about her hair, she rejoins by telling them about the issues."

Displaying her business acumen, Sheryl devised the concept of VVAF singer-songwriter benefit concerts. "She said, 'Look, Bobby, this isn't just about getting the word out, it's about making money,'" Muller recalls. To that end, acoustic sets requiring minimal amounts of stage equipment and technical support, performed in the round, and featuring major artists, amount to high-end, low-cost entertainment that provides the organization with some of the necessary funds to help effect a change.

"I love Sheryl Crow, and I feel a tremendous debt of gratitude to her," Muller remarks. "She's a smart woman, she does a tremendous interview, she's practical when it comes to the money side, and she knows how to use her talent. She has done this really for no reason other than being altruistic, and while I wish I could do something to reciprocate her consideration and kindness, she derives her sense of reward and satisfaction from knowing that she's really been a big lift for a respected and recognized cause."

Among the other causes that Sheryl has championed during the past few years is the fight against scleroderma, a chronic, degenerative, and potentially life-threatening rheumatic disease which manifests itself in the form of one or more of the following symptoms: thickening and hardening of the skin; swelling of the hands and feet; pain, stiffness, and contracture of the joints; weakness and fatigue; digestive, facial, dental, and oral problems; dry mucus membranes; and over-sensitivity to the cold. Also capable of afflicting the kidneys, heart, and lungs, scleroderma affects an estimated 300,000 people in the U.S., approximately 80 percent of them women, and there is currently no known cure.

When Sharon Monsky was first diagnosed with the illness in 1983, she was only given a couple of years to live. Today, she heads the Scleroderma Research Foundation, which she founded in 1987, and Sheryl, whom she first met in 1996, is among the handful of celebrities who've gone out of their way to help raise funds. Scleroderma affected Sheryl's life when it afflicted a longtime family friend in Kennett. He died in January 2002, but not before Sheryl had arranged for him to receive treatment in California at her own expense. Over the years she's also performed benefit concerts for the Foundation, and testified before Congress to request more money for research.

"In April of 2001, she flew from New York to Santa Barbara on a Saturday morning to play at our show, and then took the red-eye back because she had another commitment," Monsky recalls. "She didn't want to let us down, and you know, not many people do that. She has given so much back, and it's made a very important difference."

"I think that my involvement and support for charities actually just helps my spirit," Sheryl told The Waiting Room. "I don't know how much good my involvement does for different charities, except for it just makes me feel better about my life and how much has been given to me, and it's just a way of evening things out a little bit. I guess it's my karmic distribution, or my karmic offering basically."

In 2000, Sheryl also felt obligated to throw her hat into the political arena, performing at fundraisers for Democratic presidential candidate Al Gore and testifying before Congress to protest an amendment to the 1976 Copyright Act, which made sound recordings the property not of their creators, but of the record companies. This had been signed into law the previous November, drawing an immediate outcry from the National Academy of Recording Arts & Sciences (NARAS), which cited the amendment's detrimental effect on artists and lack of prior discussion on the subject as good enough reasons to repeal it.

Inside a packed Room 2141 at the Rayburn House Office Building in Washington, D.C., on May 25, Sheryl and Mike Greene, then-President/CEO of NARAS, went head to head with Hilary Rosen, President and CEO of the Recording Industry Association of America (RIAA), and Paul Goldstein, Professor of Law at Stanford Law

School. Introducing herself to the House of Representatives Subcommittee on Courts and Intellectual Property, Sheryl stated her case:

> If any of you sat in on a recording session, you would see that the artist featured on a sound recording functions as the author of the work. Without the creative contribution of the featured artist, there would be no sound recording. To legislate that the record label should be recognized and credited as the 'author' of the sound recording undermines the framers' intent of the Constitution and goes against my good Midwestern common sense. I am the author and creator of my work.... A sound recording is the final result of the creative vision, expression, and execution of one person—the featured artist...any claims to the authorship by producers, hired musicians, background singers, engineers would be false.... In short, the sound recording artist is not only the author, but is also the person in charge of all facets of production, up to the point of distribution. We give the record labels our work to exploit for thirty-five years. Like other authors, we should be able to reclaim our work as Congress intended.

The result was that legislators restored the Copyright Act to its pre–November 1999 status, leaving the issue to be decided in court at a later date; as of this writing, an artist is the owner and author of his or her own work, and can reclaim ownership of a recording after thirty-five years. However, if a record company contractually claims it as a "work for hire," which is practically a given if a new artist wants to sign a deal, that company is deemed the owner and author of the record for the full term of the copyright: ninety-five years or more. It is a far from satisfactory situation, and one of several contentious issues on the agenda of the Recording Artists' Coalition, which was co-founded by Don Henley and Sheryl Crow to fight for artists' interests, most especially those not as rich and successful as themselves.

Still, for all the enmity between the artists and their employers, Sheryl has had a pretty good relationship with her own record company, and in 1998, together with Scooter Weintraub and Jay Cooper, she negotiated a new five-album deal with A&M.

"We negotiated the hell out of that deal," recalls Al Cafaro. "I was obviously negotiating for the company, but I felt enormously responsible to her—and, in part, for her—and we went around. You know, if she felt that she deserved things then she'd fight for them, and I respected that. Scooter cut his chops with Sheryl. He was learning as she was rolling, and he is the sweetest guy you'll ever want to meet. Now, that's not always [a positive] attribute if you're a manager—it can be problematic—but Scooter has a way of being able to get what he needs to get done for his artist, and I think he's smart about it.

"Scooter would always involve me, and we were sort of like partners. You know, I was a manager with Sheryl and he was always looking out for her best interests. We would always be collaborative about where we were trying to go, and it wasn't like it was behind Sheryl's back. We would double-team her about stuff, and I'd know the stuff that he needed help with, and he always made it easy to do the best thing for his client. That is not an easy thing to do. You see, very often managers feel that they have to come in and make demands, or they have to be unreasonable, or they have to be confrontational, and that's not really the way to get shit.

"There were times when Scooter would yell and get tough, but invariably he always chose another way, and he's been great with her. He's always been there for her, even when she's kicking his ass, as every client is going to do to their manager at some point, because it's hard to get around the fact that when you're a manager you're taking a percentage of somebody else's money. You work for them, and even when she was kicking his ass Scooter always held his head up, and when he needed to he would fight back, but he would always do it in a high-minded fashion. He is a total believer. When he would play me things he would always be very, very open and honest about it."

David Anderle is in total agreement with Cafaro regarding Scooter: "I think he is absolutely the perfect manager for Sheryl Crow. He likes her music, and with Sheryl that's really important, whereas with some artists it may not be. He understands it, he has a musical history that is important to her evolution as an artist, he fought for her, and he has an understanding of the needs of the label, as well as probably those of promoters and so forth. You get that sense you can talk to him. You can tell him certain things that must be done, and even if he can't get her to do it you know that he's putting up a big fight. Vice-versa, he comes back to the label saying, 'That's not going to happen.'

"There might have been some weak areas in the beginning—I don't think he understood a lot of what we were trying to achieve, and he might have been cowed by her a little bit—but I think he grew into his shoes really well. Over time he was able to deal with her more effectively, and certainly with us more effectively, and I know he's honest. She didn't need a manager who was not going to be there, who's like one of those spiffy guys who shows up at the Grammys and at the renegotiation. She needed a day-to-day man, and Scooter was there every moment. She needed a believer, and he's a true believer, so I think it's perfect."

In May 1998, the PolyGram Corporation, which had purchased A&M nine years earlier, was merged into the Universal Music Group as part of a $10.6 billion buyout by Universal's mega-giant owner, Seagram—a case of one conglomerate being swallowed up by an even bigger one. UMG was now the world's largest music organization, and as such it wasn't long before the usual "restructuring" took place in the form of sweeping cost cuts. The A&M, Island, Mercury, and Motown labels which had been under the PolyGram umbrella were suddenly vulnerable, and on January 21, 1999, the axe fell in the form of about 500 job dismissals nationwide. Many more were to follow.

That day, about 170 A&M staffers were unceremoniously fired as the company was absorbed into UMG; arriving for work, they were met by security guards who watched over them as they packed their belongings and left. Some now-ex-employees wrapped a black banner around the revolving A&M sign on the La Brea lot. By late afternoon, the Seagram bosses had ordered it removed.

"While change is always difficult, the restructuring of the labels is necessary for us to be more competitive, develop artists' careers, and pave the way for meaningful growth," was the Universal Music Group's official statement on a bloodletting that would contribute to an estimated annual savings of around $300 million.

"The record business is changing fundamentally," Al Cafaro told the *Los Angeles Times* as he bid adieu to the company that had been a part of his life for more than two decades. "Don't think that there are calm seas on the other side of this threshold. If the quake that devoured A&M and Geffen is a 6.0 on the Richter scale, there is a 7.0 coming in this industry. It's a Wall Street world now. Get ready."

Hereafter, A&M continued to exist as a label for back-catalog reissues and for those artists who wished to align themselves with the relic of a company that, reflecting the ethics of Herb Alpert and Jerry Moss, had stood for quality, integrity, and placing music before money. Stripped of its autonomy after the purchase by PolyGram, and continually operating in the red, an independent, half-billion-dollar labor of love had evolved into corporate superfluity within just ten years.

"It's certainly sad to see what is happening today, but to tell you the truth, you could see it coming once A&M became part of the [conglomerate structure] at PolyGram," Herb Alpert told the *L.A. Times*. "I saw that train coming…the sharp contrast between the independent world and the corporate. I don't think their bottom line has much to do with music or artists. It's very black and white. I'm not speaking for all corporations, just my experience at PolyGram. It seemed like they were so bottom-line conscious that it was hard to make a decision like we used to…just from the gut, based on feeling, not whether an artist might be able to sell oodles of records."

On that "Black Thursday," Sheryl stopped by the lot to commiserate with some of her friends who'd lost their jobs. Thereafter, she had to become accustomed to life as a member of the Universal family, aligned to Interscope Records while still on the A&M label.

"She called me and she was really distraught," David Anderle recalls. "She was very unhappy. We talked a lot. She didn't say anything about wanting to switch labels. She was more concerned about her own place in terms of who she was going to interact with, so I told her I thought she would have a good relationship with [Interscope Chairman] Jimmy Iovine, who I like and who I worked with. I just said, 'You're going to have to hang there day to day, because there are going to be a lot of other artists,' and I said, 'I wouldn't even think about changing labels, because this is a very big label and you should give it a shot.'"

"Frankly, I wish I had known that the company was on the line when we negotiated Sheryl's deal," adds Al Cafaro. "I would have given her more. I mean, I was happy with the deal that we did, because a good deal is when both people feel like they've won, but I'd rather Sheryl have the money than Universal. That's just the way I feel, and I would say that to anybody.

"You have to keep in mind that I had been at A&M for twenty-two years. I believed the dream. I believed that we were all lucky to be there. I believed that artists were lucky to be there. I believed that we worked the artists and that we were fortunate to have people who could do this. I believed it, and I never stopped believing it until the very end. Still, that doesn't mean you shouldn't get a good payday. Sheryl got a really good deal, and I had to fight to get the deal 'upstairs,' and I'm glad she got it, but certainly in retrospect I wish she had got a shitload more. Because at the end of the day, if that dreamworld of mine existed, it certainly doesn't anymore."

When *The Globe Sessions* won the Grammy for Best Rock Album on February 24, 1999, Sheryl dedicated the award to her friends and associates who'd lost their jobs at A&M. Sporting a new short and shaggy hairdo, she stepped up to the microphone at the Shrine Auditorium in Los Angeles and told the audience: "I wanted to win a Grammy tonight because it is a closing of an era…I am sort of a poster child for my label and small labels like A&M.… I have to look at the label for helping me to develop from the ground up."

Al Cafaro and David Anderle were among the former execs who were on hand to hear Sheryl's acceptance speech, and both truly appreciated the gesture.

"At some level all of us executives love flattery," Cafaro admits. "At some level we want to believe that we weren't just a part of something, but instrumental to something, and most often, of course, the truth is different to that. You make a contribution and you do your job and the artists are the ones who fight the fight. Having said that, when Sheryl made her comments, what I found so moving about them—and what I think everybody found so moving about them—is that they weren't about Al Cafaro or David Anderle, they were about a place. She stepped up and said something, and she had nothing to gain by saying it. Nothing at all.

"As a matter of fact, Scooter told me that at the Grammy party afterwards—which, of course, I didn't go to—he was standing with Sheryl, and they were looking over at [Vivendi Universal Executive Vice Chairman] Edgar Bronfman, Jr., and waiting for him to come over and say hi. Well, Edgar Bronfman wasn't coming over and saying hi, and so Scooter went over to Bronfman, who was talking to [Universal Music Group Chairman and CEO] Doug Morris, and Scooter said something to Doug about coming over and saying hi to Sheryl. Doug said to Edgar, 'Let's go say hi to Sheryl,' and Edgar said, 'After her remarks, we should go say hi?' Doug asked him, 'Were you responsible for her career? Who's she gonna thank?' and so they went over and said hi. Good for them. That was the right thing to do, but I also take my hat off to Sheryl. That's what you get with her. That's what makes her so special to me. It's the highs and the lows, and it's the victories and it's the fights. There's a purpose to it all."

As it happens, Jimmy Iovine, who co-founded Interscope Records with financier Ted Field in 1990, had the kind of rock credentials that would definitely appeal to Sheryl. After cutting his musical teeth as an engineer for John Lennon and Bruce Springsteen during the mid-'70s, he'd turned his hand to production with artists such as Patti Smyth, Tom Petty, Stevie Nicks, Bob Seger, Dire Straits, The Pretenders, and U2. Now running a company that had been purchased by Universal after avoiding a buyout by Time Warner, Iovine was more than happy to welcome Sheryl Crow to an eclectic roster that would include Sting, Dr. Dre, Eminem, Nine Inch Nails, and Limp Bizkit.

"Doug Morris wanted to do the opposite of what he saw happen at other companies," Iovine says. "For example, when A&M was bought by PolyGram, Jerry Moss left. When Island was bought, Chris Blackwell left. When Geffen was bought, David Geffen served his contractual time and left. However, when Doug bought Def Jam and Interscope, he said, 'I have to ensure that the top guys stay. They are the spirit of these companies.' So, he took Interscope and put it with Geffen and A&M, and he took Def Jam and put it with Island, and he made sure that the guys who'd built those companies continued to run them. I mean, you don't buy Def Jam and get rid of Lyor Cohen. We're the people with the intrinsic taste and feel for what we helped create. Bit by bit we're rebuilding A&M. Ron Fair is the President, we're signing new artists to the label, and we're starting to get its identity back.

"Thank God, I developed a relationship with Sheryl and Sting and Jonny Lang. It took time, it took a long time, because they were nervous and they didn't know what was going to happen. With Sting, it helped that one of his closest friends happens to be Bruce Springsteen, who's known me since I engineered *Born to Run* in my early twenties. Then, with Sheryl, both she and I have produced Stevie Nicks, so Sheryl asked her, 'What's Jimmy like?' That's how things develop, and we now have a great relationship. Sheryl makes this company hum…in fact, she could run it. She wouldn't want to, but she could. She has the drive and commitment of a real thoroughbred."

In the meantime, when Sheryl hit the road to tour behind her *Globe Sessions* album, it was with yet another lineup: Jim Bogios on drums; Tim Smith on bass and guitar; Peter Stroud, formerly of Pete Droge's band, on lead guitar; Mike Rowe on keyboards; Matt Brubeck on cello; and Lorenza Ponce on violin and acoustic guitar. The latter two musicians reflected the shift in tone of Sheryl's live performances, fleshing out ballads such as "Riverwide," "The Difficult Kind," "Strong Enough," and "Home," while adding more color and depth to the overall sound. Gone from the lineup were guitarists Todd Wolfe and Jeff Trott.

"Although I love performing, I have the worst stage fright," Jeff explains. "Before going onstage I am trembling, and I've done hundreds and hundreds of shows. I've toured all over the world with Sheryl and other people, and as soon as I step onstage I'm okay. It's just getting up the stairs to the stage that's the problem. I'm thinking, 'Oh my God, am I going to suck,' and then I get out there and I just play a chord and it's like, 'Oh, I'm all right.' I think my expectations are too high.

"Then again, Sheryl's also a perfectionist on the road, and in that way she's kinda like me. You know the work that you've put into the recordings, and you just want to be able to capture a little bit of that magic live. Sometimes, when you're touring with a band of people who didn't necessarily play on the record, it has a different feel to it, which can be frustrating. The drummer has the toughest task. You know, some of Sheryl's songs have many different drum kits and different parts, and it would be physically impossible for one guy to reproduce all of that. Still, in addition to being a perfectionist, Sheryl is also a really great travel companion. I mean, we really have a pretty good time. She loves performing, and sometimes I think she likes performing better than being in the studio. She knows what it is, whereas in the studio you don't get that instant gratification from people's responses to the songs. There it's just us, and so if I'm not saying, 'Oh wow, this is so great,' then something's wrong, like it's not working."

In early 1999, Sheryl played some European dates before kicking off a U.S. tour in the spring. A May 8 show at the Palace of Auburn Hills in Michigan was captured for later release on video and DVD as *Rockin' the Globe Live,* and that summer Sheryl also joined the lineup of the third and final Lilith Fair tour, in addition to appearing at Woodstock '99 in Rome, New York. Taking to the stage in a tight white tank top and equally figure-hugging brown leather pants on Woodstock's first day, July 23, she performed a one-hour set and responded to people shouting, "Show us your tits!" by at one point stating, "You'll have to pay a *lot* more than what you did to get in here to see *my* tits." For the record, said meatheads had shelled out $150.

After winding up her North American tour in Edmonton, Canada, on August 31, Sheryl performed in Japan that October and punctuated the next couple of years with all forms of benefit gigs, ranging from one to raise funds for the St. Jude Children's Hospital in Memphis to those in aid of the fights against breast cancer and amyotrophic lateral sclerosis (a.k.a. Lou Gehrig's disease). However, it was a concert that Sheryl gave on September 14, 1999, to help American Express launch a new credit card that gained by far the most widespread attention.

Titled *American Express Brings You Central Park in Blue,* this event truly served to confirm Sheryl Crow's standing in the music business, headlining a show that was "trimulcast" live on the Fox TV network, SFX radio, and the World Wide Web, and featuring some very high-caliber "special guests": Eric Clapton, Keith Richards, Stevie Nicks, Chrissie Hynde, Sarah McLachlan, and the Dixie Chicks, introduced onstage by Bill Murray. Proceeds from the sale of tickets benefited the Elizabeth Glaser Pediatric AIDS Foundation. If ever an event helped elevate Sheryl in the eyes of the general public, this was it, and it all came together at the last minute after she'd deliberated for several weeks as to whether or not she should participate.

"You're talking about a network television special and a Central Park gig, which is a lot bigger than the Beacon Theatre," says *Central Park in Blue's* co-Executive Producer, John Cossette. "You know, the Pope plays Central Park. This would be one of the most visible things that she'd ever done, so she had reservations about whether she could make it a success, and I think any artist would have those reservations. What's more, she was traveling from city to city on the Lilith Fair tour, it was hard to focus on everything, and she wasn't sure if she'd have the time to put it together, so I totally understand what her concerns were."

Cossette, whose company produces Broadway shows and TV events such as the Grammy Awards, first became involved with the project when he and Mark Dowley, then head of an event-marketing company named Momentum, had a breakfast meeting at the Four Seasons Hotel in Beverly Hills on June 4. Dowley, who'd already used Cossette Productions to provide entertainment for the 1996 Olympic Games in Atlanta, explained that one of his clients, American Express, wanted to target a young demographic for its new "Blue" credit card by way of a major attention-getting music event.

"He told me that they had up to two hours on Fox and asked if I could put something together," Cossette recalls. "I said, 'When's the air date?' and he said, 'September 14.'

I said, 'Three whole months, huh? Well, I'll tell you what, we'll give it a go.' We set a date of August 1 to either push ahead or abort, depending on whether or not we had something together by then. That way, no money would have been spent, because by the time you're done the whole thing comes to fifteen to twenty million dollars at least."

Among the first people John Cossette considered to headline the show was Sheryl Crow, whom he'd already observed interacting with other artists at the Grammys, and whose music he considered strong enough to perform in an all-star, televised setting.

"Mark was under a great deal of pressure from the client, because they think you can snap your fingers and pull somebody out of the hat who's going to want to do this," Cossette explains. "Well, it's not that easy. We figured that Sheryl would be perfect, Scooter agreed, and both American Express and Fox loved the idea, but the only person who wasn't sold on Sheryl was Sheryl. She had to think about it for a while—a long while—and everybody was getting nervous. American Express was breathing down Mark's back, Mark was breathing down my back, and I was saying, 'Just trust me.' He was looking at me like, 'John, what's going on here?' and all I could say was 'Hey, be cool, man! I've never failed you before. Just relax.' I was calling Scooter every day, and it got to the point where I was waiting so long that I was putting all my eggs in her basket, so thank God it worked out the way it did! It took about a month—which was a week before our August 1 deadline—for Sheryl to finally say 'yes.'

"At that point, once she committed, she was a thousand percent into it. She wanted to make all the calls and get the guest stars herself. Normally we would make the calls, but she took the lead and she's the one who delivered Eric, Keith, Stevie, everybody. We put the TV part of it together, but Sheryl's the one who put it all together musically and creatively. It was that important to her career."

Getting all of the guest stars to commit was no easy task in itself—David Bowie had to pull out due to scheduling conflicts. Accordingly, it was only a couple of days before the show that all of the pieces fell into in place, and the pressure wasn't eased by the fact that Fox, which had broadcast Woodstock '99 to lousy ratings the month before, was suddenly nervous about transmitting another live music show.

"I wasn't telling Sheryl any of this, but it didn't help the process at my end very much," Cossette admits.

In any event, things went according to plan, and the show itself was a spectacular success. Duplicating the approach taken with regard to Sheryl's touring career, the organizers eliminated the risk of her playing to a less than packed venue by staging the two-hour concert in front of 25,000 people who crowded into Central Park's East Meadow. Furthermore, the tickets were given away—no more than four to a person—by American Express representatives who'd been hired to walk the city.

Sarah McLachlan was Sheryl's only guest during the first hour; this then segued into the live trimulcast, featuring all of the performers, each of whom appeared for specific songs and then disappeared, before gathering together for the closing number, a rendition of Bob Dylan's "Tombstone Blues." To avoid interruptions for the Central Park audience while ensuring that TV viewers didn't feel like they were missing out on anything, Sheryl performed three-minute, fifty-second versions of selected songs during the commercial breaks. These fillers were seamless, thanks in part to the stage manager appearing thirty seconds before they were due to go back on air and giving Sheryl a wrap-up sign, and then counting her in—"five-four-three-two-one"—for the next song. Still, the evening wasn't without its hitches.

"Bill Murray was supposed to do the introductions for both segments, but we got Sandra Bernhardt—who was a celebrity backstage—to do this for the first set as Bill wasn't there yet," John Cossette remembers. "Well, she was a little bit out of line, shall we say, and not very nice to American Express in front of all their executives. I saw my whole career flashing before my eyes, but I didn't hear anything about it. I only heard how great the show was.

"Sheryl's a consummate professional. She's unbelievable. Beforehand, she did five days of rehearsals, and I was worried about her being over-rehearsed. She knew her own material, and so most of the rehearsing had to do with the guest artists. Well, I was worried that she might lose her voice, but as things turned out, she was magic and it was a wildly successful event. When you do this kind of thing, you try to get the artists to sign contracts giving away all of the rights to make a record or anything else out of it, and needless to say, nobody will sign those things going in. However, it was such a successful night that it ended up turning into a Grammy-winning album."

In reviewing *Sheryl Crow and Friends: Live from Central Park*, which entered and peaked at No. 107 on The Billboard 200 (tallying just 368,000 U.S. sales to date), *Q* magazine alluded to "the limber momentum of the songs, no sentiment, strong emotions, the power of small detail at work in the big setting…such a groove and such deadly reportage…it really does catch Sheryl Crow close-up, right now and credibly 'au naturel.'" *Mojo* asserted that the album "has all the ramshackle enthusiasm of a concert," while *Entertainment Weekly* commented that, in spite of the all-star contributions, "the best cuts belong to [Sheryl] when she's all alone with her band."

Sheryl was happy with the concert, and so was American Express, which in 2002 funded her "Soak Up The Sun" video and used part of it for an Amex TV commercial.

Corporate Crow: There was an obvious conflict between Sheryl singing about contentment with what you've got and the public being encouraged to go on a spending spree. However, she was unapologetic.

"I used to have incredible reticence about anything that was corporate," Sheryl told *Billboard* magazine. "But you know what? In the last few years, all these rules are being rewritten. Everything is starting to overlap, whether you think it's fortunate or unfortunate. You just have to have control so you can control your integrity."

Still, at least the Blue Card commercial (and a 2000 British ad for Pantene Pro V shampoo, which used "All I Wanna Do") actually featured Sheryl's voice, as opposed to those of the soundalikes who'd cropped up on American television in recent years. Ranging from the "ask how, ask now, ask Sherwin-Williams" paint ad to the title song of the *Cinematherapy* show on the Women's Entertainment (WE) cable channel (part Sheryl, part Rickie Lee Jones—take your choice), these were all pretty feeble efforts, even if they did provide a fair indication as to how much Sheryl Crow was now a part of the social fabric and public consciousness.

Making little impact in that regard back in 1999 was her big-screen acting debut in *The Minus Man*. Written and directed by Hampton Fancher, based on a novel by Lew McCreary, this slow-paced, understated psychodrama focused on the coolly sadistic activities of serial killer Vann Siegert (Owen Wilson), whose thoughtful *modus operandi* is to terminate people who are unhappy with their lives. An asthmatic junkie named Laurie Bloom (a.k.a. Casper) is the first such person to succumb to his charms. "I've always wanted to be a junkie, but I never wanted to do the drugs," Sheryl told the *New York Daily News* about taking on the role.

As for her adequate performance, Sheryl admitted to *Musician* magazine that she wasn't "terribly extroverted when it comes to being in front of a camera, so in that way it was a really good experience.... The bottom line is, you have to be unaware of your actions and be so instinctual when you're in front of a camera and you're acting like someone else. For me to stand up and sing 'My Favorite Mistake' is me singing what I feel. I write those words from my own standpoint, so it's quite a bit different. I was not completely unaware of how it all works at least. I had some knowledge of cameras, directing, the slow pace of it, and so I wasn't completely out of my element. It's different, though, when you speak and you hear your voice come out of your body. It's something to really get used to. It's different than when you're singing...the speaking voice can be much more alarming."

*The Minus Man*, which also featured Mercedes Ruehl, Brian Cox, Janeane Garofalo, and Dwight Yoakam, premiered at the 1999 Sundance Film Festival, and went on general release in the U.S. during September and October to mixed reviews and poor box-office returns. (By October 24, the domestic gross was just $368,808.) Of far more significance to Sheryl by then, however, was the liaison that she'd begun the previous year with her leading man. One of her more high-profile relationships—she and Owen Wilson appeared together at several movie premieres and numerous other public engagements—this would end in tabloid headlines during the summer of 2000 when Wilson took up with actress Gina Gershon.

A July 27 report by E! Online gossip columnist Ted Casablanca described how "a Whiskey Bar regular" at the Sunset Marquis Hotel on the Sunset Strip saw Wilson and Gershon "very much enjoying each other's company." Then Sheryl "stopped by to ruin the mood...apparently the hip rocker was so out of it that a couple of friends had to help her stand up." Some screaming ensued and Sheryl stormed out. On the sleeve-notes to her *C'mon, C'mon* album a couple of years later, the lovelorn ballad "Safe And Sound" would be dedicated "For O."

Overall, Sheryl was enjoying more stability with her non-romantic friendships, many of them cultivated over many years. Among the more recent but certainly more invaluable of these was that with singer-songwriter Stevie Nicks, who Sheryl had idolized as a teenager when Stevie was riding high as a member of Fleetwood Mac. The two women first met in early 1995, when they were attending a party at the House of Blues in Los Angeles for the premiere of the Whoopi Goldberg/Mary-Louise Parker/Drew Barrymore buddy movie, *Boys on the Side*. The Sheryl Crow/Todd Wolfe composition, "Somebody Stand By Me," had been recorded by Stevie for the film's soundtrack, and when she spoke with Sheryl she told her that she'd like to work with her.

"That was the first time I talked to her about possible production, because I had really liked her song and really enjoyed doing it," Stevie recalled in a May 2001 interview with *Wall of Sound*. "We really planned it out; we wanted to work together and we wanted to sing together. Sheryl's a harmony singer and I'm a harmony singer; we go to harmony immediately before we go to melody. So, we thought it would be something that would be great to do."

On August 20, 1998, the two women duetted on "Strong Enough" for Sheryl's episode of VH1's *Storytellers*, taped at the Sony Studios in New York City. Beforehand, Stevie asked Sheryl to produce her recordings for the soundtrack to the Sandra Bullock/ Nicole Kidman movie, *Practical Magic*: the Nicks compositions "Crystal," which had originally been sung by Lindsey Buckingham, and "If You Ever Did Believe," which would subsequently be released as a single.

"I had two days right between my *Storytellers* and going to Europe," Sheryl recalled in her *Musician* interview. "I said, 'This is all I have, and we'll just really push the envelope and try to pull it off.' So, that's what we did."

To a VH1 interviewer, Sheryl asserted, "There is such a fabulous dynamic that happens in the studio when there are two women, two kindred spirits [with] similar mindsets."

Accordingly, in 1998 Stevie indulged that dynamic by asking Sheryl to produce her next album. The pair subsequently collaborated on a couple of Nicks compositions, "Candlebright" and "Sorcerer," before Sheryl took advantage of a break in her U.S. tour early the following year to co-produce and contribute vocal, guitar, and/or bass parts to three other tracks that ended up on the finished record: "Too Far From Texas," "That Made Me Stronger," and "It's Only Love," a tender acoustic ballad written by Sheryl and produced by her and Jeff Trott. It was at a later date that she recorded her vocals for "Candlebright" and "Sorcerer," recreating the harmonies that Lindsey Buckingham had sung on the original demos.

Released in May 2001, *Trouble in Shangri-La* was Stevie Nicks's first solo album in seven years, and in addition to having Sheryl appear with her in the video for the "Sorcerer" single and on stage during some of the shows on the *Shangri-La* tour, she also went out of her way in press and media interviews to praise the woman whom she referred to in the record's credits as "the little sister I always wanted—part of my family."

"Sheryl's brilliant," Stevie told *Billboard* in February 2001. "She's an amazing songwriter, singer, and musician. But she's also someone who gets it. She understands the life of a woman in rock 'n' roll. There's no room for playing games with her or saying, 'You don't understand what I'm going through.' She understands, and that's brought us closer than I can explain."

In the same *Billboard* piece, Sheryl returned the compliments: "She represents such a huge chunk of my life that it's almost unreal to be in the same room with her....

Stevie's just so real, so completely open as a person. And as an artist, she continues to work hard. Sometimes you meet your heroes, and you discover they've stopped growing or have gone past caring about what they do. Stevie's still so vital. She's still looking to try new things."

Indeed, such was the strength of this mutual admiration that it soon resulted in a widely reported story that Sheryl was about to replace Christine McVie as the keyboard player and co-vocalist in Fleetwood Mac. Mick Fleetwood had to issue a statement denying the rumor. Still, there could be little doubt that the Crow-Nicks bond ran extremely deep—aside from their personal and professional compatibility, both women knew what it was like to deal with troubled relationships and male-dominated work environments. The only thing Sheryl didn't know was what she was about to get into when embarking on her own new album project. It would be a harrowing experience.

# CHAPTER FIFTEEN

# Out of the Waiting Room

Accustomed to many of the tracks on her previous albums being composed in the studio, Sheryl took a different approach when embarking on a new project in the early spring of 2000. This time she wanted to come up with the material in advance, and so at the end of March she and Jeff Trott got together for a series of writing sessions at her home in the Hollywood Hills.

"Sheryl had a pretty amazing studio setup there," Jeff remarks. "She originally bought this house at the end of the street which looks a little bit European, kind of like a small château. Well, it's on the same property as a Craftsman house that was owned by Monty Montgomery, the filmmaker who's produced some of [director] David Lynch's work. When he decided to sell the house, Sheryl decided to buy it so that she wouldn't have any neighbors and have a little more privacy on this ten-acre spread in the Hills. It's really cool; desert terrain with indigenous plants everywhere, as well as incredible little trails and little hutches where you can sit back, sip a beer, and look at the city. It almost feels like you're in Mexico.

"The studio was in the living room of the main house, which has thicker walls than the Craftsman—from which the whole mountainside would have heard everything she did—but I think the home setup was a little more than Sheryl bargained for. I mean, I don't think she realized that when you have a studio in your house you've got to learn how to discipline yourself and separate work from regular life. She actually moved into the Craftsman for a short time, but then she just got so used to going to the studio and upstairs to her regular bedroom that she figured she'd stay in the big house and use the Craftsman mostly for doing yoga."

Before long, Sheryl would tire of her home studio. But in the meantime, in a couple of two-week stretches during the first half of 2000, she and Jeff wrote there while Jeff's friend Brian Scheuble took care of the engineering.

"Each day we'd get together at noon, have a little bit of lunch, sit around and talk, pick up some instruments, and then listen to some drum grooves and records," Jeff explains. "I'd sit down at the piano and sometimes the harmonium. The thing with the harmonium is that it's just a simple, melodic instrument, and it doesn't require tuning or anything. You just squeeze it and start playing. So, Sheryl would play accordion and I'd play harmonium. We'd try to ease into it and not just go running for the instruments, and then at other times I'd get an acoustic guitar and start finger-picking, but it's almost like we'd have to fool ourselves into thinking that we weren't really writing. We'd kind of pretend that we weren't really doing anything, and then it'd finally happen. I think that's the thing that frightens a lot of people when we have friends or players come in and they're not used to the unorthodox way in which we work. They kind of freak out, saying, 'What are they doing?' Eventually, by the end of the night, we've done a lot of music, but it's sort of like the little dance that animals do when they're courting. It's really a state of mind. We just don't want it to be work."

Brian MacLeod played drums and Tim Smith was on bass for some of these early writing/tracking sessions, which produced a combination of Southern rock and early-'70s-style glam rock, melding sex with attitude. However, unsure of how this—or she—could fit into a music scene that was now largely dominated by heavy-metal-rap, hip-hop, contemporary R&B, teen-oriented boy bands, and country records that sounded suspiciously like MOR pop, Sheryl soon balked at the idea of making her kind of record. Consequently, searching for an alternative while trying to deal with the aforementioned breakup of her relationship with Owen Wilson, she almost totally lost herself.

"I was stricken with melancholy on a day-to-day basis," Sheryl later recalled in an interview with *Billboard*'s Melinda Newman. "I thought I could work my way through it. I thought it would heal the bruises, but it didn't—it just made a big scab. I thought music would be my medicine, and that's just not realistic."

Unhappy with the material that she and Jeff had been collaborating on, Sheryl called him after he'd returned home to Portland and asked if he would send her some new ideas that she could embellish.

"I'd spent an entire summer coming up with music, because she didn't want me to get involved in the lyric-writing part of it," Jeff recalls. "We'd come up with twenty to thirty fairly strong ideas, but nothing was completed because she was having a really difficult time writing the lyrics. On her *Globe Sessions* record, Sheryl's songs had started becoming a little more personal, expressing her own point of view rather than a group point of view, and I think she wanted to go even further with that on the new record, which maybe wasn't the right thing to do. She said she didn't want to write an album about Owen Wilson.

"She also told me I could feel free to come up with lyrics as well as music, so I wrote two or three songs, but once I start writing it's kinda hard to not follow through and finish it. I have a hard time just coming up with half-baked ideas. I'll get one line going and that'll set me off. I'll just keep writing 'til I've got three or four verses, and then I'll choose the best verses that make the most interesting song."

Consequently, when Jeff sent Sheryl his new ideas, she complained that there was little for her to do. He'd been hoping to get a co-production credit for the songs they worked on. Now he decided it might be best to withdraw before all the discontent placed too much of a strain on their friendship. It was an ugly time, and when Trina Shoemaker visited Sheryl's house at short notice that August, she too was greeted with indifference and indecision.

"She had this real rad setup that she'd spent a lot of money on, and now she was saying, 'I don't like the studio here,'" Trina remembers. "I thought, 'Uh-oh, that's not a good sign.' Then again, as with the previous project, she was saying, 'I don't want to make the same record this time,' and so I wasn't sure if she even wanted to work with me or not.... No matter how talented you are, you cannot say, going into the studio, what record you're going to make and what it's going to sound like. You can only hope for something."

Not even sure quite what she was hoping for, Sheryl was struggling to tread water. On her previous albums, thanks to either her own initiative or that of her collaborators, she'd pursued her aims with a vengeance. Now she was drifting and achieving virtually nothing. As in the past, she thought a change of scenery might help stimulate her creative juices. Sheryl decided to quit the home setup.

"I couldn't go back in there," David Wild later quoted her saying in *Rolling Stone*. "I just didn't want to work. Every time I walked out of my house, it represented what I wasn't getting done. So I just packed up my stuff and went to New York."

Unfortunately, this move was in no way a solution to Sheryl's inner turmoil, which stemmed from her personal woes, professional concerns, and sheer overwork. Before long came the inevitable meltdown.

"There was definitely bipolar behavior during this record," Sheryl later told *Rolling Stone*'s Mim Udovitch. "I really, really hit bottom in the middle of this record, and I had to find what music meant for me, what it means to me in the present and what it's going to mean to me in the future. It's been a part of all of my relationships, it's been a part of the way I see myself in the universe, and I just got to where I didn't want to do it...."

"Chrissie Hynde actually made a very serendipitous appearance at the point where I just couldn't go on anymore. She came down and visited me at the studio in New York. And I was forcing myself to go in, trying to finish music. My heart wasn't in it, and I was trying to figure out what direction I was going in and why this was turning out to be such a hard project. And she said, 'What do you want to do?' And I said, 'Really, I want to stop.' And she said, 'Well, why don't you? You know, your music is not your life. Music is something you do, and your life is your life.' And in a weird way, it emancipated me from the whole thing. I just put so much weight in my work and let it be sort of a big Band-Aid. Whenever my relationships slowed down, I was like, 'Okay, well, I'm going to get into my work,' you know? I just walked away from it."

And by Sheryl's own admission to David Wild during her 2002 TV appearance on Bravo's *Musicians*, she also "took a few trips to Mount Sinai [Hospital] for some psychiatric help." In her interview with Mim Udovitch, she discussed the extent to which therapy has helped her cope with depression.

"All I can tell you is I never graduate with the diploma, where the guy says, 'Okay, you're free to go, you're cured,'" Sheryl remarked. "It's a good investment in your art, just to get into the inner workings of the human spirit. Although that's not why I've done it. I've had to go into therapy because—it's just such an uncomfortable topic— but really because all the applications I ever had didn't work anymore. Like, I let myself get so overwhelmed with repressing anger or depressing it. I'm really good at just going to work if I'm unhappy, or if I'm angry or if I'm frustrated or if I'm lonely, and then it gets a little bit out of control, so I have to go in to dig myself out of the cave I've built."

Her way out of the cave this time around came in the unlikely form of a sojourn at the residential studio of white rapper, Kid Rock, just north of Detroit. Rock (a.k.a. Bob Ritchie) had not only achieved success courtesy of an eclectic musical fusion of hip-hop, country, jazz, and hard rock, but he'd also cultivated what the media love to describe as a "bad-boy image," thanks to his sometimes-overtly sexual lyrics and devil-may-care attitude. It therefore made for great press copy when he and Sheryl were seen in each other's company early in 2001. During her impromptu show at the Cutting Room in New York City on April 14, Rock showed up in a bunny costume and duetted with Sheryl on a cover of Lynyrd Skynyrd's "Sweet Home Alabama." They repeated this performance when Sheryl headlined another all-star gig at New York's Shine a couple of weeks later, and they also showed up together at a New York Knicks basketball game.

"Every time I am around him I just appreciate him so much more," Sheryl told *Rolling Stone* after the Cutting Room show, when it was also reported that she and Rock would be appearing on each other's forthcoming albums. Like Julia Roberts and Lyle Lovett, Whitney Houston and Bobby Brown, here was another beauty-and-the-beast-type coupling. Never mind that both Sheryl and the Kid categorically refuted talk of anything more than a friendship; when he became entwined with actress Pamela Anderson, the tabloids asserted that Sheryl had been dumped.

In fact, her personal anguish and professional inertia had begun to dissipate after hanging out at Kid Rock's new Clarkston Chophouse studio that February. Sheryl was there to sing, and play bass and 12-string guitar, on "Picture," a plaintive, country-flavored track that would end up on his *Cocky* album. Despite the aforementioned reports, Rock wouldn't appear on Sheryl's new record, but their time together played a priceless role in stirring her to revive her own project.

"It was just so much fun," Sheryl recalled when David Wild interviewed her for *Musicians*. "It totally reminded me of what it was like when I was growing up. It was all about trucks and Camaros and Lynyrd Skynyrd and the Allman Brothers and Budweiser and hanging out with your friends, and I just felt like, 'Wow! I remember now who I am.' I think you can live in Hollywood, and you can have money and be famous, and then you start to forget who your audience is. And my audience were always the people…that drank Budweiser and listened to the Allman Brothers, just like I still do. So, it turned me around. It reminded me of what it was I'm supposed to be doing."

Still, when asked by *Rolling Stone* in March what form her long-awaited new album would be taking, Sheryl took a cynical, tongue-in-cheek swipe at the music scene in general, and the misogynistic, homophobic lyrics of then-controversial rap artist Eminem in particular. "Lots of profanity," she jokingly promised. "Lots of gay-bashing. A lot of anti-women statements. I think it's gonna be huge!"

That same month, a revitalized Sheryl resumed work on her album at Clinton Recording in New York City, where she was joined at the start of April by Trina Shoemaker, who'd been occupied with various other engineering assignments since the fall. At that point, Sheryl had only produced a couple of the tracks that would make it onto the finished record: "Safe And Sound," which would later be revamped with new guitar and drum parts at Oceanway in Nashville; and "It's Only Love," the Crow composition that had first surfaced on Stevie Nicks's *Trouble In Shangri-La* album. Sheryl had tracked a demo of "It's Only Love" and then forgotten about it, but her friend, actress Gwyneth Paltrow, hadn't. Paltrow encouraged Sheryl to rerecord the song and even critiqued her performance, while giving an outing to her own vocal talents by harmonizing on the track.

"She was so used to the way I'd sung it on the demo, that she kept coming into the studio where I was singing, or into the booth, saying, 'No, no, no, you're not singing it the way you did on the demo!'" Sheryl recalled in a videotaped interview conducted by Paul Guthrie, which was featured on her official Web site to help promote the album. "And she was kind of coaching me, which was funny."

Paltrow had displayed her vocal prowess when singing with Huey Lewis in the 2000 comedy film, *Duets*, and she did the same when partnering Sheryl on "It's Only Love" at her April 14 Cutting Room gig, where they also performed covers of numbers such as The Who's "Squeeze Box" and Ram Jam's "Black Betty." Not that Paltrow would be the only guest singer on Sheryl's new album—in addition to Stevie Nicks's contributions to "C'mon, C'mon" and "Diamond Road," there would be appearances by Lenny Kravitz on "You're An Original," Don Henley on "It's So Easy," Natalie Maines on "Abilene," Emmylou Harris on "Weather Channel," and Liz Phair on "Soak Up The Sun."

"It's kind of weird because, when I got to the end of making *C'mon, C'mon*, I realized that there were a lot of people on this album, and I got really worried about it," Sheryl remarked in a David Wild interview that was included in the record's press package. "I got worried about how they would be perceived and whether it would look like I was capitalizing on my relationships. But then I realized that, above all else, I really needed support on this record emotionally. So, I called people that were really good friends of mine, friends who have been through the struggle with me."

Given her troubled state of mind, Sheryl had originally considered naming the record *Songs from the Waiting Room*. "I have been sort of waiting around for the album to kind of reveal what it's supposed to be," she told Wild in an interview for *Rolling Stone*. "Also, there was the kind of iffy health I was in and my relationship kind of falling apart at that juncture. My cyclical depression struck very hard this time. Had Mariah Carey not done it first, I would have checked myself into a hospital."

As it turned out, Sheryl got both herself and the project back on track, utilizing not only the aforementioned guest vocalists, but also a large number of stage and studio musicians in addition to regulars like Jeff Trott, Tim Smith, and Brian MacLeod. These included Jim Bogios, Steve Jordan, Shawn Pelton, Jeremy Stacey, Jeff Anthony, and Lenny Castro playing a combination of drums and/or percussion; John Shanks, Mike Elizondo, and Dave Faragher on bass; guitarists Craig Ross, Doyle Bramhall II, Peter Stroud, and Wendy Melvoin; Benmont Tench, Doug Grean, and Keefus Ciancia on keyboards; and a variety of programmers, string players, and arrangers.

"We meandered around the globe and tried all kinds of different stuff before finally creating a cohesive album out of about twenty-two tracks that were written, recorded, and produced," says Trina Shoemaker. "For me, an incredibly important change in approach this time was having Eric Tew as the dedicated full-time Pro Tools engineer. We finally succumbed to modernization insofar as tracking everything on analog before it immediately went into Pro Tools, which we used for convenience, and Eric was absolutely crucial to this record."

"Over You," a heavy but fairly innocuous mid-tempo number in which Sheryl tells her former lover that she wants to get over him before he gets over her, was written in her New York apartment after she'd been inspired by watching the "It's Been Awhile" video by New England rock alternative band Staind on MTV.

"'Over You' really is just about being finally over a relationship, but still having the residue of it," Sheryl stated in her interview with Paul Guthrie. "Maybe not necessarily thinking about the person or wanting to be with them, but always kind of coming into the circles that you traveled in, or having the reminders around you and feeling like 'When am I actually going to have absolutely no feeling about this, so that I can move on, free and clear?'"

In the summer of 2001, having attempted to write with a number of different people, Sheryl got back in touch with Jeff Trott and told him her record lacked the kind of material that only their partnership could produce. Jeff responded by asserting that, this time, he wanted them to see all of their song ideas through to completion, even if they ultimately weren't used on the album. Sheryl agreed, and so in late July they met in L.A. By now her home studio had been completely disassembled. Therefore, plugging a guitar and drum machine into an amp, they proceeded to work in the makeshift demo facility that Sheryl had set up in her basement. A few songs resulted—including "You're An Original" and "Soak Up The Sun," both of which emanated from Jeff's melodic ideas—but then the following month, after Sheryl again had trouble coming up with lyrics on her own, she and Jeff reunited in her New York loft.

This was essentially for a lyric-writing session, although Jeff also arrived with a song named "Hybrid Lives" that he'd written just beforehand. When Sheryl heard the melancholy number she instantly liked it and began fixing some of the lyrics; retitled "Chances Are," the number would be included as a bonus track on some versions of the U.K. "Soak Up The Sun" CD single. For the latter song, Jeff had contrived the title refrain and lyrical framework before flying to New York, and the sum of these parts would comprise a highly commercial singalong number in the Beach Boys vein.

"Sheryl was in a great mood when I went out to New York, but I really thought that if we didn't come up with anything she was just going to have a nervous breakdown," Jeff remarks. "In one day we wrote all of the lyrics. We completed every single line. We were not going to leave her home until we were done, and we ended up going out to dinner, we met a couple of friends, and Sheryl was just beaming. She was like, 'I have broken through that barrier.'"

At the start of August, Sheryl had canceled a couple of live gigs due to what was officially described by the William Morris Agency as "an unavoidable medical condition that required surgery." Given her smooth-faced appearance in the "Soak Up The

Sun" video the following year, as well as in some of the album's publicity photos, there were soon rumors that what Sheryl declared to be "non-invasive surgery" was actually a facelift. She categorically denied this.

"I can always tell when people have plastic surgery," she informed Franklin Cumberbatch in an interview for VH1. "Maybe in four years people have forgotten what I look like. A lot has changed, not just for me personally. A lot's happened in the music business. It's become very visually oriented. There's a lot of attention on body and beauty. I've never relied on that part of my persona for my credibility. I'm almost anti-image. I've suffered because of it, because you're selling a product, which is yourself. Now it's gone that way even more, so it's fun to me. I feel like I'm on the outskirts of all of it. Anytime I look nice, people are like, 'What has she done?'…I haven't had anything done. I'm not a person that works out shamefully. I have good genes."

Regardless, it was while recuperating from her surgery that Sheryl worked with Jeff on "Soak Up The Sun."

"I was sick and flat on my back," she told *Billboard*'s Melinda Newman. "It was sort of a diversion, and out of that came this lyric that wrote itself very, very fast, and Jeff was howling. It could have been the medication I was on. It was the same medication I was on when I wrote 'Weather Channel.' It was definitely very freeing."

To David Wild, Sheryl commented that "The lyric came about during one of the lowest points of this record you can imagine, and it wound up being the most upbeat song. It's a social commentary on the amount of minutiae that clutters our lives and how we miss the moments that tick by. I was at a point where I was just feeling like 'Wow, I'm spinning my wheels. I'm not sure what I'm doing, and every day that goes by you can't get back.' It's really just a song about yearning for the simple things."

While working on the vocal in Studio A at Sunset Sound in L.A., Sheryl was distracted by the noise of basketball rimshots in the adjacent courtyard. When she went outside to tell the culprit to tone it down, she discovered this to be singer-songwriter Liz Phair, who was subsequently invited to make her own harmonic contribution to the song's chorus. This worked perfectly well, whereas another section in which Sheryl sang alone wasn't nearly as suitable.

"There was a very twisted outro on that song which, for obvious reasons, didn't make the mix," says Jeff Trott. "It had just an acoustic guitar and Sheryl, in a little girl's voice, singing this anti-gun thing. It was creepy, because it was like a little girl with a shotgun, and the song was not meant to be that heavy."

Largely recorded at Jeff's facility in Portland, Oregon, "Soak Up The Sun" signaled a successful rekindling of the Crow/Trott songwriting partnership, while providing him with the co-production credit that he was now insisting on when heavily involved in the creative process. Still, it took some time for Sheryl to agree to this.

"She came to me and said, 'Jeff told me he now won't write with me unless I agree to not only a co-write but a co-production in advance,'" Trina Shoemaker recalls. "I said, 'Well, that's great.' 'What do you mean?' I said, 'Sheryl, he's being up-front with you. It's better than writing a song with you and helping you get it on tape in a finished form, and then turning around later and saying, "I want a co-production." Professionals lay on the line in advance what they deserve and feel that they deserve. I admire him.' 'Really?' I said, 'Yeah! Sheryl, he's saying he wants to write with you, but that he deserves co-production, and if you don't accept that then he cannot write with you. That's not betraying you.'

"After that she loosened up a little bit. I said, 'Guess what, Sheryl. Nobody really cares about production. Everybody in the room produces the record and everybody knows it. It doesn't really matter. You're the artist and they know it's you. It's your sound. You can feel totally secure in owning that.' I mean, nobody looks and says, 'Hey, produced by Jeff and Sheryl! Whoopedy-fuckin'-doo!' Who cares?"

The point was well made. "Soak Up The Sun" and "You're An Original" would be credited as Crow/Trott co-productions—Jeff wasn't involved in the recordings of "Lucky Kid" and "Abilene," which he and Sheryl also wrote together—while John Shanks would share the production credit with her on their co-composition "Steve McQueen." Still, Sheryl's more relaxed attitude in this regard didn't cure her general restlessness, which partly accounted for the sessions switching locations several times; from Clinton and Avatar in New York to Oceanway and Emerald in Nashville, and Sunset Sound in Los Angeles.

"Different songs utilized sets of musicians who were on either the East or West Coast," Trina explains. "Plus, Sheryl needed to be in New York for a few months in the spring for personal business to do with her property. Then she needed to get out to L.A. because she was building a pool and had some gigs on the West Coast, so we moved out there. Then her sister Kathy was getting married and she lives near Nashville, so we worked there for a while. It wasn't boring, and it let me investigate a lot of great rooms in America!"

*C'mon, C'mon* turned into something of a family affair, what with middle sister Karen contributing handclaps to "Hole In My Pocket," and Sheryl co-composing "It's So Easy" with Kathy, who is a country music songwriter in Nashville.

"We actually wrote the song 'It's So Easy' for another artist," Sheryl informed David Wild, "and I called Jimmy Iovine…and I said, 'My sister and I wrote this song, and it's a really good song. It's a waltz. It's in 3.' It was 6/8, basically, really country. He said, 'Well, let me just hear it.' He loved the song, and he called me and said, 'You have to do it.'"

Sheryl was happy to take Iovine's advice, while recruiting Don Henley to duet with her and sing the second verse alone.

"The song was always kind of meant to be a duet," she told Wild. "It definitely has a male-female relationship in it. It's basically about people who are in a clandestine relationship that know it's wrong, but it's so difficult to unattach or detach from it, which is kind of a universal feeling. I don't know how many people have experienced being in an adulterous relationship, but definitely everybody has experienced being in a relationship that they knew was not suitable or whatever."

Sheryl and her colleagues were actually tracking at Emerald in Nashville on September 11, the day that terrorist-navigated planes crashed into the World Trade

Center towers in New York, the Pentagon in Washington, and a field in Somerset County, Pennsylvania, southeast of Pittsburgh.

"We were all in our hotel rooms that morning, calling each other, crying," Trina Shoemaker recalls. "When we got to the studio, we had a big wide-screen TV wheeled into the control room, there was a short-wave radio, and we were all very stunned and scared, talking to our families. We fooled around with 'Safe And Sound,' but we cut that session short for two days. Sheryl said, 'We've all got to find ways home,' so that's what we did, driving to see our folks, because we didn't know what was coming next."

On September 21, Sheryl debuted "Safe And Sound" as her contribution to *America: A Tribute to Heroes*, the two-hour multi-star telethon which was simulcast live on more than thirty networks and cable stations to raise funds for victims of the tragedy. The other musical performers were Bruce Springsteen, Billy Joel, Neil Young, Paul Simon, Mariah Carey, Jon Bon Jovi, Faith Hill, The Dixie Chicks, Enrique Iglesias, Alicia Keys, Tom Petty, Sting, U2, Eddie Vedder, Wyclef Jean, Stevie Wonder, Celine Dion, and Willie Nelson. Muhammad Ali, Julia Roberts, Clint Eastwood, Robert De Niro, Tom Hanks, Jim Carrey, George Clooney, Tom Cruise, Will Smith, and Robin Williams were among the guest speakers.

"9/11 affected the session like it affected all of our lives," says Trina Shoemaker. "It made us realize how lucky we are to live in a free country and be paid to work on music. We played 'Sweet Home Alabama' as much as possible and made up Osama bin Laden jokes, and it brought our little team closer together."

It was while in Nashville, in the wake of September 11, that Sheryl wrote the album's starkest, most stripped-down ballad, "Weather Channel," and recruited Emmylou Harris to duet with her.

"That song came in such a dark place," Sheryl told David Wild. "I called Emmylou and said, 'I really want your voice on this song,' because her voice for me exemplifies something deeper than an earthly voice. For me it's so spiritual. Her voice is so healing—if I was sick, I would just put her on a loop and listen to it over and over, and I know I would be healed."

Meanwhile, in light of all the acts of bravery that took place on September 11 and during the days and weeks that followed, Sheryl realized that the upbeat rocker, "Steve McQueen," originally written about the contemporary lack of real-life heroes, was now wide of the mark. Therefore, having already tracked the song, she went back into the studio to record some hastily revised lyrics, and retained other lines which she still considered pertinent—while likening pop stars to porn stars, the singer asserts that she still wants to have some fun.

In her promotional interview with David Wild, Sheryl described the song as "a shameless tribute to Steve Miller. Actually, Steve Miller was a name I tossed around when I was thinking about making this record. I was thinking of the albums and the music that were the soundtrack to my early rebellious years—getting my driver's license, driving around town, circling the A&W, listening to rock radio, which was *Rumours* and Heart and Steve Miller and Lynyrd Skynyrd and Peter Frampton. After coming off the Central Park gig, I really wanted to follow up with the rock feeling. I wanted to go and make that record, and to me 'Steve McQueen' is kind of Steve Miller 'Fly Like An Eagle'-ish, or something by The James Gang. And metaphorically I think the song represents a yearning to be wild and free. I think Steve McQueen was the archetypal rebellious free spirit—mysterious, heroic, American—and what he represented, in my mind at least, was just that: that free-spirited kind of no-holds-barred living, and how we lost that wide-open America. It's kind of a loss of innocence song."

"You're An Original," penned with Jeff Trott the same summer 2001 afternoon they wrote the lyrics to "Soak Up The Sun," and also recorded in Portland with Dean Baskerville as engineer, focuses on a similar theme in a different vein—the difficulty for present-day female artists to avoid being defined by their physical attributes. In interviews published at the time of the album's release, Sheryl didn't allow herself to be drawn on who the song might be referring to as dirty-mouthed and mean. However, the inspiration was Shelby Lynne, with whom Sheryl had duetted and presented an award at the 43rd annual Grammys show in Los Angeles on February 21, 2001.

The diminutive country singer with the hellraising reputation had been nominated for her Island/Def Jam album, *I Am Shelby Lynne*, produced by Sheryl's old nemesis, Bill Bottrell. Add the fact that Shelby was extremely close to Bill's wife, Betty, who wasn't particularly enamored with Sheryl, and it doesn't take a genius to figure out that the Crow/Lynne pairing contrived by Grammy producer Ken Ehrlich was less a match made in heaven than one resembling a face-off between Bette Davis and Joan Crawford.

Shelby immediately balked when she was told that Sheryl had chosen to perform one of her own compositions, the now-aptly titled "The Difficult Kind." After all, why not duet on one of Shelby's songs or even, she suggested, a track off The Beatles' *Revolver* album? That little idea went down like a lead balloon. If Shelby thought she could prevail against Sheryl, she was sadly mistaken. Sheryl simply dug her heels in and stood her ground, resulting in a stay of execution for "The Difficult Kind." Nevertheless, at the show's February 19 dress rehearsal, an intoxicated Shelby showed up three hours late, and after over-emoting during the song's run-through, walked over to the podium where she and Sheryl would announce the next set of nominees, peered at the TelePrompTer, and cried, "Goddammit! Nobody told me I had to read!" Fortunately for all concerned, things ran according to plan on the actual night, while Sheryl now had rich source material for "You're An Original."

Often working on more than one number at a time, Sheryl presented her studio colleagues with some brand-new songs during the project's later stages. Such was the case with "C'mon, C'mon," which she wrote in her Nashville hotel room one morning a few days before Christmas of 2001, and whose title was subsequently used for that of the album, reflecting the artist's reinvigorated spirit.

"We tracked it that afternoon, Sheryl recorded all of the vocals and laid down an accordion part, and it came out perfect, with a beautiful vibe," Trina Shoemaker recalls. "That's how things remained fresh."

Meanwhile, throughout the long and traumatic process of making *C'mon, C'mon*, it was Jimmy Iovine who virtually A&R'd the record, consulting with Sheryl on an almost daily basis to discuss music and strategy

"I've produced a lot of people, so although I didn't produce this record, I've been to the movie," he says. "In the end, Sheryl made a great album, but she was also terrific about accepting input. She really let me in, and I went to the studio a lot with her. I said, 'Let's not put this record out until it's right,' and to be honest, I pushed her. I think I pushed her farther than she wanted to go, telling her we needed a few more songs or that some others should be rerecorded, and she got it. 'Let's try this, let's try that.' She was fantastic."

In her publicity bio, Sheryl told David Wild that she wanted to make an album "in the flavor of '70s and '80s classic rock—when rock songs were songs that were crafted, that you could sing; songs that were the soundtrack to your summer—songs that were committed to rock." With *C'mon, C'mon* she achieved that aim, although at the expense of the country feel to which she is more innately attuned, and with little connection to the direction that she'd been given a decade earlier by the Tuesday Night Music Club. Just as she prefers to be seen with a bass guitar rather than behind the keyboards that she's more adept at playing, so it appears that Sheryl's personal tastes and self-image have led her towards a style of music that she can capably handle, but which isn't necessarily her most natural fit.

Not displaying as much light and shade as her previous albums, and more uneven in terms of the quality of raw material, *C'mon, C'mon* nevertheless has some fine moments, as well as plenty of extremely radio-friendly material that caters to an increasingly starved baby-boomer market: "Steve McQueen" and "You're An Original" are both strong rockers, "It's So Easy" is perfectly suited to Don Henley's vocal style, and "Abilene"—a Crow/Trott composition which originated during *The Globe Sessions*—finds Sheryl in more familiar, countrified territory. Other highlights include "Diamond Road," in which the penultimate line about making plans is adapted from one in John Lennon's "Beautiful Boy"; "It's Only Love," which not too surprisingly has a distinct Fleetwood Mac flavor (despite using the title of a Beatles song); and, perhaps best of all, the title track, which borrows its feel from Mac, Tom Petty, and Bob Dylan.

"Sheryl will often come in with example songs that we're not meant to rip off," Trina Shoemaker explains. "She'll say, 'I want it to feel like U2's "Elevation"' because she digs the vibe of that production, but she'll also say, 'I want the guitar sounds bigger. I want them almost like [Black] Sabbath.' 'Oh, okay.' At that point, Peter Stroud will be going, 'Cool, right on, right on,' and Shawn Pelton will be thinking about a loop, so we'll be on an aesthetic, but it'll then become utterly her own and be completely different from the example she used. All she's getting from it is a palette. She's a producer, and she comes in with an atmosphere for each song to exist within—an image or a feeling. As Jimmy Iovine says, music is an illusion, and you have to bring people where you want them to go. If they want purity, they can go see a blues show. Sheryl knows the illusion she wants to create, even if how we're going to create it is up for grabs sometimes."

"To me, Sheryl is like a combination of Tom Petty and Stevie Nicks," adds Iovine. "Not so much sound-wise, but in terms of how they work. I really like what she does, and musically it gave me a real foothold. We'd just finished working on U2 and Sting, and we'd learned so much from those records regarding the marketing—Sting's record *Brand New Day* [on A&M] sold eight million worldwide, and U2's *All That You Can't Leave Behind* [on Interscope in the U.S. and Island overseas] sold eleven million, so it was good timing. The company was really ready for Sheryl, and we had very, very high hopes for her record.

"Ron Fair has been great, and every single person at this company pulls for Sheryl. I don't know how she does it. Every person in this building wanted that record to do as well as she did. I couldn't fake that. With the marketing of the record, she was a blast."

That she certainly was, not least for the amount of self-publicity Sheryl managed to generate as a result of the apparent conflict between her public pronouncements and equally public appearances. In the March 2002 edition of men's magazine *Stuff*, she decried a contemporary scene where young female artists such as Britney Spears and Christina Aguilera are "being marketed like porn stars. I don't mean to sound like a fuddy-duddy," Sheryl continued, "but the images are pretty sleazy. It's hard for some of these young girls. Where do you go after you've been 19 and you've stuck your crotch on a camera lens in front of 20,000 people?…I'm not going to put out a high-production, X-rated commercial video just to sell records. I think it's good for your art to speak louder than your image. Otherwise you suffer the consequences."

Still, there she was, posing in underwear and cowboy boots alongside an article titled "Bare Crow," while flashing some breast and sporting the briefest of hot-pants on the magazine's cover. Celebrating her fortieth birthday in Hawaii on February 11 during the shoot of the "Soak Up The Sun" video, Sheryl was looking hotter than ever, and her *Stuff* interview/photo-feature did its job by attracting the desired widespread publicity.

"The *Stuff* cover was, for me, sort of about just taking the piss about having fun," she explained to *Rolling Stone*. "It's definitely a part of my personality, although I don't know whether it's a part of my persona."

Still, as attested to by her appearance at the Staples Center in Los Angeles on February 27, when presenting an award with the Dixie Chicks during the 44th annual Grammys ceremony, this wasn't the limit of Sheryl's fabulous-at-forty, flesh-revealing exploits. Decked out in matching black Henry Duarte hot-pants, open-fronted bustier, and cowboy boots, as well as a blue crop-duster shearling coat, she was predictably targeted by *US Weekly*'s notorious Fashion Police, while *Entertainment Weekly* likened her to "an (admittedly fetching) streetwalker."

"We're truly frightened by Sheryl Crow's getup," remarked *People* magazine when listing her among the top eight Grammy Fashion Misses. "Before the ceremony, she noted happily that she was just there to 'read the cue cards'—we wish one had advised her to change."

It was all grist to the mill. Released on April 16, 2002, *C'mon, C'mon* entered the *Billboard* charts at No. 2, the highest position for any of Sheryl's albums in the U.S., where it sold nearly 185,000 copies during its first week—another personal best.

"Given the state of the market, that kind of response was stunning," remarks Jimmy Iovine. "We were thrilled, but it's a long-term process. I mean, it took twenty months for the U2 album to be at four million units in America. We worked very hard on Sheryl's record, and we're not going to stop supporting her. We're crazy about her, and she makes you crazy about her."

Reviews for the album were mixed. "Sheryl Crow is beginning to second-guess herself, underestimating the resilience of her hardy, well-crafted tunes," stated *Rolling Stone* in its three-star review. "*C'mon, C'mon* is devoid of the dreamy first-light coherence and good-time-gal oomph that Crow can pull off so effortlessly."

"Musically, Crow skillfully taps her classic-rock influences, adding some fleeting hip-hop hues for color, without moving them forward much beyond a surprise modulation here or there," commented the *Los Angeles Times*, while English newspaper *The Guardian* asserted, "She isn't an original, but Crow's knack with a memorable pop melody serves her very well."

"Trends, be damned!" was the verdict of *Billboard*. "Crow closes a four-year gap between recordings with a set that bravely (and wisely) leaves the tail-chasing and kiddie-baiting to others. Instead, she offers a masterfully crafted collection that warmly recalls the era of album-driven FM rock radio.... A most welcome return from one of rock's most valuable players."

Booked to headline the Jeep World Outside Festival tour and open some shows for The Rolling Stones during the summer of 2002, Sheryl had again proved to herself that when the chips are down she can deliver the goods. What's more, despite changes in the marketplace, her standing remained strong on the contemporary scene, and now she was back in flight with a collection of songs that largely served as a throwback to the music of her youth.

At the age of forty, Sheryl Crow had come full circle.

# Coda

In Kennett, life carries on pretty much as normal. For although Sheryl and her childhood friends have all moved away, many of their peers have stayed put. Wendell Crow maintains his law practice, and he and Bernice are still apt to visit the Country Club on a Friday night. They no longer reside at 1201 West Washington Street; they've moved into a new property built by their son, Steven, whose construction business has done a good job in recent years of bringing an urban look to the small hometown. The old ranch-style houses are gradually being replaced, but in most other respects Kennett is the same, and the old-timers are still running the place.

Sheryl accepted a key to the city a few years back, and she makes a point of returning there every now and then. "At Midnight Mass on Christmas Eve, the entire Crow family—among others—sings in the choir at the Presbyterian church," says Debbie Welsh, "and when Sheryl goes home for Christmas Eve she goes to the church, puts on the robe, and sings. It's a very centered part of what people still do in Kennett."

Debbie now lives in Kansas City, as does Ann Cash, while Sheryl's closest childhood companion, Jo Beth Skaggs, is in Los Angeles. Carlotta Tarver lives just north of there. "The friendship is not going anywhere," says Debbie. "Sheryl knows we are here in good and in bad. This is a core group of girls who've been together through high school and college and post-college and some boyfriends and some husbands and some ex-husbands. It's pretty amazing, and the other amazing factor is that none of us have children. We don't know why. Sheryl has the most maternal instinct of any of us, but I figure we'll all be sixty years old, in matching pyjamas, and by ourselves again!"

"Sheryl's one smart, knowledgeable cookie," adds Jo Beth Skaggs. "She's much more mature, much more focused, and much more conscious of the world around her and what maybe she can do to make a difference.... She's grown so tremendously, both musically and as a person, that sometimes it just boggles my mind to think how much she's absorbed and how much she's learned."

Others who have known and observed Sheryl for a long time agree. "I would say she is a little more tamed now than when I first knew her, and she's also aware of her own shortcomings better than she was then," remarks Shelle Jensen, one of Sheryl's sorority sisters at the University of Missouri. "She's maybe more true to herself and more reflective about who she is and the issues that concern her. She's an opinionated gal, which I think is great, and while she may have had strong opinions in college, she wasn't as confident when it came to speaking up about them. Now her success enables her to do that."

Not that success has helped Sheryl overcome her lifelong struggle with depression and mood swings. Happy one moment, she can suddenly switch to darkness. When this happens, it's as if all of the lights go off in town, and those around her need to be prepared. Otherwise, it can be a disquieting experience.

"She definitely needs her space," says Betsy Lenger, another Mizzou sorority sister. "She's a very intense, moody person who is often really hard on herself and can get very sad. When she's feeling like that, she'll make it clear by just going away on her own. That has nothing to do with her being famous—it's how she always is and was—and anytime I've ever seen her being moody, her way of dealing with it is to remove herself. That's just part of her intensity."

Sheryl's professional associates are also more than a little aware of this intensity, not to mention the unpredictability of her disposition.

"Sheryl's got like a hundred different personalities all at one time, and so you don't know who you're gonna meet in the morning," remarks Trina Shoemaker. "All of them are talented, all of them are beautiful, even the mean ones. In fact, usually when she's being obnoxious she's also being funny, so it's kinda hard not to laugh. She's very, very comic, and if she's angry in the studio it doesn't come down to yelling, but more of a quiet rage. She'll either mutter that a song sucks or just sneak out of the room and go sit in the one next door. You'll be like, 'What's wrong?' 'The song blows.' 'Oh, okay. Shall I put up something else, maybe?'

"Like any artist, she can be temperamental, but she's not an asshole like some of the people I've worked with. First and foremost, it is about pleasing herself, and thinking of herself as the great writer and performer that she is. And it's also about protecting her reputation, because she is probably one of the best musicians in terms of feel and natural ability that I've ever been near. She's got this identity that she wants of Sheryl Crow the pop star, but outside of that, when she sits down at a piano and plays classically, you'll pee on yourself. She's incredible. She could have been anything, and she chose to be a pop star. She's a great talent, and great talents need to be great."

Life moves on, and so have many of the people whose lives have been impacted, for better or for worse, by Sheryl Crow. One-time fiancé Mike Rechtien, now married and working for the Muscular Dystrophy Association, recently moved back to St. Louis from Kansas City. Bill Bottrell, disenchanted with the L.A. scene, relocated himself and his studio to a tiny village near Mendocino, in one of the remotest parts of Northern California, and has since worked on records by the likes of Tom Petty, Elton John, and Shelby Lynne. David Baerwald, who's resurrected his career courtesy of some highly lucrative film music assignments, now lives in Austin, Texas, where he regularly performs live gigs and records material for release on the Lost Highway label. At his home in Beverly Hills, surrounded by oil-on-canvas portraits of the famous who've sat for him since the mid-'60s, David Anderle indulges his passion for painting. In New York City, Al Cafaro is co-president of a new venture called Big Voice Music, where he runs the company's record label.

As for Sheryl, when she's not on the road she divides much of her time between L.A. and New York. Forty and single, she's a free agent to do as she pleases: recording, touring, appearing at countless benefit gigs and charity events, attending movie premieres, associating with pop stars and presidents, chasing the next golden ring as it pertains to her career. She regularly expresses her desire to settle down with a husband and have kids, but while her biological clock is ticking, there's no apparent compromising of ambition. Sheryl's reached a pivotal stage of her life, and it'll be interesting to see which road she heads down during the next few years.

"I'm always tickled when I see these rumors in the press about the different people she might be dating," comments Ann Cash. "People will call me and say, 'Oh, your friend Sheryl is supposed to be dating so-and-so,' and it always makes me laugh. I'm like, 'Well, do you see this person going to the Kennett Country Club and shaking hands with everybody?' Because, whoever she ends up with, that's what he's going to have to do. You know, is he going to sit in the Presbyterian church? Is he going to be judged by the Kennett bridge club? If he can, then she might end up with him, but otherwise it's no big thing."

In the meantime, it's a surefire bet that Sheryl won't rest; she never has. Hand-in-hand with her ambition, music has been the driving force of her life up to this point, and almost regardless of whether she places less emphasis on the professional achievements, it's doubtful that the quest for personal happiness will stifle her natural talents.

"I'm not gonna say that she can pick up a guitar and play like Eric Clapton or Jimi Hendrix, but she's got the feel, and she could hold her own onstage with them," states Trina Shoemaker. "She could have held her own standing right next to Jimi Hendrix, playing organ while he played guitar. She's got that much feel, and she's often frustrated because she ends up around people who don't have that feel. She's always searching for them. In musical terms, there is no one outstanding quality to Sheryl Crow, but a combination of her feel, her ability to translate that onto an instrument, her sense of melody and lyric, and her incredible voice. I mean, she can sing like Aretha Franklin, and I've heard her do it, but she won't do it, because she doesn't want to be pegged as an R&B artist. She's got three octaves of full voice, and she can mimic people, too, right down to their tone."

"Because of the type of music she writes, Sheryl hasn't yet incorporated her R&B range into her work," adds Seth Riggs, the Los Angeles–based voice coach to the stars. "I mean, she's doing fine, but she's singing in a much more limited range than she's capable of. She can do a lot more, but then that might not be her interest, and if it ain't broke, why fix it?"

What Sheryl might have a hard time fixing as time marches on is the pressure to deliver—the need to live up to a reputation and her own self-image while not dropping the ball with regard to all of the people who have come to depend on her. In a business where many artists are only as good as their last record, Sheryl has compiled a body of work that should enable her to rise above any short-term setbacks—in one form or another, be it as a headlining performer or as a composer, she's going to be around for a long time. However, it's going to be her choice as to how she deals with all of the demands, many of them self-imposed.

"It's gonna get worse, it doesn't get better," asserts David Anderle. "When I was doing A&R and producing, and acts would start getting into sad stories at the very beginning, I would always say, 'These are your glory days, believe me. These are the days you can fuck up, you can fuck around; these are the days you can get away with shit. If you want to know what pressure is, wait 'til you're successful. Sure, right now you're starving, you don't know where the next meal is, you haven't got gas for the car, and those are all problems, but wait 'til you get the big problems; wait 'til people start living off you, wait 'til you get expectations. That's what Sheryl's got."

Trina Shoemaker agrees: "She feels an enormous responsibility to make hit records. She's got a huge number of people at this point who are counting on her for a living, and so if she's having a bad day it's often because she doesn't feel like she's delivering the kind of caliber writing or performances that she needs to make a hit record and maintain the empire."

In the final analysis, while Sheryl might effect some major changes in her life, along with the obligatory cosmetic variances in her clothing and the color of her hair, at her core she'll always be the same person, searching for her own persona rather than consciously reinventing herself—searching on every level. Impacted by the people she has met and situations she has found herself in as she's moved through her career, she is still learning how to compartmentalize her experiences and access them at the appropriate time.

"I always call her The Crow," says David Anderle. "Of course, she happened right when the movie happened, as well as The Black Crowes and Counting Crows. All of a sudden, out of nowhere, there were all of these crows! But she's the only one who is The Crow. I think Sheryl is one of the original watch-my-dust girls, so lots of people will be hurt, but the people who understand that will get up, dust themselves off, move on, and hopefully be happy that they had that moment with her. Because she ain't staying there for long. It's the way things are. Unfortunately, some guys find it distressing that they've been Crowed by a woman...."

# *The Albums and Live Videos*

Following are details of Sheryl Crow's albums through April 2002, including the catalogue numbers, basic track listings, and release dates pertaining to the U.S. The peak chart position in each case is taken from *Billboard* magazine.

**SHERYL CROW** (A&M Records 75021 5393 4)
**Track listing:** All Kinds Of People / Father Sun / What Does It Matter? / Indian Summer / I Will Walk With You / Love You Blind / Near Me / When Love Is Over / You Want It All / Hundreds Of Tears / The Last Time / On Borrowed Time
**Produced by** Hugh Padgham and Sheryl Crow
**Engineered by** Hugh Padgham
**Additional production by** Jay Oliver, Kevin Gilbert
**Additional engineering by** Kevin Gilbert
**Mixed by** Kevin Gilbert, except "Love You Blind" **mixed by** Hugh Padgham
**Recorded at** A&M Studios, L.A.; Brooklyn Studios, L.A.; The Townhouse Studios, London; Playhouse Alley, L.A.
**Mixed at** Andora Studios, L.A., A&M Studios, L.A.
**Scheduled release date:** September 22, 1992. UNRELEASED.

**TUESDAY NIGHT MUSIC CLUB** (A&M Records 31454 0126 2)
**Track listing:** Run, Baby, Run / Leaving Las Vegas / Strong Enough / Can't Cry Anymore / Solidify / The Na-Na Song / No One Said It Would Be Easy / What I Can Do For You / All I Wanna Do / We Do What We Can / I Shall Believe
**Produced By** Bill Bottrell
**Engineered and mixed by** Blair Lamb, Bill Bottrell
**Recorded and mixed at** Toad Hall, Pasadena
**Released:** August 3, 1993
**Peak chart position:** 3

**SHERYL CROW** (A&M Records 31454 1587 2)

**Track listing:** Maybe Angels / A Change / Home / Sweet Rosalyn / If It Makes You Happy /
Redemption Day / Hard To Make A Stand / Everyday Is A Winding Road /
Love Is A Good Thing / Oh Marie / Superstar / The Book / Ordinary Morning

**Produced by** Sheryl Crow

**Recorded by** Trina Shoemaker, Blair Lamb, Tchad Blake, Bob Salcedo

**Mixed by** Tchad Blake

**Recorded at** Kingsway Studio, New Orleans, Sunset Sound,
L.A., Sunset Sound Factory, L.A.

**Mixed at** Sunset Sound Factory, L.A.

**Released:** September 24, 1996

**Peak chart position:** 6

**THE GLOBE SESSIONS** (A&M Records 31454 0959 2)

**Track listing:** My Favorite Mistake / There Goes The Neighborhood / Riverwide /
It Don't Hurt / Maybe That's Something / Am I Getting Through (Part I & II) /
Anything But Down / The Difficult Kind / Mississippi / Members Only / Crash And Burn /
Subway Ride* / Sweet Child O'Mine**

*unlisted track ** added for 1999 re-release (A&M Records 06949 0404-2)

**Produced by** Sheryl Crow

**Recorded by** Trina Shoemaker

**Additional recording by** Husky Hoskolds

**Mixed by** Tchad Blake, except "There Goes The Neighborhood,"
"Anything But Down," "The Difficult Kind," "Mississippi" **mixed by** Andy Wallace

**Recorded at** Globe Studios, N.Y, and Sunset Sound Factory, L.A.

**Mixed at** Sunset Sound Factory, L.A. and Soundtracks, N.Y.

**Released:** September 29, 1998

**Peak chart position:** 5

**SHERYL CROW AND FRIENDS: LIVE FROM CENTRAL PARK**
(A&M Records 069490574-2)

**Track listing:** Everyday Is A Winding Road / My Favorite Mistake / Leaving Las Vegas /
Strong Enough / It Don't Hurt / A Change Would Do You Good / Gold Dust Woman /
If It Makes You Happy / All I Wanna Do / Happy / The Difficult Kind / White Room /
There Goes The Neighborhood / Tombstone Blues

**Produced by** Sheryl Crow

**Mixed by** Chris Lord-Alge at Image Recording, Hollywood, CA

**Released:** December 7, 1999

**Peak chart position:** 107

**C'MON, C'MON** (A&M Records 069493260-2)

**Track listing:** Steve McQueen / Soak Up The Sun / You're An Original / Safe And Sound / C'mon, C'mon / It's So Easy / Over You / Lucky Kid / Diamond Road / It's Only Love / Abilene / Hole In My Pocket / Weather Channel

**Produced by** Sheryl Crow except "Soak Up The Sun" and "You're An Original" **produced by** Sheryl Crow and Jeff Trott, and "Steve McQueen" **produced by** Sheryl Crow and John Shanks

**Recorded by** Trina Shoemaker with Peter Tew

**Additional engineering by** Dean Baskerville, Chris Shaw, Peter Stroud, Monique Mizrahi, Brian Scheuble, Mark Valentine, Thom Panunzio

**Mixed by** Andy Wallace, except "Steve McQueen," "It's So Easy," "Safe And Sound" **mixed by** Jack Joseph Puig

**Recorded at** Sunset Sound, Los Angeles; Clinton Recording, New York; Avatar, New York; Oceanway, Nashville; Emerald Studios, Nashville; Black Apple Studios, Portland; Henson Studios, Los Angeles; Funny Bunny Studios, London; The Sound Factory, Los Angeles; The Living Room, Los Angeles

**Mixed at** Soundtrack Studios, New York; Oceanway, Los Angeles

**Released:** April 16, 2002

**Peak chart position:** 2

Following are the concert videos/DVDs that have been released through April 2002, featuring Sheryl Crow headlining her own shows.

**LIVE FROM LONDON** (U.K.: VVL 0540883)

**Track listing:** Hard To Make A Stand / Everyday Is A Winding Road / Leaving Las Vegas / A Change Would Do You Good / Run, Baby, Run / If It Makes You Happy / Sweet Rosalyn / Redemption Day / Can't Cry Anymore / Strong Enough / Maybe Angels / All I Wanna Do / Superstar / Ordinary Morning / On The Outside

**Recorded by** PVI Recordings at the Shepherd's Bush Empire, London—November 26, 1996

**Issued on video in** U.K., **laser disc and video** in Japan, **VCD** in Taiwan

**Released:** 1997

**ROCKIN' THE GLOBE LIVE** (video: A&M Records/Image Entertainment ID8817AR) (DVD: A&M Records/Image Entertainment ID8818ARDVD)

**Track listing:** Maybe That's Something / A Change Would Do You Good / Anything But Down / My Favorite Mistake / It Don't Hurt / Riverwide / If It Makes You Happy / Am I Getting Through / Everyday Is A Winding Road / The Difficult Kind / All I Wanna Do / There Goes The Neighborhood / Strong Enough / Mississippi / Home

**Recorded at** the The Palace of Auburn Hills, Michigan — May 8, 1999.

**Produced by** Joel Stillerman

**Directed by** Lawrence Jordan

**Issued on video and DVD** in U.K. and U.S.; **DVD** in Australia, China, and Hong Kong; **VCD** in Malaysia and Indonesia

**Released:** 1999

# The Studio Recordings

Except for the tracks that were destined for the unreleased 1992 *Sheryl Crow* album, the following have all been officially issued on record through April 2002. Not included are other shelved recordings, and neither are Sheryl's guest appearances on other artists' records (for these, see Appendix D), or the songs that she's only performed on TV, radio, or in concert. (Note: Regardless of the year of release, all of the Bill Bottrell productions date from 1992 and 1993.)

**"A CHANGE" (A.K.A. "A CHANGE WOULD DO YOU GOOD")**
Written by Sheryl Crow,
    Jeff Trott, Brian MacLeod
1996 release produced by Sheryl Crow
*Sheryl Crow* album and single

**"ABILENE"**
Written by Sheryl Crow, Jeff Trott
2002 release produced by Sheryl Crow
*C'mon, C'mon* album

**"ALL BY MYSELF"**
Written by Eric Carmen, Sergei Rachmaninoff
1993 release produced by Bill Bottrell
B-side of "Run, Baby, Run" single

**"ALL I WANNA DO"**
Written by Wyn Cooper, Sheryl Crow,
    Bill Bottrell, David Baerwald, Kevin Gilbert
1993 release produced by Bill Bottrell
*Tuesday Night Music Club* album and single

**"ALL KINDS OF PEOPLE"**
Written by Sheryl Crow,
    Kevin Gilbert, Eric Pressly
Produced by Hugh Padgham,
    Sheryl Crow, Kevin Gilbert
Unreleased 1992 *Sheryl Crow* album

**"AM I GETTING THROUGH (PART I & II)"**
Written by Sheryl Crow
1998 release produced by Sheryl Crow
*The Globe Sessions* album

**"ANYTHING BUT DOWN"**
Written by Sheryl Crow
1998 release produced by Sheryl Crow
*The Globe Sessions* album and single

**"BEHIND BLUE EYES"**
Written by Pete Townshend
2001 release produced by Sheryl Crow
*Substitute: The Songs of The Who* various-artists tribute album

**"BLUE CHRISTMAS"**
Written by Billy Hayes, Jay Johnson
1997 release produced by Sheryl Crow
*A Very Special Christmas 3* various-artists benefit album

**"CAN'T CRY ANYMORE"**
Written by Sheryl Crow, Bill Bottrell
1993 release produced by Bill Bottrell
*Tuesday Night Music Club* album and single

**"CAROLINA"**
Written by Sheryl Crow
1998 release produced by Sheryl Crow
*Message in a Bottle* various-artists
    movie soundtrack and Japanese issue
    of *The Globe Sessions* album

**"CHANCES ARE"**
Written by Sheryl Crow, Jeff Trott
Produced by Sheryl Crow
Bonus track on some versions of U.K.
    "Soak Up The Sun" CD single

**"C'MON, C'MON"**
Written by Sheryl Crow, Jeff Trott
2002 release produced by
    Sheryl Crow, Jeff Trott
*C'mon, C'mon* album

**"CRASH AND BURN"**
Written by Sheryl Crow, Jeff Trott
1998 release produced by Sheryl Crow
*The Globe Sessions* album

**"DIAMOND ROAD"**
Written by Sheryl Crow, Marti Frederiksen
2002 release produced by Sheryl Crow
*C'mon, C'mon* album

**"D'YER MAK'ER"**
Written by Jimmy Page, Robert Plant,
    John Paul Jones, John Bonham
1995 release produced by Bill Bottrell
*Encomium* various-artists Led Zeppelin
    tribute album

**"EVERYDAY IS A WINDING ROAD"**
Written by Sheryl Crow,
    Jeff Trott, Brian MacLeod
1996 release produced by Sheryl Crow
*Sheryl Crow* album and single and *Erin
    Brockovich* various-artists movie soundtrack

**"FATHER SUN"**
Written by Sheryl Crow, Jay Oliver
Produced by Hugh Padgham,
    Sheryl Crow, Kevin Gilbert
Unreleased 1992 *Sheryl Crow* album

**"FREE MAN"**
Written by Sheryl Crow
1996 release produced by Sheryl Crow
U.K. and Japanese issues of *Sheryl Crow* album

**"GOOD MORNING, HEARTACHE"**
Written by Dan Fisher, Irene
    Higginbotham, Erving Drake
2001 release produced by Phil Ramone
*Playin' with My Friends: Bennett Sings the Blues*
    Tony Bennett various-artists duets album

**"HARD TO MAKE A STAND"**
Written by Sheryl Crow, Bill Bottrell,
    Todd Wolfe, R.S. Bryan
1996 release produced by Sheryl Crow
*Sheryl Crow* album and non-US single

**"HOLE IN MY POCKET"**
Written by Sheryl Crow, Peter Stroud
2002 release produced by Sheryl Crow
*C'mon, C'mon* album

**"HOME"**
Written by Sheryl Crow
1996 release produced by Sheryl Crow
*Sheryl Crow* album and single, and *Women
    Talking Dirty* various-artists movie soundtrack

**"HUNDREDS OF TEARS"**
Written by Sheryl Crow, Bob Marlette
Produced by Hugh Padgham, Sheryl Crow
Unreleased 1992 *Sheryl Crow* album and
    *Point Break* various-artists movie soundtrack

**"I SHALL BELIEVE"**
Written by Sheryl Crow, Bill Bottrell
1993 release produced by Bill Bottrell
*Tuesday Night Music Club* album and *Roswell*
    various-artists TV tie-in album

**"I WANT YOU"**
Written by Sheryl Crow
2002 release produced by Sheryl Crow
U.K. issue of *C'mon, C'mon* album

**"I WILL WALK WITH YOU"**
Written by Sheryl Crow
Produced by Hugh Padgham, Sheryl Crow
Unreleased 1992 *Sheryl Crow* album

**"IF IT MAKES YOU HAPPY"**
Written by Sheryl Crow, Jeff Trott
1996 release produced by Sheryl Crow
*Sheryl Crow* album and single

**"I'M GONNA BE A WHEEL SOMEDAY"**
Written by Dave Bartholomew,
    Roy Hayes, Antoine Domino
1994 release produced by Pete Smith
*Fast Track to Nowhere* various-artists
    TV tie-in album

**"INDIAN SUMMER"**
Written by Sheryl Crow, Jay Oliver
Produced by Hugh Padgham, Sheryl Crow
Unreleased 1992 *Sheryl Crow* album

**"IN NEED"**
Written by Sheryl Crow
1996 release produced by Sheryl Crow:
    B-side of assorted non-US singles
1998 remake produced by Sheryl Crow:
    *Hope Floats* various-artists movie soundtrack

**"IT DON'T HURT"**
Written by Sheryl Crow, Jeff Trott
1998 release produced by Sheryl Crow
*The Globe Sessions* album

**"IT'S ONLY LOVE"**
Written by Sheryl Crow
2002 release produced by Sheryl Crow
*C'mon, C'mon* album

**"IT'S SO EASY"**
Written by Sheryl Crow, Kathryn Crow
2002 release produced by Sheryl Crow
*C'mon, C'mon* album

**"JUANITA"**
Written by Chris Hillman, Gram Parsons
1999 release produced by Sheryl Crow,
    Emmylou Harris
*Return of the Grievous Angel: A Tribute to
    Gram Parsons* various-artists album

**"KEEP ON GROWING"**
Written by Eric Clapton, Bobby Whitlock
1994 release produced by Stephen
    "Scooter" Weintraub
*Boys on the Side* various-artists movie soundtrack

**"KISS THAT GIRL"**
Written by Sheryl Crow
2001 release produced by Sheryl Crow, Jeff Trott
*Bridget Jones's Diary* various-artists
    movie soundtrack

**"LEAVING LAS VEGAS"**
Written by Sheryl Crow, Bill Bottrell, David
    Baerwald, Kevin Gilbert, David Ricketts
1993 release produced by Bill Bottrell
*Tuesday Night Music Club* album and single

**"LONG GONE LONESOME BLUES"**
Written by Hank Williams
2001 release produced by Sheryl Crow
*Tribute* various-artists Hank Williams
    tribute album

**"LOVE IS A GOOD THING"**
Written by Sheryl Crow, Tad Wadhams
1996 release produced by Sheryl Crow
*Sheryl Crow* album

**"LOVE YOU BLIND"**
Written by Sheryl Crow, Jay Oliver
Produced by Hugh Padgham,
    Sheryl Crow, Jay Oliver
Unreleased 1992 *Sheryl Crow* album

**"LUCKY KID"**
Written by Sheryl Crow, Jeff Trott
2002 release produced by Sheryl Crow
*C'mon, C'mon* album

**"MAYBE ANGELS"**
Written by Sheryl Crow, Bill Bottrell
1996 release produced by Sheryl Crow
*Sheryl Crow* album

**"MAYBE THAT'S SOMETHING"**
Written by Sheryl Crow, Jeff Trott
1998 release produced by Sheryl Crow
*The Globe Sessions* album

**"MEMBERS ONLY"**
Written by Sheryl Crow
1998 release produced by Sheryl Crow
*The Globe Sessions* album and *Shallow Hal*
    various-artists movie soundtrack

**"MISSING"**
Written by Sheryl Crow
2002 release produced by Sheryl Crow
U.K. issue of *C'mon, C'mon* album

**"MISSISSIPPI"**
Written by Bob Dylan
1998 release produced by Sheryl Crow
*The Globe Sessions* album

**"MOTHER NATURE'S SON"**
Written by John Lennon, Paul McCartney
2002 release produced by Sheryl Crow
*I Am Sam* movie soundtrack

**"MY FAVORITE MISTAKE"**
Written by Sheryl Crow, Jeff Trott
Produced by Sheryl Crow
*The Globe Sessions* album and single

**"NEAR ME"**
Written by Sheryl Crow, Jay Oliver
Produced by Hugh Padgham, Sheryl Crow
Unreleased 1992 *Sheryl Crow* album

**"NO ONE SAID IT WOULD BE EASY"**
Written by Sheryl Crow, Bill Bottrell,
    Kevin Gilbert, Dan Schwartz
1993 release produced by Bill Bottrell
*Tuesday Night Music Club* album

**"OH MARIE"**
Written by Sheryl Crow,
    Jeff Trott, Bill Bottrell
1996 release produced by Sheryl Crow
*Sheryl Crow* album

**"ON BORROWED TIME"**
Written by Sheryl Crow
Produced by Hugh Padgham, Sheryl Crow
Unreleased 1992 *Sheryl Crow* album

**"ON THE OUTSIDE"**
Written by Sheryl Crow, Jeff Trott
1996 release produced by Bill Bottrell
*Songs in the Key of X* TV tie-in album

**"ORDINARY MORNING"**
Written by Sheryl Crow
1996 release produced by Sheryl Crow
*Sheryl Crow* album

**"OVER YOU"**
Written by Sheryl Crow
2002 release produced by Sheryl Crow
*C'mon, C'mon* album

**"REACH AROUND JERK"**
Written by Sheryl Crow,
    Bill Bottrell, Dan Schwartz
1993 release produced by Bill Bottrell
Track on four-song "Run, Baby, Run" U.K.
    single

**"REDEMPTION DAY"**
Written by Sheryl Crow
1996 release produced by Sheryl Crow
*Sheryl Crow* album and *Erin Brockovich*
    various-artists movie soundtrack

**"RESUSCITATION"**
Written by Sheryl Crow, Jeff Trott
1998 release produced by Sheryl Crow
*The Faculty* various-artists movie
    soundtrack and non-U.S. issues
    of *The Globe Sessions* album

**"RIVERWIDE"**
Written by Sheryl Crow
1998 release produced by Sheryl Crow
*The Globe Sessions* album

**"RUN, BABY, RUN"**
Written by Bill Bottrell,
    David Baerwald, Sheryl Crow
1993 release produced by Bill Bottrell
*Tuesday Night Music Club* album and single

**"SAD SAD WORLD"**
Written by Sheryl Crow,
    Jeff Trott, Brian MacLeod
1996 release produced by Sheryl Crow
Some non-U.S. issues of *Sheryl Crow* album

**"SAFE AND SOUND"**
Written by Sheryl Crow
2002 release produced by Sheryl Crow
*C'mon, C'mon* album

**"SOAK UP THE SUN"**
Written by Sheryl Crow, Jeff Trott
2002 release produced by
    Sheryl Crow, Jeff Trott
*C'mon, C'mon* album and single

**"SOLIDIFY"**
Written by Sheryl Crow, Kevin Hunter,
    Bill Bottrell, David Baerwald, Kevin Gilbert,
    David Ricketts, Brian MacLeod
1993 release produced by Bill Bottrell
*Tuesday Night Music Club* album

**"SOLITAIRE"**
Written by Neil Sedaka, Philip Cody
1994 release produced by Matt Wallace
*If I Were A Carpenter* various-artists
    tribute album

**"STEVE McQUEEN"**
Written by Sheryl Crow, John Shanks
2002 release produced by
    Sheryl Crow, John Shanks
*C'mon, C'mon* album and single

**"STILL"**
Written by Sheryl Crow
1999 release produced by Sheryl Crow
*Dill Scallion* movie soundtrack

**'STRAIGHT TO THE MOON"**
Written by Sheryl Crow, Jeff Trott
1998 release produced by Sheryl Crow
*King of the Hill* TV tie-in album

**"STRONG ENOUGH"**
Written by Sheryl Crow, Bill Bottrell,
    David Baerwald, Kevin Gilbert,
    David Ricketts, Brian MacLeod
1993 release produced by Bill Bottrell
*Tuesday Night Music Club* album and single

**"SUBWAY RIDE"**
Written by Sheryl Crow
1998 release produced by Sheryl Crow
*The Globe Sessions* album

**"SUPERSTAR"**
Written by Sheryl Crow, Jeff Trott
1996 release produced by Sheryl Crow
*Sheryl Crow* album

**"SWEET CHILD O' MINE"**
Written by Izzy Stradlin, Steve Adler,
    Duff McKagan, Axl Rose, Slash
1999 release produced by Rick Rubin,
    Sheryl Crow
*Big Daddy* various-artists movie soundtrack,
    U.S./U.K. re-release of *The Globe Sessions*
    album, and single

**"SWEET ROSALYN"**
Written by Sheryl Crow, Jeff Trott
1996 release produced by Sheryl Crow
*Sheryl Crow* album

**"THE BOOK"**
Written by Sheryl Crow, Jeff Trott
1996 release produced by Sheryl Crow
*Sheryl Crow* album

**"THE DIFFICULT KIND"**
Written by Sheryl Crow
1998 release produced by Sheryl Crow
*The Globe Sessions* album

**"THE JOKER"**
Written by Steve Miller, A. Ertegun, M. Curtis
1996 release produced by Sheryl Crow
*The Pompatus of Love* various-artists
    movie soundtrack

**"THE LAST TIME"**
Written by Sheryl Crow
Produced by Hugh Padgham, Sheryl Crow
Unreleased 1992 *Sheryl Crow* album

**""THE NA-NA SONG"**
Written by Sheryl Crow, Bill Bottrell,
    David Baerwald, Kevin Gilbert,
    David Ricketts, Brian MacLeod
1993 release produced by Bill Bottrell
*Tuesday Night Music Club* album

**"THERE GOES THE NEIGHBORHOOD"**
Written by Sheryl Crow, Jeff Trott
1998 release produced by Sheryl Crow
*The Globe Sessions* album and single

**"TIME HAS COME TODAY"**
Written by Joseph & Willie Chambers
2000 release produced by The Twangtrust
*Steal This Movie* various-artists
    movie soundtrack

**"TOMORROW NEVER DIES"**
Written by Sheryl Crow, Mitchell Froom
1997 release produced by Mitchell Froom
*Tomorrow Never Dies* various-artists movie
    soundtrack and single

**"VOLVO COWGIRL 99"**
Written by Sheryl Crow, Bill Bottrell,
    David Baerwald, Kevin Gilbert,
    David Ricketts, Brian MacLeod
1993 release produced by Bill Bottrell
B-side of U.K. "What I Can Do
    For You" single

**"WE DO WHAT WE CAN"**
Written by Sheryl Crow, Bill Bottrell,
    Kevin Gilbert, Dan Schwartz
1993 release produced by Bill Bottrell
*Tuesday Night Music Club* album

**"WEATHER CHANNEL"**
Written by Sheryl Crow
2002 release produced by Sheryl Crow
*C'mon, C'mon* album

**"WHAT DOES IT MATTER?"**
Written by Sheryl Crow
Produced by Hugh Padgham, Sheryl Crow
Unreleased 1992 *Sheryl Crow* album

**"WHAT I CAN DO FOR YOU"**
Written by David Baerwald, Sheryl Crow
1993 release produced by Bill Bottrell
*Tuesday Night Music Club* album and U.K./
    European single

**"WHEN LOVE IS OVER"**
Written by Sheryl Crow
Produced by Hugh Padgham, Sheryl Crow
Unreleased 1992 *Sheryl Crow* album

**"WHO WILL THE NEXT FOOL BE?"**
Written by Charlie Rich
2001 release produced by Ahmet Ertegun
*Good Rockin' Tonight: The Legacy of Sun Records*
    various-artists tribute album

**"YOU ALWAYS GET YOUR WAY"**
Written by Sheryl Crow
1998 release produced by Sheryl Crow
B-side of U.K. "There Goes The
    Neighborhood" single

**"YOU WANT IT ALL"**
Written by Sheryl Crow, Michael Lunn
Produced by Hugh Padgham, Sheryl Crow
Unreleased 1992 *Sheryl Crow* album

**"YOU'RE AN ORIGINAL"**
Written by Sheryl Crow, Jeff Trott
2002 release produced by Sheryl Crow, Jeff Trott
*C'mon, C'mon* album

**"YOU'RE NOT THE ONE"**
Written by Stevie Nicks,
    Sheryl Crow, Jeremy Stacey
Produced by Sheryl Crow
Japanese issue of *C'mon, C'mon* album
    and bonus track on some versions of U.K.
    "Soak Up The Sun" CD single

# *The Live Covers*

Following are Sheryl's stage or television performances of other composers' songs—not recorded in the studio—which have been officially released through April 2002. (Ensemble and backing performances are not included.)

**"FLESH AND BLOOD"** with Emmylou Harris, Mary Chapin Carpenter, Mary Stuart
Written by John R. Cash
*An All-Star Tribute to Johnny Cash* video (1999)

**"GOLD DUST WOMAN"** with Stevie Nicks
Written by Stevie Nicks
*Sheryl Crow and Friends:*
*Live from Central Park* album (1999)

**"GOOD MORNING, HEARTACHE"**
Written by Dan Fisher, Irene Higginbotham, Erving Drake
*Stormy Weather* album of Walden Woods Project benefit concert (1998)

**"HAPPY"** with Keith Richards and Chrissie Hynde
Written by Keith Richards, Mick Jagger
*Sheryl Crow and Friends:*
*Live from Central Park* album (1999)

**"JACKSON"\*/"ORANGE BLOSSOM SPECIAL"\*\*** with Willie Nelson and The Mavericks
\*Written by Billy Edd Wheeler, Jerry Leiber
\*\*Written by Ervin T. Rouse
*An All-Star Tribute to Johnny Cash* video (1999)

**"LÀ CI DAREM LA MANO"** with Luciano Pavarotti
Written by Wolfgang Amadeus Mozart
*Pavarotti & Friends for War Child* benefit album and video (1996)

**"LITTLE WING"** with Eric Clapton
Written by Jimi Hendrix
*Eric Clapton and Friends in Concert* album, video, DVD (1999)

**"MERRY CHRISTMAS BABY"** with Eric Clapton
Written by John Dudley Moore, Lou Baxter
*A Very Special Christmas Live from Washington D.C.* album (1998)

**"ONE LESS BELL TO ANSWER"**
Written by Burt Bacharach, Hal David
*Burt Bacharach: One Amazing Night* album, video, DVD (1998)

**"ROCKIN' AROUND THE CHRISTMAS TREE"** with Mary J. Blige
Written by Johnny Marks
*A Very Special Christmas Live from Washington D.C.* album (1998)

**"RUN RUDOLF RUN"**
Written by Marvin Brodie, Johnny Marks
*A Very Special Christmas 5* album (2000)

**"TOMBSTONE BLUES"** with Natalie Maines, Chrissie Hynde, and Sarah McLachlan on vocals
Written by Bob Dylan
*Sheryl Crow and Friends:*
*Live from Central Park* album (1999)

**"WHITE ROOM"** with Eric Clapton
Written by Jack Bruce, Pete Brown
*Sheryl Crow and Friends:*
*Live from Central Park* album (1999)

# *The Guest Appearances*

Following are Sheryl Crow's appearances on other artists' records through April 2002. (Greatest hits albums are not included.)

ARTIST: **One 2 Many**
ALBUM: *Mirror* (A&M, 1988)
SC backing vocals on some tracks

ARTIST: **Johnny Mathis**
ALBUM: *Once in a While* (Columbia, 1988)
SC backing vocals on "Just Like You"
and "Love Brought Us Here Tonight"

ARTIST: **PM**
ALBUM: *PM* (Warner Brothers, 1988)
SC backing vocals on "Say It Again,"
"Nothing," "The Wanting," and
"Love Is A Stranger"

ARTIST: **Don Henley**
ALBUM: *The End of the Innocence*
(Geffen, 1989)
SC backing vocals on "If Dirt Were Dollars"

ARTIST: **Jimmy Buffett**
ALBUM: *Off to See the Lizard* (MCA, 1989)
SC backing vocals on some tracks

ARTIST: **Neal Schon**
ALBUM: *Late Nite* (CBS, 1989)
SC vocals and backing vocals on some tracks

ARTIST: **Steve Thomson**
ALBUM: *Steve Thomson*
(CMC International, 1989)
SC backing vocals on some tracks

ARTIST: **Nancy Wilson**
ALBUM: *Lady with a Song* (Sony, 1990)
SC backing vocals on some tracks

ARTIST: **Kenny Loggins**
ALBUM: *Leap of Faith* (Columbia, 1991)
SC vocals on "I Would Do Anything";
other tracks feature SC on backing vocals

ARTIST: **Taj Mahal**
ALBUM: *Like Never Before*
(Private Music, 1991)
SC backing vocals on some tracks

ARTIST: **Vinx**
ALBUM: *Rooms In My Fatha's House*
(Pangea, 1991)
SC backing vocals on some tracks
(credited as Cheryl Crowe)

ARTIST: **Patty Smyth**
ALBUM: *Patty Smyth* (MCA, 1992)
SC backing vocals on some tracks

ARTIST: **Foreigner**
ALBUM: *The Very Best . . . And Beyond*
(Atlantic, 1992)
SC backing vocals on "Soul Doctor"

ARTIST: **Farm Dogs**
ALBUM: *Last Stand in Open Country*
(Discovery, 1996)
SC backing vocals on some tracks

ARTIST: **Ron Sexsmith**
ALBUM: *Other Songs* (Interscope, 1997)
SC accordion on some tracks

ARTIST: **TDF (Eric Clapton
and Simon Climie)**
ALBUM: *Retail Therapy* (Reprise, 1997)
SC spoken vocal on "What She Wants"

ARTIST: **Dwight Yoakam**
ALBUM: *Under the Covers* (Reprise, 1997)
SC vocals on "Baby Don't Go"

ARTIST: **Salt 'N Pepa**
ALBUM: *Brand New* (Red Ant, 1997)
SC vocals on "Imagine"

ARTIST: **Gregg Rolie**
SC backing vocals on studio demos (1997)

ARTIST: **Scott Weiland**
ALBUM: *12 Bar Blues* (Atlantic, 1998)
SC accordion on "Lady, Your Roof
Brings Me Down"

ARTIST: **Mitchell Froom**
ALBUM: *Dopamine* (Atlantic, 1998)
SC vocals on "Monkey Mind"

ARTIST: **Waylon Jennings**
ALBUM: *Closing in on the Fire*
        (ARK 21, 1998)
SC and Sting vocals on "She's Too
Good For Me"

ARTIST: **Stevie Nicks**
ALBUM: *Practical Magic* soundtrack
        (Warner Brothers, 1998)
SC vocals on "If You Ever Did Believe"
and "Crystal"

ARTIST: **Salt 'N Pepa**
ALBUM: *Our Friend Martin* soundtrack
        (Motown, 1999)
SC vocals on "Imagine (Remix)"

ARTIST: **David Baerwald and the
New Folk Underground**
ALBUM: *A Fine Mess* (1993–1999
        publishing demos, Palindrome, 1999)
SC backing vocals on "Smart In A Stupid Way"

ARTIST: **Taj Mahal**
ALBUM: *Blue Light Boogie*
        (Private Music, 1999)
SC vocals on some tracks

ARTIST: **Indigo Girls**
ALBUM: *Come On Now Social* (Epic, 1999)
SC backing vocals on "Gone Again" and
"Cold Beer And Remote Control"

ARTIST: **The Artist Formerly
Known as Prince**
ALBUM: *Rave Un2 The Joy Fantastic*
        (NPG, 1999)
SC vocals and harmonica on "Baby Knows"

ARTIST: **Zucchero**
ALBUM: *Overdose d'Amore: The Ballads*
        (ARK 21, 1999)
SC vocals on "Blue"

ARTIST: **Los Lobos**
ALBUM: *El Cancionero: Mas y Mas*
        (2000, Rhino)
SC vocals on "What's Going On"
(live, from 1997)

ARTIST: **Maceo Parker**
ALBUM: *dial:MACEO* (ESC, 2000)
SC and Prince vocals on "Baby Knows"

ARTIST: **Stacey Earle**
ALBUM: *Dancin' With Them That Brung Me*
        (Gearle, 2000)
SC backing vocals on "Kiss Her Goodnight"

ARTIST: **Dan Zanes & Friends**
ALBUM: *Rocket Ship Beach*
        (Festival Five, 2000)
SC vocals on "Polly Wolly Doodle"

ARTIST: **Johnny Cash**
ALBUM: *American III: Solitary Man* (Sony, 2000)
SC vocals on "Field Of Diamonds" and
accordion on "Mary Of The Wild Moor"
and "Wayfaring Stranger"

ARTIST: **Bob Dylan**
ALBUM: *Love and Theft* (Columbia, 2001)
SC vocals on "Mississippi"

ARTIST: **Neil Finn**
ALBUM: *One Nil* (Parlophone, 2001, U.K.);
        *One All* (Nettwerk, 2002, U.S.)
SC vocals on "Turn And Run" and "Driving
Me Mad," and accordion on "Into The Sunset"

ARTIST: **Stevie Nicks**
ALBUM: *Trouble in Shangri-La* (Reprise, 2001)
SC vocals and guitars on "Candlebright" and
"Sorcerer," bass on "Too Far From Texas,"
acoustic guitar on "That Made Me Stronger,"
guitars and backing vocals on "It's Only Love,"
and backing vocals on "Fall From Grace"

ARTIST: **Kid Rock**
ALBUM: *Cocky* (Atlantic, 2001)
SC vocals, 12-string guitar, and bass on "Picture"

ARTIST: **Willie Nelson**
ALBUM: *The Great Divide* (Lost Highway, 2002)
SC vocals on "Be There For You"

ARTIST: **Steve Earle**
ALBUM: *Sidetracks* (Artemis, 2002)
SC vocals on "Time Has Come Today"

ARTIST: **Counting Crows**
ALBUM: *Hard Candy* (Interscope, 2002)
SC vocals on "American Girls"

# *The Videos*

Following are the promotional videos that Sheryl Crow has starred in through April 2002. The songs they relate to haven't all been officially released as singles worldwide (in America, for instance, "Run, Baby, Run" was only issued as a promo single), but this list gives a fair indication as to the tracks that have led the way commercially. Sheryl's appearances in the videos of other artists are not included.

**LEAVING LAS VEGAS** (1993)
Directed by David Hogan

**ALL I WANNA DO** (1994)
Directed by David Hogan

**RUN, BABY, RUN** (1994)
Directed by David Hogan, David Cameron

**STRONG ENOUGH** (1994)
Directed by Martin Bell

**CAN'T CRY ANYMORE** (1995)
Directed by Elizabeth Bailey

**WHAT I CAN DO FOR YOU** (1995)
Directed by Jeff Richter

**IF IT MAKES YOU HAPPY** (1996)
Directed by Keir McFarlane

**TOMORROW NEVER DIES** (1997)
Directed by Daniel Kleinman

**EVERYDAY IS A
WINDING ROAD** (1997)
Directed by Peggy Sirota

**A CHANGE** (Version I – 1997)
Directed by Michel Gondry

**A CHANGE** (Version II – 1997)
Directed by Lance Acord, Sheryl Crow

**HARD TO MAKE A STAND** (1997)
Directed by Matthew Amos

**HOME** (1997)
Directed by Samuel Bayer

**MY FAVORITE MISTAKE** (1998)
Directed by Samuel Bayer

**THERE GOES THE
NEIGHBORHOOD** (1998)
Directed by Matthew Rolston

**ANYTHING BUT DOWN** (1999)
Directed by Floria Sigismondi

**SWEET CHILD O'MINE** (1999)
Directed by Stephane Sednaoui

**SOAK UP THE SUN** (2002)
Directed by Wayne Isham

**STEVE McQUEEN** (2002)
Directed by Wayne Isham

# *Index*